The

Ideal
Element
in Law

ROSCOE POUND

The
Ideal
Element
_in_ Law

Roscoe Pound

Liberty Fund

INDIANAPOLIS

© 2002 Liberty Fund, Inc. All rights reserved.
Originally published by the University of Calcutta Press in 1958.

Frontispiece courtesy of Art & Visual Materials, Special Collections
Department, Harvard Law School. Portrait of Roscoe Pound
by Charles Sydney Hopkinson, 1929.

Printed in the United States of America

06   05   04   03   02   C   5   4   3   2   1
06   05   04   03   02   P   5   4   3   2   1

Library of Congress Cataloging-in-Publication Data

Pound, Roscoe, 1870–1964.
The ideal element in law/Roscoe Pound.
p.   cm.
Originally published: [Calcutta]: University of Calcutta, 1958.
Includes bibliographical references and index.
ISBN 0-86597-325-3 (alk. paper) — ISBN 0-86597-326-1 (pbk.: alk. paper)
1. Jurisprudence.   2. Law — Philosophy.   I. Title.
K230.P67   A35   2002
340'.1 — dc21
2001050518

Liberty Fund, Inc.
8335 Allison Pointe Trail, Suite 300
Indianapolis, Indiana 46250-1684

Contents

Foreword

Roscoe Pound (born on October 27, 1872, in Lincoln, Nebraska; died on July 1, 1964, in Cambridge, Massachusetts), practically unknown among the general American population today, was the most famous American jurisprudential thinker of the first half of the twentieth century. He was also the greatest twentieth-century dean of the Harvard Law School (1916–36). Through his work in building faculty and programs and in seeking international students, he made Harvard the first of the world-class American law schools. His name now graces one of Harvard's buildings, an honor accorded to only a handful of legal greats. Pound was the principal architect of a legal philosophical approach he called "sociological jurisprudence," which sought to make the law more responsive to changes in society, while still maintaining its authoritative traditional and moral character. Pound is the spiritual father of the still dominant school of American legal thought now known as "legal realism," but he might have regarded legal realism as a prodigal son.[1]

Legal realism, as practiced in the 1930s, maintained that a sensible and "realistic" jurisprudence ought to result in altering law and legal institutions to meet the needs of the times, and ought not to pay excessive deference to older concepts such as freedom of contract and restraints on the interference of state and federal governments with private agree-

1. A valuable recent biography of Pound is David Wigdor, *Roscoe Pound, Philosopher of Law* (Westport, Conn.: Greenwood Press, 1974). Pound's thought, and that of the legal realists, is nicely analyzed in N. E. H. Hull, *Roscoe Pound and Karl Llewellyn: Searching for an American Jurisprudence* (Chicago: University of Chicago Press, 1997).

ments. If Pound's work was an inspiration for legal realism, then Pound is due some of the credit for laying the foundations of legal realism's greatest triumph, President Franklin D. Roosevelt's New Deal. During the New Deal, lawyers trained in legal realism expanded the role of the federal government through plastic interpretations of the U.S. Constitution and the creation of a myriad of new administrative agencies. Still, late in life Pound turned against legal realism and expressed uneasiness with the increasingly centralized federal control of American life the New Deal had spawned.

Though Pound always believed in the need for sensible legal reform, there was a tension in Pound's reformist jurisprudence, because along with his fervor for modernizing the law, Pound had a healthy respect for what he called the "taught legal tradition." Roscoe Pound favored the slow and orderly change of the law through the courts and other established legal institutions, rather than the New Deal era's radical shift of legal power from the states to the federal government. *The Ideal Element in the Law*, a series of lectures delivered at the University of Calcutta in 1948, and first published ten years later, contains a concise, and yet a mature and thorough statement of the basic tenets of Pound's jurisprudence. It is an extraordinary survey of the development of jurisprudence in Greece, Rome, Continental Europe, England, and America, and a treasure trove of information about the law with value for both lawyers and laymen. It reflects what were for Pound the most important jurisprudential problems in his last years — what goals should law and legal institutions have? How can the law be used to preserve liberty and avoid tyranny? These questions, of great concern before, during, and after World War II, the period of time when Pound developed the analysis in these lectures, are no less important now.

Pound was the son of a prominent Nebraska judge, who wanted his boy to follow in his footsteps and study the law. Pound did become a lawyer, but his love of his native prairie environment also led him to become a professionally trained and highly regarded botanist. He received a B.A. (1888) and a Ph.D. (1897) in botany from the University of Nebraska. Pound was the brightest star in a small galaxy of talented botanists at Nebraska, and had as his mentor Professor Charles Bessey, an early follower of Charles Darwin. For some time Pound appears to have vacillated between the law and botany. He studied law for one year at Harvard (1889–90), when Harvard's great innovator, Dean Christopher Columbus Langdell, had introduced the case method and Socratic teaching, and was pioneering the study of law as if it were an evolutionary science. Pound did well at Harvard, and would likely have been invited to join the *Harvard Law Review* (the most prestigious honor, then and now, that a Harvard law student can secure), but was forced to return home to Lincoln, Nebraska, because of the ill-health of his father. Pound became a member of the Nebraska bar even as he continued his study of botany. He taught law at the University of Nebraska from 1890 to 1903, but also served as the director of Nebraska's state botanical survey. Along with a fellow botanist, Pound wrote a path-breaking book on plant life in Nebraska, *Phytogeography of Nebraska* (1898),[2] treating botany not as a sterile field concerned only with taxonomy and classification, but rather encompassing an understanding of the organic and evolutionary relationship among all plant life.

Pound's training as a natural scientist, and as a Darwinist under the influence of Bessey, predisposed him to see the law in terms of organic growth and to understand that only those parts of the law should survive that were useful. This was a perspective he never abandoned, as readers of this book will understand. But readers will also not be surprised to learn that while Pound understood the fact of organic change in botany and law, he never wavered from a conviction that in both fields of study there were constant principles which determined change, a constant striving toward stability and equilibrium, and a constant existence of underlying truths which could be revealed by careful observation, classification, and analysis.

Just as Pound had learned botany in the field, he learned several institutions of the law firsthand, as he helped to form the Nebraska Bar As-

2. Roscoe Pound and Frederick E. Clements, *Phytogeography of Nebraska* (Lincoln, Neb.: privately published, 1900).

sociation in 1900; served, in the capacity of an appellate judge, as the youngest member of the Nebraska Supreme Court Commission (a reform panel created to eliminate the backlog of cases in the Nebraska Supreme Court) from 1901 to 1903; and, from 1904 to 1907, served as a commissioner on uniform state laws for Nebraska, in which position he began his efforts to modernize American law. Pound was appointed dean of the Nebraska College of Law in 1903, and instituted many of the same reforms in legal education he had observed at Harvard, including close study of cases and the Socratic method of teaching. Pound also changed the course of study of the law from two to three years at Nebraska, and required every student who matriculated to be a high school graduate. At about the time Pound became dean, all that was really necessary to be admitted to practice law in Nebraska was that one be able to read, but Pound was in the forefront of a movement to make the bar more professional in character, the better to perform the job of improving the law Pound believed essential.

In August 1906, Dean Pound addressed the annual convention of the American Bar Association in St. Paul, Minnesota. His talk was titled "The Causes of Popular Dissatisfaction with the Administration of Justice," and was his first major exposition of what would become known as sociological jurisprudence. Because his talk advocated what appeared to be major changes in the law and legal practice, in order to take advantage of modern science, it struck many of Pound's listeners as radical, and some objected to its publication. Nevertheless, others who heard the talk or read the text understood that Pound was one of the most significant contemporary legal thinkers, and it immediately catapulted Pound to national notice. One important result of the talk was an offer from the dean of the Northwestern University School of Law, John Henry Wigmore, to join Northwestern's faculty. Wigmore, the author of the most famous American legal treatise, *Wigmore on Evidence*,[3] was,

3. John Henry Wigmore, *A Treatise on the Anglo-American System of Evidence in Trials at Common Law: Including the Statutes and Judicial Decisions of All Jurisdictions of the United States*, 4 vols. (Boston: Little, Brown, 1904–5).

when he hired Pound, the leading American legal scholar, and Wigmore had brought Northwestern to the forefront of national efforts to improve law and legal institutions.[4] Pound taught at Northwestern from 1907 to 1909, then at the University of Chicago for a year, and then accepted an appointment at Harvard in 1910.

To return to Harvard seems to have been Pound's goal since his untimely exit before he could receive his law degree, and once back at Harvard, Pound continued his work in legal reform, most significantly in criminal law and civil procedure. Pound believed that many legal practices of pleading and trial conduct could be improved, made simpler, and made more sure and certain. During the latter part of Pound's deanship at Harvard, however, he sought to distance himself from the more extreme of the legal realists, who were building on his sociological jurisprudence to argue for giving judges much more discretion to decide cases, and to argue that it was time to abandon the notion that the law contained within itself timeless moral and philosophical truths. The most radical of their number, Jerome Frank, argued that established legal rules, reason, and timeless truths played no role in formulating judicial decisions, which were actually, according to Frank, after-the-fact rationalizations designed to disguise judges' naked personal policy preferences.[5] Pound's disagreement with the legal realists became increasingly more strident, as he concluded that their efforts would undermine the organic character of the law, and lead to arbitrary and dangerous judicial behavior.

Following his service as Harvard Law School's dean, in 1936 Pound became the first University Professor at Harvard, and thereby was permitted to teach in any of the school's academic units. By that time he had practically become the voice of jurisprudence for the entire country. His administrative duties ceased, but his efforts at scholarship remained

---

4. For Wigmore and his career at Northwestern, see generally William R. Roalfe, *John Henry Wigmore, Scholar and Reformer* (Evanston: Northwestern University Press, 1977).

5. Jerome Frank, *Law and the Modern Mind* (New York: Brentano's, 1930).

strong, and many of his most significant books were published after his retirement as dean.[6]

Pound delivered the lectures that comprise *The Ideal Element in Law* at the ripe old age of seventy-six. They still reflect Pound's early training in botany, and his emphasis on the importance of classification, but they also illustrate Pound's early-developed attention to the organic nature of the legal system, its constant principles, and its vitality. These lectures are clearly those of a mature thinker at the height of his powers, speaking to us from an earlier and, in some ways, a wiser era. The lectures were delivered in 1948, six years *before Brown* v. *Board of Education* (1954),[7] and they are blessedly free of the arrogance of the kind of imperative legal theory that began with that case. In *Brown*, for the first time, the United States Supreme Court, profoundly influenced by the kind of legal realism practiced by Frank, wholly embraced social science (in that case the nascent discipline of social psychology) as a guide for refashioning constitutional law. *Brown* based its decision to end racial segregation in the nation's public schools not on the basis of the original understanding of constitutional provisions, nor on the basis of established legal doctrines, but rather on the work of a group of social psychologists who had argued that racial separation resulted in educational disadvantages for black children. In doing so, the Supreme Court made no real pretension of exercising the traditional passive role of judges, or of following the taught legal tradition, but boldly embarked on a program of essentially legislative change that would eventually extend to ordering modifications of state criminal procedure, the abolition of the practice of allowing prayer and Bible readings in public schools, and, finally, to prohibiting states from outlawing abortion.

While all of that was in the future when Pound wrote *The Ideal Element in Law*, there were, at the time, plenty of advocates urging the activist role for the courts which was eventually manifested by *Brown* and

6. See, e.g., Roscoe Pound, *An Introduction to the Philosophy of Law* (New Haven, Conn.: Yale University Press, 1954); Roscoe Pound, *The Formative Era of American Law* (Boston: Little, Brown, 1938); Roscoe Pound, *Jurisprudence*, 5 vols. (St. Paul, Minn.: West Publishing Co., 1959).

7. *Brown v. Board of Education*, 347 U.S. 483 (1954).

its progeny. These lectures are best understood, then, as part of Pound's broader efforts to defend the taught legal tradition, the common law method of adjudication in particular, and the Anglo-American juris-prudential tradition in general, as the best guarantor of liberty. Pound saw those urging the courts to undertake a program of radical social change, and in particular, the legal realists who disparaged the decisive role of legal doctrines in determining the outcome of court cases, as a real danger to American legal institutions.

The most important theme in these lectures, then, is Pound's sus-tained attack on these legal realists. Pound tended to rework the same materials over many decades, subtly spinning out the implications of his arguments. These lectures are a much more fully developed expression of the ideas that Pound had quickly penned in a 1931 essay.[8] That essay had been designed to rebut the wilder claims of some legal realists, most notably Jerome Frank, the author of a best-selling (for a work on the law) volume called *Law and the Modern Mind*.[9] As indicated, Frank had ar-gued that certainty in any field of the law was an illusion, and that those who argued that the legal doctrines led to sure results, were simply vic-tims of a frustrated childhood desire to have an omnipotent father. This purported insight of Frank's, which he borrowed from Freudian psy-chology, was used by Frank expressly to criticize Roscoe Pound, whose defense of the certainty in commercial and property law Frank derided as the "prattling" of a "small boy" in search of a perfect father. Readers of *The Ideal Element* will note the clear and elegant manner in which Pound skewers Frank's theories, and suggests the immature and silly na-ture of Frank's analysis.[10]

But if Pound has harsh words for psychological legal realists such as Frank, it is nevertheless true that *The Ideal Element in Law* also seeks to further the work of and to praise the efforts of some of the calmer legal

8. Roscoe Pound, "The Call for a Realist Jurisprudence," 44 HARVARD LAW REVIEW 697 (1931), excerpted in Stephen B. Presser and Jamil S. Zainaldin, *Law and Jurispru-dence in American History*, 4th ed. (St. Paul, Minn.: West Publishing Co., 2000), 789–805.

9. See above, note 5.

10. See generally *The Ideal Element in Law*, pp. 120–27, 288–299.

realists, such as Karl Llewellyn.[11] Llewellyn, like the young Pound when he was a champion of sociological jurisprudence, recognized the important role of stable, traditional elements in American law, and also the obvious fact that many areas of the law did allow courts to engage in certain and sensible decision making.[12] Unlike Frank, Llewellyn enjoyed the friendship and, to a certain extent, the patronage of Pound, and was prepared to concede that the legal rules were, in the main, the cause of particular legal decisions. Still, Llewellyn was aware that American legal institutions could be encouraged to develop law that was more in keeping with twentieth-century needs. Llewellyn, then, like the mature Pound, appreciated both the traditional and organic as well as the evolutionary nature of the law, and Pound was determined to further efforts like Llewellyn's and disparage those like Frank's.[13]

These Indian lectures appear to have been intended as a summing of Pound's jurisprudential perspective, and it is something of a tragedy that they never received wider circulation in America. By the time they were first published, Pound's influence had begun to fade, but had they been widely disseminated, it is possible that his essentially conservative vision might have given some pause to those who sought in the 1950s, 1960s, and 1970s to use the courts to further radical social change, in the service of a renewed populism. The last few pages of this book, building on all that has gone before, comprise one of the best warnings against the tyranny of the majority, against the excesses of the welfare state, and against authoritarianism in general, that any legal scholar has ever penned.

In keeping with Pound's concerns late in his life, the book is a stirring argument for the preservation of liberty, but it is also a humbling demonstration of the cosmopolitanism and sheer learning that characterized some of the early twentieth-century legal titans such as

11. Ibid., pp. 289, 312–13.

12. See, e.g., Karl N. Llewellyn, *The Common Law Tradition: Deciding Appeals* (Boston: Little, Brown, 1960).

13. For the interesting triangular relationship among Pound, Frank, and Llewellyn, see Hull, *Roscoe Pound and Karl Llewellyn*, pp. 173–222.

Holmes,[14] Wigmore, and Pound himself. The breadth of their legal knowledge, especially when compared to legal writers of the late twentieth century, is nothing short of breathtaking. In these lectures Pound uses Greek, Roman, medieval, European, and American materials with an equal command, and it is obvious that he has been able to read many of the works on which he relies in their original languages. He gives us a picture of what a real legal scholar used to be able to do, and shames virtually all of us in the academy who look only to America (and post-1954 America, at that) for jurisprudential principles.

Whether or not Pound's sociological jurisprudence, and his inspiration of the Progressives in the beginning of the century, led inevitably to Franklin Roosevelt's New Deal, in *The Ideal Element in the Law*, Pound argues convincingly that the welfare state (or the "service state" as he calls it) cannot do everything. This book is, then, among other things, a powerful argument against redistribution, or what Pound calls the "Robin Hood" principle.[15] From the beginning of his work in the law, Pound was skeptical of populism, its expressed desire for redistribution, and its attacks on established centers of wealth and power in society. In *The Ideal Element*, Pound devotes substantial space to expounding his lifelong view that the desire for equality should not be pushed so far that it ends up destroying liberty, and Pound hints darkly that we have already gone too far down that road. In these lectures he provides very good examples not only from political mistakes of European nations, but also from the common law doctrines themselves, as they have been skewed in American jurisprudence, most clearly in torts and contracts. What Pound said in 1948 still rings remarkably true in the early twenty-first century.

Pound must have demanded a great deal of concentration from those who heard these lectures, and even one who has the text before him or her will discover that keen attention and perhaps even multiple readings

---

14. Holmes's erudition is displayed at its peak in Oliver Wendell Holmes, Jr., *The Common Law* (Boston: Little, Brown, 1881).

15. See, e.g., *The Ideal Element in Law*, p. 340, 357–67.

are required before Pound's arguments emerge with clarity. By the time one finishes the book, though, Pound's organizing principles should have become clear, and these lectures should easily be seen to be at least a tour de force, and, most probably, a landmark in modern jurisprudence. *The Ideal Element in Law* foreshadows or anticipates the celebrated works by Lawrence Friedman[16] and Grant Gilmore[17] on the "Death of Contract," in which they described the manner in which twentieth-century American judges eroded the theories of bargain and exchange that dominated the nineteenth century. Pound's treatment is more satisfying than Gilmore's or Friedman's, however, because Pound better understands the aspirational element of contract (the furthering of both human freedom and ordered liberty) that is missing in most contemporary analysis, and especially in the works of latter-day legal realists like Friedman and Gilmore.

The Ideal Element in Law relates the classical American efforts of Story and Blackstone to a two-thousand-year jurisprudential tradition, and its publication, at this troubled time, might make some modest steps back toward encouraging us to regard the practice of law as a calling instead of a business. While the book is accessible to anyone with an interest in law or philosophy, it ought to be required reading for anyone embarking on the professional study of law, because it gives an essential grounding in legal philosophy and legal history that are too often missing from the increasingly pragmatic American law schools.

In his prime (the period from about 1920 to 1960) Pound towered over the legal academy in a manner even greater than that of the most visible contemporary American law professors such as Richard Posner,[18]

16. Lawrence M. Friedman, *Contract Law in America: A Social and Economic Case Study* (Madison: University of Wisconsin Press, 1965).

17. Grant Gilmore, *The Death of Contract* (Columbus: Ohio State University Press, 1974).

18. Richard Posner was for many years a professor at the Law School of the University of Chicago, and was then a judge and Chief Judge of the United States Court of Appeals for the Seventh Circuit. He was the major moving force behind the development of the legal academic specialty law and economics. For a sampling of Posner, see, e.g., *Eco-*

Laurence Tribe,[19] Alan Dershowitz,[20] or Ronald Dworkin.[21] Most of them have achieved fame through a fairly narrow series of endeavors either as professors, judges, or practitioners. Pound was all of those, as well as an inspired writer, lecturer, law school administrator, and almost tireless laborer on countless local, national, and international reform commissions.

Most academics have ignored Pound in recent years, and the flashiest late twentieth-century school of legal thought, the left-leaning "critical legal studies," all but trashed him. With the availability of *The Ideal Element in Law*, this modest "summa" of a lifetime of jurisprudential work in the trenches and in the study, however, Pound's indispensability to anyone who seeks to grasp the nature of American law should once again become clear. What Pound railed against as the "sporting theory of litigation," the notion that litigation ought to be a ruthless tool to achieve partisan ends, now is everywhere in evidence in twenty-first-century America, extending even, in 2000, to the election

nomic Analysis of Law, 5th ed. (New York: Aspen Law & Business, 1998); *The Problems of Jurisprudence* (Cambridge, Mass.: Harvard University Press, 1990); *Sex and Reason* (Cambridge, Mass.: Harvard University Press, 1991).

19. Laurence Tribe, a professor at the Harvard Law School, is perhaps the leading Supreme Court advocate for what might be regarded as the liberal position on constitutional law issues. He is often invited by members of the Democratic Party to appear as their witness before Congressional hearings. His major work is Laurence H. Tribe, *American Constitutional Law*, 3rd ed. (New York: Foundation Press, 2000).

20. Alan Dershowitz, also a Harvard Law School professor, is best known for his representation of defendants in criminal trials, most notably O. J. Simpson. He is a frequent guest on cable-television network news programs, and is not known for his professional modesty. See, e.g., Alan M. Dershowitz, *Chutzpah* (Boston: Little, Brown, 1991).

21. Ronald Dworkin, for many years, divided his time between law professor duties at New York University School of Law and Oxford University. He is widely regarded as one of the leading jurisprudes of the late twentieth century, having produced scholarship that might be described as an attempt to defend the activist jurisprudence of the Warren Court by suggesting that it was grounded in natural law theory. Dworkin also has been a frequent contributor to the *New York Review of Books*. See, e.g., R. M. Dworkin, *Freedom's Law: The Moral Reading of the American Constitution* (Cambridge, Mass.: Harvard University Press, 1996).

of the United States president. A healthy dose of Pound's wisdom, available in these lectures, might do wonders in reminding a new generation of American law students and lawyers how law ought properly to be used to preserve and protect American traditions, the rule of law, and liberty.

Stephen B. Presser
Northwestern University
School of Law

Table of Cases

The

Ideal
Element
in Law

Is There an Ideal Element in Law?

Whether there is an ideal element in law depends not a little on what is meant by the term 'law.'

Historically the oldest and longest continued use of the term 'law' in juristic writing is to mean the aggregate of laws, the whole body of the legal precepts which obtain in a given politically organized society. This meaning was generally assumed in definition of law from the Middle Ages to the end of the eighteenth century. Law was an aggregate of laws and a law was an authoritative rule of conduct for the individual man. Bentham put it so[1] and such was generally the position of the English analytical jurists. It became a practical question recently in what is likely to prove a leading case under the new constitution (1947) of the State of New Jersey.[2] The constitution provided: "The Supreme Court shall make rules governing the administration of all courts in the state and, subject to law, the practice and procedure in such courts." The court held that the words 'subject to law' referred to substantive law; not to future or past legislation as to details of procedure but to substantive law established either by common law or by legislation. Law is a broader term than 'laws' or than 'a law.' The latter term refers to single items of one element in law in but one of three senses of that term which must be distinguished.

1. *Principles of Morals and Legislation* (1879 ed.) 324.
2. *Winberry v. Salisbury*, 5 N.J. 240 (1950).

One of those meanings is what is now called 'the legal order'—*ordre juridique, Rechtsordnung*, the regime of adjusting relations and ordering conduct by systematic application of the force of a politically organized society. This regime is the most highly developed form of social control in the modern world. It is a specialized form of social control, carried on with a body of authoritative precepts, applied in a judicial and administrative process. After law had been defined by Greek philosophers and Roman jurists, and by philosophers, publicists, jurists, and lawyers, from Thomas Aquinas to Grotius and Pufendorf and Hobbes and Blackstone in terms of laws or rules of law, Kant at the end of the eighteenth century applied the term to the condition which the body of precepts brings about or seeks to bring about and so came near to the idea of the legal order.[3] Later formulas were put in terms of the legal order, thought of as a process rather than a condition.[4] Kohler expressly defines the legal order as such and assumes that no further definition of law is required.[5] Also Kelsen uses 'law' in this sense in his theory of the unity of law, that is, the unity of the legal order.[6]

As was said above, a second sense of the term law, is to mean the authoritative materials by which controversies are decided and thus the legal order is maintained. It is the sense in which law is said to be an aggregate of laws. But in truth here also there is no simple conception. I undertake to say that law in that sense is made up of precepts, technique, and ideals. There is a body of authoritative precepts, developed and applied by an authoritative technique, in the light of authoritative traditional ideals. Law in the second sense is commonly thought of as simply

3. *Metaphysische Anfangsgründe der Rechtslehre* (1797) 27.
4. Gareis, *Enzyklopädie der Rechtswissenschaft* (1887) § 5 ; I Dernburg, *Das bürgerliche Recht der deutschen Reichs und Preussens* (1903) § 16; 3 Berolzheimer, *System der Rechts- und Wirtschaftsphilosophie* (1906) § 17. I have discussed this in *Interpretations of Legal History* (1923) 151–53.
5. *Einführung in die Rechtswissenschaft* (1902) § 1.
6. As to Kelsen's theory of law, *see* an excellent discussion by Lauterpacht in *Modern Theories of Law*, 105–38.

a body of authoritative precepts. But the technique of developing the precepts, the art of the lawyer's craft, is quite as authoritative and no less important. Moreover, the ideal element of law in the second sense, the body of received, authoritative ideals, which is the background of interpretation and application of legal precepts and is crucial in new cases in which it is necessary to choose from among equally authoritative starting points for legal reasoning, often has more significance in the administration of justice according to law than the text of the precepts applied.

As a consequence of development of the functional attitude toward the science of law, there began a generation ago to be increased attention to the phenomena of the actual administration of justice as contrasted with exclusive attention to the authoritative materials for guidance of judicial action. Accordingly much which has been written about 'law' has had to do with what Mr. Justice Cardozo has taught us to call the 'judicial process.'[7] But today we must take account also of what we may call the 'administrative process.' We must think of maintaining the legal order by a process of adjusting relations and determining controversies whether it is done judicially or through administrative agencies. Writers on jurisprudence from a psychological standpoint are concerned chiefly with the judicial process or with both the judicial and the administrative processes as phases of one type of governmental activity. Hence, in the neo-realist writing, of which there has been so much in America in the past twenty-five years, the term 'law' is used in a third sense. As Llewellyn has put it, "What officials do about disputes is . . . the law itself."[8]

Much of what has been written about the 'nature of law' has been vitiated by taking all three of these meanings as included in the one term and then assuming that the whole may be defined by defining the authoritative materials for guidance of judicial and administrative deter-

7. Cardozo, *The Nature of the Judicial Process* (1921).
8. *The Bramble Bush* (1930) 3.

mination in terms of one item of the precept element in those materials, namely, rules of law. In truth, the precept element itself is complex, composed of rules in the strict sense, precepts prescribing definite detailed legal consequences for definite detailed states of fact; principles, *i.e.*, authoritative starting points for legal reasoning; precepts defining conceptions, *i.e.*, authoritative categories into which states of fact may be put with the consequence that certain rules or standards become applicable to them; and precepts establishing standards, *i.e.*, measures of conduct from which one departs at his peril of answering for resulting damage or of legal invalidity of what he does.

In arguing for and discussing an ideal element in law one must look into all these meanings of 'law.' But one must be concerned specially with one ingredient of law in the second sense, namely, laws, the body of authoritative norms or models or patterns of decision applied by the judicial organs of a politically organized society in the determination of controversies so as to maintain the legal order. This precept element may be looked at with respect to the form in which the laws are expressed, reflecting the source of their authority, or with respect to the point of view from which we regard them. They have looked very different to jurists according to the form looked at or the standpoint of observation chosen.

Law as an aggregate of legal precepts may be defined with reference to the source of authority or with respect to the form regarded as typical. When thought of in terms of the authority which promulgates it and puts coercion behind it, jurists have spoken of enactment or promulgation by the ruling organ of a politically organized society. Hence, we get definitions of a law in terms of the imperative type of legal precepts.[9] But

---

9. "What the ruling part of the state enacts after considering what ought to be done," Xenophon, *Memorabilia*, i, 2, § 43; "an ordinance of reason for the general good, emanating from him who has the care of the community," Thomas Aquinas, *Summa Theologica*, I, 2, q. 90, art. 4; "Civil law is to every subject those rules which the commonwealth hath commanded him . . . to make use of for the distinction of right and wrong," Hobbes, *Leviathan*, chap. 46; "A command proceeding from the supreme authority of

jurists who looked instead at the form in which precepts are expressed have thought of traditional or customary precepts, expressing reason or good morals as the type and so have defined law as a body of traditional or moral rules of conduct formulated by some authority of politically organized society but having a deeper foundation in reason.[10]

More significant differences, however, come from the standpoint of purpose from which legal precepts may be regarded. One such standpoint is that of the citizen or subject who wishes to know what he should do, as an upright and law-abiding person, at the crisis of action. To him a law is a rule of conduct.[11] On the other hand, Mr. Justice Holmes thought the question as to the nature of a law should not be put from the standpoint of the conscientious good man, seeking guidance as to what is right, but from the standpoint of the unconscientious bad man who seeks to know how far he may do what he wishes to do with impunity or at least a reasonable prospect of impunity. To such a person law is a body of threats of what the public authorities may do or a person aggrieved may do to him if he does some particular thing he has in mind or does not do something he wishes to avoid doing. This threat theory of a law has been much urged in the present century.[12]

In the same paper Mr. Justice Holmes speaks of a law from another standpoint, namely, the standpoint of a counselor, advising clients as to their rights and liabilities. From this standpoint, he says, a law is a pre-

---

a State, and addressed to the persons who are the subjects of that authority." Amos, *Science of Law*, 48.

10. "The highest reason, implanted in nature, which commands what ought to be done and prohibits the contrary," Cicero, *De legibus*, i, 6; "a rule of moral actions obliging to that which is right," Grotius, *De iure belli ac pacis*, I, 1, 9, § 1; "The expression of the idea of right involved in the relation of two or more human beings," Miller, *Lectures on the Philosophy of Law*, 9.

11. Xenophon, *supra* n. 9; Cicero and Grotius, *supra* n. 10; "A holy sanction commanding what ought to be done and prohibiting the contrary," Fortescue, *De laudibus legum Angliae*, cap. 3; "a rule of civil conduct . . . commanding what is right and prohibiting what is wrong," Blackstone, *Commentaries on the Laws of England*, I, 44.

12. Holmes, *The Path of the Law*, 10 HARVARD LAW REV. 457, 457–61.

diction of what the courts or administrative agencies will do, given a particular state of facts or particular situation.[13] But it is the counselor who does the predicting, not the law. Hence, Mr. Justice Cardozo combined the threat idea and the prediction idea, saying that a law is a rule of conduct so established as to justify a prediction with reasonable certainty that it will be enforced by the courts if its authority is challenged.[14]

Another standpoint from which the nature of a law may be looked at is that of the judge, called upon to decide a case pending before him and looking for an authoritative ground of decision. He may think of a rule of conduct which is, therefore, a rule of decision. Or he may think of a model or pattern of decision of such cases as the one before him.[15] It is because judges feel bound to and do normally give effect to these rules or decide in accordance with these models or patterns that they may serve as rules of conduct for the good man or threats to the bad man or bases of prediction to the counselor.[16]

Finally, there is the standpoint of the jurist or the law teacher who seeks to put the body of legal precepts in the order of reason for the purposes of systematic exposition. Today jurists have come generally to think of a legal precept as an authoritative pattern of what ought to be in conduct, in official action and in decision.

In whichever of these five senses we understand the body of legal precepts which is commonly taken to be meant by the term 'law,' when we come to study it functionally, we find that we must inquire as to certain ideals of the end or purpose of social control and so of the end or purpose of the legal order (law in the first sense), of the judicial process (law in the third sense), and hence of the authoritative materials of judicial decision and administrative action (law in the second sense). We find

13. *Ibid.* 460–61.

14. *The Growth of the Law,* 52.

15. "The sum of the rules administered by courts of justice." Pollock and Maitland, *History of English Law,* 1 ed. (1895), 1, XXV.

16. Gray, *Some Definitions and Questions in Jurisprudence,* 6 HARVARD LAW REV. 21, 24 (1892).

that we must take account of certain ideals of what those authoritative materials should be and how they should be understood and applied in order to achieve the end and purpose of the legal order by means of the judicial process. For example, we find that in the judicial process a highly significant role is played by ideals with reference to which the starting points for legal reasoning are chosen, by ideals which determine what is 'reasonable,' by ideals by which the 'intrinsic merit' of competing interpretations is determined, and by ideals which lead tribunals to extend one precept by analogy while restricting another to the narrow bounds of its four corners.

What is an 'ideal' as I am using the term in connection with theories of the nature of 'law'? The term comes from a Greek word meaning basically something one sees. Applied to action, it is a mental picture of what one is doing or why, to what end or purpose, he is doing it. Postulating a good lawmaker and a good judge, it is a picture of how the one ought to frame the laws he enacts and how the other ought to decide the cases that come before him. But behind these pictures of what ought to be the enacted or the judicially formulated precept for the case in hand is a basic mental picture of the end or purpose of social control—of what we are seeking to bring about by adjustment of relations and ordering of conduct by social pressure on the individual and so immediately of what we are seeking to achieve through adjustment of relations and ordering of conduct by systematic application of the force of politically organized society.

Such ideals may be the avowed basis of determination or may be held and made the background of their decisions by judges unconsciously or, one might say, half consciously, being taken for granted as a matter of course without conscious reference to them. Often they have a traditional authority from having been received in the thinking and understanding of practitioners and judges—an authority, therefore, quite as legitimate as that of traditionally received precepts. Often they have been assumed in a long course of teaching and writing so that lawyers and judges, perhaps for generations, have assumed them as a matter of course as the criteria of valuing claims or expectations, of deciding upon the intrinsic merits of competing interpretations, of choosing from among possible starting points of legal reasoning or among competing analogies and of determining what is reasonable and just. Sometimes we may find this body of received ideals referred to in the lists of *subsidia* in codes or in authoritative or semiauthoritative expositions of codes.[17]

Are ideals of this sort a part of the law? Are we to say, with Bentham, that law is nothing but "the sum total of a number of individual laws taken together"?[18] Shall we say that they are wholly outside of the law, that is, are no part of the authoritative materials established or received for the guidance of judicial or administrative action, or shall we say that so far as they are received and generally recognized by lawyers and judges they are inside of the body of the law, using that term in the second of the three senses set forth above? Shall we say that the ideals which enter into the judicial process in action are partly inside and partly outside of the law? Some, shall we say, are felt by lawyers and judges to be authoritative so that they ought to be applied in adjudication, while others are subjective and personal to particular judges and magistrates and can properly operate no further than to shape or help shape judicial action in matters which the law commits to discretion?

Because men tend to do what they think they are doing, professional and judicial ideals of the social and legal order have been and are a decisive factor in legal development. Such ideals may be so generally and firmly established with the weight of authoritative tradition behind them as to be a form of law in the strictest analytical sense. No consideration of the 'pure fact of law' takes account of the whole fact if it omits these authoritative materials. They are often quite as generally and authoritatively received as the legal precepts whose applications they determine and shape and content they fix. If it is said that many formula-

17. 2 Austin, *Jurisprudence*, 3d ed., 695. Of the examples Austin gives from the lectures by the drafters upon the project of the French Civil Code, the first *subsidium*, natural equity and natural law, is in point, if we bear in mind what those terms meant in France in 1804.

18. *Principles of Morals and Legislation* (1879 ed.) 324.

tions of such ideals fail of acceptance and many ideals are urged which remain wholly subjective and are never authoritatively received or established, the same is true of proposed formulations of legal principles, of attempts to define the limits of legal standards, and of precise statements of rules of law. Everything which is urged in the name of the law does not succeed in establishing itself among the authoritative legal materials. Thus, merely from the analytical standpoint we need to distinguish between these ideals which are received and established and thus have become a part of the 'pure fact of law' and those which might be called sources rather than forms[19] of the ideal element of a given body of law. In the case of legal precepts I have preferred to use 'forms of law' to mean the authoritative shapes which they take, the forms in which they are expressed and to which courts are referred in the decision of controversies. Sources then would be the unauthoritative materials from which the authoritative forms get their content. Ideals which are being urged in current juristic or judicial or professional thought, and so are beginning to influence judicial action without determining it (in the same way as a statement of a suggested rule of law in an Anglo-American text book may influence a court's thinking more or less without being taken up as a ground of decision and formulated in the judgment of a court of ultimate review)—such ideals may be thought of as analogous to the sources of legal precepts. The ideal element in law, if I am right, should have the same thoroughgoing analytical study which has been given to the precept element. We should be studying whence came our received ideals and the newer formulations which are pressing upon tribunals. We should investigate how they have taken form and how they are used. Much study of legal precepts in action has missed effectiveness because it has ignored this element.

My point may be made best from the American cases because in the formative era of American law the courts were seeking to develop a common law for independent America from the common law of England as

---

19. I use these terms in the meanings first well distinguished by Clark, *Practical Jurisprudence*, 196–201 (1883).

it had taken form in the seventeenth and eighteenth centuries. What they thought they were doing and why they were doing it had a special importance in the performance of such a task.

Ideals to which American judges have sought or tended to make the traditional or the enacted legal precepts conform may be ideals of the social order, and so of the end of law, or they may be ideals of the authoritative materials by application of which to the adjustment of relations and ordering of conduct that order is maintained and the end is to be achieved. The latter are more articulate in the reports. Moreover they reflect and help us understand the former. Let us, then, look first at judicial ideals of the content of the precept element of American law. Let us scrutinize judicial pictures of the materials in which the judges held themselves bound to find the grounds of deciding cases. What did they take these materials to be? How did they conceive of the content of the body of legal precepts they were administering?

One way of looking at a body of legal precepts is ethical. It has commonly been put in terms of 'natural law.' It finds natural law by reasoning on the basis of the 'nature of man,' using 'nature' to mean an ideal. It assumes an ideal body of legal precepts derived by reason from an ideal of what a perfect man would do and would not do. This is the classical natural law of the eighteenth century. Let us recall the task of the formative era of American law in which this ideal was dominant. It was necessary to make the common law of England, heavily burdened with the formalism of the strict law, shaped by ideals of the relationally organized society of the Middle Ages, speaking from an era of organization, applicable in a time of commercial development, to the needs and ideas of men who were opening up the wilderness in an oncoming era of individualism. In our social development we began with a pioneer society struggling to subdue the wilderness and defend against the Red Men. Then followed a time of settled agriculture, an era of small towns. Upon this followed a period of commercial progress, involving the rise of seaport cities and trade centers. Then came industrial supremacy and the rise of great metropolitan centers. Some of these stages have followed rapidly at times and in places and more slowly in others. They called for ideas of adaptability tempered by considerations of the stability required by the economic order. Such ideas were drawn from the ideas of the jurists of the eighteenth-century law-of-nature school. Their 'natural law' was set forth at the beginning, and for a long time thereafter, in American introductions to the study of law and elementary law books.[20]

But our American course of judicial decision began after the doctrine of this school was losing its vogue and it seldom appears as such in the law reports. Usually the ethical approach is put in terms of 'the nature of justice' or of 'natural rights.' Here 'nature' means ideal. The law is taken to be a body of reasonable precepts expressing an ideal of justice or a body of precepts expressing an ideal of rights—an ideal of secured moral claims or expectations. The former was commonly given a content from a philosophical version of the historical common law, or sometimes from comparative law. The latter was likely to get a politico-legal content from the bills of rights.

Ethical natural law with a philosophical-historical content seemed to have warrant of authority in the common law doctrine, as laid down by the English courts in the seventeenth century, that an Act of Parliament making a person judge in his own case would not be given effect by the courts,[21] and Blackstone's version of those cases as a rule of interpretation.[22] The refusal of the seventeenth-century courts to enforce a statute 'against common right and reason' meant that legal precepts were pronouncements of common right and reason and to be interpreted and applied as such.[23] More commonly interpretation and application were referred to the 'nature of justice,' that is, an ideal of justice, or the 'nature

20. Full statements may be found in 1 Blackstone, *Commentaries on the Laws of England*, 42; 1 Wilson, *Lectures on Law*, chap. 2, 1 *Works* (1804) 55 ff.; Walker, *American Law* (11 ed. 1905) §§ 10, 11.

21. *Bonham's Case*, 8 Co. Rep. 107a, 113b; *Day v. Savadge*, Hob. 85 (1615); *City of London v. Wood*, 12 Mod. 669 (1701).

22. 1 Blackstone, *Commentaries on the Laws of England*, 91.

23. Examples of this in earlier American decisions are: *Ham v. M'Claws*, 1 Bay, 93, 98 (S.C. 1789); *Bank v. Cooper*, 2 Yerg. 599, 603 (Tenn. 1831); License Tax Cases, 5 Wall. 462, 469 (U.S. 1866).

of things,' that is, an ideal of the moral and social order.[24] A 'natural-rights' way of thinking, a picture of a body of precepts of universal inherent authority, securing ideal fundamental interests or expectations, going back to Grotius[25] by way of Blackstone,[26] was specially manifest in interpretation of the Fourteenth Amendment to the Constitution of the United States,[27] in the application of which it played a great part.[28]

A closely related type of thinking proceeds on a postulated religious natural law. In America it conceived of an ideal Christian society and so of the legal precepts which would obtain in such a society.[29] There was some historical warrant in the old English law books for saying that Christianity was part of the common law.[30] This might mean that the

24. In the Supreme Court of the United States: Johnson, J., in *Fletcher v. Peck*, 6 Cranch. 87, 143 (1810); Story, J., in *Terrett v. Taylor*, 9 Cranch. 43, 50 (1815); *Hurtado v. California*, 110 U.S. 516, 535 (1884); *Arndt v. Griggs*, 134 U.S. 316, 321 (1890); *Turpin v. Lemon*, 187 U.S. 51, 60 (1902); *Watson v. Maryland*, 218 U.S. 173, 177 (1910); *Simon v. Southern R. Co.*, 236 U.S. 115, 122 (1915). In state courts: *Holden v. James*, 11 Mass. 396, 405 (1814); *Dash v. Van Kleeck*, 7 Johns. (N.Y.) 477, 502–9 (1811); Kent, C., in *Gardner v. Newburgh*, 2 Johns. Ch. (N.Y.) 162, 166–67 (1816); *Matter of Albany St.*, 11 Wend. (N.Y.) 149, 151 (1834); *Ervine's Appeal*, 16 Pa. St. 256, 263 (1851); *State Bank v. Cooper*, 2 Yerg. (Tenn.) 599, 602–3 (1831); Baldwin, C.J., in *Hoxie v. New York, N.H. & H.R. Co.*, 82 Conn. 352, 359–60 (1909).

25. Grotius, *De iure belli ac pacis*, I, 1, 4 (1625).

26. 1 Blackstone, *Commentaries on the Laws of England*, 123–26 (1765).

27. See Pound, *Liberty of Contract*, 18 YALE LAW JOURN. 454, 455–58, 464–68 (1909).

28. See for example *United States v. Cruikshank*, 92 U.S. 542, 554 (1875); Field, J., in *Butcher's Union Co. v. Crescent City Co.*, 111 U.S. 746, 756 (1884); *West v. Louisiana*, 194 U.S. 258, 263 (1904); *Rogers v. Peck*, 199 U.S. 425, 434 (1905); *Ballard v. Hunter*, 204 U.S. 241, 262 (1907); *Franklin v. South Carolina*, 218 U.S. 161, 164–65 (1910); *American Ry. Express Co. v. Kentucky*, 273 U.S. 269, 273 (1927); *Commonwealth v. Perry*, 155 Mass. 117, 125 (1891); *People v. Marx*, 99 N.Y. 377, 386 (1885).

29. For an extreme example *see* Turney, J., in *Lanier v. Lanier*, 5 Heisk. (52 Tenn.) 462, 472 (1871). After quoting from the Bible (Matthew 19:3–10) he continues: "Now I must elect between a statutory regulation demoralizing in its every influence and tendency . . . and an express divine law. I do not hesitate to disregard the one and observe the other." He goes on to quote Blackstone: "Upon these two foundations, the law of nature and the law of revelation, depend all human laws — that is, no human law shall be suffered to contradict these." 1 Blackstone, *Commentaries on the Laws of England*, 42.

30. *Taylor's Case*, 1 Vent. 293 (1676). See Story, J., in *Vidal v. Girard*, 2 How. 127, 198 (1843); *Updegraph v. Commonwealth*, 11 Serg. & R. (Pa.) 394 (1824); *Zeisweiss v. James*, 63 Pa. St. 465 (1870).

common law of England presupposed a Christian society and hence its received ideals were those of such a society.[31] But it was obviously another matter to maintain an ideal of a Christian society, as one received as part of the authoritative materials of judicial and administrative determinations in an American state in the nineteenth century.[32] The proposition has never had much currency.

A type which has been most in evidence in American judicial decisions may well be styled a political natural law. In one form it proceeds upon the nature (*i.e.*, ideal) of a politically organized society, commonly referring to the 'social compact,' which is frequently cited with assurance as something given us as authoritatively in all its details as the Statute of Wills.[33] Sometimes it goes on the nature (*i.e.*, ideal) of American institutions.[34] Usually it is put more universally as drawn from the nature (*i.e.*, ideal) of 'free institutions' or of 'republican government.'[35]

31. Kent, C.J., in *People* v. *Ruggles*, 8 Johns. (N.Y.) 290, 294–95 (1811); Doe, J., in *Hale* v. *Everett*, 53 N.H. 9, 202–11 (1868); *Commonwealth* v. *Kneeland*, 20 Pick. (Mass.) 206, 220–21 (1835).

32. Doe, J., in *Hale* v. *Everett*, 53 N.H. 9, 208–11 (1868); *Bloom* v. *Richards*, 2 Ohio St. 387 (1853); Jefferson's Note, 2 Jeff. (Va.) 137–42 (1772).

33. Vanhorne's *Lessee* v. *Dorrance*, 2 Dall. (U.S.) 304, 310 (1795); *Fletcher* v. *Peck*, 6 Cranch (U.S.) 87, 135, 139 (1810); *Goshen* v. *Stonington*, 4 Conn. 209, 225 (1822); *Welch* v. *Wadsworth*, 30 Conn. 149, 155 (1861); *Wheeler's Appeal*, 45 Conn. 306, 315 (1877); *Regents* v. *Williams*, 9 Gill & J. (Md.) 365, 408–9 (1838). Compare Webster, *arguendo* in *Dartmouth College* v. *Woodward*, 4 Wheat. (U.S.) 518, 581 (1819): "The general rules which govern society." Choate, *arguendo*, in *Pollock* v. *Farmers' Loan & Trust Co.*, 157 U.S. 429, 532, 534 (1895) puts it on the basis of the nature (*i.e.*, the ideal) of civilized government.

34. *Holden* v. *James*, 11 Mass. 396, 405 (1814); *Sohier* v. *Massachusetts General Hospital*, 3 Cush. (Mass.) 483, 493 (1849); *Gillilan* v. *Gillilan*, 278 Mo. 99, 111–13 (1919). In this last case primogeniture in estates tail was held "contrary to the theory on which this and other commonwealths were built" (p. 112). The statute read: ". . . and the remainder shall pass in fee simple absolute to the person to whom the estate tail would on the death of the first grantee, devisee or donee in tail first pass according to the course of the common law." Such a provision had been held elsewhere to give the first taker an estate for life and the common-law heir in tail a fee simple." The Supreme Court of Missouri changed the legislatively prescribed course of descent to fit its idea of an ideal social-political theory.

35. In the Supreme Court of the United States: Chase, J., in *Calder* v. *Bull*, 3 Dall. (U.S.) 386, 388–89 (1798); *Wilkinson* v. *Leland*, 2 Pet. (U.S.) 627, 658 (1829); *St. Louis* v.

This ideal was invoked to exclude all arbitrary or unreasonable legislative or executive action, *i.e.*, contrary to a traditional standard of reasonableness, and the phrase 'due process of law' in the constitution, bills of rights, federal and state, was construed as declaratory thereof.[36]

For more than a century this was so universally received and so completely established in American constitutional law that we may well say the ideal was formulated as a standard for judging of legislative and administrative action. If this construction has a historical background in the contests between the Stuart kings and the courts, Coke's Second Institute, and the contests between the colonists and the Crown and Parliament, yet it should be noted that history gave us nothing more than a doctrine of holding the ministers and agents of the Crown to the legal limits of the authority the Crown could give them, refusal to give effect to Royal assumption of the powers of Parliament, and assertion of judicial power to refuse to give effect to legislative action beyond the limits of temporal authority or in derogation of common right and reason. The

---

The Ferry Co., 11 Wall. (U.S.) 423, 429 (1870); Field, J., in Slaughter-House Cases, 16 Wall. 36, 95 (1872); Miller, J., in *Loan Assn. v. Topeka*, 20 Wall. 655, 663–64 (1874); *Monongahela Navigation Co. v. United States*, 148 U.S. 312, 324 (1893); *Chicago B. & Q.R. Co. v. Chicago*, 166 U.S. 226, 235–41 (1897); *Holden v. Hardy*, 169 U.S. 366, 389 (1898); *Madisonville Traction Co. v. St. Bernard Min. Co.*, 196 U.S. 239, 251–52 (1905). In state courts: *In re* Dorsey, 7 Port. (Ala.) 293, 377–78 (1838); *Jeffers v. Fair*, 33 Ga. 347, 367 (1862); *State v. Barker*, 116 Ia. 96, 105; *State v. Nemaha County*, 7 Kan. 542, 555–56 (1871); *White v. White*, 5 Barb. (N.Y.) 474, 484–85 (1849); *Benson v. Mayor*, 10 Barb. 223, 245 (1850); *Nunnemacher v. State*, 129 Wis. 190, 197–202 (1906). In *Jeffers v. Fair* this ideal was used to read an extreme doctrine of states' rights into the Confederate constitution without regard to any language of that instrument.

36. Bradley, J., in *Davidson v. New Orleans*, 96 U.S. 97, 107 (1877); *Ex parte* Wall, 107 U.S. 265, 303 (1882); Field, J., in *Butchers' Union Co. v. Crescent City Co.*, 111 U.S. 746, 759 (1884); *Barbier v. Connolly*, 113 U.S. 27, 31 (1885); *Yick Wo v. Hopkins*, 118 U.S. 356, 369–70 (1886); *Leeper v. Texas*, 139 U.S. 462, 468 (1891); *Lawton v. Steele*, 152 U.S. 133, 137 (1894); *Dobbins v. Los Angeles*, 195 U.S. 223, 236 (1904); *Chicago B. & Q.R. Co. v. McGuire*, 219 U.S. 549, 569 (1911); *Truax v. Corrigan*, 257 U.S. 312, 332 (1921); *Barbour v. Louisville Board of Trade*, 82 Ky. 645, 648 (1884); *Sears v. Cottrell*, 5 Mich. 251, 281 (1858); *Stuart v. Palmer*, 74 N.Y. 183, 190 (1878); *In re* Jacobs, 98 N.Y. 98, 110 (1885); *Norman v. Heist*, 5 Watts & S. (Pa.) 171, 173 (1843); *Dunn v. City Council*, Harper (16 S.C. Law) 189, 199–201 (1824); *State Bank v. Cooper*, 2 Yerg. (Tenn.) 599, 611 (1831).

interpretation of the limits imposed upon the federal and state governments in America by constitutional provisions for due process of law, as securing against what the courts regarded as arbitrary and unreasonable exercise of powers, was derived not from the historical materials of Anglo-American public law, but from an ideal of political action in the New World.

In suits to enjoin expulsion from clubs or societies or voluntary associations, where no property rights are involved but expulsion is a serious injury to the personality of the member expelled or threatened with expulsion, both English courts and American courts have spoken of the rules under which expulsion was threatened or proceedings whereby it took place as 'contrary to natural justice,' deriving an ideal of justice in such matters from the doctrines and methods of process and hearing in the courts.[37] In one case the Master of the Rolls founded his determination on an ideal of the course of action which British officers and gentlemen would pursue.[38]

Closely related to the political-philosophical natural law is an economic-philosophical type in which the doctrine of *laissez faire*, as set forth in the classical political economy, is taken as the ideal of an economic order under an American constitution, and constitutional guarantees are taken to be declaratory thereof. In the statement which has had the most influence, Field, J., quoted from Adam Smith's *Wealth of Nations*.[39] This ideal of the economic order, as a legal ideal to be used as the background of interpreting and applying the provisions of a constitution, was put in almost the very words of the nineteenth-century texts on economics in an advisory opinion by the Supreme Court of Maine in 1871.[40] After this statement of the classical economic doctrine the justices said: "The less the state interferes with industry, the less it di-

37. Brett, L.J., in *Rigby v. Connol*, 14 Ch. D. 482 (1880); *Universal Lodge v. Valentine*, 134 Md. 505 (1919); *Loubat v. LeRoy*, 40 Hun. (N.Y.) 546 (1886); *Grassi Bros. v. O'Rourke*, 89 Misc. (N.Y.) 234 (1915).

38. Jessel, M. R., in *Fisher v. Keane*, 11 Ch. D. 353, 357–59 (1878).

39. *Butchers' Union Co. v. Crescent City Co.*, 111 U.S. 746, 756–57 (1884).

40. *Opinion of the Justices*, 58 Me. 590, 597 (1871).

rects and selects the channels of enterprise, the better. There is no safer rule than to leave to individuals the management of their own affairs. Every individual knows best where to direct his labor, every capitalist where to invest his capital. If it were not so, as a general rule guardians should be appointed, and who would guard the guardians?"[41] There are many other examples in the books.[42] Applied to legislation it is expressed in the doctrine that statutes in derogation of the common law are to be strictly construed.[43] Applied to constitutions it conceives that idealized principles of the traditional law are guaranteed by the bills of rights and are beyond the reach of legislative innovation.[44]

Two typical cases are the decisions upon the first Married Women's Acts in the fore part of the nineteenth century and the earlier decisions upon Workmen's Compensation or Employers' Liability Acts in the present century. To this day the law as to legal transactions of married

41. *Id.* at 598.

42. Peckham, J., in *Lochner v. New York*, 198 U.S. 45, 57 (1905); *State v. Haun*, 61 Kan. 146, 161 (1899); O'Brien, J., in *People v. Coler*, 166 N.Y. 1, 14–17 (1901); Landon, J., *ibid.* 23; Dodge, J., in *State v. Kreutzberg*, 114 Wis. 530, 536–37 (1902). In *People v. Coler*, O'Brien, J., says that the "maxim that the government governs best which governs the least," as an ideal, "was always present to the minds of the men who framed the Constitution, and it is proper for courts to bear it in mind when expounding that instrument." 166 N.Y. at 14. But the eighteenth-century jurists and publicists held to a natural-law creed in which it was a prime article that the reason of the lawmaker could discover and formulate the details of a perfect code. To attribute to them the nineteenth-century distrust of legislation is to read a nineteenth-century ideal into eighteenth-century natural law as well as into the Constitution. As Holmes, J., put it, the constitutions are made to declare, not the doctrines current when they were enacted, but Spencer's Social Statics. *Lochner v. New York*, 198 U.S. 45, 75 (1905).

43. Dwarris, *General Treatise on Statutes*, Potter's ed. 185 (1875). As to this doctrine and its history, *see* Pound, *Common Law and Legislation*, 21 HARVARD LAW REV. 383, 386–402 (1908); Allen, *Law in the Making*, 5 ed. 434–35 (1951).

44. Miller, J., in *Pumpelly v. Green Bay Co.*, 13 Wall. 166, 177 (1871); McKenna, J., dissenting in Arizona Employers' Liability Cases, 250 U.S. 400, 436–37 (1919); *Taylor v. Porter*, 4 Hill (N.Y.) 140, 144–47 (1843); *Ives v. South Buffalo Ry.*, 201 N.Y. 271, 287–89, 293–96, 298 (1911); *Durkin v. Kingston Coal Co.*, 171 Pa. St. 193, 202–3 (1895); Baldwin, J., in *Hoxie v. New York, N.H. & H.R. Co.*, 82 Conn. 352, 359–60 (1909).

women is made difficult by the attitude taken by the courts when these acts first came before them.[45] It is significant to compare the way in which the operation of these statutes was held down, as in derogation of the common law, with the willingness of the courts to go beyond the letter of the statutes in giving effect to laws abrogating or altering rules of the feudal property law.[46] The ideal of an American society, in the minds of the judges, pictured a simple ownership of land freely transferable, as the chief asset of a pioneer society, relieved of rules appropriate to a society ruled by great landowners, and devolving at death in the same way in which personal property was distributed. On the other hand, it pictured women as in the home, not about in the world entering into all manner of legal transactions. The one set of statutes conformed to the picture and was given more than full effect. The other did not and was held down in operation. Both were in derogation of the common law. But it is significant that the doctrine of strict construction of statutes in derogation of the common law was not applied to the laws which overhauled the law of real property and purged it of archaisms. Married Women's Acts were no more radical in their departure from the common law than the statutes which made over descent of land. The difference in judicial treatment is not to be explained analytically by the common-law canons of interpretation.

When Married Women's Acts first came before American courts they were looked at jealously with respect to rights of husbands,[47] just as Workmen's Compensation and Employers' Liability Acts were at first

45. There is a good discussion in Tiffany, *Persons and Domestic Relations*, (3 ed. 1921) §§ 82–83.

46. Compare, for example, the way in which the court went beyond the statute reforming the law as to estates tail in *Gillilan v. Gillilan*, 278 Mo. 99, 111–13 (1919) with the attitude of the same court toward a Married Women's Act in *Leete v. State Bank*, 115 Mo. 184 (1893).

47. E.g., *Erwin v. Puryear*, 50 Ark. 356 (1887); *Farrell v. Patterson*, 43 Ill. 52, 58 (1857); *Coombs v. Read*, 16 Gray (Mass.) 271 (1800); *Carter v. Carter*, 14 Smedes & M. (Miss.) 59 (1850); *Leete v. State Bank*, 115 Mo. 184 (1893); *Westervelt v. Gregg*, 12 N.Y. 202 (1854); *White v. White*, 5 Barb. (N.Y.) 474 (1849).

held unconstitutional for want of due process of law as infringing the liberty and taking away the property of employers. It would have been quite possible to uphold the Married Women's Acts as adopting the equitable as against the common-law view with respect to the property of married women and so not depriving husbands of substantial vested rights but giving the substantial claims of the wife better security than could be afforded in equity. That seems to have been the theory on which the statutes were drawn, as shown by the title: "An Act for the More Effectual Protection of the Property of Married Women."[48]

In the same way the Workmen's Compensation and Employers' Liability Acts might have been upheld, as in the event they came to be, on more than one common-law analogy, notably that of liability without fault of the master or principal for the tort of a servant or agent.[49] The assertion of the writer of the opinion in the New York case that "when our Constitutions were adopted it was the law of the land that no man who was without fault or negligence could be held liable in damages for injuries sustained by another"[50] overlooks well-established common law liabilities without fault which had always obtained in New York: An owner of cattle was bound 'at his peril' to keep them from trespassing;[51] an infant too young to have fault imputed to him was liable in tort;[52] a lunatic, who would not be responsible criminally was liable for tort;[53] one who carried on blasting operations was held for resulting damages without regard to fault.[54] The proposition that there can be no liability without fault was not an established common-law principle. It rested on an ideal of what the law of torts should be, drawn from Continental metaphysical jurisprudence, by which the analytical and historical ju-

---

48. Laws of New York, 1848, p. 307. *See* 1 Spence, *The Equitable Jurisdiction of the Court of Chancery*, 595–97 (1846).

49. Holmes, J., in Arizona Employers' Liability Cases, 250 U.S. 400, 432 (1919).

50. Werner, J., in *Ives v. South Buffalo Ry.*, 201 N.Y. 271, 293 (1911).

51. *Tonawanda R. Co. v. Munger*, 5 Denio (N.Y.) 255, 267 (1848).

52. *Bullock v. Babcock*, 3 Wend. (N.Y.) 391 (1829).

53. *Williams v. Hays*, 143 N.Y. 442 (1894).

54. *Sullivan v. Dunham*, 161 N.Y. 290 (1900).

rists of the nineteenth century were seeking to overhaul the law.[55] In the case of the laws as to inheritance on the one hand and the Married Women's Acts on the other, the courts chose different starting points guided by an ideal of the legal and social order with which the statutes were felt to be in or out of accord.

In contrast to the ethical ideal which derived from eighteenth-century natural law, and the political ideal, which was closely connected with the historical and metaphysical thought of nineteenth-century jurists, a picture of law as a body of logically interdependent precepts, authoritatively established and self-sufficient, without the need of ideals, had much vogue in the last century. It goes back to the medieval conception of the Corpus Iuris as a complete and authoritative body of rules, to be interpreted and applied by a logical process and admitting only of development by an authoritative technique. From this standpoint the nineteenth-century analytical jurists took the science of law to be a mere comparative anatomy of developed systems of legal precepts. They rigidly excluded all questions of what ought to be. Any ethical consideration was irrelevant. Jurist and lawyer and judge were concerned only with the 'pure fact of law.'[56] It was enough to dispose of sociological jurisprudence to say that it was (in Bentham's phrase) de-ontological. It had to do with what ought to be, and what ought to be was not law.[57] Law was an aggregate of laws, logically interdependent and self-sufficient for yielding grounds of decision for any case when logically manipulated. From the latter part of the nineteenth century this conception of the science of law and its ideal of the legal order have been under vigorous attack from many sides. We see clearly enough to-day that the analytical jurist's logically interdependent body of precepts, conforming to a universal plan and potentially covering every conceivable case, is not in the least a 'pure fact.' It is an ideal. It is a picture of a body of law as it is conceived it ought to be. It is no more a fact than the

---

55. See Pound, *Interpretations of Legal History*, 34–37 (1923).
56. Amos, *Systematic View of the Science of Jurisprudence*, 1 (1871).
57. Gray, *Nature and Sources of the Law*, 2 ed. 139, n. 1 (1921).

body of ideal precepts discoverable in detail by reason believed in by jurists in the eighteenth century. The analytical jurist did not discover a universal plan of which each particular legal precept as it actually obtains is a part, as, for example, one of the fragments is a part of a picture puzzle. He sets up a logical plan which will explain as much as possible of the actual norms or models of decision employed in the administration of justice, and criticizes the unexplained remainder for logical inconsistency therewith.

For example, such books as Gray's *Restraints Upon Alienation of Property* or Gray on *The Rule Against Perpetuities,* did not state legal precepts which actually obtain just as they obtain in any one jurisdiction in any one exact time. They set forth the author's conception of what legal precepts ought to obtain in an ideal common-law jurisdiction in which there was an ideal logically interdependent body of legal precepts upon those subjects, logically deducible from the classical common-law authorities. No such system exists anywhere, nor did it ever exist. To postulate such a system serves excellently to organize and make available the authoritative materials of judicial decision. But the postulated ideal system is no more 'pure fact of law' than a historically derived ideal system, such as the historical jurists pressed upon us, or a philosophically constructed ideal system such, for example, as is urged upon us today by the advocates of revived natural law. Moreover, such books postulate traditional ideas of the end of law which give content to the abstract precepts which the analytical jurist conceives to be the 'pure fact of law.' Thus in the preface to the second edition of his *Restraints Upon Alienation*[58] Professor Gray tells us that his critique of the decisions as to spendthrift trusts proceeds on a philosophical theory of the end of law which is assumed to be a cardinal principle of the common law. Such 'principles' may or may not be authoritatively received ideals, established as part of the taught legal tradition. At any rate the one Professor Gray invokes is generically the same as the ethical ideals and political

---

58. Gray, *Restraints Upon Alienation of Property,* 2 ed. 1895, xviii, ix.

ideals above considered. It is a philosophical-economic conception to which it is conceived the administration of justice ought to conform. This analytical ideal, as would be expected where the English legal tradition prevails, proves at bottom, when compared with the ethical and political ideals of law, to be political.[59] It is an ideal of a legal order in an ideal politically organized society in which relations are governed, conduct is regulated, and differences are adjusted by fixed rules, attaching definite detailed consequences to definite detailed states of fact, and of uniform application, so that every personal element in the administration of justice is eliminated. It pictures a legal order as part of the political order portrayed by the political natural law which has given content to the phrase 'due process of law.' For that type of juristic and judicial thinking has behind it an ideal of a politically organized society in which governmental power of every sort is wielded upon careful weighing of all the interests involved and a reasoned striving to give effect to all of them; in which, therefore, arbitrary or capricious selection of the interests to be secured, and securing of some without regard to the effect upon others, does not take place.

Although the ideal of a body of law held by the analytical jurists in the nineteenth century had behind it a picture of politically organized society, it was a picture drawn from the nationalist polities of the sixteenth century. But three governing ideas as to the nature of law, that is, as to the nature of the body of authoritative materials for the guidance of judicial and administrative action, which obtained in the later Middle Ages, have been more widely accepted and have been persistent in legal and juristic thought.

First, there is the universal idea, the ideal of law as a body of precepts of universal authority, universal content, and universal applicability. Second, there is the idea of relationship, the ideal of law as a body of precepts dealing with relations and flowing from or attaching to relations; as a body of precepts governing men because of the relations in which

59. See Pound, *Interpretations of Legal History*, lect. 3 (1923).

they find themselves. Medieval society was relationally organized. Evidently this ideal of law proceeded from an idealizing of existing society as did the ideal of the end of law held at the same time. It should be contrasted with the nineteenth-century idea of law as deduced not from relation but from freedom; as expressing not the duties of men in relations but the rights of independent, self-sufficient, free-willing entities. Third, there is the idea of authority, the ideal of a body of precepts authoritatively imposed upon men from without by an unchallengeable authority, to be interpreted and applied but not subject to local change nor to be added to or subtracted from in this or that place.

Thus in the latter Middle Ages there was, in the first place, an ideal of a universal body of precepts resting on an external universal authority governing all Christendom. Jurists postulated a universal church, with exclusive jurisdiction over matters of spiritual cognizance, and in consequence its own body of universal law. Also they postulated a universal empire, an academic conception of Christendom as an empire continuous with that of Augustus, of Constantine and of Justinian, and hence governed by Justinian's law books as authoritative legislation for that empire. Also along with these ideas, in part flowing from the same ideal and in part competing with them, there was the Germanic idea of law as an expression of the justice and truth of the Creator, having an authority above kings and lawmakers and of universal force because of the universal authority of God's justice and God's truth.[60]

In the politics and law of the Middle Ages the distinction between the spiritual and the temporal, between the jurisdiction of religiously organized Christendom and the jurisdiction of the temporal sovereign, that is, of a politically organized society, was fundamental. It seemed as natural and inevitable to have church courts and state courts, each with their own field of action and each, perhaps, tending to encroach upon the other's domain, but each having their own province in which they were paramount, as it seems to Americans to have two sets of courts, federal courts and state courts, operating side by side in the same territory,

---

60. Heusler, *Institutionen des deutschen Privatrechts* (1885–86) § 1.

each supreme in their own province. When the medieval English courts held acts of Parliament 'impertinent to be observed' where they sought to effect results in matters spiritual[61] they did what a court, state or federal, would do in the United States if a state legislature were to seek to prohibit interstate commerce by putting an embargo on imports from a neighboring state.

How the ideal of a universal church gave a stamp to doctrines and institutions which has endured ever since may be seen in the law of marriage. The academic teachers of law, the doctors of the civil and canon law in the universities, had before them the ideal of a universal law, and the doctrine of the twelfth-century canonists has maintained itself everywhere as the basis of the law on this important subject. It is significant that in the face of the ultra-individualism of nineteenth-century law, in the face of the general emancipation of women and straining of the last century to treat all things in terms of the individual will, the idea of marriage as a condition which cannot be terminated by the act of the parties but only by nature or the law was able to persist.[62] If we contrast the theory of marriage and the conception of marriage as creating a condition of the parties, not merely an obligation, which came into the law of all Christendom from the Middle Ages, with the utter diversity of divorce laws, from country to country and in the United States from state to state, speaking from the era of nationalism after the Reformation, the difference will tell us something of the power of an ideal of a universal law.

Again the medieval academic teaching of law postulated the continuity of the empire. This was a juristic ideal of a universal law for the temporal concerns of all Christendom; an ideal of Christendom ruled by one law to be found in the law books of Justinian. The development of the texts of the Corpus Iuris to this ideal gave a body of received, au-

61. *Rous* v. *An Abbot*, Statham, Abr., Annuity, 11; Fitzherbert, Abr. Annuity, 41, Easter, 27 Hen. 6 (1449); *Prior of Castleacre* v. *Dean of St. Stephens*, Y.B. 21 Hen. 7, 1 (1506).
62. Even the Soviet Civil Code of 1926 preserves much of the general doctrine which obtained elsewhere by derivation from the canonists. 1 Gsovski, Soviet Civil Law, 116 (1948).

thoritative grounds of judicial decision which has endured as the basis of the legal system in half of the modern world. More than this it gave a basis for utilizing the juristic thought of any part of Christendom in any other. The reason of any law teacher anywhere, exerted upon the texts of the Roman law with reference to any legal problem of medieval Europe, was available to any jurist or any tribunal anywhere else when confronted with the same problem or one analogous. Thus the ideal of universality, an ideal of the universities, which taught one law wherever situated, enabled the law in each locality to develop by availing itself of the sum of juristic activity everywhere.

We have had a similar phenomenon in American legal history. The ideal of a general common law, held by Kent and Story, and governing in American law schools under the leadership of those which have taught from a national standpoint, made possible the rapid development of a law for the new world by enabling the courts in the newly peopled and newly organized states to use the whole judicial experience, not merely of the older states but of the English-speaking world. What the ideal of a universal law could do for a great department of the law throughout the world is illustrated in the conflict of laws. The commentators in the Middle Ages drew a universal theory from the Roman texts so well, on simple lines so generally acceptable,[63] that this great subject has kept to those lines ever since. This is perhaps the one subject in the law governing private relations where common-law lawyer and civilian understand each other and where Story[64] and Savigny[65] are cited equally throughout the world.

Elsewhere I have spoken at length of the idea of relation as the basis of much of our thinking in Anglo-American law.[66] Where the Pandectist thought in terms of will, the common-law lawyer has characteristically spoken in terms of relation. In that idea he has found a starting

63. Bartolus in *The Conflict of Laws*, transl. by Beale (1914).

64. Story, *Commentaries on the Conflict of Laws*, Foreign and Domestic (1834).

65. Savigny, *System des heutigen römischen Rechts*, vol. 8 (1849), English transl. by Guthrie as *A Treatise on the Conflict of Laws* (2 ed. 1880).

66. Pound, *The Spirit of the Common Law* (1921), 20–31.

point for judicial and juristic reasoning which has come down from the Middle Ages and grown out of a medieval ideal. It may suggest Spencer's proposition that law is a government of the living by the dead. But Mr. Justice Holmes has given us the answer: "Continuity with the past is only a necessity and not a duty."[67] It is not, for any great part, that rules prescribing definite, detailed legal consequences for definite, detailed states of fact, made by or for the dead are governing the living. It is rather that the past has given us analogies, starting points for reasoning and methods of developing legal materials that have proved themselves in experience and are still serviceable.

A third medieval shaping juristic idea was the idea of authority. Philosophically this idea had in itself the seeds of its own undoing. But it has maintained itself in law and, as the medieval lawyer worked it out as a received ideal, has endured as part of the legal equipment of the modern world.

For example, compare the seventeenth-century commentary of Coke on Littleton's *Tenures,* the oracle of the law of real property in the English-speaking world for three centuries, with the gloss of the Italian law teachers on Justinian's *Digest* in the twelfth century. Coke assumed that Littleton's treatise was "the most perfect and absolute work that was ever written in any human science," that it was a work of "absolute perfection in its kind," and "free from error."[68] Postulating this, he analyzed it section by section and developed the content of each section and sentence and phrase so as to make it the basis of English land law down to 1926[69] and of American land law in most of our states today. He did for Littleton what the glossators had done for the *Digest.*[70] To those who are familiar with the doctrinal development of the Continental codes in the

67. *Law in Science and Science in Law,* 12 HARVARD LAW REVIEW, 443, 444 (1899).

68. Coke on *Littleton,* preface (1628) Hargrave and Butler's 18th ed. xxxvi.

69. *Law of Property Act,* 12 & 13 Geo. 5, chap. 16 (1922), put into effect by 15 Geo. 5 chaps. 18, 19, 20, 21, 22, 23, 24, to go into effect in 1926.

70. 1 CONTINENTAL LEGAL HISTORY SERIES, *General Survey,* 124–42; Vinogradoff, *Roman Law in the Middle Ages,* 44–58; 5 Savigny, *Geschichte des römischen Rechts in Mittelalter,* 222–40; Salvioli, *Storia del diritto italiano,* 8 ed. §§ 105–12.

nineteenth century one need say no more. To the Anglo-American lawyer I would say compare Story's Commentaries on the Constitution of the United States[71] or compare a commentary on the Uniform Negotiable Instruments Law or the Uniform Sales Act today. In each case some text is postulated as of final authority and we develop its content analytically and by logical unfolding. The philosophical science of law of the seventeenth and eighteenth centuries and the historical method of the nineteenth century each added something to our technique. But the medieval method of postulating authority, or postulating a text which can only be interpreted, which is self-sufficient, which contains in itself expressly or by implication a complete body of precepts covering the whole matter with which it deals, is one that must be employed when applying such an instrument as a written constitution or such statutes as the American Uniform State Laws, or in applying the traditional materials governing such subjects as property in land.

It must not be forgotten that this self-sufficiency of the authoritative text is but an ideal. It is a postulate for certain practical purposes. It is not an assertion of absolute fact. It may be shown that the ideals, or, if you will the postulates of straight lines and planes and perpendiculars do not conform to the facts of Einstein's curved universe. Yet these ideal lines and planes and perpendiculars are exceedingly useful for many practical purposes. Likewise it is no matter that the postulates of our technique of interpreting and applying authoritative legal texts may be shown not to accord precisely with reality. It is easy to point out that a chief difficulty in interpreting and applying a text assumed to be complete and self-sufficient is that it presupposes an intention as to every detail on the part of the framers of the text, whereas what calls for interpretation is very likely the circumstance that as to the point in controversy they had none. The particular situation of fact did not occur to them.[72] It has been easy to show that the glossators and commentators and the nineteenth-century Pandectists made the texts of the Di-

71. First ed. 1833, 5 ed. 1891.
72. Gray, *Nature and Sources of the Law*, 2 ed. 172–73 (1921).

gest announce propositions which were not the Roman law of antiq-uity.[73] It has often been shown that Coke's versions of the medieval En-glish law were sometimes adaptations to the exigencies of the judicial process in the seventeenth century.[74] But the answer is that in postulat-ing intention of the lawmaker we are doing so as a means toward certain practical results. Law in each of its three juristic meanings is a practical matter. For practical purposes the postulates involved in the ideal of au-thority come as close to the phenomena of finding and applying the law, the phenomena of the judicial process, as the postulates come to the phenomena in any body of organized knowledge. The medieval idea of authority has given an instrument of enduring usefulness in the doctri-nal development of the law and in the judicial process.

At the Reformation authority broke down on every side. In religion the north of Europe substituted unauthoritative private interpretation of the Scriptures for authoritative interpretation by the church. In phi-losophy the scholastic dialectical development of authoritative starting points gave way to new methods. Aristotle ceased to be 'the philosopher.' Philosophy was used to challenge authority, not merely to uphold it. The canon law lost its sanction and came to have little more than his-torical interest except as it continued to govern the internal organization of the Roman Church. Presently also the Roman law lost its theoretical binding force in western Europe with the disappearance of the aca-demic dogma of the continuity of the empire. The universal idea and the idea of authority gave way to two ideas which proved adequate to achieve stability and to direct growth for the next two and one-half cen-turies. These were (1) the political idea, the idea of a national or local law, with a sufficient basis in the power of the local political authority,[75] and (2) the idea of reason, the idea of law as a formulation of the rea-

---

73. Buckland, *Wardour Street Roman Law*, 17 LAW QUARTERLY REVIEW, 179 (1901), *More Wardour Street Roman Law*, 31 LAW QUARTERLY REVIEW, 193 (1915).

74. Allen, *Law in the Making*, 5 ed. 425–28 (1951); Plucknett, *Bonham's Case and Ju-dicial Review*, 40 HARVARD LAW REVIEW, 30 (1926).

75. Hobbes, *Leviathan* (1651); Bentham, *Principles of Morals and Legislation* (1780); Austin, *The Province of Jurisprudence Determined* (1832).

sonable, deriving its authority from its inherent reasonableness, and putting in legal form the ideal precepts which are identifiable and to be identified by a sheer effort of reason.[76]

Thus the medieval idea of authority went on in juristic nationalism or even localism, the political idea. The universal idea of the Middle Ages went on in what I have called positive natural law, an ideal of a universal superlaw, discoverable by reason, to which local law ought to conform and of which the local law at its best is a reflection.

Nationalism, in the form of faith in a self-sufficient local law, took a strong hold upon the imagination of Americans in the nineteenth century. For a long time the several states took a certain pride in anomalies of local decision and local legislation as things to be cherished for their own sake. As late as the beginning of the present century there was in many quarters a sort of cult of local law.[77] Even now, when this worship of local legal anomalies has become a thing of the past through the teaching of a general common law in university law schools which have taken the lead in training for the legal profession, effects of the cult of local law embarrass business and enterprise in more than one connection. For example, the Uniform Negotiable Instruments Law has been on our state statute books for more than half a century. It lays down detailed rules which have been adopted usually in identical language by the legislatures of the several states with the avowed purpose of making the law on this subject uniform throughout the United States. Yet this statute, very much needed and urged by bankers and business men, has not completely achieved the desired uniformity. Courts have been so tenacious of the anomalies of the local law that in one way or another they have adhered to them in the teeth of the statute.[78] When a subject

76. Grotius, *De iure belli ac pacis* (1625); Pufendorf, *De iure naturae et gentium* (1672); Burlamaqui, *Principes du droit naturel* (1747); Wolff, *Institutiones iuris naturae et gentium* (1750); Rutherforth, *Institutes of Natural Law* (1754–56); Vattel, *Le Droit des gens, Préliminaires* (1758).

77. "In all that is good, Iowa affords the best." Motto on the title page of Ebersole, *The Iowa People's Law Book* (1900).

78. There is a full discussion in Beutel's Brannan, *Negotiable Instruments Law*, 80–90 (1948).

so vital to business as the law of bills and notes can remain in that condition although a uniform statute has been on the books since 1896, it is evident that the idea of intrinsic validity and value of local law had taken deep root.

Throughout the world there has been a revival of the universal ideal. In the United States, where the idea of the intrinsic value of local law had been strongest, no less than four countermovements have been making for a swing back to the idea of a general law. These are: (1) the movement for uniform state legislation promoted by the National Conference of Commissioners on Uniform State Laws, (2) the restatement of American common law recently under the auspices of the American Law Institute, (3) the influence of national as contrasted with local law schools, becoming marked after 1890, and (4) the revival of interest in comparative law. In the formative era of American law comparative law was resorted to in order to find the rule of natural law, dictated by reason, of which a rule of positive law was bound to be declaratory. After decades of neglect following a general giving up of eighteenth-century natural law throughout the world, comparative law has been taking on a new life. It is not the least of the forces in the law of today which are bringing back the universal ideal to meet the needs of a unifying world.

Again the idea of authority is taking on new form and may be seen at work in juristic thought on every hand. A postulated ultimate practical source of rules and sanctions, a postulated form of law to which other guides to judicial and administrative action must be subordinated, raise questions very like those to which medieval ideas of authority were addressed. Ever since the Reformation the emphasis has been on change. The Reformation, the Puritan Revolution, the English Revolution of 1688, the American Revolution, the French Revolution, the Russian Revolution—six major revolutions in four hundred years, or roughly one in every other generation—have made violent change seem the normal course of things and stability seem stagnation. But there have in the past been eras of legal and political stability. Like our own time, moreover, they have been eras of bigness and of wide economic unification, not of self-sufficing small politically organized societies and neighborhood economic independence. If we are moving toward stress on peace and stability, shall we not turn to an ideal of authority? Likewise there is a revival of the idea of relation.[79] The nineteenth-century ideal of the abstract free individual will is manifestly giving way before a renewed tendency to think of men not as isolated in abstract ideal conditions but as in concrete relations; to think of them as in a society in which they are all in every sort of relation with their fellow men and their most significant activities for the legal order take place in or have to do with these relations.[80] This revived idea of relation is connected with an ideal of co-operation, one might say of co-operative effort to maintain, further, and transmit civilization. In all parts of the world economic unification and organization of industry are affecting the received conception of the relation of man to man in society. The received ideal of free competitive activity of individual self-sufficing units is being redrawn as one of adjusted relations of economically interdependent units.

To show that such ideals are by no means wholly realized in practice in the course of judicial decision does not dispose of them. They or some of them are as much a part of the authoritative traditional legal materials by which justice is administered as the authoritative starting points for legal reasoning which are chosen by reference to them, or the authoritative rules which are selected, interpreted and applied to conform to them. An ideal of the end of law, and hence of what legal precepts should be and how they should be applied, set forth in the formative era of American law by Kent[81] and Story,[82] developed by Cooley,[83] applied to new areas of the law by Dillon,[84] and constantly recurring in the re-

---

79. Pound, *The Spirit of the Common Law*, lect. 1 (1921); id. *The New Feudalism*, 16 AM. BAR ASSN. JOURN. 553 (1930).

80. Ehrlich, *Fundamental Principles of the Sociology of Law*, transl. by Moll, chap. 3 (1936).

81. *Dash v. Van Kleeck*, 7 Johns. (N.Y.) 477 (1811); 1 Kent, *Commentaries on American Law*, 455 (1826).

82. *Wilkinson v. Leland*, 2 Pet. (U.S.) 627, 658 (1829).

83. *Constitutional Limitations*, chap. 11 (1868).

84. *Municipal Corporations*, §§ 104–5 (1872).

ported judicial decisions as the avowedly determining element, is too significant a phenomenon to be overlooked in a scientific account of American law. I undertake to add that as much may be said for any developed system of law. The existence of such ideals should be recognized as one authoritative form which legal materials may take. Their history should be traced as we trace the history of legal precepts. Their operation in action should be studied as we study the operation in action of legal precepts. In the past, philosophical jurisprudence has been concerned with the ethical and philosophical bases of legal institutions and legal precepts and the principles and method of criticism with reference to those bases. Today we should be employing philosophical method in jurisprudence to set off and criticize the ideal element in systems of developed law, to organize that element, as in the last century we organized the precept element, to give it definiteness, and to work out a critique no less assured and thorough than that to which the apparatus of rules and doctrines has long been subjected.

TWO

Natural Law

Law as a body of authoritative grounds of or guides to decision and administrative action under a legal order, as has been said in the first lecture, is made up of three elements: A precept element, a body of authoritative norms, *i.e.*, models or patterns of decision in adjusting relations and ordering conduct, a technique element, an authoritative technique of developing, interpreting and applying the precepts, and an ideal element, a body of received and traditionally authoritative or taught ideals with respect to which the precepts are developed, interpreted, and applied.

In a developed body of law the first and the third elements, the precept element and the ideal element are of chief importance. Likewise the ideal element has a special relation to one of the two forms of legal precept. Legal precepts, as to their form, may be, on the one hand, enacted or imperative, or, on the other hand, traditional or habitual. The first is the modern element in a body of legal precepts today and, so far as the form of the law is concerned, is tending to become predominant. The second is the older or historical element upon which juristic development of the law proceeds by analogy. In the process of time consciously made and promulgated laws, legislation, becomes absorbed in the traditional material of the legal system. The enacted rule becomes a traditional principle. Thus in Roman law in its maturity the *leges* of the republic and the *senatus consulta* of the early empire have long ceased to be referred to according to their texts. "They were recognized only in the form in which they had been embodied in the writings of the jurisconsults, and were regarded as part of the *ius* or jurisprudential law rather than of the *leges* or statute law."[1] Also English statutes prior to colonization and to some extent prior to the Declaration of Independence are part of American common law in the form in which they were construed at the Revolution.[2] The older English statutes are part of English common law in the way in which they were worked into it by Coke.[3] There is a gradual transformation of the imperative into the traditional element of the legal system. On the other hand, as the traditional element is developed by judicial experience and juristic science and its principles are worked out into detailed rules, these rules are in time given imperative form by legislation, so that there is a gradual transformation of the traditional into the imperative. Examples may be seen in the English Bills of Exchange Act and Sale of Goods Act and the American Negotiable Instruments Law, Uniform Sales Act, and like statutes promoted by the Conference of Commissioners on Uniform State Laws.[4]

At first the traditional element rests upon the usage and practice of tribunals or the usage and customary modes of advising litigants on the part of those upon whom tribunals rely for guidance.[5] Later it comes to rest upon juristic science and the habitual modes of thought of a learned profession. Thus the basis of its authority comes to be reason and conformity to ideals of right.[6] On the other hand, the imperative element

1. Muirhead, *Historical Introduction to the Private Law of Rome*, § 84, p. 404 (1 ed. 1886).

2. *Patterson v. Winn*, 5 Pet. (U.S.) 533 (1831); *Spaulding v. Chicago & N.W.R. Co.*, 30 Wis. 111 (1872).

3. Thus the Statute, 34 Hen. 8, c. 34 (1540) is always discussed in terms of *Spencer's Case*, 5 Co. 16a (1583), and the Statute, 13 Eliz. c. 5 (1570) in terms of *Twyne's Case*, 3 Co. 80b (1601).

4. The Acts are set out in full, together with the corresponding English Acts, in the series *Uniform Laws Annotated*, published by Edward Thompson Co., Brooklyn, N.Y.

5. *Interpretatio* of the *ius ciuile* during the Roman republic may be instanced. *Dig.* I, 2, 2, §§ 5, 6.

6. "For reason is the life of the law, nay the common law itselfe is nothing else but reason," *Co. Lit.* 97b. "The common law is the absolute perfection of reason; for nothing that is contrary to reason is consonant to law." Wood, *Institute of the Laws of En-*

rests immediately upon enactment — upon the expressed will of the sovereign. The basis of its authority is the power of the state.[7] In consequence of these two elements in a developed legal system and of the different bases upon which their authority is rested, two distinct ideas of law in the second of the three senses in which lawyers use the term, are to be found throughout the history of juristic science.

Corresponding to these ideas and corresponding to the two elements in the body of authoritative legal precepts, two distinct words, originally expressing two distinct ideas, are to be found in most languages spoken by peoples among whom law in the lawyer's sense has had any great development. One set of words, τὸ δίκαιον, *ius, Recht, droit, diritto, derecho*, has particular reference to the idea of right (what is right) and justice. The leading notion of this set of words is ethical. Hence these words have three meanings. First they mean *right* — that which accords with our ethical ideas. Second they mean *a right*, a reasonable expectation of the individual under the circumstances of life in a civilized society — a right, moral or legal, that is, a capacity which the moral sense of the community or the power of the state confers in order to bring about right. Third they come to mean law, that is, a system of principles or body of precepts designed to enforce rights and bring about right. In other words, each of this set of words means primarily right and refers to an idea of right and justice, but comes to be used also to mean law in general. It is appropriate to and is on the whole the prevailing word in periods of legal history in which law is formative or is expanding and developing through juridical exposition or some other non-imperative agency. The other set of words νόμος, *lex, Gesetz, loi, legge, ley*, refers primarily to that which is enacted or set authoritatively, but tends to mean law as a whole. It is appropriate to periods of enacted law and to

---

gland, Introduction (1722). "The word law is used in many senses. One sense is when that which is always equitable and just is called law, as, for instance, natural law." Paul, in *Dig.* I, 1, 11, pr.

7. Compare the dictum of Hobbes that authority not truth makes the law. 2 English Works, 185, 6 *id.* 26.

periods of legal history in which the growing point of law is in legislation.

As now one and now the other of the elements of a developed legal system has prevailed for the time being, now one and now the other name has come to be used for the whole. The classical period of Roman law was marked by juristic rather than by legislative activity, and the classical period of the modern Roman law was similarly characterized. Hence the preponderance of *ius* and its equivalents in the languages of Continental Europe. On the other hand, in England, where a strong central authority took the administration of justice in hand under the Normans and through the king's courts and the king's writs created a vigorous system which attained fixity before juristic development had gone far enough to exert an influence, *law*, a word of the second type,[8] became the general term, and *right*,[9] never acquired more than an ethical signification.

I have spoken of the traditional element in a legal system as rested upon usage. Thus it is a product of experience. At Rome it grew out of the experience of jurisconsults in answering questions as to actual controversies litigated in the forum. In Anglo-American law it has grown out of decision of cases in the courts and the endeavour to find in recorded judicial experience the principles of deciding new questions arising in concrete experience in concrete controversies. The imperative element, on the contrary, is immediately the work of a lawmaker or lawmaking body. The lawmaker may be advised or guided by a philosopher. But he is likely to think of himself as invested with a power to command. Thus we have law as ascertainment and formulation of just precepts on the basis of experience and law as command of what the lawmaker holds

8. As distinguished from *a law*. Etymologically, however, *law* is a word of the first type. Clark, *Practical Jurisprudence* 67–70 (1883).

9. As distinguished from *a right* which may be thought of as moral or as legal. In Scotland, however, where Continental influence was strong from the sixteenth century, *Recht*, *droit*, and *diritto* are often translated by *right*. E.g., Lioy, *Philosophy of Right*, transl. by Hastie (1891).

to be just precepts. For judge, jurist, and lawmaker seek to establish just precepts, and each is governed by some ideal.

From the Greek philosophers through the greater part of the history of juristic thought the ideal, both for judge and jurist and for legislator has been provided, in various forms by the theory of natural law, a theory of a body of ideal precepts of universal validity for all peoples, for all times, and for all places, derived from ideas of what an ideal man would do and would not do, would claim and would concede as the claims of others, and arrived at wholly or at least in large part by pure reason.

Civilization, the development of human powers to continually greater completeness, the maximum of human control over external or physical nature and over internal or human nature of which men are for the time being capable, seems to me the starting point for the social sciences. So much, I submit, we can learn from the Neo-Hegelians even if we do not arrive at it nor justify it after the manner of Hegel. It is the control over internal nature which has enabled man to inherit the earth and to maintain and increase that inheritance. The social sciences have to do with this achieved mastery over internal or human nature. They study and teach what it is, how it has come about, and how it is and may be maintained, furthered, and transmitted. Immediately civilization is maintained by social control, by the pressure brought to bear upon each man by his fellow men, the major agencies of which are morals, religion, and law. In the beginnings of law these are not differentiated. Even in so advanced a civilization as the Greek city-state one word is used to mean religious rites, ethical custom, the traditional course of adjusting human relations, the legislative regulations of the city to promote the general security, and all these looked on as a whole. All the agencies of social control and the means of exercising them are included in the one term which we translate as 'law.'[10] The beginnings of philosophical

10. This is well brought out in Plato's *Minos*, now considered not a genuine work of Plato and variously dated from as early as about 350 B.C. to as late as about 250 B.C.

jurisprudence are in Greek philosophical thinking upon social control.

Greek definitions of law vary greatly. Some are imperative,[11] some are in terms of agreement, one might say social contract, which would include custom along with legislation,[12] some speak of discovery of the natural, universal ethical precept,[13] and some of universal rules not only to govern human conduct but governing all things, and so the phenomena of physical nature as well.[14] Demosthenes, not a philosopher or jurist, but an orator, *i.e.*, advocate, argued to what may be likened to a jury that they should enforce the law, not run away with it, as both Greek dicasts and Anglo-American jurors will, gave the term almost every meaning that has ever been attributed to it. Law, he said, was something "which men ought to obey for many reasons, and chiefly because every law is both a discovery and a gift of God, and a teaching of wise men and a setting right of wrongs, intended and not intended, but also a common agreement of the state, according to which every one in the state ought to live."[15]

But the permanent Greek contribution to juristic thought about law was made by Aristotle. Reflecting on the adjustment of relations and ordering of conduct in the Greek city-state he distinguished two types of precepts in a discussion which became fundamental. He said "Of political justice part is natural, part legal — natural that which everywhere has the same force and does not exist by people's thinking this or that, legal, that which is originally indifferent, but when it has been laid down is not indifferent, *e.g.*, that a prisoner's ransom shall be a *mina*, or that a goat and not two sheep shall be sacrificed, and again all the laws that are

11. "What the ruling part of the state enacts after considering what ought to be done is called law." Xenophon (B.C. c. 429–c. 356) *Memorabilia*, 1, 2, § 43.

12. "A definite statement, according to a common agreement of the state, giving warning how everything ought to be done." Anaximenes (B.C. c. 560–c. 500) quoted by Aristotle, *Rhetoric to Alexander*, I.

13. Plato (B.C. 427–347) *Minos*, 315 A.

14. Chrysippus (B.C. 287–209) quoted by Diogenes Laertius, VII, 88.

15. Demosthenes (B.C. 384–322) *Oration Against Aristogeiton*, 774.

passed for particular cases, *e.g.*, that sacrifice shall be made in honor of Brasidas[16] and the provisions of decrees."[17]

Here Aristotle points out that of the precepts according to which social control was exercised by the politically organized society of a Greek city-state part had the same form everywhere, *i.e.*, in all civilized societies, while part was established by some ruling authority, moral or legal. The text speaks of a natural element, which has the same force everywhere and does not depend on what people think here and there, and an element established by custom of this or that people or community by the local lawmaking authority. The natural is contrasted with the legal or conventional; the universal which had its basis in nature, with the legal or conventional which depended on how men habitually acted in their relations with each other and on how they voted in the lawmaking assemblies or decreed as rulers or as magistrates. This idea of a universal natural law had a strong hold in Greek thought as illustrated in the oft-quoted words which Sophocles puts in the mouth of Antigone: "The unwritten steadfast precepts of the gods."[18] The precept here enjoined upon kinsmen burial of their dead. It was to the Greeks a universal religious precept. The Stoics said that "law was by nature and not by imposition."[19]

16. When the Spartans captured Amphipolis, an Athenian colony, in B.C. 424, the Athenian colonists were driven out and their place was taken by new colonists. The Greeks thought of a city-state as a group of kindred, descended from a common ancestor to whom ancestor worship was due. Those who repeopled Amphipolis came from different communities and could claim no common ancestor. Hence they chose the Spartan general Brasidas, who had taken the city, as their eponym. Aristotle puts the law providing for sacrifice to Brasidas as eponym as an example of a legal (or today we should say positive) precept as distinguished from a natural one.

17. *Nicomachean Ethics*, V, 7, translation in McKeon, *Basic Works of Aristotle*, 1014 (1941). On Greek ideas of natural law, *see* Hildebrand, *Geschichte und System der Rechts- und Staatsphilosophie*, I, DAS KLASSISCHE ALTERTUM, §§ 1–122 (1860); Sauter, *Die philosophischen Grundlagen des Naturrechts*, chaps. 1–2 (1931); Burle, *Essai historique sur le développement de la notion de droit naturel dans l'antiquité grecque* (1908); Ehrenberg, *Die Rechtsidee im früheren Griechentum* (1921).

18. Sophocles, *Antigone*, 454.

19. Stobaeus, *Ecologae*, ii, 184.

As to how such precepts were found, the doctrine was not so clear. They might be legal-ethical precepts given to men by the gods, or found by reason, or general religious-ethical or legal-ethical customs, put as ideal universals. Aristotle in another work contrasts the proper law of a particular city-state with the law common to the Greek city-states which is said to be in accord with nature.[20] It seems from this text that he thought of 'common law' (κοινός) as 'natural law' (νόμός καταφύσιν). This suggests a like tendency of Roman jurists to identify *ius naturale* and *ius gentium*.

Democritus had said that "rules of law (νόμιμα) are made by men; atoms and void (*i.e.*, the unoccupied space in which the atoms exist) exist by nature."[21] What, then, did the Greek philosophers mean by 'nature'? Certainly it was not what it meant to the biological evolutionary thinking of the nineteenth century. To the latter the 'natural' apple would be the wild crab apple, from which the apple of the orchard has been developed by cultivation. To the Greek very likely it would have been the golden apple of the Hesperides. In Latin φύσις (literally growth) is translated as *natura*. Lucretius translated the περίφύσεος of Epicurus as *de rerum natura*. How things grew, or perhaps how they came into existence, could be expressed by how they were born. Applied to things 'nature' seems to be the ideal of the thing in its highest perfection. Applied to laws and institutions it appears to have meant the law or institution in its most perfect form.

A distinction which Aristotle drew in the passage quoted from the Nicomachean Ethics came down into modern law as a distinction between *mala in se* and *mala prohibita*. As Blackstone put it, the former are actions which are naturally and intrinsically wrong while the latter are actions which are in themselves indifferent but become wrong "according as the municipal legislator sees proper for promoting the welfare of the society and more effectually carrying on the purposes of civil

---

20. Aristotle, *Rhetoric to Alexander*, I, 14, 16.
21. *Diogenes Laertius*, IX, 45.

life."[22] What this came to is that the older infringements of the social interest in the general security were recognized in the formative era of American criminal law as *mala in se*. But newer methods of infringement, becoming antisocial under the conditions of today, in which all manner of mechanical means of endangering life and limb are invented and in operation, have to be the subject of legislation and are said to be *mala prohibita*.[23] The distinction in this form has not been satisfactory in its results.

"Law must be stable and yet it cannot stand still. Hence all thinking about law has struggled to reconcile the conflicting demands of the need of stability and of the need of change." Thus I began my lectures on interpretations of legal history a generation ago.[24] Aristotle might have said that the universal precepts of the natural or general (κοινός) part of law, being immutable, maintained stability, while the part which rested on opinion for the time being and took form in legislation responded to the need of change. Here an analogy was made use of which has played a great part in juristic thought — the analogy of three regular and predictable phenomena of physical nature: the return of the seasons, the succession of the phases of the moon, day and night. As Socrates is reported in Plato's Minos to have put it, fire burns and water flows in Greece, in Persia, and at Carthage. The analogy of the physical order of the universe to the moral order and to the legal order has always appealed strongly. Indeed as the psalmist reflected on it and thought of the order of the universe as reflected in the moral law, as it stands in the Psalm *de profundis* in the Vulgate, he exclaimed, "Because of Thy law have I abided Thee, O Lord." Because of the stable character of the phenomena of external nature and of the moral order he had faith in the Eternal that makes for righteousness.

Differentiated social control in the stage of the strict law led to distinction of the enacted or imperative from the traditional element in the

22. 1 Blackstone, *Commentaries*, 54–55 (1765).

23. *Com. v. Adams*, 114 Mass. 323 (1873); *State* v. *Horton*, 136 N.C. 588 (1905); *Com.* v. *Romig*, 22 Pa. D. & C. 341 (1934); Contra *Com.* v. *Williams*, 133 Pa. Super. 104 (1935).

24. Pound, *Interpretations of Legal History*, 1 (1923).

positive law. A resulting exclusive preoccupation of jurists with positive law led analytical jurists to develop a distinction suggested by Aristotle. Austin distinguished what he called 'necessary' principles, notions, or distinctions, which were inevitable constituents of any system of law, since no "system of law as evolved in a refined community" could be imagined coherently "without conceiving them as constituent parts of it." On the other hand, he saw other principles, notions, and distinctions which were not necessary in that "an expanded system of law could be imagined without conceiving them as constituent parts of it." He considered that these "rest upon grounds of utility which extend through all communities" and, "as they are obvious in all refined communities . . . occur very generally in matured systems of law."[25] Austin's necessary constituents of a matured legal system are deduced from his definition of law as the aggregate of rules established by political superiors, that is, "by persons exercising superior and subordinate government in independent nations or independent political societies."[26] Both the necessary and the general principles, notions, and distinctions may in form be either traditional or legislative. But the distinction is made as to positive law. The necessary principles are logically necessary as involved in the very idea of a system of positive law. The general but not necessary principles, as Austin saw them, were established on general grounds of utility as it made itself felt among different peoples. Both would be included in Aristotle's κοινὸν δίκαιον.

It may be that an idea that the method of dichotomy is the exclusive method of classification, an idea no longer held,[27] is the explanation. At any rate, except as Aristotle suggests, without expressly setting them forth separately, three categories, namely, natural, general, and local, more or less, however, identifying the general type with the universal, but setting it between the natural as resting on customs of all civilized peoples, and the local resting on local usage and local legislation, philo-

25. 2 Austin, *Jurisprudence* (5 ed. 1885) 1072–74.
26. Austin, *The Province of Jurisprudence Determined*, 2 (1832).
27. Joseph, *Introduction to Logic*, 107 ff.; Schiller, *Formal Logic*, chap. 6, § 9.

sophical jurists from the Greeks to the present have generally distinguished two types, natural and positive. In the last century Austin distinguished necessary from general precepts and institutions. Historical jurists distinguished traditional from imperative precepts and institutions.

These distinctions, philosophical, analytical, or historical, belong to later modes of juristic thinking. But the distinction made by Aristotle in the Nicomachean Ethics has had a long and fruitful as well as eventful history in the science of law and is the subject of lively debate today. Aristotle's idea of a law common to the Greek city-states appears in the Roman law books as an idea of a *ius gentium*. We first find this term in Cicero. But he implies clearly that it was older than his time, telling that it was distinguished from *ius ciuile*, the strict law of the Roman city-state, by the *maiores*, the lawyers of the past.[28] In another place he speaks of it as a body of legal precepts assumed to exist everywhere.[29] It is true in a number of places he assumes that the *ius gentium* is universal because it is natural; because it has its basis in natural reason.[30] In one place he speaks of it as a matter of natural law.[31] Thus like Aristotle he was not assured as between a threefold strict law, law of peoples, and natural law, or a twofold positive law and natural law in which the positive law had a universal element and natural law that element as something dictated by nature. Pomponius, in the second half of the second century, uses the term to mean legal institutions known among all peoples.[32] In the Veronese codex of the Institute of Gaius, the Roman Blackstone,[33] there is a chapter heading (in a later hand) *de iure ciuili et naturali*, but the first section of Book I speaks only of the *ius gentium*. The first and part of the second sentence of the section have disappeared in the only manuscript. But they are quoted by Justinian and the section no doubt read

28. Cicero, *De legibus*, iii, 17, 69.
29. *Partitiones oratoriae*, xxxvii, 130.
30. *De officiis*, iii, 5, 23; *De republica*, iii, 27, 33; *Tusculan disputations*, i, 13, 30.
31. *De haruspicum responsis*, xiv, 32.
32. *Dig.* i, 1, 1, 3.
33. His principal works were written between A.D. 130 and 180.

thus: "Every people that is governed by statutes and customs observes partly its own peculiar law and partly the common law of all men; but what natural reason establishes among all men is equally followed by all peoples and is called *ius gentium*, as the law which all peoples make use of."[34] He often seems to identify *ius gentium* with *naturalis ratio*. But it is not so clear that he identifies *ius gentium* with *ius naturale*. *Naturalis ratio* is put as what establishes *ius gentium* among all men.[35] But the later jurists of the classical period often speak of the *ius gentium* as a branch of the positive Roman law to which they refer different doctrines and institutions.[36]

Although the extent to which a general body of precepts derived from contact with Greek traders, merchants, and bankers, and affected by reading Greek philosophers, existed as a recognized part of the Roman law of the end of the republic, may have been exaggerated in the last century, the extreme skepticism which would label Gaius's statement contrasting the *ius ciuile* with the *ius gentium* and his promise to tell us to which of the two the several legal institutions he will expound belong, 'pure fantasy,'[37] seems equally exaggerated. Such a combination of comparative jurisprudence and rational speculation is not an isolated phenomenon in legal history. An example may be seen in the development of Anglo-American commercial law out of the contact of the English common-law courts with foreign traders and bankers and reading by judges and lawyers of the Continental texts on commercial law.

At any rate, the idea of a *ius gentium*, a rationally derived common law of the civilized world, became a fruitful idea in the later medieval and seventeenth-century development of the received Roman law.

In its distinctive sense in the later Roman law books the *ius gentium* was a part of the positive law. On the other hand, the *ius naturale* was a speculative body of principles serving theoretically as the basis of law-making, juristic doctrine, and criticism, regarded as potentially appli-

34. *Gaius*, i, § 1.
35. *Id.* ii, §§ 65–69, iii, § 154; *Dig.* i, 1, 4, ix, 3.
36. E.g., *Dig.* xli, 1, l; xlvi, 4, 8, 4; xlviii, 19, 17; xlviii, 22, 15.
37. Schulz, *History of Roman Legal Science* (1946) 73, 162–63.

cable to all men, in all ages, among all peoples, derived from reason and worked out philosophically. The proof of the *ius gentium* was in its acceptance and application as positive law among civilized peoples. The proof of *ius naturale* was in reason applied to the nature of things.

Roman jurists of the period of the strict law were little, if at all, affected by Greek philosophical ideas of natural law. What Cicero has to say about *ius naturae*[38] is said from the standpoint of an orator and of a philosopher on the basis of Greek theories rather than of Roman law. In the classical period we hear much about natural law. But 'the nature of things' was thought of with reference to Roman legal institutions and legal conceptions, *e.g.*, the nature of property and ownership and the nature of legal transactions, such as contract.[39] Roman natural law seems a natural law drawn from idealized positive law, like what I have called 'positive natural law' as it was developed in American law in the nineteenth century.[40] In the later empire Greek philosophical ideas affected the Greek teachers of law in the postclassical law schools and were applied to the classical texts.[41] Yet the texts had repeatedly made the distinction that slavery exists by virtue of the *ius gentium* whereas slavery is contrary to *ius naturale*.[42] Likewise they contrasted natural law with positive law in case of agnation and cognation.[43]

In Cicero we see the idea, which was to become strong in the Middle Ages and in the modern world, that *ius naturale* is the basis of all law and may not be set aside by the law of the state.[44] The same idea appears fre-

---

38. As to this and the Greek originals on which he drew, *see* Senn, *De la justice et du droit* (1927).

39. The idea of natural law as a law applying to all animate creation, quoted in the Digest from Ulpian's Institutes (*Dig.* i, 1, 1, 3), is thought to be a postclassical interpolation. Maschi, *La concezione naturalistica del diritto* (1937) 162 ff.

40. Pound, *Natural Natural Law and Positive Natural Law* (1952) 68, Law Quarterly Review, 330.

41. *See* Maschi, *La concezione naturalistica del diritto* (1937).

42. *Inst.* i, 2, 2, i, 3, 2; *Dig.* i, 1, 4, pr. i, 5, 4, 1, xii, 6, 64, xvi, 3, 31, pr., xviii, 1, 34, 1.

43. *Gaius*, i, § 158.

44. Cicero, *De inuentione*, ii, 22, 65; *De legibus*, ii, 5, 11.

quently in the later law books.[45] There was an ideal to which the law was to be shaped. But the law was not automatically abrogated by an appeal to natural law. Buckland puts the matter well: "The name *ius naturale* expresses a tendency in the trend of legal thought, a ferment which was operating all over the law."[46] It was not, however, a part of the positive law, as was the *ius gentium*. A pact might be binding by natural law and yet not create necessarily a *naturalis obligatio* in the positive law.[47]

The history of the modern science of law begins with the revival of the study of Roman law in the Italian universities of the twelfth century. From the twelfth to the seventeenth century there were two parallel lines of juristic development, one legal and the other philosophical. In the legal line of development the text of the Corpus Iuris was taken to be authoritatively binding. It could only be interpreted. But the texts spoke of reason, and in philosophy authority was held a ground of reason and church doctrine was declaratory of reason. As it was put by Erigena, the teachings of the fathers of the church, which rest on their authority, were discovered by them with the aid of reason.[48] Anselm sought to prove the teachings of the Scriptures and of the fathers through reason so as to convince even the unbeliever.[49] A revival of natural law came with study of the Institutes and Digest and was furthered by acceptance of Aristotle as authority in philosophy. Natural law was given a purely theological basis. But philosophy was turned to in order to reinforce theology and later was used as the foundation of a science of law which gradually cut loose from theology. Thus Lord Acton was moved to say that not the devil but St. Thomas Aquinas was the first Whig.

Thomas Aquinas (1225–1274) divided the old *ius naturale* into two: (1) *lex aeterna*, the eternal law, the "reason of the divine wisdom governing the whole universe," and (2) *lex naturalis*, natural law, the law of human

45. *Gaius*, i, § 158; *Inst.* i, 2, 11; *Dig.* iv, 5, 8.
46. *Text-Book of Roman Law* (2 ed. 1932) 55.
47. *Dig.* xlv, 1, 1, 2, xlvi, 1, 5, 6, pr.
48. Johannes Scotus Erigena, *De divisione naturae*, i, 69 [c. 875].
49. St. Anselm (1033–1109) *Cur Deus homo*, 12.

nature, proceeding ultimately from God but immediately from reason and governing the actions of men only. Positive law was a mere recognition of the *lex naturalis* which was above all human authority.[50]

It will be noted that Thomas Aquinas writes of *lex naturae*, not of *ius naturale*, or *ius naturae*. The law teaching of the medieval universities thought of law as legislation of the Emperor Justinian. It was not traditional in origin or in form. It was legislation, "proceeding from him who has the care of the community and promulgated."[51] The law imposed on Christendom by Justinian was analogous to the eternal law which the Creator had laid down for the universe. The *lex naturae* was the body of command imposed on mankind by the ultimate lawmaker, in part revealed and for the rest discoverable through reason.

It could be assumed that the legislation of the Christian emperor was declaratory of reason. But it was positive law, and appeal to the conscience against details of the positive law could be made in the name of natural law. The teaching of the Roman books as to the immutable precepts of natural law, beyond the reach of the lawmaker, was reinforced by theology. A precept contrary to natural law had no legal validity.[52] But interpretation of and commentary on the text of the Corpus Iuris was enough for a general law for Continental Europe for three centuries before effective use could be made of the proposition. In England it came to be used to reinforce an idea of the reciprocal duties of lord and man when the king from the ultimate landlord was transformed into a governor ruling, as Sir Edward Coke told James I, under God and the law,[53]

---

50. "A law is a rule and measure of acts, whereby one is induced to act or is restrained from action. Now the rule and measure of human action is reason: it being the part of reason to direct to the end, which is the first principle of conduct. Hence a law must be some function of reason." *Summa Theologica*, i, 2, qu. 90, art. 1 (Rickaby's transl.). "Every law framed by man bears the character of a law exactly to that extent to which it is derived from the law of nature. But if on any point it is in conflict with the law of nature it at once ceases to be a law: it is a mere perversion of law." *Id.* i, 2, q. 95.

51. *Id.* i, 2, q. 90, art. 4.

52. *Id.* i, 2, q. 95.

53. Prohibitions del Roy, 12 Co. 63 (1612).

and was used to uphold the authority of the church against encroachments by Parliament in Acts "impertinent to be observed,"[54] from which
in the right line of juristic descent we come to a fundamental doctrine
of American law.[55]

The taught law of the medieval universities in Continental Europe
was in a stage of strict law. As was said above, the Corpus Iuris was a body
of legislation to be interpreted and applied. But there was no competent
lawmaking authority in the polity of the time which could add to it or alter it. While the method of the academic expositors of Roman law was
the scholastic method of formal logic applied to authoritative texts, like
the Roman jurists of the republic, they were little influenced by philosophy. Hence the juristic function of natural law in the Middle Ages was
limited. In legal history, when the balance of stability and change is
overweighted on the side of stability, positive natural law is found organizing the body of stable precepts in their interpretation and application. When it is overweighted on the side of change we find natural natural law a directing agency of growth.

But theological natural law could operate indirectly through the
canon law. What a good Christian would do and would not do gave an
ideal that in one situation played a significant role. There were differences on moral grounds between the civilians and the canonists on the
confines between law and morals.[56] The civilians felt bound to adhere

54. Fitzherbert, *Abridgement*, Annuity, 41. Statham, *Abridgement*, Annuity, Easter, 27
Hen. 6; *Prior of Castleacre v. Dean of St. Stephens*, Y.B. 21 Hen. 7, 1. After the Reformation this became a doctrine that statutes "against common right and reason," such as to
enact that "those who do not offend shall be punished," *Lord Cromwell's* Case, 4 Co. 12b
(1578), or to make one a judge in his own case, *Bonham's* Case, 8 Co. 118a, (1610); *Day
v. Savadge*, Hob. 87 (1614); *City of London v. Wood*, 12 Mod. 669, 687–88 (1701), would
not be enforced by the courts.

55. This history is well brought out in Coxe, *Essay on Judicial Power and Unconstitutional Legislation*, chaps. 13–20 (1893).

56. Galoanus Bononiensis (14th century canonist) *De differentiis legum et canonum*,
no. 67 in 1 TRACTATUS UNIVERSI IURIS (1584) fol. 189; Hieronymus de Zannettinis (died
1493) *De differentiis inter ius canonicum et ciuile*, nos. 83, 97, id. fol. 202; Gregorius de

to the Roman doctrine that a bare pact was not legally enforceable and to argue that this was in accord with reason,[57] while the canonists regarded a promise as binding on the conscience and so to be given legal effect on grounds of religion, natural law, and the practice of civilized peoples.[58] Ultimately the canonist idea prevailed in Continental Europe. In the eighteenth century, Pothier, in the era of the law-of-nature school of jurists, explained that the Roman categories of enforceable pacts were very far from being in accord with nature and reason.[59]

We have seen that Greek philosophy gave Roman legal science two significant ideas: natural law or the law of nature, a universally valid body of ideal legal precepts, grounded in reason, and a body of legal precepts lying between natural law and the positive law of the particular state, on the one side more or less identical with natural law and on the other side received or recognized as positive law — a body of precepts common in varying degrees to the positive law of civilized peoples.

In England where from the thirteenth century the law was the law of the king's courts and was taught by practicing lawyers in societies of lawyers and law students, lawyers did not trouble themselves about philosophy. Until the latter part of the sixteenth century or even till the seventeenth century English law was in the stage of strict law. In theory the courts applied the common custom of England. There was no such gen-

---

Megalottis (died 1537) *Tractatus securitatis ac salviconductis*, ii, 29, 11 Tractatus Universi Iuris, pt. 1, fol. 236.

57. Andreas ab Exea (16th century jurist) *De pactis*, 294, 296, 6 Tractatus Universi Iuris, pt. 2, fol. 9; Caccialupi (jurist, died 1496) *De pactis*, xi, 7, 6, 6 Tractatus, pt. 1, fol. 13; Duarenus (François Duaren, French jurist, 1509–1559) *De pactis*, vi, 1, 6 Tractatus, pt. 1, fol. 15.

58. Antonius Corsetus Siculus (15th century canonist) *De iuramento et eius privilegiis*, no. 76, 4 Tractatus, fol. 364; Conradus Brunus (Braun, 16th century jurist) *Tractatus de seditionibus*, ix, 15, 11 Tractatus, pt. 1, fol. 132; Gulielmus Redoanus (16th century Bishop of Nebio in Corsica) *De simonia mentali*, ii, 4, 15, 15 Tractatus, pt. 2, fol. 60, no. 15. Redoanus adds that as to merchants and money changers *nuda pacta* are actionable. *Id.* no. 16. This was urged also as a proposition of natural law and a dictate of reason. Nicolaus Moronus, *Tractatus de treuga et pace*, q. 17, 2, 11 Tractatus, pt. 1, fol. 420. *See also* Andreas ab Exea, *De pactis*, note 57 *supra*.

59. Pothier, *Traité des obligations*, i, 1, 1, § 1 (1761).

eral body of custom common to all England — certainly not on many matters on which the courts had to pass. What the courts administered was a custom of judicial decision, not a custom of popular action. But it was the belief that judicial decision was ascertaining and declaring the established custom of the land that made it possible for the custom of decision to establish itself as law.

On the Continent, where the law that prevailed was a law of the universities, the academic law teachers were in immediate contact with theology and many of them were doctors of the canon law as well as of the civil law, jurisprudence was thought of as applied theology. The ideal element in law was supplied by a theological natural law. This mode of thought had some influence in the development of equity as part of the Anglo-American common law system. In Doctor and Student,[60] a foundation book in the history of English equity, a philosophical justification of the equity administered in the Court of Chancery was put in the principle of the canon law that the circumstances of human life vary so infinitely that general rules cannot be made to cover all of them. This was a characteristic idea of the canon law. Discretion guided by conscience was held necessary to justice and equity was to be governed by conscience. The idea of equity as correction of that wherein rules of law by reason of their generality are deficient goes back to Aristotle[61] but got a theological color in the canon law.[62] Conduct conforming to equity and good conscience and decision according to the Chancellor's conscience guided by principles became ideals of Anglo-American equity.

At the Reformation the two parallel lines of development of a science of law, the practical and the philosophical, converged. The authoritative basis of practical exposition of law had failed. The doctrine of continuity of the empire and consequent binding force of the Corpus Iuris

60. St. Germain, *Dialogues between a Doctor of Divinity and a Student of the Common Law* (1528, revised ed. 1532).
61. *Nicomachean Ethics*, v, 9, transl. in McKeon, *Basic Works of Aristotle*, 1019–20 (1941).
62. *See* 4 Holdsworth, *History of English Law*, 279–81.

was given up. The law was emancipated from the text of Justinian.[63] The authoritative basis of philosophical speculation had likewise given way. The method of the scholastic philosophers had been superseded. The unchallengeable authority of Aristotle and of the fathers of the church no longer afforded a basis for infallible deduction. The Protestant jurist-theologians of the north of Europe did not hesitate to declare that there was a sufficient basis for natural law apart from the Scriptures.[64] Grotius even went so far as to say that he could conceive of natural law if there were no God.[65] In the seventeenth and eighteenth centuries the science of law and the authority of legal precepts were rested solely upon reason. Lip service was long done to theology by naming revelation along with reason as the foundation of what was essentially a rationalist natural law.[66]

For two centuries, in the era of what is called the law-of-nature school,[67] jurists believed that a complete and perfect system of legal precepts could be built upon principles of natural law discoverable by reason and derived from the ideal of the abstract man. Thus the seventeenth and eighteenth centuries are in many respects comparable to the classical era of Roman law. The fields of jurisprudence and ethics were taken to be the same. Jurists sought to make law coincident with morals. It was sought to make legal precepts conform to what each particular writer thought on ethical grounds they should be. An era of creative law-making resulted, the influence of which is still felt in law and in the sci-

63. Hotman, *Anti-Tribonianus* (1567) chaps. 1–2, 7–9, 12–13; Conring, *De Origine Iuris Germanici* (1643), chaps. 21–27, 32–34.

64. Hemmingius (Hemmingsen) *De lege naturae apodictica methodus* (1562) q. 9; 2 Kaltenborn, *Die Vorläufer des Hugo Grotius*, 31.

65. Grotius, *De iure belli ac pacis* (1625) Prolegomena, § 11.

66. 1 Blackstone, *Commentaries on the Laws of England* (1765) 39–41; 1 Wilson, Works (Andrews' ed.) 105–6 (law lectures delivered in 1791).

67. Grotius, *De iure belli ac pacis* (1625); Pufendorf, *De iure naturae et gentium* (1672); Burlamaqui, *Principes du droit naturel* (1747); Wolff, *Institutiones iuris naturae et gentium* (1750); Rutherforth, *Institutes of Natural Law* (1754–56); Vattel, *Le droit des gens*, Préliminaires (1758).

ence of law. Reason provided systematic organization of the body of legal precepts in place of the order of the titles in the Digest, an arrangement which had been taken from the praetor's edict since the most used treatises of the classical era were commentaries on the edict. Hence from the sixteenth century the great law books on the Continent are treatises on the law as a whole, not commentaries on the Digest, and in England, instead of the commentary style of Coke's Commentary on Littleton and Coke's Second Institute,[68] and the alphabetical arrangement of the abridgements,[69] there came to be systematic expositions of the law as a whole even if they sometimes keep the name of commentaries.[70]

Five notable juristic achievements stand to the credit of the law-of-nature school: The founding and development of international law, the eighteenth-century codifications on the Continent, Lord Mansfield's rationalizing and modernizing of much of English law, the building of an American common law in the fore part of the nineteenth century from the English law of property and English legal procedure of the seventeenth century under the influence of natural law theories expounded by Blackstone and Kent, and the development of constitutional law in America on the basis of Coke's Second Institute and Blackstone's exposition of the common-law rights of Englishmen, taking the common-law rights of Englishmen to be the natural rights of man, under the influence of Continental treatises on natural law.

By general consent international law, as it has been known and accepted since the seventeenth century, begins with the great work of

---

68. Coke, *Commentary on Littleton* (1628); Second Part of the Institutes of the Lawes of England, containing the exposition of Many Ancient and Other Statutes (1642), a commentary on *Magna Carta* and on the great statutes of Edward I.

69. As to these *see* Holdsworth, *Sources and Literature of English Law*, 104–11 (1925).

70. Blackstone, *Commentaries on the Laws of England* (1765–69); Wood, *Institute of the Laws of England; or Laws of England in their Natural Order* (1724); Wooddeson, *Systematical View of the Laws of England* (1792–93). *Compare also* Kent, *Commentaries on American Law* (1826–30).

Grotius.[71] But no less by general consent that work marks the beginning of the law-of-nature school of jurists which held the ground in jurisprudence for two centuries and was a strong competitor for half a century more.[72] The analogy of the moral duties of men in their relations with one another was made to point out the moral duties of states in their relations with other states, and an idealized form of the precepts of the matured Roman law governing the relations and conduct of individuals was taken to show what reason prescribed as the basis of positive law.

Working out of elaborate detailed systems of natural law and a confident faith in the possibility of formulating natural law in a complete body of positive legal precepts, in a time when Continental states with well-developed legal systems seemed to have exhausted the possibilities of juristic development through the traditional element and to require a new basis for a new juristic development, together with need for one law in countries whose several political subdivisions had divergent local laws, led to a strong and general movement for codification in the eighteenth century. An Austrian Civil Code was projected in 1713. A draft was published in 1767 and a partial new draft in 1787. The code was put in force in 1811. Frederick the Great held that his legal advisers could draw up a perfect code which would require no judicial developing or interpretation and would need only to be applied. A draft was published in 1749 and a code was put in force in 1780–94. But the outstanding work of this era of codification was the French Civil Code of 1804, commonly known as the Code Napoléon. A French Civil Code was projected under Louis XIV in 1667–70, and the foundation was laid in a series of royal ordinances codifying particular subjects and by the writings of Pothier.[73] At the Revolution a code was demanded as a means of unifi-

71. 2 CONTINENTAL LEGAL HISTORY SERIES, *Great Jurists of the World*, 169–84, 305–44; Lysen, *Hugo Grotius* (1925); Vreeland, *Hugo Grotius* (1917); Knight, *Life and Works of Hugo Grotius* (1925).

72. Pound, *Grotius in the Science of Law*, 19 AMERICAN JOURNAL OF INTERNATIONAL LAW, 685 (1925).

73. Robert Joseph Pothier (1699–1772) professor of law in the University of Orleans and judge of the Presidial Court of Orleans. His treatise on obligations is still cited, and

cation and after much delay on the part of the commission, the draft was promulgated in 1804 through the intervention of Napoleon.[74] This code still in force, though with many amendments, was copied extensively in Europe and Latin America and set the fashion until a new model was set by the German Civil Code published in 1896 and in effect in 1900.

William Murray, Earl of Mansfield (1705–1793), Chief Justice of the King's Bench, 1756–88, an outstanding figure in the judicial history of England, learned in Roman and Continental as well as in English law, looked at the common law from the standpoint of the law-of-nature jurisprudence of his time and did much to rationalize and liberalize the law of his time. He put the law merchant in its place in the common-law system, restating it by making intelligent use of the Continental treatises, and infused equitable principles into more than one part of the general law, notably quasi contract.[75]

In America natural-law thinking held the field undisputed in the three generations after independence. Blackstone was the law student's first book in the law office and in most law schools until the end of the nineteenth century. Select chapters from Grotius and Pufendorf were in law school curricula till 1850. Grotius, Pufendorf, Rutherforth, Burlamaqui, and Vattel were read by law students at least to the time of the American Civil War. There can be no doubt that the believers in eighteenth-century natural law did great things in the formative era of American law because that theory gave them faith that great things could be done. Application of reason to the details of the received common law made the work of the legislative reform movement (1776–1875) enduring. In the formative era American lawyers formulated authoritatively much which jurists had reasoned out in the treatises on the law of nature in the seventeenth and eighteenth centuries. Even more it led to independent creative lawmaking such as had not proceeded from law-

much of his treatises and monographs on French law was incorporated almost in his words in the Civil Code.

74. See *Livre centenaire du code civil français* (1904).

75. Birkenhead, *Fourteen English Judges*, 180; 3 Lord Campbell, *Lives of the Chief Justices*, 274 ff. (3 ed.); Fifoot, *Lord Mansfield*.

makers after the era of the Civil War until the Workmen's Compensation Acts.[76]

But it is significant that each of these achievements had in it the seeds of its own undoing.

It has become increasingly manifest that a chief obstacle to an effective legal regime of international justice is lack of an international law adapted to the world it is to govern. In the seventeenth century Grotius wrote in an era of absolute personal sovereigns. The monarch of the seventeenth century, the Spanish king after Charles V, the French king of the old regime, the Stuart king in England, the Hapsburg ruler in Austria, was analogous to the masterful head of a Roman household. The relations of Philip and Louis, and James and Ferdinand with each other were enough like those of the Roman *paterfamilias* to his neighbor to make the precepts worked out by Roman jurists for the latter when idealized prove applicable to the former. So long as the political organization of society and political ideas remained much that they had been, the law of nations worked out by Grotius and developed by his successors served its purpose well. But with changed political ideas throughout the world it has become increasingly inadequate to its tasks. Its fundamental idea is out of line with the democratic organization of societies of today. It has, therefore, conspicuously failed in the present century. If a regime of legal adjustment of relations and ordering of conduct of self-governing peoples is to achieve its task competently in the world of today it must proceed on a different theoretical basis.[77] Natural law, thought of as eternal and immutable, is not equal to such a change of base.

Nor could the eighteenth century codes achieve the completeness of statement or permanence of content expected of them. They were chiefly successful in unifying the law where there had been an inconvenient diversity of local law. They have had to be amended and sup-

---

76. Pound, *The Formative Era of American Law* (1938) 27.

77. Pound, *Philosophical Theory and International Law*, 1 BIBLIOTHECA VISSERIANA, 71 (1923).

plemented and a mass of doctrinal and judicial interpretation and application has had to grow up around them and new codes have had to be drawn up and more are urged upon wholly new lines and theories. Lord Mansfield's attempt to settle all parts of English common law on rational principles, although it achieved much, especially in commercial law, on the whole failed.[78] Pure reason and the example of the modernized Roman law of the Continent did not suffice to enable him to make the common-law courts into courts of equity, to do away with the technical medieval rules of the law of real property, nor to put the common law as to simple contracts on a rational and moral basis. He was more than a century ahead of his time. What he sought to do and much more has been done since under the auspices of a different philosophy.

Likewise the natural-law theory of American constitutional law had ill results from which administration of justice in America has been suffering for two generations. It led to a doctrine of constitutional provisions as declaratory of natural law and so to an ideal of the common law as in its main lines and characteristic doctrines an embodiment of universal precepts running back of all constitutions. Thus certain common-law doctrines and traditionally received ideals of the profession were made into a superconstitution by which the social legislation of the last decade of the nineteenth century and of the first third of the present century was to be judged.[79]

At the end of the eighteenth century Kant undermined the method of the law-of-nature school of the two preceding centuries.[80] For a time the place held by theology in the Middle Ages and by reason in the seventeenth and eighteenth centuries was taken by history and philosophical jurisprudence was carried on by a metaphysical school which sought to work out an ideal critique of legal institutions, legal doctrines and legal precepts deduced from a metaphysically given fundamental

---

78. See 7 Holdsworth, *History of English Law*, 44–45.

79. Werner, J., in *Ives v. South Buffalo R. Co.*, 201 N.Y. 271, 285–87, 293–95; Winslow, J., in *Nunnemacher v. State*, 129 Wis. 190, 199–202; *Noel v. Ewing*, 9 Ind. 37, 61; *In re Moore's Estate*, 114 Or. 444; *Smith v. Smith*, 48 N.J. Eq. 566, 590.

80. Kant, *Metaphysische Anfangsgründe der Rechtslehre* (2 ed. 1798).

idea of right or some simple fundamental formula of justice.[81] Where
the law-of-nature school thought of an ideal body of detailed legal precepts, the metaphysical jurists thought rather of an ideal element in the
law and a critique of legal precepts on the basis of that element. Conceiving of the ideal element as the significant part of the law they rejected the law-of-nature theory of law made consciously to the pattern of
rationally discovered universally valid precepts and held with the historical jurists that law was found not made. It was found by experience,
said the historical jurists,[82] and in that experience, said the Hegelian
later metaphysical jurists, an ideal of right or an idea of freedom was realizing itself.[83] In England and the United States it has been customary
to speak lightly of this school and to assume that their speculations were
wholly in the air.[84] It is true they did not directly and immediately affect
the actual course of judicial decision and juristic writing. But Kant formulated the idea of justice which was universally accepted in the nineteenth century and obstinately held on in American constitutional law
in the first third of the present century. Through their influence upon
the historical school of jurists, which was dominant in the latter part of
the nineteenth century, they fixed the lines of the ethical interpretation
of legal history and gave content to the idea of freedom which historical
jurists postulated as unfolding in legal development. Maine's famous
generalization that the history of law is the record of a progress from status to contract[85] simply puts in concrete form the cardinal idea of the
metaphysical school.

81. Hegel, *Grundlinien der Philosophie des Rechts* (1821), transl. by Knox (1942);
Ahrens, *Cours de droit naturel* (8 ed. 1892); Boistel, *Cours de philosophie du droit* (1870,
new ed. 1899); Bonnecase, *La notion de droit en France au dix-neuvième siècle*, chaps.
1–3.

82. This was so put by Mr. Justice Holmes in his historical period: *The Common Law*,
1 (1881).

83. I have considered this at length in *Interpretations of Legal History*, lects. 2–3
(1923).

84. Bryce, *Studies in History and Jurisprudence* (American ed.) 631–34; Pollock, *Essays in Jurisprudence and Ethics*, 28–30; Gray, *Nature and Sources of the Law* (1 ed.)
§§ 7–9.

85. Maine, *Ancient Law*, last paragraph but one of chap. 5 (1861).

At the end of the nineteenth century the then dominant historical school of jurists all but displaced philosophical jurisprudence. In
the present century a revived philosophy of law took form in a social-
philosophical school, social utilitarians, Neo-Kantians, and Neo-
Hegelians,[86] more or less merging later in a neo-idealist type.[87] In the
fore part of the nineteenth century lines of cleavage involved in divergent aspects of eighteenth-century philosophical jurisprudence and different phases of reaction from the law-of-nature school, brought about a
separation of jurists into three well-defined schools: historical, metaphysical, and analytical.[88] The nineteenth century was the century of
history as the thirteenth was the century of theology, at any rate in jurisprudence, and the seventeenth and eighteenth centuries were the
centuries of reason. The historical jurists carried forward the doctrine of
those eighteenth-century jurists who held that legislation and precepts
of positive law were merely declaratory. The law-of-nature jurists said
they were declaratory of reason. The historical jurists said they were declaratory of social experience in the administration of justice in which
an idea of right or an idea of freedom was unfolding. The metaphysical
school sought to demonstrate an unchallengeable basis to replace pure
reason and thus provide an assured critique of law from the outside. The
analytical school carried forward another trend in eighteenth-century
theory which had conceived of an authoritative declaration of natural
law by the sovereign. Thus all three of the nineteenth-century schools
have the doctrine of the law-of-nature school in their pedigree. Bentham taught something very like a natural law derived from his theory
of utility. Austin[89] and Holland[90] gave us what was very like a *ius gen-*

---

86. I have considered these fully in *The Scope and Purpose of Sociological Jurisprudence*, 25 HARVARD LAW REVIEW, 140–58 (1911) and *Fifty Years of Jurisprudence*, 51 HAR-
VARD LAW REVIEW, 444–53 (1938).

87. *See* my paper, *Fifty Years of Jurisprudence*, 51 HARVARD LAW REVIEW, 444, 454–63
(1938).

88. I have considered these schools in detail in *The Scope and Purpose of Sociological Jurisprudence*, 24 HARVARD LAW REVIEW, 591, 595–611 (1911).

89. *Jurisprudence* (5 ed. 1885) the first six lectures published in 1832 under the title of
The Province of Jurisprudence Determined.

90. *Elements of Jurisprudence* (1880, 13 ed. 1924).

tium, a system of law reached by reason applied to comparative law. The metaphysical school, the philosophical school of the last century, definitely disappeared by the beginning of the twentieth century. The historical school and the analytical school still have adherents, but both have been largely superseded by new types of juristic thought.

In social philosophical jurisprudence the most influential group has been the Neo-Kantians. Their founder and leader, Rudolf Stammler (1856–1938) sought to work out a universally valid method of judging as to the justice obtained by application of legal precepts in the time and place. He spoke of a natural law with a changing content. As contrasted with the eighteenth-century conception of universally valid ideal precepts, and Kant's essay at a universal critique, Stammler sought a universally valid method of developing a relative critique whereby justice might be achieved in the time and place. His enduring work has been in formulation of the social ideal of the time and place, and his theory of the application of legal precepts where the last century thought simply of their nature. Nineteenth-century philosophical jurisprudence asked whether a particular legal precept was just. Stammler asked whether and how far justice may be attained by means of the precept. Where nineteenth-century jurists thought that if rules were abstractly just the results of the application of the rules in particular cases need not be looked into, he taught the present century to seek just results by means of legal precepts conforming to and administered in the light of social ideals.[91]

Josef Kohler (1849–1919) was the leader of the Neo-Hegelians. He recognized that law, while it must be stable, must nevertheless constantly change. He thought of law as a product of the civilization of a people in the past and of attempts to adjust the results of that past civilization to the civilization of the present. The adjustment must be made with reference to recognition of a continually changing civilization. The traditional legal materials must be shaped so as to further rather than retard

---

91. Stammler's chief writings: *Wirtschaft und Recht* (1896, 5 ed. 1924); *Lehre von dem richtigen Rechte* (1902, 2 ed. 1926) transl. by Husik as *Theory of Justice* (1925); *Lehrbuch der Rechtsphilosophie* (1922, 2 ed. 1923).

developing culture. His most important contribution to jurisprudence is his theory of the jural postulates of the civilization of the time and place. He considers it a task of the jurist to find and formulate the principles of right assumed in or expressed by a given civilization. These postulates may serve as a critique of legal precepts. But even more received ideals may be tried with reference to them and thus clear outline may be given to the ideal of the legal order which is so large an element in the development and application of legal precepts.[92]

More recently there has been a tendency to merge the formerly distinct types of social-philosophical jurisprudence in what may be called a neo-idealism, which seeks to understand, organize, and criticize the ideal element in law and, in particular, to transcend nineteenth-century individualism and nineteenth-century orthodox socialism by a conception which shall neither measure community values and civilization values in terms of personality values nor personality values and civilization values in terms of community values, but shall conceive of civilization as the end toward which both a maximum of free individual self-assertion and an efficient social organization are but means. Here belongs Gustav Radbruch (1878–1950),[93] whom I should put first among contemporary philosophers of law. He points out that justice, the ideal relation among men, morals, the highest development of individual character, and security, each demands the others and yet each if carried to its full logical development negates the others. This must be recognized and the three must be kept in mind in a view of the whole. Of three theories of the binding force of law, (1) that law has binding force only when commanded by a force imposing itself on all other forces, (2) that its obligatory force is based on consent, and (3) that it may be de-

---

92. Kohler's chief writings on the philosophy of law: *Einführung in die Rechtswissenschaft* (1902, 5 ed. 1919); *Rechtsphilosophie und Universalrechtsgeschichte*, in 1 Holtzendorff, ENZYKLOPADIE DER RECHTSWISSENSCHAFT (6 ed. 1904, 7 ed. 1913); *Moderne Rechtsprobleme* (1907, 2 ed. 1913); *Lehrbuch der Rechtsphilosophie* (1908, 3 ed. by Arthur Kohler, 1923, the first ed. transl. by Albrecht as Kohler's *Philosophy of Law*, 1914).

93. *Grundzüge der Rechtsphilosophie* (1914); *Rechtsphilosophie* (3 ed. 1932); *Vorschule der Rechtsphilosophie* (1947). See Pound, *Fifty Years of Jurisprudence*, 51 HARVARD LAW REVIEW, 444, 454–63 (1938).

duced directly from justice and owes its binding force thereto, he holds that no one of them by itself can give a satisfactory answer. He points out series of legal precepts dictated preponderantly by each of these principles. But there is only a preponderant dictation. There is no complete dictation by any one of them.

In France the revival of philosophy at the beginning of the present century led to what has been called a revival of natural law — not, however, a revival of the law-of-nature school. In this revival there were two outstanding leaders: François Gény (1861–1944)[94] and Léon Duguit (1859–1928);[95] the one writing from the standpoint of a neo-scholastic, the other from the standpoint of a positivist-sociological, natural law.

Gény in his philosophical work (Science et technique) subjects social life, that is, the life of the individual man as a moral entity in society, as a moral phenomenon, to the scrutiny of reason in order to discover principles which may be used to establish norms, *i.e.*, patterns or models, for lawmaking, law finding, and the application of law.[96] One might say that in Stammler's phrase they are to give us the social ideal or in Kohler's the jural postulates of civilization except that Stammler sought the social ideals of the epoch and Kohler the postulates of the civilization of the time and place. As a Catholic neo-scholastic jurist Gény had faith he could do more. Scholasticism was a method of formal logical development of authoritative texts. It postulated twofold truth: Revealed truth, that is, revealed in the Scriptures as interpreted in the writings of the fathers, and discovered truth, that is, truth discovered by reason, scrutinizing the universe. In the subjects of the social sciences this means scrutinizing human life. But this life is a life in society. Hence Gény insists on society as a prime factor to be scrutinized in setting up any theory of values. Thomas Aquinas sought the 'ought' which reason

94. *Science et technique en droit privé positif* (vol. I, 1914, vol. II, 1915, vol. III, 1921, vol. IV, 1924). See Pound, *Fifty Years of Jurisprudence*, 51 HARVARD LAW REVIEW, 444, 464–66 (1938).

95. *L'état, le droit objectif, et la loi positive* (1901); *Le droit social, le droit individuel et la transformation de l'état* (3 ed. 1922); *Les transformations du droit privé* (1912). See Pound, *Fifty Years of Jurisprudence*, 51 HARVARD LAW REVIEW, 444, 454–60 (1938).

96. 2 *Science et technique*, § 117.

addresses to a reasonable creature. He went on the basis of the individual man as a moral entity. Gény goes on social life as a moral phenomenon — something given us as a fundamental truth which may be developed logically into its consequences. On this revived scholastic basis he calls for recognition of the element in a body of law which consists in traditional views as to the end of law and traditional pictures of the legal and social order and seeks to give us a firmer grasp of them. In his third volume Gény treats of the technique of positive law. He holds that free scientific research yields starting points for juristic and judicial construction. These starting points (donnés) are fundamental, but a technique of construction is required to build on them.[97] The finding of a donné is a matter of intelligence. The technique is a matter of will. It is something done by choice, "guided only by the predetermined ends of the legal order."[98] This recognition of the process of finding starting points for legal reasoning by choice from among competing starting points by a technique in the light of received ideals is a contribution of the first importance. It brings out the most effective role of the ideal element of the law in the administration of justice. It may be added that the present day tendency of juristic thought in France seems to be to move over from the dominant positivism of the last of the nineteenth century and first decades of the present century to or toward neo-scholasticism.[99]

Duguit's system is called a system of natural law because he conceives of everything in law as deriving its validity from and to be judged by a fundamental rule or principle of right-and-law. Philosophically he was a thoroughgoing positivist. Following Comte, he sought to arrive at his fundamental principle by observation and to verify it by further observation. But Gény justly observes that his règle de droit is supposed, as

97. 3 id. chap. 1.

98. Ibid., 20, 23.

99. See Renard, La théorie de l'institution (1930); Le Fur, les grands problemes du droit (1938); Bonnard, L'Origine de l'ordonnancement juridique, in MELANGES MAURICE HAURIOU, 31 (1929); Delos, La théorie de l'institution (1931) in ARCHIVES DE PHILOSOPHIE DU DROIT ET DE SOCIOLOGIE JURIDIQUE, 96; Réghlade, Valeur sociale et concepts juridique, norme et technique (1950); Horvath, Social Value and Reality in Current French Legal Thought, 1 AM. JOURN. COMP. LAW, 243 (1952).

Duguit in many places vehemently insists, to be derived by observation of a verified fact of social interdependence, whereas in truth it comes in by an unconscious metaphysics and is given a content of the social interdependence from which it purports to be derived.[100]

As Duguit sees it, observation of the phenomena shows that there are no such things as rights, much less natural rights, or sovereign or subjects.[101] Also observation shows there is no such thing as the distinction between public law and private law. All such ideas must be given up. We must start anew from the observed and verified fact of social interdependence through similarity of needs and diversity of functions, or, as it has become, in the industrial society of today, similarity of interest and division of labor. From this comes the rule or principle of right-and-law binding all members of a society to act so as to further this social interdependence and not to do anything that impairs it.[102] As one would expect in a system of natural law, a legislatively enacted precept, although it may conform to the constitution, is not binding unless it tends to further (rather than impair or hinder) social interdependence. Hence he suggests that there should be a tribunal composed of representatives of all social classes to "judge of the legality of the law," i.e., its natural legality, not whether it conforms to the constitution but whether it conforms to the natural-law requirement of promoting social interdependence. Observation of American experience of judical determination whether social legislation conformed to a requirement of reasonableness, or was contrary to "common right and reason" does not give one much faith in the suggestion.

Duguit's ideal picture of the social and legal order is an idealization of a modern industrial city and the country dependent upon it in which everything turns upon efficient production in the greatest possible quantity.

100. 2 *Science et technique en droit privé positif*, 248. See Duguit, *L'état, le droit objectif, et la loi positive*, 18–19.
101. *L'état, le droit objectif, et la loi positive*, chaps. 4, 5.
102. *Les transformations du droit privé depuis le Code Napoléon*, 24.

It should be added that there has been a steady growth of natural-law thinking in one form or another in many countries since 1920.[103]

I have suggested elsewhere that we should distinguish what I have called natural natural law from what would then be called positive natural law.[104] According to this distinction natural natural law is ideal law simply as ideal. It is a body of ideal precepts derived independent of the actual positive law by some method which is regarded as guaranteeing universal moral validity and applicability. Positive natural law, which is what has usually gone by the name of natural law, is an idealized version of the positive law in which the jurist was brought up, in which, postulating that it is declaratory of natural law, and that it derives its force from the ideal precepts it declares, he sets out the positively established precepts, or some of them in universal form. These idealized precepts of a positive law in which the jurist was trained are now made to appear as universal, unchallengeable and unchangeable. Thus there are two sides to natural law as we see the idea at work in legal history. For example, the lawyers, judges and teachers in the formative era of American law found their creating and organizing idea in the theory of natural law. This theory of an ideal universal law, to which an appeal lay from the received precepts of the inherited English law, was at work in legislation, in judicial decision, and in doctrinal writing and guided the creative process of applying reason to experience which has been the life of the law. But at the end of the formative era natural law became a stabilizing, not a creative, theory. It led to an idea of the constitution as declaratory of an ideal of the Anglo-American common law as in its main lines and characteristic doctrines an embodiment of universal, immutable pre-

---

103. Leibholz, *Les tendences actuelles du droit public en Allemagne* (1931) in ARCHIVES DE PHILOSOPHIE DU DROIT ET DE SOCIOLOGIE JURIDIQUE, 207–24; Carlo, *Il diritto naturale nell' attuale fase del pensiero Italiano* (1932); Mendizábaly Martin, *El indestructibile derecho natural* in 2 STUDI FILOSOFICI GIURIDICI DEDICATI A GIORGIO DEL VECCHIO, 92. For America *see* the ethical-rationalist natural law of Morris R. Cohen, *Law and the Social Order*, 165–247 (1933).

104. Pound, *Natural Natural Law and Positive Natural Law*, 68 LAW QUARTERLY REVIEW, 330 (1952).

cepts "running back of all constitutions."[105] Thus certain common-law doctrines and traditionally received ideals of the profession were made a superconstitution by which the social legislation of the end of the nineteenth century and fore part of the present century was to be judged.[106]

Natural natural law has been rested wholly on revelation, or on revelation supplemented by reason, or wholly upon reason. But the number of problems confronting the lawyer which can be solved from the Scripture is too small for practical purposes. The attempt to administer justice in the simple pious society of colonial New England from "the word of God" proved vain. Likewise the number which pure reason, either supplementing revelation or by itself, can solve satisfactorily is very small. Indeed, Kant at the end of the eighteenth century effectively demonstrated the limitations of pure reason. For the greater part we have to find by experience workable adjustments of relations and orderings of conduct which will satisfy the most of the expectations incident to life in civilized society with the least friction and waste. From antiquity one of the foundations of natural law was found in the universal and unchallengeable obligation to keep a promise.[107] But humanitarian ideas of the full individual social and economic life and psychological juristic ideas of frustration have been creating all over the world what has been called "the right not to pay debts."[108] The attempt to solve all legal liabilities for loss and injury by a moral proposition that liability was necessarily and solely a corollary of fault, put as a fundamental prin-

105. Harlan, J., in *Railway Co. v. Chicago*, 206 U.S. 226, 227.

106. *See* Pound, *Liberty of Contract*, 18 YALE LAW JOURNAL, 454 (1909).

107. Plato, *Republic*, i, 330 ff.; Cicero, *De officiis*, i, 7; Thomas Aquinas, *Summa Theologica*, D. ii, Q. cx, Art. 1, § 5; Grotius, *De iure belli ac pacis*, ii, 11, 1, 1; *id.* ii, 11, 1, 3–5; *id.* ii, 11, 4, 1 (1625); Hobbes, *Leviathan*, chaps. 14, 17 (1651); Rousseau, *Contrat Social*, i, chaps. 4, 5 (1762); Strykius, *Dissertationes Hallenses*, Disp. xxii, cap. 4, § 24 (1715), 7 *Opera omnia* (Florence ed. 1839) 919.

108. 2 Planiol, *Traité élémentaire de droit civil*, revision by Ripert and Boulanger, 4 ed. §§ 443–80 (1952); 2 Josserand, *Cours de droit civil positif français*, (3 ed. 1939) §§ 402–5 *bis.*

ciple in the Code Napoléon, has failed everywhere.[109] Often the problem is one of fixing the incidence of a loss among a number of innocent victims. Where no one has been at fault the humanitarian thought of today is not satisfied to leave the burden of a loss upon the luckless victim on whom it fell. Even when an individual has brought an injury upon himself in whole or in part by culpable failure to exercise reasonable care and diligence the humanitarian morals of the time shrink from making him bear the whole burden. What it comes to is that we make the best practical adjustment we can by experience developed by reason and reason tested by experience in order to solve practical problems in a complex social and economic order which do not admit of satisfying solution by simple moral maxims of universal validity. But we must have rules of decision if social control is to be maintained. Men will not long submit to arbitrary subjection of their wills to the wills of others.

In urging this I am not for a moment preaching against conformity of law and of the application of laws to an ideal of justice. Indeed, it is such conformity, so far as we can bring it about, that makes social control through the force of politically organized society tolerable. Does not this mean that natural law has its real function as a critique of the ideal element in the positive law rather than as a test of the validity of positive laws or an authoritative guide to all lawmaking and all application of laws? When we do more we ask too much of natural law and impair its effectiveness for what it can do.

109. I have considered this at length in *New Paths of the Law* (1950) lect. 2. *See also* Friedmann, *Law and Social Change in Contemporary Britain* (1951) 73–101.

THREE

Law and Morals

Throughout the world today law, legal institutions, and justice according to law have been under attack for a generation. People are dissatisfied with law and have been willing to try experiments in government without law because they have felt that the law was not operating lawfully. Especially in dealing with the many new questions and providing for newly pressing interests involved in a changing economic and social order, law has been falling short of what was expected of it. We see clearly enough that the received idea which governed in the last century and had been taking form since the sixteenth century is not a true picture of the society of today. But we have not as yet been able to draw an exact picture of that society to take the place of the old one. Perhaps the change has not gone far enough so that we can expect to draw the new picture with assurance. In consequence solution of new legal problems comes to be too much at large. With no well-understood ideal to guide exercise of the force of a politically organized society its exercise becomes personal to those who wield it and arbitrary and so at variance with the very idea of law. A regime of force is substituted for a regime of law. If we are inclined to think badly of the regime of law as it operated in the latter part of the last century, we must nevertheless admit that it achieved much more toward civilization than the regimes of force have been achieving today.

The idea of civilization, the raising of human powers to constantly greater completeness, the maximum of control over external or physical nature and over human or internal nature, of which men are for the time being capable, seems to me the starting point for understanding the social sciences. These two sides of civilization are interdependent. Without the control over internal nature which men have developed, they could have done little toward the conquest of external nature. If men had to go about armed in fear of attack, if they could not assume that others will commit no intentional aggression upon them and will exercise due care not to cast unreasonable risk of injury upon them, it would not be possible to carry on the research and experiment and investigation which have made possible the harnessing of so much of physical nature to man's use. Thus control over internal nature has made it possible for enormous populations which now occupy the earth to maintain themselves. It has enabled man to inherit the earth and to maintain and increase that inheritance. What this mastery over internal nature is, how it has been achieved, and above all how it may be maintained, furthered and transmitted are the subject matter of the social sciences.

Immediately control over internal nature is maintained by social control; by the pressure upon each man brought to bear by his fellow men in order to constrain him to do his part in upholding civilized society and to deter him from conduct at variance with the postulates of the social order. The major agencies of social control are religion, morals, and law. In the beginnings of law these are not well differentiated. They are increasingly differentiated with the development of politically organized society and after the sixteenth century law becomes more and more the paramount agency.

But organized religion is by no means the least of the three agencies. For a long time in the history of civilization it carries the greater part of the burden of social control. Much of the beginnings of law took over religious institutions and religious precepts and put the force of the state behind them. In the beginnings of English law we find one of the Anglo-Saxon kings exhorting his people as Christians to keep the peace instead of commanding them to do so as subjects.[1] On the downfall of the

---

1. Laws of Edward, 4, 1 Thorpe, *Ancient Laws and Institutes of England* (1840) 161–64; Laws of Aethelstan, I, 1 Thorpe, 193.

Roman empire in the West the church was the chief agency of social control for some six centuries, and in the later Middle Ages the courts of the church and the law of the church divided jurisdiction over adjustment of relations and ordering of conduct not unequally with the courts of the state. Religion still has an intimate relation to the ideal element in law. One of the leading jurists of today tells us that for our measure of values, which he considers philosophy cannot give us, we must turn to religion.[2]

There has been no such effective organization behind morals as an agency of social control as there has been everywhere behind religion. But in kin-organized societies the kin-group disciplined the kinsman whose conduct brought reproach upon his kindred. At Rome a power of censorship over morals, which had belonged to the king as patriarchal head of the Roman people, passed to one of the magistrates of the republic and left remnants in the law which came down to the modern world. If such things as kin-group discipline and official censors of morals no longer exist in a politically organized world, yet trade and professional associations, trade unions, social clubs, and fraternal organizations, with their codes of ethics, or their law or their standards of conduct or canons of what is done and what is not done, exercise, although in subordination to the law of the state, an increasing measure of control of individual conduct.

In the modern world political organization of society has become paramount. It has, or claims to have and on the whole maintains, a monopoly of force. All other agencies of social control are held to exercise disciplinary authority subject to the law of the state and within limits fixed by that law. The English courts will review disciplinary expulsion from clubs or associations for want of conformity to "natural justice."[3] Also English and American courts have decided whether property given

2. Radbruch, *Rechtsphilosophie* (3 ed. 1932) § 12.
3. *Fisher v. Keane*, 11 Ch. D. 353 (1878); *Labouchere v. Earl of Wharncliffe*, 13 Ch. D. 346 (1879).

in trust for church purposes was being used according to the tenets of the church for which it was given.[4] The household, the church, the associations which serve to some extent to organize morals in contemporary society, operate as agencies of social control within legally prescribed limits.

Nevertheless it would be a mistake to assume that politically organized society and the law by which it brings pressure to bear upon individuals are self-sufficient for the tasks of social control in the complex society of the time. The law must operate on a background of other less direct but no less important agencies, the home and home training, neighborhood opinion, religion, and education. If these do their work properly and well the task of the law is greatly lightened. Much of ill-adjusted relations and antisocial conduct is obviated by bringing up and training and teaching leading to life measured by reason. But conditions of urban life in industrial communities have seriously affected home training. Moreover the general secularization, distrust of creeds and dogmas, and hard boiled realism of the present time have loosened the hold of religious organizations. Education is thought to be our main reliance for the background of social control. But that, too, is secularized and has not found itself equal to training in morals. The problem of enforcing the precepts of morals has become acute as law more and more takes the whole field of social control for its province.

When law is the paramount agency of social control it means that the main reliance of society is upon the force exercised by its political organization. Relations are to be adjusted and conduct is to be ordered through the orderly and systematic application of that force. But if law as a mode of social control has the strength of force, it has also the weakness of dependence on force. That something resting on ascertained and declared moral duty very like law can exist and prove effective without any political organization behind it and so without any backing of

---

4. *General Assembly of Free Church of Scotland v. Lord Overtoun* [1904] A.C. 515; *Miller v. Gable*, 2 Denio (N.Y.) 492 (1845).

force, is shown by the achievements of international law from the seventeenth century to the first World War.

Neither ethics nor jurisprudence can give a complete and self-sufficient system of social control. In their beginnings they were not differentiated. Ethical customs, laws, and usages unrelated to social control might be covered in Greek by the one word we translate as "law," so that Socrates could speak of a cookbook as the laws of cooking and a gardener's manual as the laws of horticulture.[5] Even after differentiation has gone on there have been times in the development of jurisprudence in which jurists have sought to identify law and morals. At other times some have sought to make law achieve its task taking no account of morals. If neither of these extreme positions is taken, the relation of morals to the ideal element of law is nonetheless manifest. If we look on law and morals as co-equal co-workers in the task of social control, we shall need to inquire how they co-operate with or affect each other, what are their respective provinces, whether exclusive or overlapping or co-incident. Such questions have troubled jurists from the beginnings of a science of jurisprudence. The relation of law and morals was one of three subjects chiefly argued by the contending schools of jurists in the nineteenth century.[6]

Jhering said that the relation of law and morals was the Cape Horn of jurisprudence.[7] The juristic navigator must round it, but in doing so he ran great risk of fatal shipwreck. Commenting on this Ahrens said that the question called for a good philosophical compass and strict logical method.[8] But Jhering showed later that if the philosophical compass had often been untrustworthy, the linguistic charts had also been de-

---

5. Plato, *Minos*, 321 A. This dialogue is now held not a work of Plato but of one of his school somewhat later than his time.

6. The other two were: The nature of law, *see* Pound, *Social Control Through Law* (1942) 35–62; Pound, *What Is Law* (1940) 47 WEST VIRGINIA LAW QUARTERLY, 1; and the interpretation of legal history, *see* Pound, *Interpretations of Legal History* (1923).

7. 2 *Geist des römischen Rechts*, § 26, p. 48 (1854).

8. 1 *Naturrecht oder Philosophie des Rechts und des Staats* (6 ed. 1870) 308.

ceptive.[9] The root of the difficulty lay in juristic and ethical vocabulary. There was poverty of terms which required one word which we translate as "law" to carry many meanings. To compare with it there was in German an abundance of words of different degrees of ethical connotation with meanings not always clearly differentiated.[10] He points out that the Greeks had but one word on the ethical side of the relation (δικη). The Romans had two (*ius, mores*). German has three (*Richt, Sitte, Moral*).[11] English has two: morality, morals. But morality and morals are not thoroughly distinguished in general English usage. It is, however, a useful distinction to use "morality" for a body of accepted conduct and "morals" for systems of precepts as to conduct organized by principles as ideal systems. Thus "morals" would apply to "the broad field of conduct evaluated in terms of end, aims, or results," while "morality" would refer to a body of conduct according to an accepted standard. So conventional morality would be a body of conduct approved by the custom or habit of the group of which the individual is a member. Christian morality would be conduct approved by Christians as in accordance with the principles of Christianity.[12] In this way of putting it, "morality" would not be an ideal but an actual system. As jurists would say, it is "positive" while morals are "natural," that is, according to an ideal, not necessarily practiced nor backed by social pressure as to details. Systems of morals, however, are likely to be in the main idealizings of the morality of the time and place.

From the standpoint of the historical school in the nineteenth century law and morality have a common origin but diverge in their development. In the first stage of differentiation morality is much more advanced than law. In the beginnings of Roman law *fas* and *boni mores* do much of what becomes the task of *ius*, and such matters as good faith in

---

9. Jhering, *Der Zweck im Recht* (1883) 15–95.
10. *Ibid.*, 49–58.
11. *Ibid.*, 56.
12. Lee, *Morals, Morality, and Ethics: Suggested Terminology* (1928) 38 INTERNATIONAL JOURNAL OF ETHICS, 451, 452–53.

transactions, keeping promises, performing agreements, are left to *boni mores* rather than to *ius*.[13] There is no law of contracts in Anglo-Saxon law. In the earlier Middle Ages enforcement of informal contracts was left to the church.[14] When a distinct legal development begins, since remedies and actions exist but rights are not yet worked out, rigid rules are the only check upon the magistrate. Presently law in this stage is outstripped by the development of moral ideas and has no means of sufficiently rapid growth to keep abreast. Interpretation of the Twelve Tables could not provide a better order of inheritance based on blood relationship when succession of the agnates and the *gentiles* became out of accord with moral ideas. There are no generalizations in the earlier stages of law and the premises are not broad enough to allow of growth by interpretation beyond narrow limits. Common-law ideas of property could not give effect to the purely moral duties of a trustee. No development of the common-law writs could give equitable relief against fraud. On the other hand, in a later stage the law sometimes outstrips current morality, as in the case of the duty of disinterested benevolence exacted of directors and promoters of corporations by Anglo-American equity.

Four stages in the development of law with respect to morality and morals may be recognized. First, there is a stage of undifferentiated ethical customs, customs of popular action, religion, and law; what analytical jurists would call the pre-legal stage. Law is undifferentiated from morality.[15] Second, there is a stage of strict law, codified or crystallized custom, which in time is outstripped by morality and has not sufficient power of growth to keep abreast. Third, there is a stage of infusion of morality into the law and of reshaping by morals, in which ideas of equity and natural law are effective agencies of growth. Fourth, there is a

---

13. *Aulus Gellius*, vii, 18, 1, xx, 20, 1, 39; Cicero, *De officiis*, i, 7, 23, iii, 31, 11; *Livy*, i, 21; *Dion. Hal.* i, 40.

14. *Decret. Greg.* i, 35, 1 and 3.

15. As sociologists commonly use the term 'law' for all social control, Malinowski does not admit this. *Introduction to Hogbin, Law and Order in Polynesia* (1934). But the matter is conclusively set forth in Llewellyn and Hoebel, *The Cheyenne Way* (1941) 233–38.

stage of conscious, constructive lawmaking, the maturity of law, in which it is urged that morals and morality are for the lawmaker, and that law alone is for the judge.

As soon as morality and law are differentiated a progression begins from moral ideas to legal ideas from morality to law.[16] Thus in Roman law by the strict law manumission could only be made by a fictitious legal proceeding, by entry on the censor's register, or by a formal provision in a will.[17] An irregular manumission was void. The rise of ethical ideas as to slavery gave rise to equitable freedom, in case of manumission by letter or by declaration before friends (*i.e.*, witnesses), recognized and protected by the praetor. This was made a legal freedom by the *lex Iunia*. In the common law, seisin of estates in land was protected by real actions which became obsolete, possession of land by ejectment and trespass, and of chattels by trespass de bonis and trover. All this left gaps which could not be filled by fictions or interpretation. Moral ideas were later taken up by equity and gave rise to a doctrine of constructive trusts. Again, at common law easements could only be created by grant or by adverse user. The enforcement of restrictive covenants in equity against purchasers with notice gave rise to equitable easements or servitudes. At length zoning laws made such restrictions legal.[18]

This progress goes on in all stages of legal development. In what I have noted above as the third stage, however, there is a wholesale taking over of purely moral notions under an idea that law and morals (more or less identified with morality) are identical. The historical jurist, therefore, taught that morality was potential law. That which started with a moral idea became an equitable principle and then a rule of law, or later became a definite precept of morality and then a precept of law.

In general, in the strict law the law is quite indifferent to morals. In the stage of equity and natural law it is sought to identify law with

16. This is well put in Millar, *Historical View of the English Government* (1879) bk. ii, chap. 7.

17. Gaius, i, § 17.

18. Van Hecke, *Zoning Ordinances and Restrictions in Deeds* (1928) 37 YALE LAW JOURNAL, 407.

morals. In the maturity of law it is insisted that law and morals are to be kept apart sedulously. Morality and morals are conceived of as for the legislator or the student of legislation, the one making laws out of the raw materials of morality, the other studying how this is done and how it ought to be done. But it is urged that they are not matters for the judge or for the jurist. It is held that the judge applies (or ought to apply) the rules that are given him, while the jurist studies these rules, analyzes and systematizes them and works out their logical content. This assumes that law in the second sense is a body of rules. Such was Austin's first assumption, taken from Bentham.[19] Analytical jurists continue to insist vigorously on this separation of law and morals, even after the law has definitely passed into a new stage of development.[20] They are zealous to point out that a legal right is not necessarily right in the ethical sense; that it is not necessarily accordant to our feelings of what ought to be. They are zealous to show that a man may have a legal right which is morally wrong, and to refute the proposition that a legal right is not a right unless it is right. This could stand as an analysis of legal systems in the nineteenth century. But, as will be seen presently, the sharp line between making or finding the law and applying the law which the analytical jurist drew cannot be maintained in this connection. Whenever a legal precept has to be found in order to meet what used to be called a "gap in the law," it is found by choice of an authoritative starting point for reasoning from among competing starting points, a choice governed by considering how far application of the result reached from one or another will comport with the received ideal. Thus morals were a matter for judge and jurist as well as for legislator. Yet it was necessary for sound thinking to perceive that moral principles are not law simply because they are moral principles.

On the other hand, the circumstance that "a right" and "law" and what is "right" in the ethical sense were expressed by the same word in

---

19. Austin, *The Province of Jurisprudence Determined* (1832) 2; 1 Bentham, *Works,* Bowring's ed. 141.

20. E.g., Kelsen, *Reine Rechtslehre* (1934) 25–26.

Latin, and that "a right" and what is "right" in the ethical sense are expressed by the same word in English, has had not a little influence in the history of law in bringing rights and law into accord with ideas of right.

In the nineteenth century philosophical discussions of the relation of jurisprudence and ethics, of law to morality and morals,[21] were much influenced by German discussions of the relation of *Recht* to *Sitte*. Neither of these words translates exactly into a single English word. *Recht* does not mean law as the precepts which the courts recognize and apply but means more nearly what the courts are seeking to reach through judicial decision. *Sitte* might be rendered "ethical custom."[22] So the question which German philosophers of the last century were debating came to this: Is what the courts are trying immediately to attain identical with morality or a portion of the broad field of morals or is it something which may be set over against them?

Philosophical jurisprudence arises in the stage of legal development in which attempt is made to treat legal precepts and moral precepts as identical; to make moral precepts as such legal precepts. Hence at first philosophers of law assumed that jurisprudence was a branch of ethics and that legal precepts were only declaratory of moral precepts. They assumed that a norm or pattern of decision in the courts could not be a legal precept unless it was a moral precept; not merely that it ought not to be a legal precept if it ran counter to a moral precept. They assumed also that moral precepts as such were legally obligatory. This was derived from the treatment of jurisprudence as a department of theology before the Reformation.

From the standpoint of seventeenth- and eighteenth-century jurisprudence positive law gets its whole validity from being declaratory of natural law. But conceding that this theory that the validity of a legal pre-

---

21. Green, *Principles of Political Obligation*, §§ 11–31 (lectures delivered 1879–80); Hegel, *Grundlinien der Philosophie des Rechts* (1821) §§ 105–14; Miller, *Lectures on the Philosophy of Law* (1884) lect. 13.

22. *See* Haldane, *Higher Nationality: A Study in Law and Ethics* (1913) 38 REPORT, AMERICAN BAR ASSOCIATION, 393, 403–5.

cept as such is to be tested by its conformity to moral principles did much service in the seventeenth and eighteenth centuries in promoting liberalization through bringing law abreast of morality and seeking to conform it to ideals of morals, the theory is tolerable only when absolute ideas of morals are held universally. If all men or most men agree in looking to some ultimate authority for decisive pronouncements on the content and application of moral principles the theory may be tolerable in practice. In practice the theory meant that each philosophical jurist made his own ethical views, largely an ideal form of the doctrine or institutions which he had been taught or with which he was familiar, the test of the validity of legal precepts. The real value of the theory was that it led each jurist to work out ideal standards which could serve for a critique. Bentham said that the natural-law exponent of ethics held himself one of the elect so that one who wished to know what was right had only to consult him as a divinely instructed authority.[23] When and where there are absolute theories of morals as to which all men are agreed it may be possible to find Bentham's man who was one of the elect. From such a source authoritative natural law may be drawn without impairing the general security. But when absolute theories are discarded and no authorities are universally or even generally recognized, when, moreover, classes with divergent interests hold diverse views on fundamental points, natural law in the eighteenth-century sense would make every man a law unto himself. Accordingly historical jurists and analytical jurists in the nineteenth century threw over ideals of law entirely and the metaphysical jurists sought to deduce an ideal critique from some fundamental conception of right or justice given us independently and having independent validity. They held that both law and morals were deductions from the fundamental conception, but differed in that in morals the deductions had reference to the motives of conduct, while in law they had reference to the outward results of conduct.[24]

23. *Introduction to the Principles of Morals and Legislation* (Clarendon Press ed. 1876) 17 n. 3.
24. Ahrens, *Cours de droit naturel* (8 ed. 1892) § 21, II.

Already at the beginning of the eighteenth century Thomasius began to insist upon distinguishing law and morals.[25] Kant made a clear distinction. He begins with a proposition that a man in endeavoring to bring his animal self and his rational self into harmony is presented to himself in two aspects, an inner and an outer, so that his acts have a twofold aspect. On the one hand they are external manifestations of his will. On the other hand they are determinations of his will by motives. On the one hand he is in relation to other beings like himself and to external things. On the other hand he is alone with himself. The law, says Kant, has to do with his acts in the former aspect. Morals have to do with them in the latter aspect. The task of the law is to keep conscious, free-willing beings from interfering with one another. It is so to order their conduct that each shall exercise his freedom in a way consistent with the freedom of all others, since all others are to be regarded equally as ends in themselves. So law has to do with outward acts. It reaches no further than the possibility of outward compulsion.[26]

In the maturity of law in the nineteenth century, the same circumstances which led analytical jurists to adopt the idea of distinguishing law and morals led to philosophical attempts to express the relation between them by contrasting them. According to Hegel what we seek to attain through law is the possibility of liberty. Morals determine not what is externally possible but what internally ought to be. So law and morals are in contrast as the possible of external realization and the internally obligatory. The opposition disappears in the highest unity of the ethical social habit which obtains in an association such as the family or civil society.[27] This is a metaphysical way of putting what sociological jurists put by saying that law and morals are agencies of social control.

In the latter part of the nineteenth century, as abstract individualist theories begin to be replaced by theories which proceed not upon a

---

25. *Fundamenta iuris naturae et gentium,* i, 1, 4, §§ 89–91, i, 1, 5, § 47, i, 1, 6, §§ 3, 32–43, 64–66, 74–75 (1 ed. 1705, 4 ed. 1718).

26. Kant, *Metaphysische Anfangsgründe der Rechtslehre* (1797) introduction, §§ B–D.

27. *Grundlinien der Philosophie des Rechts* (1821) §§ 104–14. *See* Reyburn, *Ethical Theory of Hegel* (1921) 118–21.

principle of individual independence but upon a basis of the social interdependence of men, attempts to oppose or to contrast law and morals are given up and we come upon a new phase of attempts to subordinate law to morals.

This begins with Jellinek as far back as 1878. Law, he said, is a minimum ethics. The field of law is that part of the requirements of morals observance of which is indispensable in the given stage of social development. By "law" here (*Recht*) he meant law as we try to make it; the idea of law. The actual body of legal precepts may fall short of or in places or at times may go beyond this ethical minimum. The field of law is only a part of the field of ethical custom, namely, the part which has to do with the indispensable conditions of the social order.[28] As distinguished from law, morals include only the excess beyond the indispensable minimum. This excess, desirable but not indispensable, he terms an "ethical luxury." The minimum represents what we may expect to give effect to through legal precepts.[29] In a broader view morality is made to embrace the whole. In this doctrine there are characteristic features of the nineteenth century. It assumes that the scope of law is to be held down to the smallest area possible. This was a postulate of metaphysical jurisprudence. Law was thought of as a systematic restriction of freedom in the interest of free individual self-assertion. It was necessary and yet was in some sort an evil, and was not to be suffered to extend itself beyond what was obviously necessary.[30]

28. Compare a like view held by Malinowski, *Introduction to Hogbin, Law and Order in Polynesia* (1934) xxv–xxvii.

29. Jellinek, *Die sozialethische Bedeutung von Recht, Unrecht, und Strafe*, chap. 2 (1878, 2 ed. 1908). *See also* Demogue, *Les notions fondamentales du droit privé*, 13 ff. "The endeavor to find any other differences between law and morals, and especially between customary law and ethical custom, than a higher or lesser importance for the ordering of the common life has not thus far proved successful." Radbruch, *Einführung in die Rechtswissenschaft* (5–6 ed. 1925) 21.

30. "Reduced to these terms the difference between morality and right (*diritto*, right-and-law) is a difference in degree and not of essence. Yet it is a very important difference, as it reduces the power of coercion to what is absolutely necessary for the harmonious co-existence of the individual with the whole." 1 Lioy, *Philosophy of Right* (transl. by Hastie 1891) 121. *See also* Beudant, *Le droit individuel et l'état* (3 ed.) 148 (1 ed. 1898, 3 ed. 1926).

Turning to the social philosophical jurists of the end of the last and fore part of the present century, to Jhering the immediate task of the law is to secure interests—claims or wants or demand. We must choose what interests we will recognize, fix the limits within which we will recognize them, and must weigh or evaluate conflicting or overlapping interests in order to secure as much as we may with the least sacrifice. In making this choice, in weighing or valuing interests, whether in legislation, or in judicial decision, or in juristic writing, he maintains that we must turn to ethics for principles. Morals is an evaluation of interests. Law is or seeks to be a delimitation in accordance therewith.[31] Thus we come back in substance to a conception of jurisprudence as on one side a branch of applied ethics.[32]

Again, as Stammler, the leader of the Neo-Kantians put it, we seek justice through law. But to attain justice through law we must formulate the social ideal of the epoch and endeavor to insure that law is made to advance it and secure it in action. These ideals are developed outside of the law. They are moral ideals and so jurisprudence is dependent upon ethics so far as ethics has to do with these goals which we seek to attain and with reference to which we measure legal precepts and doctrines and institutions in order to make them agencies of progress toward the goals, while jurisprudence has to do rather with the means of attaining them.[33] Although he insists on separation of jurisprudence from ethics and that each must have an independent method,[34] he comes finally to the proposition that "just law has need of ethical doctrine for its complete realization."[35]

According to Kohler, the leader of the Neo-Hegelians, government, law, and morality are forces working toward the attainment of an ideal of civilization. So jurisprudence "must appreciate these ideal ends to-

31. This is well put in Korkunov, *General Theory of Law* (transl. by Hastings 1909) 521. *See* Everett, *Moral Values*, 7.

32. 2 Jhering, *Der Zweck im Recht* (1883) 15–134.

33. Stammler, *Wirtschaft und Recht* (1895) §§ 102–3.

34. *Lehre von dem richtigen Rechte* (1902) bk. i, pt. 2, pp. 55–92. The second edition (1926) is much altered.

35. *Ibid.*, 87.

ward which society strives."[36] Perhaps he alone of the leaders of philosophical jurisprudence in the fore part of the present century did not
more or less avowedly go back in some degree to subordination of jurisprudence to ethics. Law and morals, he taught, express and also further a progressive civilization.[37] Hence jurisprudence and ethics are
both subordinated to a universal history of civilization and to a philosophy of right and economics from which we determine the jural postulates—the presuppositions as to right conduct—of the civilization of
the time and place.[38] More than one contemporary book on ethics, however, presupposes very nearly what he called for[39] and the practical result is to make jurisprudence more or less dependent on a science which
a modern type of ethical philosophers would be likely to claim as
theirs.[40]

After the first World War the dominance of Neo-Kantian thinking in
the social sciences and stress upon methodology led to a revival of the
nineteenth-century contrasting of law and morals and cutting off of jurisprudence from ethics. Thus Radbruch holds that law and morals are
an irreducible antinomy;[41] that legal precepts and moral precepts coincide only by chance;[42] and that the problem of values is wholly outside
the science of law. Kelsen, in the same way, and from a Neo-Kantian
starting point, holds that all we have to consider is "that it is laid down
in a rule of law, as a condition of a specific result, that the positive legal
order react to that behavior with an act of coercion."[43]

Nineteenth-century analytical views of the relation of law and morals
were strongly influenced by the assumption of the separation of powers
as fundamental for juristic thinking, not merely a constitutional device.

---

36. *Moderne Rechtsprobleme* (1907) §§ 1–7; *Rechtsphilosophie und Universalrechtsgeschichte*, in 1 Holtzendorf, ENZYKLOPADIE DER RECHTSWISSENSCHAFT (6 ed. 1904) § 9.
37. *Lehrbuch der Rechtsphilosophie* (1 ed. 1909) 2.
38. *Rechtsphilosophie und Universalrechtsgeschichte*, § 2.
39. E.g., Dewey and Tufts, *Ethics* (1908).
40. Lévy-Bruhl, *La morale et la science des moeurs* (5 ed. 1913).
41. *Rechtsphilosophie* (3 ed. 1932) § 9.
42. *Ibid.*, § 6.
43. *Reine Rechtslehre* (1934) 26.

Accordingly assuming an exact, logically defined separation of powers, the analytical jurist contended that law and morals were distinct and unrelated and that he was concerned only with law.[44] If he saw that their spheres came in contact or even overlapped in practice, he assumed that it was because while in a theoretically fully developed legal system judicial and legislative powers are fully separated, this separation has not been realized to its full extent in practice. So far as and where this separation was still incomplete there was confusion of or overlapping of law and morality and morals. He saw four such points of contact: (1) in judicial lawmaking or law finding, (2) in interpretation of legal precepts, (3) in application of legal standards, and (4) in judicial discretion. At these four points, he considered, there was a border zone, where the separation of powers was not complete. So far as the separation of judicial and legislative functions was complete, law was for courts, morals and morality were for legislators; legal precepts were for jurisprudence, moral principles were for ethics. But so far as the separation was not yet complete, and in what he took to be the narrowing field in which judges must make as well as administer legal precepts, morality had to stand for the law which ought to but did not exist as the rule of judicial determination.[45]

It was natural that Austin should have thought of judicial decision as turning precepts of "positive morality" into legal precepts since he could see some such process actually taking place in the work of the Judicial Committee of the Privy Council in appeals from newly settled areas in which the British were setting up courts for the first

---

44. 2 Austin, *Jurisprudence* (5 ed. 1885) 1072–73.

45. As to the points of contact, *see* 1 Austin, *Jurisprudence* (5 ed. 1885) lects. 37, 38, and note on interpretation, 2 *ibid.*, 989–1001; Amos, *Science of Law* (1874) 34–42. Austin argued for a codification which should be 'a complete and exclusive body of statute law.' 2 *Jurisprudence* (5 cd. 1885) 660. He held that the 'incognoscibility' of 'judiciary law' was due to the legislator's negligence. *Ibid.*, 654. Until such a code, the judges, in the absence of legislation, "impress rules of positive morality with the character of law through decision of causes." 1 *ibid.*, 36. *See also* Markby, *Elements of Law* (6 ed. 1905) §§ 25–30. "As the development of law goes on, the function of the judge is confined within ever narrowing limits; the main source of modifications in legal relations comes to be more and more exclusively the legislature." Sidgwick, *Elements of Politics* (2 ed. 1897) 203.

time.[46] A like situation arose later in a case where a succession was governed neither by English nor by Hindu nor by Mohammedan law. Lord Westbury said that it must be determined "by the principles of natural justice."[47]

With such cases before them we may understand how the first English analytical jurists like the historical jurists, thought that judicial making or finding of law was no more than a reaching out for precepts of positive morality and in the absence of authoritative grounds of decision giving them the guinea stamp of precedent. But the doctrine that morals were to be looked to only in an immature stage of legal development before the separation of powers is complete involves two other false assumptions, one, the possibility of a complete analytical separation of powers, the other, the possibility of a complete body of legal precepts which will require no supplementing and no development by judicial action.

Yet granting that these two assumptions are not well taken we do not wholly dispose of the contention of the analytical school. For there is a difference of the first moment between legislative lawmaking and judicial lawmaking. The legislative lawmaker is laying down a rule for the future.[48] Hence the general security does not require him to proceed on

46. Thus at Penang, when newly settled, there was a mixed population and no native law for the whole, since people had come in from different parts, from which they were often refugees, and had brought no law with them. The home government recommended to the judge on the spot that where the parties were of different native laws, decision be made according to 'the laws of universal and natural justice.' *See* introduction to 1 Kyshe's *Reports* (Straits Settlements) ix (1885). See *Palangee* v. *Tye Ang* (1803) 1 Kyshe, xix.

47. *Barlow* v. *Orde*, L.R. 3 P.C. 164, 167 (1870). Natural justice proved to require something very like the English law as to wills and succession, *ibid.*, 189. Also in *Palangee* v. *Tye Ang*, supra, note 46, "natural justice called for wills and probate and letters of administration." In other words, the court applied positive natural law.

48. Unless constitutions forbid, he may lay down rules by which the past is to be judged. But such legislation is universally reprobated, and has been forbidden in formulations of fundamental law from the Twelve Tables to modern constitutions. *The French Civil Code*, art. 2, provides: "The enacted rule only makes dispositions for the future; it has no retroactive effect." It is said of this: "In a well organized society individuals ought not to be exposed to having their condition or fortune compromised by a

predetermined premises or along predetermined lines. He can take his premises from whencesoever expediency or his wisdom dictates and proceed along the lines that seem best to him. On the other hand the judicial lawmaker is not merely making a rule for the future. He is laying down a legal precept which will apply to the transactions of the past as well as to the future, and he is doing so immediately with reference to a controversy arising in the past.[49] Hence the social interest in the general security requires that he should not have the same freedom as the legislative lawmaker. It requires that instead of finding his premises where he will or where expediency appears to him to dictate, he finds them in the authoritatively recognized legal materials or by a process recognized by the legal system. It requires that instead of proceeding along the lines that seem best to him, he proceeds by using the authoritative legal technique upon authoritative legal materials.[50]

Thus the proposition that a judicial decision is only evidence of the law, the doctrine that judges find the law and do not make it, are not purposeless dogmatic fictions. If they are dogmatic fictions, they do more than enable us to arrange the phenomena of the administration of justice in a convenient, logically consistent scheme. They express a sound instinct of judges and lawyers for maintaining a paramount social interest. They serve to safeguard the general security by requiring the grounds of judicial decision to be as definite as is compatible with the attainment of justice in results. They serve to make judicial action pre-

---

change of legislation. There must be some security in transactions; but there is none if laws may operate retroactively, for the right I have acquired today in conformity to the provisions of the existing law may be taken from me tomorrow by a law which I could not have taken into account since it was impossible to foresee it." 1 Baudry-Lacantinerie, *Précis de droit civil* (12 ed. 1919) no. 46. *See* XII Tab. ix, 1, 1 Bruns, *Fontes Iuris Romani Antiqui* (7 ed. 1909) 34; Clark, *Australian Constitutional Law* (1901) 28 ff.; *Constitution of Brazil*, arts, 15, 791.

49. "It must be observed that a judicial decision *primae impressionis* or a judgment by which a new point of law is for the first time decided, is always an *ex post facto* law." 1 Austin, *Jurisprudence* (5 ed. 1885) 487.

50. "The law is progressive and expansive, adapting itself to the new relations and interests which are constantly springing up in the progress of society. But this progress must be by analogy to what is already settled." Greene, C.J., in *Hodges v. New England Screw Co.*, 1 R.I. 312, 356 (1850).

dictable so far as may be. They serve to hold down the personality of the magistrate. They constrain him to look at causes objectively and try them by reasoned development of legal materials which had taken shape prior to and independent of the cause in hand. Hence where rules are laid down for the future only, the lawmaker is given entire freedom, subject in America to a few reservations in bills of rights. Where, as in judicial lawmaking, rules are laid down for past as well as for future situations, the lawmaker is held to traditional premises or traditional lines and modes of development to the end that those who know the tradition and are experienced in the technique may be able within reasonable limits to forecast his action.

A second point of contact between law and morals is to be found in interpretation. Interpretation has been thought of as including the process of finding or making rules for new cases or reshaping them for unusual cases considered above. This is called interpretation by a dogmatic fiction because in the analytical theory of the last century the law was complete and all cases were at least covered by the logical implications of pre-existing rules or the logical content of legal principles. Austin set it off under the name of "spurious interpretation."[51] Here the contact between law and morals is obvious since the process is in substance one of lawmaking. But in what Austin called "genuine interpretation"[52] — search for the actual meaning of the one who prescribed a rule admittedly governing the case in hand — the final criterion, when literal meaning and context fail to yield a satisfactory construction, is found in the "intrinsic merit" of the various possible meanings.[53] The court or jurist assumes that the lawmaker's ideal and that of the tribunal or the writer are in substantial accord; that each holds to the same ideal

---

51. 2 *Jurisprudence* (5 ed. 1885) 991–95.

52. *Ibid.*, 989–91.

53. 1 Savigny, *System des heutigen römischen Rechts* (1840) §§ 34, 37; Clark, *Practical Jurisprudence* (1883) 234–35. Among the five means of genuine interpretation in French law it is said the fourth is to "weigh the consequences which the legal precept would produce according to whether one understood it in the one sense or in the other." 1 Baudry-Lacantinerie, *Précis de droit civil* (12 ed. 1919) no. 103, p. 56.

pattern of law or ideal picture, moral, political, or social, of the end of law. But the political and the social ideals have a predominant moral element. Thus, however much the analytical theory of "genuine interpretation" may purport to exclude the moral ideas of the court, and to insure a wholly mechanical logical exposition of a logically implied content of legal precepts, two doors are left open. The court must determine whether the criteria of the literal meaning of the words and of the text read with the context yield a "satisfactory" solution.[54] If the court finds they do not, it must inquire into the "intrinsic merit" of the competing interpretations. In practice "satisfactory" will almost always mean morally satisfactory. "Intrinsic merit" will always tend to mean intrinsic moral merit.[55]

Another point of contact is in the application of standards. Analytical jurists have liked to think of the application of legal precepts as a purely mechanical process. Such things as the margin of discretion in the application of equitable remedies, the appeal to the ethical in the maxims of equity, and the ethical element in such equitable doctrines as those with respect to hard bargains, mistake coupled with sharp practice, and the like, were distasteful to them. Partly under their influence and partly from the same spirit of the maturity of law that led to the analytical way of thinking, in the last quarter of the nineteenth century, some American courts sought to eliminate, or at least minimize the scope of these doctrines and to make equitable relief, once jurisdiction was estab-

54. This is obvious in extreme cases like the statute for rebuilding the Chelmsford jail, Serjeant Robinson, *Bench and Bar: Reminiscences of One of an Ancient Race* (3 ed. 1891) 229, or the statute against discharging firearms upon the highway. Pound, *A Hundred Years of American Law*, in 1 *Law: A Century of Progress, 1835–1935*, 8. It may be seen, however, in everyday cases in the courts.

55. See *e.g.* Brett, M.R., in *Plumstead Board of Works* v. *Spackman*, 13 Q.B.D. 878, 886–87 (1884); *River Wear Com'rs* v. *Adamson*, 2 A.C. 743 (1877), opinions of Lord O'Hagan (757–59, 761) and Lord Blackburn (770–72); Blandford, J., in *Lombard* v. *Trustees*, 73 Ga. 322, 324 (1884); *Flint River Co.* v. *Foster*, 5 Ga. 194, 201–4 (1848); Parsons, C.J., in *Richards* v. *Daggett*, 4 Mass. 534, 537 (1808); Graves, J., in *Perry* v. *Strawbridge*, 209 Mo. 621, 628–29 (1907); *Ham* v. *McClaws*, 1 Bay (1 S.C. Law) 93, 96 (1789); *Griffin* v. *Interurban St. R. Co.*, 179 N.Y. 438, 449 (1904). *See also* the remarks of Lord Watson, as to the 'intention of the legislature,' *Salomon* v. *Salomon & Co.* [1897] A.C. 22, 38.

lished, as much a matter of course as damages at law.[56] But this equitable or individualized application of legal precepts is called for more and more in the law of today. It is the life of administration, whether executive or judicial. The lack of power of individualization in judicial administration in the nineteenth century has contributed to a multiplication of administrative agencies and tribunals and a transfer to them of matters formerly of judicial cognizance which is sufficient testimony to the futility of the attempt in the last century to make the courts into judicial slot machines.[57]

In fact, the ethical element in application of law was never excluded from the actual administration of justice.[58] It will suffice to note two aspects of application of law in which the ethical element has always been decisive: The application of legal standards and judicial exercise of discretion. A great and increasing part of the administration of justice is achieved through legal standards. These standards begin to come into the law in the state of infusion of morals through theories of natural law.[59] They have to do with conduct and have a large moral element. The standard of due care in the law of negligence, the standard of fair competition, the standard of fair conduct of a fiduciary, the Roman standard of what good faith demands in a particular transaction, the Roman standard of use by a prudent usufructuary and of how a prudent and diligent head of a household (i.e., person sui juris) would act under the given circumstances, all involve an idea of fairness or reasonableness. Like all moral precepts they are individualized in their application.

56. See 4 Pomeroy, *Equity Jurisprudence* (3 ed. 1905) § 1404 and note 2. The book was first published in 1881–82. Compare the arbitrary rule as to "mutuality of equitable relief" which developed in nineteenth-century American decisions with the remarks of Cardozo, J., in *Epstein v. Gluckin*, 233 N.Y. 490, 494 (1922).

57. See Pound, *Justice According to Law — Executive Justice* (1913) 14 COLUMBIA LAW REVIEW, 12; Pound, *Administrative Law* (1942) 37–40.

58. Dillon, *Laws and Jurisprudence of England and America* (1894) 17; Fry, *Memoir of Sir Edward Fry* (1921) 67.

59. For their origins in Roman Law in the formula in actions *bonae fidei*, see *Gaius*, iv, § 47; Inst. iv., 6 §§ 28, 30; Cicero, *De officiis*, iii, 17, 70.

They are not applied mechanically to a set of facts looked at in the abstract. They are applied according to the circumstances of each case, and within wide limits are applied through an intuition of what is just and fair, involving a moral judgment upon the particular item of conduct in question.[60]

No less clearly there is a point of contact between law and morals in matters which are left to the discretion of the court. In cases where there is a margin of discretion in the application of legal precepts, as in applying or molding equitable remedies, we speak of "judicial discretion." Here there are principles (*i.e.*, starting points for reasoning) governing judicial action within the discretionary margin of application, although at bottom there is not a little room for personal moral judgment.[61] There are many situations, however, where the course of judicial action is left to be determined wholly by the judge's individual sense of what is right and just.[62] The objections to any considerable scope for this element in the judicial process are obvious.[63] It has been said it is "the law of tyrants."[64] But hard as we tried in the last century to reduce it to the vanishing point, there proved to be a point beyond which rule and me-

60. The application of the standard of due care involves a moral judgment, but not a purely moral judgment. Holmes, *The Common Law* (1881) 107 ff. As to standards applicable to public utilities, and to unfair competition, *see* Pound, *Administrative Application of Legal Standards* (1919) 44 REP. AM. BAR ASSN. 445, 456. In case of fiduciary relations courts of equity enforce duties of good faith 'in aid of general morals.' W. W. Story, *Equity Jurisprudence* (1835) § 431. As to the standard of good faith in certain relations and transactions in Roman law *see* Cicero, *De officiis*, iii, 17, 70; *Gaius*, iv, § 62; *Inst.* iv. 6.

61. "Because the matter is left in the discretion of the court, it does not mean that the court is free to do exactly what it chooses, to indulge in sympathies or to invent some new equitable doctrine between the parties. It means that discretion is to be exercised upon judicial grounds in accordance with the principles that have been recognized in this court." Langton, J., in *Greenwood v. Greenwood* [1937] P. 157, 164.

62. See Isaacs, *The Limits of Judicial Discretion* (1923) 32 YALE LAW JOURNAL, 339.

63. *See* the remarks of Lord Penzance in *Morgan v. Morgan*, L.R. 1 P. & D. 644, 647 (1869).

64. Lord Camden, quoted by Fearne, *Contingent Remainders* (10 ed. 1844) 534 note t. It need not be said that the law of property is not a suitable field for discretion.

chanical application are impotent. The tendency today is to extend rather than to restrict its scope. We must find how to make it tolerable. The history of Anglo-American equity shows this may be done by developing through experience principles of exercise of discretion and recognizing that because there is no rule in the strict sense it does not follow that a tribunal must have unlimited power of doing what it chooses. It is to reach a reasoned decision in the light of those principles. As Kelsen has pointed out, when a legal precept leaves some matter to discretion, if the ground of decision lies outside of the body of authoritative guides to decision (law in the second sense) it does not lie outside of the legal order (law in the first sense).[65]

In the analytical account of the points of contact between law and morals the matter is put as if there were three or four restricted areas in which exceptionally such contact may take place.[66] Occasionally it may happen that a case arises for which there is no applicable legal precept and the court must work one out for the case from the legal materials at hand by a certain traditional technique of analogical development of the precedents. Occasionally, too, it may happen that an authoritatively established legal precept is so ill expressed that genuine interpretation becomes necessary. In this process it may happen that as a last resort the court must pass upon the relative merit of the several possible interpretations from an ethical standpoint. Also in those exceptional cases for which ordinary legal remedies are not adequate, a court of equity may have a certain margin of power to go upon the moral aspects of a case in granting or denying extraordinary relief. In a few matters there are "mixed questions of law and fact" where the trier of fact, in adjusting a legal standard to the facts of a particular case, may find opportunity for an incidental moral judgment. Finally some matters of administration must be left more or less to the court's personal sense of what is right. All this is put as if in its everyday course judicial justice was quite divorced

65. *Reine Rechtslehre* (1934) 99.
66. 2 Austin, *Jurisprudence* (5 ed. 1885) 638–41.

from ideas of right and morals, with intrusion of morals into the legal domain only in a residuum of cases for which adequate provision had not been made, or in which an administrative element still lingered in the courts instead of being committed to the executive. But this plausible account represents juristic desire for a certain uniform, predictable justice much more than it represents the judicial process in action. In appellate tribunals the difficulty that brings the cause up for review is usually that legal rules and legal conceptions have to be applied by analogy to causes that depart from the type for which the precept was devised or given shape. Such departures vary infinitely. Hence choice from among competing analogies and choice from among competing modes of analogical development are the staple of judicial opinions.[67] The line between "genuine" and "spurious" interpretation can be drawn only for typical cases. They shade into one another and a wide zone between them is the field in which a great part of appellate decision must take place. Likewise the extraordinary relief given by courts of equity has be-

67. In six significant cases in the law of torts note how each involves choice between two possible lines of analogical reasoning and sets the law on some point upon a path leading from some one analogy rather than from another. In *Pasley v. Freeman*, 3 T.R. 51 (1789) as between an analogy of warranty and one of assault, as between a contractual or relational and a delictal analogy, the court chose the latter and established a liability for intentional deceit although the defendant had not profited by the deceit and was under no contract duty and was in no relation which called on him to speak. Thus we get a principle of liability for aggression upon another. In *Lumley v. Gye*, 2 E. & B. 216 (1853), the court chose the analogy of injury to tangible property and applied the same principle to intentional interference with contract relations. In *Brown v. Kendall*, 6 Cush. 292 (Mass. 1850) the court chose decisively between substantive conceptions, on the one hand, and procedural distinctions, on the other hand, as the basis of liability for injuries due to culpable carrying out of a course of conduct not involving aggression. In *Heaven v. Pender*, 11 Q.B.D. 103, Brett, L.J., gives a thoroughgoing rational exposition of the resulting principle. *Rylands v. Fletcher*, L.R. 3 H.L. 330 (1868) involved a choice between the analogy of liability for culpable conduct and the analogy of liability, regardless of culpability, for failure to keep in hand something maintained which has a tendency to escape and do damage. *Davies v. Mann*, 10 M. & W. 545 (1842) involved a choice between a procedural analogy of a bar to recovery and a substantive analogy of liability for culpably caused injury.

come the everyday form of justice for large classes of controversies and legislation has been adding new classes.[68] Moreover, transition to an urban, industrial society has called increasingly for administrative justice and tribunals with flexible procedure and wide powers of discretionary action have been set up everywhere in increasing number. In fact, there are continual points of contact with morals at every turn in the ordinary course of the judicial process. A theory which ignores them or pictures them as few and of little significance is not a theory of the actual law in action.[69]

Morals are more than potential material for the legislative lawmaker. Ethics can serve us more than as a critique of proposed measures of lawmaking as presented to the legislator. To that extent the analytical jurist was wrong. But in another respect to some extent he was right. When we have found a moral principle we cannot stop at that. There is more to do than formulate it in a rule of law. We must ask how far it has to do with things that may be governed by rules of law. We must ask how far legal machinery of rule and remedy is adapted to the claims the principle recognised and would secure. We must ask how far if we formulate a precept in terms of our moral precept it may be made effective in action.[70] Even more we must consider how far it is possible to give the moral principle legal recognition and legal efficacy by judicial decision or juristic reasoning on the basis of the received legal materials and with the received legal technique without impairing the general security by unsettling the legal system as a whole.[71] As a fifteenth-century lawyer put

---

68. *See* the remarks of Lord Ellesmere in *Earl of Oxford's Case* (1616), 2 White and Tudor, *Leading Cases in Equity* (8 ed. 1910–12) 773, 779. *See also* 2 Chafee and Simpson, *Cases on Equity* (3 ed.) 1176–1218.

69. This has been well put by a practitioner and judge of long experience: "Ethical considerations can no more be excluded from the administration of justice, which is the end and purpose of all civil laws, than one can exclude the vital air from his room and live." Dillon, *Laws and Jurisprudence of England and America* (1894) 17.

70. Pound, *The Limits of Effective Legal Action* (1917) 3 AM. BAR ASSN. JOURNAL, 55, 27 INT. JOURNAL OF ETHICS, 150.

71. *See* Pound, *The Theory of Judicial Decision* (1923) 36 HARVARD LAW REVIEW, 940, 943–49.

it, some things are for the law of the land, some things are for the Chancellor and some things are between a man and his confessor.[72]

Assuming that their provinces are neither identical nor wholly distinct, what sets off their respective domains? If there are two forms or modes of social control, each covering much of the same ground, yet each having ground that is peculiarly its own, what determines the boundary between them? Is it a distinction in subject matter or in application of legal precepts and moral precepts, or is it in both? Analytical jurists have maintained that it is in both.

With respect to subject matter it is said that morals have to do with thought and feeling, while the law has to do only with acts; that in ethics we aim at perfecting individual character, while law seeks only to regulate the relations of individuals with each other and with the state. It is said that morals look to what is behind acts rather than to acts as such. Law, on the other hand, looks to acts, and only to thoughts and feelings so far as they give character to acts and determine the threat to the general security which they involve.[73] The act with malice or *dolus* is more antisocial than the one with mere stupidity or a slow reaction time behind it. Hence the criminal law calls usually for a guilty mind behind the act. But in a crowded community where mechanical agencies of danger to the general security are in everyday use and many sorts of activity incidentally involve potential infringement of social interests, thoughtlessness and want of care, or stupidity, or even failure to control one's agent or to keep in hand an agency one maintains, may be as antisocial as a guilty mind, and so a group of legal offences may be defined which take no account of intent.[74]

---

72. Fineux, *arguendo*, in Anonymous, Y.B. Hil. 4 Hen. 7, pl. 8, fol. 5 (1490).

73. "The object of the law is not to punish sins, but is to prevent certain external results." Holmes, J., in *Com. v. Kennedy*, 170 Mass. 18, 20 (1897). Some illegal act must have followed the wrongful thought. 4 Blackstone, *Commentaries* (1769) 21; 1 Bishop, *Criminal Law* (9 ed. 1923) § 204. *See also* Stone, *Law and Its Administration* (1915) 33–35.

74. "Public policy may require that in the prohibition or punishment of particular acts it may be provided that he who shall do them shall do them at his peril and will not

Next it is said that as between external and internal observance of the dictates of morals the law has to do with the former only. Thou shalt not covet thy neighbor's ox is a moral rule. But unless the covetousness takes outward form, *e.g.*, in larceny, the law does not and indeed cannot deal with it.[75] Not that the law necessarily and wholly closes its eyes to the internal. But law operates through sanctions; through punishment, substitutional redress, specific redress, or forcible prevention. Hence it must have something tangible upon which to go. Prosecution of Mr. Pecksniff for hypocrisy would achieve more harm than good. The story of the schoolmaster who said, "Boys be pure in heart or I'll flog you," is in point.[76] Purity in speech and act is the most the penalty of flogging can insure. The lawmaker must have in mind the practical limitations involved in application and administration of laws. He must not suppose he can bring about an ideal moral order by law if only he can hit upon the appropriate moral principles and develop them properly by legislation.

But nineteenth-century jurists were inclined to carry this too far and to ignore moral considerations simply on the ground of a distinction between the legal and the moral. Because it is impracticable to make the moral duty of gratitude into a legal duty, it does not follow that the law is to deal only with affirmative action and not seek to enforce tangible moral duties not involving affirmative action, even though enforcement may be practicable.

For example take the case of damage to one which is clearly attributable to willful and morally inexcusable inaction of another. Suppose a case where there is no relation between the two except that they are both human beings. If the one is drowning and the other is at hand and sees a rope and a life belt in reach and is inert, if he sits on the bank and smokes when he could act without the least danger, the law has gener-

---

be heard to plead in his defence good faith or ignorance." *Shevlin-Carpenter Co. v. Minnesota*, 218 U.S. 57, 70 (1910). See also *Hobbs v. Winchester Corporation* [1910] 2 K.B. 471; *State v. Quinn*, 131 La. 490, 495 (1912); *Wells Fargo Express v. State*, 79 Ark. 349, 352 (1906); *Welch v. State*, 145 Wis. 86 (1911); *State v. Laundy*, 103 Ore. 443 (1922).

75. Pollock, *First Book of Jurisprudence* (6 ed. 1929) 46–47.

76. *Ibid.*, 47, note 1.

ally refused to impose liability. As Ames put it, "He took away nothing from a person in jeopardy, he simply failed to confer a benefit upon a stranger. . . . The law does not compel active benevolence between man and man. It is left to one's conscience whether he will be the good Samaritan or not."[77]

What difficulties are there here to make legislatures and courts and jurists hesitate? To some extent there are difficulties of proof. We must be sure the one we hold culpable was not dazed by the emergency.[78] Again he who fails to act may assert some claim which must be weighed against the claim of him whom he failed to help. In the good Samaritan case[79] the priest and the Levite may have had cause to fear robbers if they tarried on the way and were not at the inn before sunset. Also it may often be difficult to say upon whom the legal duty of being the good Samaritan shall devolve. If a woman has a fit in a bank, does the duty fall upon the bank as a corporation or on the bank officers and employees present, as individuals, or on the bystanders? Or, take a case where a man was severely injured, without fault of the employees of a railroad company, while attempting to cross ahead of a moving car.[80] Why should the moral duty to be good Samaritans fall upon the employees as servants of the company rather than upon them as individuals? However, the case of an athletic young man with a rope and life belt at hand who sits on a bench in a park along a river bank and sees a child drown does not present these difficulties. Yet the law has made no distinction. Practical difficulties are not always or necessarily in the way. In the case put there is nothing intrinsic in the moral principle which should prevent legal recognition of it and the working out of appropriate legal pre-

77. Ames, *Law and Morals* (1908) 28 HARVARD LAW REVIEW, 97, 112. *See* Bohlen, *The Moral Duty to Aid Others as a Basis of Tort Liability* (1908) 56 UNIV. OF PENN. LAW REVIEW, 217, 316; Bruce, *Humanity and the Law*, 73 CENTRAL LAW JOURNAL, 335; *Osterlind v. Hill*, 263 Mass. 73 (1928).

78. *See* Rivers, *Instinct and the Unconscious* (1921) 55.

79. Luke 10:30–36.

80. *Union Pac. Ry. Co. v. Cappier*, 66 Kan. 749 (1903). *See* the duty of saving life at sea prescribed by *U.S. Salvage Act*, 1912, chap. 268 § 2, 37 Stat. 242, 3 *U.S. Code*, tit. 46, § 728, p. 3977. The duty is imposed upon "the master or person in charge of a vessel" and subjects him to liability to fine or imprisonment.

cepts to give it effect. Indeed, a cautious movement in this direction may be seen in American decisions. In most of the cases there was a relation — husband and wife,[81] employer and employee,[82] or carrier and passenger.[83] One case, master or owner and seaman, has been settled from of old in the sea law.[84] But there are cases in which there was no relation.[85] We must reject the opposition of law and morals when pushed so far as to justify ignoring the moral aspects of these cases where no practical difficulty is in the way. The cases which make the notion of a necessary contrast or opposition between law and morals appear well founded are cases in which the practical limits of effective legal action, the exigencies of enforcement through the judicial process, preclude not so much legal recognition as legal sanctioning of particular moral precepts.[86]

We are not so sure of the opposition of law and morals with respect to application as we were in the nineteenth century. Thus, in illustrating the distinction, Sheldon Amos said: "The same penalty for a broken law

81. *Territory v. Manton*, 8 Mont. 95. See *Rex v. Russell* [1933] Vict. L.R. 59.

82. *Ohio R. Co. v. Early*, 141 Ind. 73 (1894); *Carey v. Davis*, 190 Ia. 120 (1921); *Raasch v. Elite Laundry Co.*, 98 Minn. 357 (1906); *Hunecke v. Meramec Quarry Co.*, 262 Mo. 560 (1914); *Salter v. Nebraska Tel. Co.*, 79 Neb. 373 (1907).

83. *Yazoo-M.R. Co. v. Byrd*, 89 Miss. 308 (1906); *Birmingham Electric Co. v. Driver*, 232 Ala. 36 (1936); *Middleton v. Whitridge*, 213 N.Y. 499 (1915); *Layne v. Chicago R. Co.*, 175 Mo. App. 34, 41 (1913); *Szabo v. Pennsylvania R. Co.*, 132 N.J. Law, 331 (1945).

84. The Iroquois, 194 U.S. 240 (1903); *Cortes v. Baltimore Insular Line*, 287 U.S. 367 (1932); *United States v. Knowles*, 4 Sawy. 517 (1864); *Scarff v. Metcalf*, 107 N.Y. 211 (1887).

85. *Southern R. Co. v. Sewell*, 18 Ga. App. 544 (1916); *Depue v. Flatau*, 100 Minn. 299 (1907); *Whitesides v. Southern R. Co.*, 128 N.C. 229 (1901); *Taylor v. Slaughter*, 171 Okl. 152 (1933).

86. On this much discussed subject: *Netherlands Penal Code*, art. 450; *German Civil Code*, § 826; Stammler, *Lehre von dem richtigen Rechte* (2 ed. 1926) 302; Liszt, *Die Deliktsobligationen im System des bürgerlichen Gesetzbuchs* (1898) 72; Bentham, *Introduction to the Principles of Morals and Legislation* (Clarendon Press reprint 1876) 322–23; Bentham, *Theory of Legislation* (transl. by Hildreth, 5 ed. 1887) 65–66; 2 Livingston, *Complete Works on Criminal Jurisprudence* (Draft Code of Crimes and Punishments for the State of Louisiana) (1873) 126–27; Macaulay, *Notes to Draft of Indian Penal Code*, chap. xviii, § 294 and note M (pp. 53–56) 7 *Complete Works* (ed. 1875) 493–97; American Law Institute, 1 *Restatement of the Law of Torts* (1934) § 314.

is exacted from persons of an indefinite number of shades of moral guilt."[87] He says this as if it showed conclusively that law would not take cognizance of shades which morals would recognize. No doubt Amos's generation took the statement that the law does not recognize shades of guilt as axiomatic. But today, through probation, parole, administrative agencies and more enlightened penal treatment, the legal order is coming more and more to fit the treatment to the criminal and to do for individual offenders what had been assumed to be beyond the competency of legal administration of justice.[88] We have always had some degree of individualization of legal precepts in courts of equity.[89] Today the rise of administrative tribunals and the tendency to commit subjects to them that were once committed to the courts bear witness to a demand for individualized application at many points. The administrative process is not outside of the legal order and can be and should be carried on so that its individualized applications nonetheless apply and give effect to the body of authoritative grounds of decision which is commonly meant by the term "law."[90]

Nineteenth-century science of law assumed that all legal precepts were potentially in the jurist's head and were discovered by a purely logical process. With the breakdown of this notion of the absolute finality of legal premises and logical existence of all legal precepts from the beginning, much of the significance of the distinction in application between legal precepts and moral principles disappears. Rules of property, rules as to commercial transactions, the rules which maintain the security of acquisitions and security of transactions in a society of complex economic organization, may be and should be of general and absolute application. But such rules are not the whole of the law nor may they be

---

87. Amos, *The Science of Law* (2 ed. 1874) 33–34.
88. *See* Sutherland, *Principles of Criminology* (3 ed. 1939) 380–408, 524, 553, 613–34.
89. W. W. Story, *Equity Jurisprudence* (1836) § 742.
90. Note the review of sentences by the English Court of Criminal Appeal and the individualization with reference to the offender which goes on there, *e.g.*, Thomas, 28 CRIMINAL APPEAL REPORT 21 (1941); Burton, *id.* 89 (1941); Duerden, *id.* 125 (1942); Betteridge, *id.* 171 (1942); Billington, *id.* 180 (1942).

taken for the type of all legal precepts as the analytical jurist sought to do. Precepts for human conduct, precepts determining for what conduct one shall respond in civil proceedings and how he shall respond, may admit of a wide margin of individualized application. Indeed, in this connection, the law often employs standards rather than rules. In case of negligence the law applies the standard of the conduct of a reasonable, prudent man under the circumstances and puts it to a jury, largely in effect as a moral proposition, to decide (within limits) on their individual notions of what is fair and reasonable in the particular case. So in Roman law, where a standard of what a prudent husbandman would do is applied to a usufructuary, or the standard of a prudent and diligent head of a household is applied to the parties to a transaction of good faith. The opposition between law and morals with respect to application is significant only in the law of property and in commercial law, subjects which were to the fore in the nineteenth century, and tends to disappear in the law as to civil liability for action injurious to others, the subject in which growth is going on today.

It is equally a mistake to separate wholly law and morals, as the analytical jurists sought to do, and wholly to identify them, as the natural-law jurists sought to do. For granting all that has been said as to the analytical distinction between law and morals with respect to subject matter and application, there remain three points at which ethical theory can be of but little help to the jurist and with respect to which important areas in the law will have at least a non-moral character. In the first place, in order to maintain the social interest in the general security, to prevent conflict, and to maintain a legal order in place of private war, the law must deal with many things which are morally indifferent. In many cases in the law of property and in the law of commercial transactions the law might require either of two alternative courses of action or patterns of decision with equal justice, but must choose one and prescribe it in order to insure certainty and uniformity. In such cases developed legal systems often exhibit the greatest diversity of detail. Usually the only moral element here is the moral obligation attaching to the legal precept merely as such because of the social interest in the security of social institutions, among which law is fundamental. Aristotle saw this in drawing his distinction between that which is just by nature or just in its idea and that which derives its sole title to be just from convention or enactment.[91]

Again, the law does not approve many things which it does not expressly condemn. Many injuries are out of its reach. They are not susceptible of proof or they are inflicted by means too subtle or too intangible for the legal machinery of rule and sanction. Many interests must be left unsecured in whole or in part because they require too fine lines in their delimitation, or they are infringed by acts too intangible to admit of securing them by legal means. Such things as the long hesitation of American courts to deal adequately with nervous illness caused by negligence without any bodily impact, using language of the past which was belied at every point by modern physiology and psychology,[92] or the reluctance of some courts to give adequate legal security to personality, especially to the individual claim to privacy,[93] demonstrate the practical importance of insisting that our science of law shall not ignore morals. So long as for good reasons we cannot deal with such things legally, we must fall short of the moral order. But we must not allow an analytical distinction between law and morals to blind us to the need of legal treatment of such cases whenever the onward march of human knowledge puts it in our power to deal with them effectively.

Thirdly, law has to deal with incidence of loss where both parties are morally blameless.[94] In such cases it may allow the loss to remain where it falls or it may seek to secure some social interest by changing the in-

---

91. *Nicomachean Ethics*, v, 7.

92. *See* Goodrich, *Emotional Disturbance as Legal Damage* (1922) 20 MICHIGAN LAW REVIEW, 497.

93. *See* Pound, *Interests of Personality* (1915) 28 HARVARD LAW REVIEW, 343, 362–64.

94. *See* Ballentine, *A Compensation Plan for Railway Accident Claims* (1916) 29 HARVARD LAW REVIEW, 705; Marx, *Compulsory Compensation Insurance*, 25 COLUMBIA LAW REVIEW, 164; Report of the Committee to Study Compensation for Automobile Acci-

cidence of the loss. A large part of the legal difficulty arises from the very circumstance that the parties may be equally blameless.[95] This is notable in what was at one time called "the insurance theory of liability," a theory I shall consider at length in a later lecture. Here it is enough to say that it presupposes that we all of us should bear the losses incident to life in civilized society instead of leaving many, at least, to be borne by the one who happens to be injured. There has been a growing tendency in this direction. Juristically these liabilities thus far have been incident to some relation. Also the reasons for legislative imposings of them have been primarily economic. Very likely the juristic and economic considerations may be given an ethical formulation. Nevertheless one may suspect that in this case ethics has followed jurisprudence and that ethical theory does not help us here beyond recognizing the moral quality of obedience to the legal rule. Thus *respondeat superior* is not a universal moral rule.[96] Shifting the burden to the employer under the Workmen's Compensation Acts, no matter how careful and diligent he may have been and how free from fault, proceeds on the basis of the social interest in the general security, which is maintained best by holding those who conduct enterprises in which others are employed to an absolute liability for what their servants do in the course of the enterprise. Such, at any rate, was the reason formerly given. But with the coming of collective bargaining, closed shops, and employee control of conditions, this reason is ceasing to obtain. Evidently the basis of liability may have to be found in the so-called insurance theory. The law is to pass the burden back to all of us by imposing liability upon some one who is in a po-

dent, *Columbia Council for Research in the Social Sciences* (1932) and review by Thurston (1933) 43 YALE LAW JOURNAL, 166.

95. "It is for the legislature to determine . . . upon which of two innocent persons the loss in such cases should fall, whether upon those who are compelled to take a pilot whom they have no power of selecting, or upon those who are injured by the ship which has that pilot on board." The Ocean Wave, L.R. 3 P.C. 205, 211 (1870).

96. The various speculative justifications of the doctrine are criticized in Baty, *Vicarious Liability* (1916) chap. viii ("Justification in Ethics').

sition to bear it in the first instance and impose it ultimately upon the public in the form of charges for services rendered. But this proposition will be considered in a later lecture.

Such cases require definite rules in order to prevent arbitrary action by the magistrate. They differ from cases, such as negligence, where the moral quality of acts is to be judged with reference to a legally fixed standard applied to the circumstances. In the latter, within wide limits each trier of fact may have his own ideas. In the former, this could not be tolerated. The most we may ask in the former is that our measure for maintaining the general security be not ethically objectionable. Whenever we make a rule for a case of the former type, we are not unlikely to provide a legal which is not a moral rule.

A closely related situation which has given much difficulty arises where both parties to a controversy have been at fault and the law must fix the incidence of loss in view of the culpability of each. It might be allowed to rest where it falls (contributory negligence)[97] or the whole might be cast on the one more culpable (comparative negligence)[98] or the one last culpable (last clear chance)[99] or the loss may be divided[100] or apportioned[101] (as in the civil law and in admiralty) or recovery may be abated in view of the negligence of the complaining party,[102] or, without regard to contributory negligence of the injured person the whole burden may be put upon an enterprise conducted for public advantage which is in a position to pass the loss on to the public at large.[103] If we had any machinery for accurate quantitative or qualitative measure-

97. *Neal v. Gillett*, 23 Conn. 437 (1855).

98. Cooper, J., in *Louisville R. Co. v. Fleming*, 82 Tenn. (14 Lea) 128, 235 (1884); 1 Shearman and Redfield, *Law of Negligence* (6 ed. 1913) §§ 102, 103.

99. *Davies v. Mann*, 10 M. & W. 546 (1842).

100. The Max Morris, 137 U.S. 1 (1890).

101. Scott, *Collisions at Sea Where Both Ships Are at Fault* (1897) 13 LAW QUARTERLY REVIEW, 17.

102. *Cameron v. Union Automobile Ins. Co.*, 210 Wis. 659 (1933)—statutory.

103. The 'humanitarian doctrine.' *Hutchinson v. St. Louis R. Co.*, 88 Mo. App. 376 (1901). *British Maritime Conventions Act* (1911) § 1.

ment of culpability in such cases the rule of the civil law would be required on ethical grounds. It is because all apportionment in such cases is theoretical, and at best arbitrary, that the law is troubled what to do.[104] The fact that seven doctrines have obtained on this subject speaks for itself.[105]

In addition there is a characteristic of law that makes for a certain opposition or at least contrast between the legal and the moral. The very conception of law, whether as legal order or as a body of laws or as the judicial process, involves ideas of uniformity, regularity, and predictability. In other words, it involves rule, using that word in the wide sense. Administration of justice according to law is administration of justice in accordance with legal precepts and largely by rules in the strict sense. But even the most flexible of mechanisms will operate more or less mechanically, and it is not easy to make legal machinery flexible and at the same time adequate to the general security. The requirements of particular cases must yield more or less to the requirements of generality and certainty in legal precepts and of uniformity and equality in their application. Hence even though in general the law tends to bring about results accordant with the moral sense of the community, the necessarily mechanical application of legal rules will in particular cases produce situations where the legal result and the result demanded by the moral sense of the community are out of accord. When such

104. *See* the reasons stated in *Needham v. San Francisco R. Co.*, 37 Cal. 409, 419 (1869); *Kerwhacker v. Cleveland R. Co.*, 3 Ohio St. 172, 188 (1854); *Heil v. Glanding*, 42 Pa. St. 493, 498 (1862).

105. Compare the different solutions of the questions involved in union of materials of different owners and expenditure of labor on materials of another. The Roman jurists of the classical era were not agreed and Justinian adopted a solution differing from that of either school. *Dig.* xli, 1, 7, § 7; id. x, 4, 12, § 3; *Inst.* ii, 1, §§ 25, 26. The modern codes do not agree with the Roman law nor with each other. *French Civil Code*, art. 561–72, 576; *German Civil Code*, §§ 950, 951. The common law does not agree wholly with the Roman law nor with any modern code, nor do the common-law authorities agree with each other. 2 Blackstone, *Commentaries* (1766) 404; *Betts v. Lee*, 5 Johns. (N.Y.) 348 (1810); *Wetherbee v. Green*, 22 Mich. 311 (1871); *Silsbury v. McCoon*, 3 N.Y. 79 (1850). No rules have ever proved wholly satisfactory. But titles cannot be left in uncertainty. There must be rules in each jurisdiction.

things happen it is often because some particular legal precept has survived the social or economic conditions to which it was shaped. But to a certain extent they are an inevitable by-product of justice according to law.[106]

So much must be conceded to the analytical jurist. Yet we must not omit to note that in the last century he pressed these points too far. Thus a writer on ethics, who shows in marked degree the effects of analytical jurisprudence, says: "The law protects contracts which were made in legitimate business without regard to whether their provisions still conform to justice or not. Owing to unforeseen circumstances things may have so changed as to cause the ruin of one of the contracting parties without substantially benefitting the other party. The law is not concerned with that."[107] The proposition is true of the strict law. But if the promisee went into a court of equity for his only effective and adequate remedy (specific performance) he would encounter the chancellor's margin of discretion in the application of that remedy and the doctrine that supervening circumstances may make a bargain so hard that the court will refuse to enforce it.[108] The passage quoted sounds very like the pronouncements of lawyers in the stage of the strict law, when the line between legal and moral was drawn so sharply.[109] Something of this spirit was to be seen in the last century. But in the present century administrative moratoria in the civil law, limitations on the power of creditors to exact satisfaction both in civil-law systems and in the common-law world, and the development of the doctrine of frustration,[110]

106. I have treated this point more fully in a paper, *The Causes of Popular Dissatisfaction with the Administration of Justice* (1906) 29 REP. AM. BAR ASSN. 395, 397–98.

107. Paulsen, *Ethics* (Thilly's transl. 1899) 629. The influence of Jhering on Paulsen's views as to the relation of law and morals is manifest. His position is substantially that of the analytical jurists. *Ethics*, Thilly's transl. 624–27.

108. *Willard v. Tayloe*, 8 Wall. 557 (1809).

109. *See* Replication of a Serjeant to Doctor and Student, Hargrave, *Law Tracts*, 823.

110. American Law Institute, 1 *Restatement of the Law of Contracts* (1932) §§ 454–69. The law has gone even further in France, 2 Planiol, *Traité élémentaire du droit civil*, revised by Ripert and Boulanger (4 ed. 1952) §§ 443–80; 2 Josserand, *Cours de droit civil français* (3 ed. 1938) §§ 402–5.

mitigate the enforcement of hard bargains. The law in action is not as harsh as the author would have us believe.[111]

Yet there are too many points, such, for example, as the Anglo-American law with respect to promises made in the course of business but without a technical consideration, where the last century did not exert itself, as it should have done, to bring the legal and the moral into accord.[112] The philosophical jurist was too prone to find ingenious philosophical justification for rules and doctrines and institutions which had outlived the conditions for which they arose and had ceased to yield just results. The historical jurist was too prone to find a justification for an arbitrary rule by showing that it was the culmination of a historical development. The analytical jurist banished all ethical considerations, all criticism of legal precepts with reference to morals, from the law books. If a precept could be fitted logically into a logically consistent legal system it was enough. Such things are intelligible as a reaction from extravagances of the law-of-nature school. They are intelligible also in a period of legal development when it was needful for a time to assimilate and systematize the results of creative judicial and juristic activity. But it cannot be more than temporary. They cannot be suffered to become permanent features of a science of law.

A view of the relation between law and morals coming to a result not unlike that from the analytical approach is reached by Radbruch from a Neo-Kantian starting point. He tells us that there is an irreducible antinomy between law and morals. He thinks of justice as the ideal relation among men; of morals as the ideal development of the individual character; of the legal order as maintained security. No one of these, he says, can be carried out to a full logical development except at the expense of one or both of the others. As no logical line can be drawn and full logical development of any one negates the others, he holds that it

111. I have brought together many examples in *The End of Law as Developed in Legal Rules and Doctrines*, 27 HARVARD LAW REVIEW, 195, 231–33 (1914). *See* further references in my *Outlines of Lectures on Jurisprudence* (5 ed. 1943) 45–46.

112. See Pound, *Introduction to the Philosophy of Law* (1922) lect. 6, especially pp. 267–84.

follows that justice has to do with the formal notion of law, the end with measuring the value of the content of law, and security with the binding force of law. Law will draw its own lines as to where and how far, if at all, to recognize the other two. This is an example of Neo-Kantian logicism, putting logic much where the eighteenth century put reason. Hence, given Kantian definitions of justice, morals, and law, the next step is to develop each logically. But when this is done each conflicts with the others. Hence each must go its own path. There is, he holds, no way of reconciling them.[113]

Kant started with the conscious ego as something not open to challenge. The ideal relation between such egos was one permitting each the most freedom of will consistent with the like freedom of will of all others. The ideal development of each was the one which permitted that freedom. Law was the maintaining of that relation and its development by universal rule. But if we hold that no ultimate starting point can be proved logically, we have nothing to go on but the three, which cannot be carried out logically consistently with each other.

For example: The ideal relation among men would hold them liable to each other only for undertaking or for fault. But security requires us to impose liabilities without fault — crimes without a guilty mind, liability of the owner for injury by a borrowed automobile negligently operated by the borrower, and the like. Again, the ideal development of the individual calls for free self-determination, e.g., liberty of contract. But the ideal relation, made to include equality, may require limitation of free contract. The law must determine for itself which of these directions to take in different typical situations. Again, security carried to a full logical development might require us to allow summary convictions after administrative criminal investigation, or to extort confessions by the "third degree," or to procure evidence by unreasonable searches and seizures. Thus each one, if it is carried out logically, is independent of the others. Kelsen, also from a Neo-Kantian standpoint, makes this the

113. Radbruch, *Rechtsphilosophie* (1932) § 10. In the end he modified his view somewhat. *Vorschule der Rechtsphilosophie* (1947).

basis of a complete ignoring of morals in a pure science of law.[114] I shall endeavor to show in another connection how the three ideas may be reconciled.[115]

It remains to speak of the sociological view — the approach and point of view of the sociologists.[116]

In sociological jurisprudence all social control taken as a whole is looked at functionally. So law in the lawyer's sense and morality are forms of social control; simply different levels of social control or of what the sociologist calls law in its widest sense. This is a development in the light of sociology of the doctrine of the historical school in the nineteenth century. But it has been chiefly a development in sociology rather than in jurisprudence and so is not wholly satisfying from a juristic standpoint. Recent sociologists have drawn their juristic ideas from the historical jurists and so have left out of account the overlappings and points of contact in some connections and the distinct fields in others which have been brought out in analytical jurisprudence. Max Weber follows Vinogradoff, much more historian than jurist, as to law and "custom," i.e., ethical custom or morality.[117] The latter, however, is speaking of the Middle Ages and of the words used in the lan-

114. Reine Rechtslehre (1934) 12–18, 21.

115. I have touched on this in the past: The Spirit of the Common Law (1921) 91–93, 197–203; Introduction to the Philosophy of Law (1922) 90, 96; Interpretations of Legal History (1923) 158–64; Social Control Through Law (1942) 63–80; A Survey of Social Interests (1943) 57 HARVARD LAW REVIEW, 1.

116. Cardozo, The Nature of the Judicial Process (1921) lect. 3; Ehrlich, Grundlegung der Soziologie des Rechts (1913) chap. 4, Moll's transl. as Fundamental Principles of the Sociology of Law (1936) pp. 39–60; Pound, Social Control Through Law (1942) lect. 1; Kornfeld, Soziale Machtverhältnisse (1911) § 16; Wurzel, Das juristische Denken (1904) 62–66, translated in Science of Legal Method, 9 MODERN LEGAL PHILOSOPHY SERIES, 371–77; Gurvitch, L'idée du droit social (1932) 95–113; id. Sociology of Law (1942) 298–301; Horvath, Rechtssoziologie (1934) 213–14; Timasheff, Introduction to the Sociology of Law (1939) 143–46, 159–67; Petrazycki, Methodologie der Theorien des Rechts und der Moral, in OPERA ACADEMIAE UNIVERSALIS JURISPRUDENTIAE COMPARATIVAE (1933) Ser. 2, studia, fasc. 2; id. Ueber die Motiven des Handelns und über das Wesen der Moral und des Rechts, transl. from the Russian by Balson (1907).

117. Wirtschaft und Gesellschaft in Grundriss der Sozialökonomie (2 ed. 1925).

guages of Continental Europe derived from the Middle Ages and the religious-ethical ideas of that time. Hence he tells us of "the derivation of law from moral habits,"[118] rejecting, along with Ehrlich, Maine's theory that the judge precedes the law.[119] He points out how this is connected with the words used to express the medieval conceptions; words which go back to an undifferentiated social control. *Recht* "means what is right in social relations, what should be established and supported as right by social organization."[120] *Droit* (Latin *directum*) "is the direction of social relations in the right way. *Pravo* in the Slavonic group stands for both *iustum* and *dextrum*."[121] He adds: "All these terms and notions are not simply juridical, they belong also to the domain of morals, and the expressions pointing to right are clearly allied to words used to designate moral habits."[122] Furthermore, he proceeds, "In the term right itself the personal claim [subjective right] and social order [objective right] have their root in moral sense — in the ethics of social intercourse."[123] Accordingly sociologists in writing on law usually adopt the view of the historical jurists as to sanction.[124] Ehrlich distinguishes norms for decision from rules for conduct, the latter including morality.[125] Tönnies distinguishes true moral precepts — rules of behavior recognized and imposed by social groups — i.e., law and positive morality as Austin would put it — from individual ideas of what should be moral precepts, individual ethical theories, *i.e.*, morals.[126] To show how

118. 2 *Collected Papers* (1928) 467.

119. Ehrlich, *Fundamental Principles of the Sociology of Law* (transl. by Moll, 1936) 37–38. *Cf.* Maine, *Ancient Law* (1861) chap. I. But *see* vindication of Maine's view, Llewellyn and Hoebel, *The Cheyenne Way* (1941) 276–83.

120. 2 Vinogradoff, *Collected Papers* (1928) 466.

121. *Ibid.*, note 3.

122. *Ibid.*, 467.

123. *Ibid.*

124. *E.g.*, Ehrlich, *Fundamental Principles of the Sociology of Law* (transl. by Moll) chap. 4. "The conception of law as a coercive order . . . is based upon the fact that its exponents have one-sidedly taken into consideration only those portions of the law which derive their force solely from the state." *Ibid.*, 75.

125. *Ibid.*, 81.

126. Tönnies, *Thomas Hobbes* (3 ed. 1925) 205.

far this may be carried, what Jhering calls customary rules of polite-ness,[127] Petrazycki calls "rules of unofficial law."[128] It is significant that while Jhering distinguishes law and morality, although seeing their re-lation, sociologists have commonly used the discussion of morality in the second volume of *Der Zweck im Recht* as the basis of discussion of law as something including both.[129] By making the term "law" so all-inclusive, sociologists revert to much of the confusion in the books on the law of nature from which analytical jurists reacted to the other ex-treme.[130] If Austin and Kelsen have gone too far, it has not been with-out provocation. How confusion can result from the words used is well brought out by Llewellyn.[131]

It is to more purpose that Timasheff points out three stages or levels in social control: first, morality or ethical custom, with diffuse sanctions, second, law, organized power with organized sanctions, but not neces-sarily sanctions of a politically organized society, and third, morals, de-veloped religious and philosophical theories.[132] It is important for the jurist to bear in mind, what the sociologists insist upon, that the inner order of groups and associations other than the political organization of a society, and religious and philosophical ideals play a large and often controlling part in the ordering of society in comparison with law in the lawyer's sense.[133] Yet Ehrlich gives us a needed caution as to morals, "a preachment or teaching, as compared with morality within a group," and vouches the treatment of natives by the whites in every part of the world where they have come in contact, as showing "the depths to which the morality of modern man may sink where there are no associ-

---

127. 2 *Zweck im Recht* (3 ed. 1893–98) 480–559.

128. *See* Timasheff, *Introduction to the Sociology of Law* (1939) 149, note 2.

129. *Ibid.*, 149 ff.

130. *See* review of Salmond, *First Principles of Jurisprudence* (1894) 10 LAW QUAR-TERLY REVIEW, 89.

131. Llewellyn and Hoebel, *The Cheyenne Way* (1941) 275–76.

132. *Introduction to the Sociology of Law* (1939) 143. *See also* Gurvitch, *Sociology of Law* (1942) 299.

133. Ehrlich, *Fundamental Principles of the Sociology of Law* (transl. by Moll, 1936) 64–71.

ational bonds."[134] Conflicts between morals and law in the lawyer's sense are an old theme.[135] It is an old observation that law in the lawyer's sense commonly lags behind morality and morals. Morals grow ahead of both morality and law and this growth is an important factor in bringing about changes in law. As Gurvitch puts it, morals are "more dynamic, more revolutionary, more mobile, more directed toward the future . . . than is the law. The latter is more attached to traditional practices than to acts of innovation, more dependent on intellectual representations and the balance of forces than is morality."[136] Yet, he goes on to say, there have been cases where "an advanced law" has overcome current morality so that law has become a factor in moral change. This has happened at times during revolutions or major reform movements, when legislation or intuitive development of an inner order behind it, goes forward at a bound beyond the old law and the morality it expressed.[137] Such advanced lawmaking, however, has difficulty in maintaining itself.[138]

In conclusion, following Radbruch, in the making of rules of law and finding grounds of decision, in applying rules and grounds of decision, and in exercise of discretion in the judicial and in the administrative process, in each of these four tasks of the administration of justice, there are three things to be regarded: (1) Justice, the ideal relation between men; (2) morals, the ideal development of individual character; and (3) security. What is meant by security must be left to a later lecture. These three: justice, morals, security, have to be kept in balance. The answer to the proposition that there is here an irreducible antinomy is that we cannot ignore any one of them at the expense of the others.[139] Morals,

---

134. *Ibid.*, 75.
135. See Tufts, *America's Social Morality* (1933).
136. Gurvitch, *Sociology of Law* (1942) 300.
137. *Ibid.*, 300–301.
138. *See e.g.*, the duty of disinterested benevolence required of trustee by ultra-ethical chancellors and correction in recent times by legislation. Maitland, *Lectures on Equity* (revised by Brunyate, 1947) 90; id. *Selected Essays* (1936) 173; 1 Scott, *Trusts* (1939) § 742.
139. Radbruch, *Rechtsphilosophie* (1932) § 9.

which give us ideals, morality in which justice and morals are reflected in the time and place, are not to be left out of account in any of the four tasks. But in no one of them will morality or morals suffice of themselves. Security has also to be kept in mind, and if its dictates have to be tempered by morals and morality, theirs have to be tempered by those of security and measured by what is practicable in a legal order. The practical limitations on effective achievement of results by the judicial or the administrative process require us not to attempt too much by means of law (in the lawyer's sense) but to bear in mind that there are other agencies of social control that may sometimes do better what morals and morality require.[140] Yet we should not be too patient under lag of the law behind morality and morals. Beyond reasonable regard for security any manifest lag should be corrected. By excluding all questions of improvement of the law (in the sense of the body of authoritative guides to determination) and of the judicial and administrative processes, a science of law may be more teachable and logically satisfying to students. But jurisprudence is a practical science. As such, it must consider the end of law, the measure of valuing interests, and the adaptability of systematic application of the force of politically organized society to achieving the end and applying the measure of values. It cannot dispense with ethics. It cannot depend wholly upon ethics.

---

140. Pound, *The Limits of Effective Legal Action* (1917) 27 INTERNATIONAL JOURN. OF ETHICS, 150, 3 AM. BAR ASSN. JOURNAL, 55.

FOUR

Rights, Interests, and Values

A right is a juristic concept.[1] Such concepts are to be distinguished from legal concepts. Legal concepts are legally defined categories into which facts may be put, whereupon a series of rules, principles, and standards become legally applicable.[2] Juristic concepts are not prescribed and defined by law as legal concepts are. They are worked out by jurists in order to systematize and expound the phenomena of the legal order, the body of authoritative grounds of or guides to decision, and the operation of the judicial process. It is their primary function to provide a basis for understanding and developing law in the second sense.[3]

1. What I am here calling juristic concepts are often spoken of as jural relations (*Rechtsverhältnisse*). I prefer not to use this term since it suggests the theory of a right as a relation. With some hesitation I have preferred to follow Bierling who speaks of "juristic fundamental concepts" (*juristische Grundbegriffe*) *Kritik der juristischen Grundbegriffe*, 3–4 (1883). But he also uses *Rechtsverhältnisse*. 1 *Juristische Prinzipienlehre*, § 9 (1884). As to the latter term *see* 1 Savigny, *System des heutigen römischen Rechts*, §§ 4, 52 (1840); Savigny, *Jural Relations*, transl. by Rattigan 1–2 (a translation of book 2 of Savigny's System, 1884) the part cited being § 60 of the original; 1 Ahrens, *Cours de droit naturel* (8 ed. 1892) § 23 — *rapport de droit*, *i.e.*, relation of right and law; 2 Wigmore, *Select Cases on Torts* (1911) §§ 4–8; Kocourek, *Jural Relations* (1927) chaps. 1, 3.
2. Examples are sale, trust, bailment. Here there is no definite detailed legal consequence attached to a definite detailed state of facts nor is there a starting point for legal reasoning. The law defines these categories and defines what rules, principles, and standards are applicable to them.
3. Jhering, *Geist des römischen Rechts* (5 ed. 1891) § 3, particularly pp. 36–43, 2 II *id.* (5 ed. 1898) §§ 39–41, but these two sections are reprinted from part II of vol. 2 as it stood

Historically law in the second sense precedes these juristic concepts which we reach by analysis and postulate as the logical bases of legal precepts. The logical sequence is interest, right, duty, action, remedy. In order to secure the interest recognized and delimited by the law, it confers a legal right, secured by imposing a corresponding duty. To enforce the duty it allows an action, which has for its end a legal remedy. But historically the order of development is the reverse. In English law, for example, one complained to the king who gave a writ affording a remedy. Out of the writ an action developed.[4] Behind the action men came to see a duty to be enforced and a correlative right was found by jurists behind the duty. Since Jhering it has been seen that behind the right is an interest (claim or demand or expectation) which is recognized and delimited by the law. But if the law confers legal rights and powers and privileges, imposes legal duties and liabilities and recognizes legal liberties, it does not create or define the concepts of legal right, legal duty, or power, privilege or liberty. It prescribes when men may constrain the action of others with the backing of the force of politically organized society, when they may create or alter or direct capacities of such constraints, when men are subject to them, on what occasions men are exempt from them, and in what fields of human activity the law will keep its hands off. Jurists analyze these prescribings of law in the second sense and find in them, rights, powers, liberties, privileges, duties and liabilities, which as concepts are not defined by the law but by the jurists. They belong to the science of law rather than to the law. Hence jurists may hold different ideas with respect to them without affecting the law.

It has come to be well understood that there is no more ambiguous word in legal and juristic literature than the word "right."[5] In its most

---

in 4 ed. (1883); 1 Gény, *Science et technique en droit privé positif* (1914) 145–64; 3 ed. (1921) 175–257; 4 (1924) 23–46; Hohfeld, *Fundamental Legal Conceptions* (1923) 63–64.

4. The Register of Writs was "the core of nearly every other attempt at legal literature between the beginning of the thirteenth and the end of the sixteenth century." Winfield, *The Chief Sources of English Legal History* (1925) 286.

5. Hohfeld, *Fundamental Legal Conceptions as Applied in Judicial Reasoning* (1923); Pound, 26 INTERNATIONAL JOURNAL OF ETHICS, 92 (1915); 1 Beale, *Conflict of Laws* (1935) 62–70, 79–86.

general sense it means a reasonable expectation involved in life in civilized society. As a noun it has been used in the law books in five senses. (1) One meaning is interest, as in most discussions of natural rights. Here it may mean (*a*) an interest one holds ought to be recognized and secured. It is generally used in this sense in treatises on ethics. Or (*b*) it may mean the interest recognized, delimited with regard to other recognized interests and secured. (2) A second meaning is a recognized claim to acts or forbearances by another or by all others in order to make the interest effective, (*a*) legally, through application of the force of a politically organized society in order to secure it as the law has delimited it, or (*b*) morally, by the pressure of the moral sentiment of the community or of extra-legal agencies of social control. Analytical jurists have put this as a capacity of influencing others which is recognized or conferred in order to secure an interest. (3) A third use is to designate a capacity of creating, divesting, or altering rights in the second sense and so of creating or altering duties. Here the proper term is "power." (4) A fourth use is to designate certain conditions of general or special non-interference with natural faculties of action; certain conditions or situations, as it were, of legal hands off, *i.e.*, occasions on which the law secures interests by leaving one to the free exercise of his natural faculties. These are better called liberties and privileges — liberties, general conditions of hands off as to certain situations; privileges, special conditions of hands off exempting certain persons or persons under certain situations from the rules which apply to persons generally or apply to all persons in ordinary situations. In addition "right" is used as an adjective to mean that which accords with justice or that which recognizes and gives effect to moral rights. In Latin *ius* has the further ambiguity of also meaning law, and this is true of the corresponding words in modern languages, *Recht, droit, diritto, derecho, direito.* An example of use of "a right" to include the second, third, and fourth meanings, or in other words, the complex of concepts by which a right in the first sense is secured, may be seen in the conventional civilian analysis of *dominium* or the right of ownership.[6] According to this analysis *dominium* includes (1) *ius possidendi* (a

6. See Hearn, *Theory of Legal Duties and Rights* (1883) chap. 10.

legal right — second meaning), (2) *ius utendi* (a liberty — fourth meaning), (3) *ius fruendi* (a liberty — fourth meaning), (4) *ius abutendi* (a liberty — fourth meaning), (5) *ius disponendi* (a power — third meaning), and (6) *ius prohibendi* (a legal right — second meaning). But all are said to make up the content of a right of ownership.

I have discussed the general theory of interests and the classification of interests in other places.[7]

For the present purpose an interest may be defined as a demand or expectation which human beings, either individually or through groups or associations or in relations seek to satisfy, of which, therefore, the adjustment of human relations and ordering of human behavior by politically organized society must take account. Law, whether in the sense of the legal order or in the sense of the authoritative guides to or models or patterns of determination of controversies, does not create these interests. There is so much truth in the idea of a state of nature and natural rights. Interests in this sense would exist even if there were no legal order and no body of authoritative guides to conduct or to decision. Claims of human beings to have things and do things have existed wherever a plurality of human beings have come into contact. It has never been possible for every one to have everything that he wanted or to do everything he sought and urged a claim to do. Hence there is constant competition in the endeavor to satisfy the claims and demands and expectations involved in life in civilized society. In the endeavor to satisfy human claims and demands and expectations, individuals compete with each other and with groups or associations or societies and the latter compete with each other.

I admit some skeptical realists dispute this proposition, telling us that the claims men make to control things are a consequence of the law, not a cause of it. They say I claim and expect to hold and control the use of my watch because the law has taught me and others to claim things as

---

7. *Social Control Through Law* (1942) 63–80; *The Spirit of the Common Law* (1921) 91–93, 197–203; *Introduction to the Philosophy of Law* (1922) 90–96; *Interpretations of Legal History* (1923) 158–64.

owners and that, having been so taught to claim things, we work out a justification by attributing to ourselves an antecedent moral claim of right which we then say is secured by the state. If the state did not assign control of things to us we should not be claiming them.[8] But working-men claimed a vested right in their jobs long before recent legislation, after much strife and controversy, recognized and gave effect to it. The law did not teach workers to conduct sit-down strikes. They asserted the claim before the law had heard of such a thing and had to be taught by the law that the claim could not be allowed. Among the miners on the public domain of the United States, before government was at hand to establish law, the mining customs recognized and protected the miner in physical control for the time being of the spot where he was digging. The law did not teach the miners. The miners taught the law. After government had taken over the mining country the law books laid down later that the prospector was protected by law in his *pedis possessio* while searching for mineral.

We must begin, then, with the proposition that the law does not create these interests. It finds them pressing for recognition and security. It classifies them and recognizes a larger or smaller number. It fixes the limits within which it endeavors to secure the interests so selected, in view of other interests which are also recognized and in view of the possibility of securing them effectively through the judicial or administrative processes. It works out the means by which the interests may be secured when recognized and delimited. It prescribes canons of value for determining what interests to recognize, for fixing the limits of securing recognized interests, and for judging of the weight to be accorded in any given case to the practical limits on effective legal action.

Interests, that is, the claims or demands or expectations for which or about which the law has to make some provision if civilization is to be maintained and furthered, are asserted by individual human beings.

---

8. Lundstedt, *The General Principles of Civil Liability in Different Legal Systems, The False Idea of Right*, 2 ACTA ACADEMIAE UNIVERSALIS JURISPRUDENTIAE COMPARATIVAE 366, 371 (1934).

But they are not for that reason all of them individual interests. We must not confuse interest as claim or demand or expectation, as jurists use the term, with interest as advantage, as economists use it. The law cannot avoid taking at least some account of insistent human demands or expectations by the easy method of telling those who urge them that what they claim has no advantage for them. Thinking, then, of the claims or demands or expectations men actually urge, interests fall into three classes, individual interests, public interests, and social interests. Some are claims or demands or expectations involved immediately in the individual life and asserted in title of that life. Others are claims or demands or expectations involved in life in a politically organized society and asserted in title of that organization. They are commonly treated as the claims of a politically organized society thought of as a legal entity. Others, or some of the same in other aspects, are claims or demands or expectations involved in social life in civilized society and asserted in title of that life. It is not uncommon to speak of them as the claims of the whole social group as such.

This does not mean, however, that every claim or demand or expectation which human beings assert must be put once for all for every purpose into one of the three categories. For some purposes and in some connections it is convenient to look at the same claim or demand or expectation, or the same type of claims or demands or expectations from one of the other standpoints. They are all urged by individuals but are urged by them in different titles. When it comes to weighing or valuing them with respect to other demands or claims or expectations, we must be careful to compare them on the same plane. If we put one as an individual interest and the other as a social interest, we may seem to decide the question in advance in our very way of putting it. For example, in the liberty of contract cases which ceased to be controversial more than a generation ago,[9] one might think of the claim of the employer to make contracts of employment freely as an individual interest of substance. In that event we must weigh it with the claim of the individual

9. See Pound, *Liberty of Contract*, 18 YALE LAW JOURNAL, 454 (1909).

employee not to be coerced by economic pressure into making contracts to take his pay in orders on a company store, thought of as an individual interest of personality. If we think of either in terms of a policy
we must think of the other in the same terms. If we think of the employee's claim in terms of a policy of assuring a minimum or standard
human life, we must think of the employer's claim in terms of a policy
of free self-determination in entering into relations and engagements. If
one is thought of as a right and the other as a policy, or if the one is
thought of as an individual interest and the other as a social interest, our
way of stating the question may leave nothing to decide.

In the law books of the English-speaking world it has been usual to
speak of social interests under the name of "public policy."[10] Thus when
a great American judge was called on to weigh certain claims with reference to the social interest in the security of political institutions, he
said that a "great and overshadowing public policy" forbade applying to
the case one of the fundamental principles of the law.[11] Again, when it
seemed to a majority of the Supreme Court of the United States that the
validity of an acquisition from the Federal Government ought to be put
at rest as against a claim of fraud, although limitation did not run against
the Government, the court spoke of the "policy" behind the statute of
limitations and invoked the doctrine of election of remedies as expressing the same policy.[12] So also when a great teacher of law wished to say
that another fundamental legal doctrine, as it was then considered, was
sometimes limited in its application because of the social interest in the
general security, he stated that "except in certain cases based on public

10. "Public policy . . . is that principle of the law which holds that no subject can lawfully do that which has a tendency to be injurious to the public or against the public
good. . . ." Lord Truro in *Egerton* v. *Lord Brownlow*, 4 H.L. Cas. 1, 196 (1853). "Whatever
is injurious to the interests of the public is void on the grounds of public policy." Tindal,
C.J., in *Horner* v. *Graves*, 7 Bing. 735, 743 (1831). ". . . Wherever any contract conflicts
with the morals of the time and contravenes any established interest of society, it is void,
as being against public policy." W. W. Story, *Contracts* (1831) § 675.

11. Breese, J., in *People* v. *Brown*, 67 Ill. 435, 438 (1873).

12. Sutherland, J., in *United States* v. *Oregon Lumber Co.*, 260 U.S. 290, 299–302
(1922).

policy" the law makes liability dependent upon fault.[13] But this limitation of the application of principles, or setting off of exceptions, on grounds of public policy, was felt to be something abnormal. The classical expression of this feeling is in the opinions of the judges in *Egerton v. Lord Brownlow.*[14] Although the case was decided ultimately on the ground of public policy, the remarks of the judges have colored all subsequent judicial thinking on the subject. From the seventeenth century to the end of the nineteenth century, juristic theory sought to state all interests in terms of individual natural rights. Moreover, the nineteenth century, under the influence of Hegel, wrote history as the unfolding in human experience of an idea of liberty, as an outcome of the clash of individual free wills, leading to discovery of the invisible bounds within which each might realize a maximum of free self-assertion.[15] Thus for a time social interests were pushed into the background. It was said that public policy was "a very unruly horse, and when you get astride it you never know where it will carry you."[16] It was felt that a court should be slow and cautious in taking public policy into account, and that if rules of law were to be limited in their application, or if exercise of individual faculties of action was to be held down upon such grounds the matter ought to be left to the legislature.[17]

Questions of public policy came to courts in three forms:—(1) in connection with the validity of legal transactions (*Rechtsgeschäfte, actes jurisdiques*); (2) in connection with the validity of conditions in con-

13. Ames, *Law and Morals*, 22 HARVARD LAW REVIEW, 97, 99 (1908).

14. 4 H.L. Cas. 1, 70, 123 (1853).

15. See, *e.g.*, 1 Savigny, *System des heutigen römischen Rechts* (1840) § 52.

16. Burrough, J., in *Richardson v. Mellish*, 2 Bing. 229, 252 (1824). See also *Fender v. St. John-Mildmay* [1938] A.C. 1; *Mamlin v. Genoe*, 340 Pa. 320 (1941).

17. "Public policy is not a safe or trustworthy ground of decision." Lord Halsbury, C., in *Janson v. Driefontein Consolidated Mines* [1902] A.C. 484, 491–92, 495–97. One way of escape was to put 'policies' as 'rights.' *E.g.*, one court put security of acquisitions as 'an inherent right' of property, saying: "And the law punishes the larceny of property, not solely because of any rights of the proprietor, but also because of its own inherent legal rights as property. . . ." Cushing, J., in *Commonwealth v. Rourke*, 10 Cush. (Mass.) 397, 399 (1852). These 'inherent rights' are the social interest in the security of acquisitions.

veyances and testamentary gifts; (3) in connection with the validity of testamentary dispositions. Thus different social interests were weighed against a policy in favor of free contract ("right" of free contract) and a policy of free disposition of property which was taken to be involved in the security of acquisitions and to be a corollary of individual interests of substance ("rights" of property). Accordingly distrust of public policy grew out of a feeling that security of acquisitions and security of trans-actions were paramount policies: ". . . if there is anything," said Sir George Jessel, "which more than another public policy requires it is that men of full age and competent understanding shall have the utmost lib-erty of contracting, and that their contracts . . . shall be enforced by the courts of justice."[18] Here social interests are thought of in terms of *lais-sez faire* economics of the last century as giving the ideal by which a scheme of social interests is to be valued.

In truth, the nineteenth-century attitude toward public policy was only the expression of a public policy. It resulted from a weighing of the social interest in the general security against other social interests which men had sought to secure through an over-wide discretion in the era of the law-of-nature jurists.

There is no escape in the science of law from the problem of values. Every adjustment of relations and ordering of conduct has behind it some canon of valuing conflicting and overlapping interests. It may be merely keeping the peace. It may be preserving the social *status quo*. It may be promotion of a maximum liberty of individual self-assertion. It may be giving effect to the self-interest of a dominant social or economic class or of one seeking to become dominant. It may be maintaining and furthering the power of an established political organization. At times and in places such canons of value have been held more or less uncon-sciously. But with the advent of lawgiver and jurist they have increas-ingly been given systematic development and formulation and have been brought increasingly into relation with the postulates of life in civ-ilized society. In what might be called the classical era of legal history

18. *Printing and Numerical Registering Co.* v. *Sampson*, L.R. 10 Eq. 462, 465 (1875).

both in antiquity and in the modern world, demonstration or criticism or logical application of such canons of value have been a chief activity of jurists. The contact of Roman lawyers with Greek philosophy, the teaching of Roman law side by side with the teaching of theological ethics in the medieval universities, the emancipation of jurisprudence from theology and of law in Continental Europe from the text of the Corpus Iuris, with the coincident rise of rationalist philosophy, and the rise of historical jurisprudence with coincident metaphysical theories of liberty, mark epochs in the science of law because in each case canons of value were applied to the tasks of the law and juristic problems of the time, and the law was brought into accord with the social ideal of the time and place.

Jurists have conceived of a legal order patterned upon a divine order and so have turned to authority to provide a canon.[19] They have thought of conformity to a moral order revealed by the analogy of the order of physical nature or as partly ascertained from revelation and partly discoverable by reason.[20] At other times they have thought of the legal order as a rational order and so of a canon of values derived from pure reason.[21] In this mode of thought reason was held to reveal a natural or ideal law of universal and unchangeable validity, which, as we see it now, was in reality an ideal version of the positive law of the time and place. Thus in effect it found a canon of values in rational exposition of the positive law.[22] At still other times they have thought of the legal order as resting upon experience in adjusting relations and ordering conduct through political and legal institutions, put into formulas by lawmakers and judges and doctrinal writers and criticized and systematized by jurists. Thus they have conceived of the legal order as a historical order.[23] The

19. Thomas Aquinas, *Summa Theologica*, I, 2, qq. 92–95.

20. Grotius, *De iure belli ac pacis*, Prolegomena, 30, 40, bk. I, chap. I, 9–12 (1625).

21. Vattel, *Le droit des gens*, préliminaire (1758).

22. This has been discussed *ante* in lecture II. *See also* Bentham, *Principles of Morals and Legislation* (Clarendon Press ed. 1876) 17 n. 1.

23. *See* Pound, *Interpretations of Legal History* (1923) 9–10.

English utilitarians employed a canon of utility. Bentham said: "A measure of government . . . may be said to be conformable to or dictated by the principle of utility when . . . the tendency which it has to augment the happiness of the community is greater than any which it has to diminish it."[24] But this requires a definition of happiness and canon of happiness of the community. This, it seemed to him was "the sum of the interests of the several members who compose it."[25] And happiness was taken to be absence of "all restrictions on the actions of an individual which are not necessary for securing the like freedom on the part of his neighbors."[26] In the nineteenth century jurists generally, of all schools, came to think of the legal order as an order of freedom; as a regime of securing to every one the maximum of free exertion of his will consonant with a like measure of free exertion of his will by every one else.[27] In this view there is a canon of values in terms of individual liberty demonstrated by metaphysics. More recently there have been attempts to found a canon of values upon economics[28] or to derive one from a theory of class war, attributing value to a class rather than to individuals and to claims and expectations urged in title of a class rather than in title of individual life or of social life looking at society as a whole.[29]

Today Neo-Thomists urge a return to natural law. At the other extreme Neo-Kantians argue on epistemological grounds that it is impossible to arrive at any measure of values. Values are subjective and relative.[30] Others on the basis of Freudian psychology hold that it is not

24. *Introduction to the Principles of Morals and Legislation* (Clarendon Press ed. 1876) 3.

25. *Ibid.*

26. Dicey, *Law and Public Opinion in England* (2 ed. 1914) 134–49, is a summary of Bentham's doctrine. The extract quoted is on p. 146.

27. I have considered this at length in *The End of Law as Developed in Juristic Thought* (1916) 30 HARVARD LAW REVIEW, 201.

28. *E.g.*, Brooks Adams in *Centralization and the Law* (1906) 45, 68; Laski, *Studies in Law and Politics* (1932) 278.

29. *E.g.*, Rodell, *Woe unto You Lawyers* (1939) chap. 10.

30. *See* Pound, *Fifty Years of Jurisprudence* (1938) 51 HARVARD LAW REVIEW, 444, 455.

possible for judges and officials to adhere to a measure of values even if one is established. Whatever the criterion of values in the books, the actual behavior of judges and officials will be motivated by wish, and reason and authority will be conjured up afterward to satisfy another wish, namely, to appear reasonable. They interpret judicial and administrative action in terms of individual psychology and so conceive of an order of impulse.[31]

Mr. Justice Holmes, from the standpoint of analytical jurisprudence as against the metaphysical jurisprudence of the nineteenth century, wrote more than once in terms which seem to reduce law in all its senses to force. For example: "It seems to me clear that the *ultima ratio* not only *regum* but of all private persons is force." But this does not mean that force is the ultimate measure of values. It means that the measure of values, in order to be an effective measure, must in the end be backed by force. Again, he said: "When it comes to the development of a *corpus juris*, the ultimate question is what do the dominant forces of the community want and do they want it hard enough to disregard whatever inhibitions stand in the way?" What the dominant forces of the community have wanted has in the past been put in an ideal form by jurists, and the legal measure of values has been found in conformity to that ideal rather than in concrete wants in cases as they arose. But the doctrine, much urged today, that each single decision or administrative determination, carrying out a threat or expressing a concrete wish in the case in hand, treated as unique, is of itself the law, goes much further than Mr. Justice Holmes toward putting the legal order as a simple order of force. He thought of morality as "a check on the ultimate domination of force."[32] In the very beginnings of the common law it was laid down that

31. Frank, *Law and the Modern Mind* (1930) 1–203, 243–52; Robinson, *Law and the Lawyers* (1935) 1–19, 46–121, 284–323; Arnold, *The Symbols of Government* (1935) 1–104, 199–288.

32. The fullest statement of his views is in *The Path of the Law, Collected Papers*, 167–202 (1920). Note especially his idea of a legal precept as a threat (*ibid.* 160) and his proposition of looking at law not from the standpoint of the good man who looks to the law to

the king was "under God and the law."[33] The founders of the American constitutional legal polity laid down that the Constitution and laws made in pursuance thereof should be the supreme law of the land, a check upon exercise of force by those who wielded the authority of politically organized society,[34] and established a system of legal checks and balances accordingly.[35] But a much urged doctrine of the moment is that such checks are illusions. Force exerted by agents of a politically organized society is law.[36]

It may be admitted that we cannot demonstrate an ultimate absolute measure of values as something every one must accept for all time. But we are not bound for that reason to hold the legal order in abeyance until philosophers have achieved that impossible task. Law is a practical matter. If we cannot establish a demonstrated universal legal measure of values to which every one will agree, it does not follow that we must give up and turn the adjustment of relations and ordering of conduct in civilized society over to unchecked force. There have been centuries of experience of securing, so far as may be, conflicting and overlapping human claims and expectations in civilized society by law. Also we have learned to develop that experience by reason tested by further experience and to make use of it in weighing and valuing interests, and thus have been able continuously to keep the category of recognized and secured expectations in touch with the expanding claims and demands made upon the legal order resulting from the growth of population, occupation of more and more of the earth's surface, and constantly greater harnessing of physical nature to human use.

All this has been done although no absolute measure of values universally applicable has been able to maintain itself. Nor need we forgo

---

guide him in the right path but from that of the bad man who cares nothing for ethical rules but is deterred from antisocial conduct by threats of public force (*ibid.* 171–73).

33. Bracton, fol. 74, quoted in Prohibitions del Roy, 12 Co. 63 (1612).

34. *Constitution of the United States*, art. VI, § 2.

35. Brandeis, J., dissenting in Myers v. *United States*, 272 U.S. 52, 292–95 (1926).

36. See Gsovski, *The Soviet Concept of Law* (1938) 7 FORDHAM LAW REVIEW, 1, 29–43.

the practical task of the law on that account. Einstein has taught us that we live in a curved universe in which there are no straight lines or planes or right angles or perpendiculars. Yet we do not on that account give up surveying. Straight lines and planes may not exist. But as postulates of a practical activity they are near enough to the truth for its practical needs. So it is with the measures of values postulated or accepted in systems of law. They have varied from time to time and from place to place and have been relative to times, places, and degrees of economic and cultural development. They could not be proved as absolute and universal. But they could be used as sufficiently near the truth.

How have men gone about finding and applying a measure of valuing conflicting or overlapping competing interests in practice? Looking at the actual working out, development, and application of legal precepts rather than at juristic theory, we may see that there have been three methods. One is finding out by experience what will achieve an adjustment of conflicting and overlapping interests with the least impairment of the scheme of interests as a whole and giving that experience a reasoned development. Thus the measure becomes a practical one of what will adjust relations and order conduct with the least friction and waste. In application there is a method of finding out by trial and error, largely by judicial inclusion and exclusion, what will best serve. A second is to value with reference to the jural postulates of civilization in the time and place. Newly arising claims and newly urging expectations are measured by these postulates when they press for recognition. When recognized they are adjusted to other recognized interests by this measure. When they are delimited with reference to other interests the means of securing them are determined according to this same measure. A third measure of values, used in the classical era of Roman law and again in the classical era of modern law, the era of the law-of-nature school, and well established in the nineteenth century, is found in a received, traditionally received idea of the social order, and so of what legal institutions and doctrines should be and what should be the results of applying them to controversies.

An example of the first method was given by Dicey in his account of English legislation and judicial decision as to labor and as to defamation. In the first it became necessary to bring into harmony two conflicting interests, as Dicey put it, the right to individual freedom and the right of association, using "right" as is done so often, in the sense of recognized interest. What was done was to work out "a rough compromise between them." Likewise in the second, he tells us, the English law of libel is a "rough compromise between the right of X to say or write what he chooses and the right of A not to be injured in property or character by X's free utterance of his opinion." On the whole Dicey found the compromises had been successful.[37]

To a large extent the legal order actually functions in this way. Courts, jurists, and lawmakers have been proceeding in this way at least since the Roman jurisconsults of the first century. In the whole development of modern law courts and lawmakers and law teachers, very likely often with no clear theory of what they were doing, but guided by a clear instinct of practical purpose, have been at work finding practical adjustments and reconcilings and, if nothing more was possible, practical compromises of conflicting and overlapping interests. Many of the adjustments worked out by Roman jurists in the first two and one-half centuries of the Christian era, have stood the test of time and have survived all manner of social and economic and political changes, and obtain throughout the world today. There is at any rate an engineering value in what serves to eliminate or minimize friction and waste.[38] William James held that there was an ethical value in what gives the most effect to human demand with the least sacrifice.[39] If one accepts the civilization interpretation of the Neo-Hegelians, he may hold that this adjustment of competing interests with a minimum of waste makes for civilization and so has a philosophical value.

37. Dicey, *Law and Public Opinion in England in the Nineteenth Century* (1905) 468.
38. I have discussed this at length in *Interpretations of Legal History* (1923) 151–65.
39. James, *The Will to Believe*, 195–206.

But the practical process of the legal order does not stop at finding by experience what will serve to adjust conflicting and overlapping interests. Reason has its part as well as experience. Hence the second method. Jurists work out the jural postulates, the presuppositions as to relations and conduct, of civilized society in the time and place, and arrive in this way at starting points for judicial reasoning. Experience is developed by reason on this basis, and reason is tested by experience.

We owe the working out of this method to Kohler. As a Neo-Hegelian he held that the idea which was unfolding or realizing itself in legal history was the idea of civilization. He argued that we are not merely a mob of individuals each trying to perfect himself. There is an idea of civilization at work. A whole people, a whole race is trying to lift itself up by developing its powers to their highest unfolding. It is not merely that politically organized society keeps the peace while each prosecutes his individual search for perfection. Rather each and all are developing the whole through many means, among them legal situations and political institutions which express, maintain, and further, or are designed to further civilization as it is understood by them in their time and place. According to Kohler, then, the task of the legal order is twofold. First, it is to maintain existing values of civilization. Second, it is to create new ones; to carry forward the development of human powers.[40] How this is made effective for the finding and making of law through formulation of the jural postulates of the civilization of a time and place, belongs to a later lecture.

As to the third method, it need scarcely be said pictures of an ideal social order which come to enter into the law as part of the authoritative guides to determination of controversies are not photographs or even idealized photographs of the social order of the time and place. Much more usually they are idealized pictures of the social order of the past, undergoing a gradual process of retouching with reference to details of the social order of the present. Thus the received ideals of American law, as they took shape in the formative era in the fore part of the nineteenth

40. Kohler, *Lehrbuch der Rechtsphilosophie* (1909) 1.

century, are much closer to the pioneer agricultural society of our past than to the typically urban industrial society of twentieth-century America. In general men have sought to explain the institutions of the present in terms of a picture of the social order of the past.

Thus, Plato's Republic is a picture of an ideal Greek city-state. Aristotle's Politics is a treatise on government in terms of the Greek city as an independent, politically and economically self-sufficient unit. Each had in mind Sparta when the Spartan type of state was passing. Each had in mind the Greek city-state when the days of such states were over. Again, the medieval jurists had before their minds the academic conception of the "empire." They thought of an empire embracing all Christendom and continuous with that of Augustus and Constantine and Justinian. In consequence, they held to an idea of universal laws for all Christendom. There was the universal civil law, the universal sea law, and the universal law merchant. Also there was taken to be a universal fundamental law, expressing the eternal reason of the Creator, having authority beyond that of kings and lawmakers and carrying a name derived from the Roman law books. This ideal of universality left its mark enduringly upon the taught traditions which are part of the taught law of the world today. But it arose and was given shape when the Roman empire of which it was an idealization, was not only utterly in the past but the western world was on the eve of the nationalism which followed the Reformation.

A like story can be told of the picture behind our classical seventeenth-century law books, the received ideals of the social and legal orders as they appear in Coke on Littleton and Coke's Second Institute. In our formative period these books were oracles in the new world for our private law and public law alike. Certainly they were far from comporting with any true picture of colonial American society. Nor were they written on a background of Elizabethan society. The social and economic systems described in Littleton's Tenures was moribund when the book was written. It is no more in the spirit of the England of Shakespeare than the pedantic formal logic of Coke on Littleton was anything but an anachronism in the days of Bacon. Yet this spirit of medieval England, this idealized picture of pre-Reformation England, was an enduring element in the body of legal materials which came to govern English-speaking peoples everywhere.

International law gives us another example. The seventeenth century when Grotius wrote was an era of absolute personal sovereigns. The monarch of that era, the Spanish King after Charles V, the French King of the old regime, the Stuart King in England, and the Hapsburg ruler in Austria was analogous to the masterful head of a Roman household. The relations of Philip and Louis and James and Ferdinand with each other were enough like those of a Roman *paterfamilias* to his neighbor to make precepts worked out by Roman jurists for the latter give useful analogies for the former. The problem of international law was one of adjusting the relations and guiding the international conduct of those personal sovereigns. They made war with highly trained armies. They represented their several countries so completely that for practical purposes international relations could be treated as relations between sovereigns, and the rules of war as limitations on the belligerent conduct of sovereigns. International law grew up to this picture and we still think and speak to its pattern. But with changed political ideas it became increasingly inadequate to its tasks. Its fundamental idea is out of line with the democratic organization of societies of today. The picture of seventeenth-century Europe which served for its ideal long ago ceased to portray reality. It is no wonder that it has conspicuously failed in the present century.[41]

So much that had been held impossible has been brought to pass in these days that one must hesitate to give up anything that men have dreamed of almost as long as they had dreamed of flying. We may concede, however, that so far as we can see there is no absolute value. Value is relative to something. Perhaps in the science of law it is relative to civ-

---

41. I have considered this point fully in *Philosophical Theory and International Law* (1923) 1 BIBLIOTHECA VISSERIANA DISSERTATIONUM IUS INTERNATIONALE ILLUSTRANTIUM, 71–90.

ilization. Yet civilization is not something fixed once for all. It is something growing and is itself relative to prior stages of human development. Proximately value in jurisprudence is relative to the task of the legal order; to the task of enabling men to live together in civilized society with a minimum of friction and a minimum of waste of the goods of existence. What accords with the presuppositions of the right and just in the time and place has juristic value. If it will work in adjusting relations and ordering conduct so as to eliminate or minimize friction and waste, it is a useful measure for a practical activity.

But I do not give up faith in philosophical jurisprudence because so many fashionable philosophies of the moment despair of doing anything for law. In the legal-political constitutional polity which is spreading over the world today, questions of reasonableness have to be determined with respect to new types of legislation in the service state. More and more in the ordering of conduct, especially the conduct of enterprises, the law today relies on standards rather than on rules. Also constitutional provisions designed to maintain a balance of national and local government have to be interpreted. Application of standards and interpretation of constitutional provisions must be done with reference to received ideals; authoritative pictures of the social order. It cannot be said too often that these received ideals are as much part of the law as rules and principles and technique. It is here that most of what creates dissatisfaction with the work of the courts has its origin. If philosophy cannot give us an ultimate assured measure of values, it can give us a useful critique of the traditional ideals of the law. Administration of justice everywhere does not need reversion to justice without law which is an incident of political absolutism. It needs rather a redrawing of the received picture of the society in which justice is administered. It is bad social engineering to administer justice to a blueprint of a society of the past as a means of maintaining the jural postulates of civilization in a different society of the present.

Critique of received measures of value, however, is not all that is needed to enable the legal order better to perform its task of adjusting conflicting and overlapping expectations. We must never lose sight of the limitations of effective legal action.[42]

Three important limitations of law as an enforcing agency of social control must be borne in mind in determining what interests the legal order may secure and how it may secure them. These limitations grow out of (1) the necessity under which the law operates, as a practical activity, of dealing only with acts, with the outside and not the inside of men and things; (2) the nature of certain interests pressing upon the law for recognition and securing which in their nature do not admit of effective securing through the machinery of the legal order; and (3) the necessity under which law operates of relying on some external agency to put its machinery in motion, since legal precepts do not enforce themselves. The first requires us to note the distinction between law and morals in respect of application and subject matter which has been gone into sufficiently in the third lecture. The second requires us to consider the limitations upon law as an agency of social control which are involved in application and subject matter.[43]

There is a close connection between the problem of how to enforce the body of precepts for adjusting relations and ordering conduct by the force of politically organized society (law in the second sense) and the question how far all that we style law and seek to give effect as social control through the force of the state is capable of enforcement. When we look into the history of the subject we soon see that much of the problem of enforcing law is really a problem of intrinsic limitations in view of the nature of many of the interests to be weighed and secured and in

42. Pound, *The Limits of Effective Legal Action*, 3 AMERICAN BAR ASSN. JOURN., 55, 57. 27 INTERNATIONAL JOURNAL OF ETHICS, 150 (1917); id. *The Task of the Law* (1944) chap. 3.

43. Bentham, *Theory of Legislation*, transl. by Hildreth, *Principles of Legislation*, chap. 12 (1865); Pollock, *First Book of Jurisprudence* (6 ed. 1929) pt. 1, chap. 2; Amos, *Science of Law* (1874) chap. 3; Green, *Principles of Political Obligation* (1911) §§ 11–31; Korkunov, *General Theory of Law*, transl. by Hastings, §§ 5–7 (1909); Johnsen (compiler) *Selected Articles on Law — Enforcement* (1930); *National Commission on Law Observance and Enforcement, Report on the Enforcement of the Prohibition Laws of the United States*, 43–60, 91–98 (1931); Radin, *The Lawful Pursuit of Gain* (1931).

view of the nature of legal precepts and of the means of applying them. Historically it is significant that while complaint of non-enforcement of legal precepts is as old as the law, it has been heard chiefly in periods when the law was seeking ambitiously to cover the whole field of social control or in transition to such periods. But without going into this it will be enough to set forth analytically the limitations inherent in the administration of justice according to law which preclude complete securing through law of all interests which ethical considerations or social ideals indicate as proper to be secured.

One set of limitations grows out of the difficulties involved in ascertainment of the facts to which legal precepts are to be applied. This is one of the oldest and most stubborn problems of the administration of justice. At first the law sought to settle the facts by mechanical devices, by some conclusive test which involved no element of personal judgment on the part of the magistrate and could not be challenged for partiality.[44] At times and places the oath has been relied on as a guarantee of the truth.[45] In England the Chancellor believed that he could "search the conscience of a party" and the answer in chancery had to be under oath.[46] In the civil-law system of Continental Europe an oath in terms of the issue was a mode of proof and is still in use to some extent.[47] But the ideas which made an oath effective to assure the truth have at least lost much of their strength, and perjury, false testimony, and fabricated documents put serious obstacles in the way of throughgoing attainment of the end of law.[48] Bentham said paintings or engravings of the death of

---

44. E.g., ordeal, casting of lots, and the like. 1 Holdsworth, *History of English Law* (3 ed. 1922) 310, 311; 2 Pollock and Maitland, *History of English Law* (2 ed. 1898) 596–97; Lea, *Superstition and Force* (4 ed. 1892) 247–48.

45. 6 Wigmore, *Evidence* (3 ed. 1940) § 1815 and references in note 11; Buckland, *Text-Book of Roman Law* (2 ed. 1932) 633, 659.

46. Langdell, *Summary of Equity Pleading* (2 ed. 1883) § 78.

47. 2 Planiol, *Traité élémentaire de droit civil* (11 ed. 1932). nos. 31–34.

48. "The Psalmist said in his haste 'all men are liars.' No doubt the allegation thus baldly stated is too wide, and even thrown off hastily and without due consideration as is the case with the *obiter dicta* of many other less distinguished persons. It is, however, by no means improbable that if David had sat in the courts over which I presided, what

Ananias and Sapphira, "capitally punished on the spot by divine justice for mendacious testimony of the self-investitive or self-exonerative kind," ought to be hung in every courtroom.[49] To guard against this unreliability of oral evidence, the law often requires certain transactions to be evidenced by writing.[50] Also it requires witnesses to certain instruments other than the parties and requires some transactions to be entered into before a magistrate or official.[51] But these necessary precautions, while they prevent frauds, may often preclude the establishment of meritorious claims.[52] Again, the law has had to proceed cautiously in securing against nervous and mental injuries and injuries to sensibilities because of difficulty or supposed impossibility of clear proof in the absence of objectively manifest illness.[53] Nor is the difficulty merely one of false swearing. Mistaken observation, mistaken identification, misunderstanding or misinterpretation of what has been seen and heard afford many opportunities for honest testifying at variance with the facts.[54] Criminal procedure provides many checks for the protection of accused persons in view of the dangers involved in the testimony upon which tribunals must perforce rely. But in spite of them conviction of the innocent is by no means unknown.[55]

A second set of limitations grows out of the intangibleness of duties which may be morally of great moment but defy legal enforcement. I

---

he said in his haste would have been his considered judgment, subject to certain qualifications and exceptions." Crawford, *Reflections and Recollections* (1936) 124. *See also* Purrington, *The Frequency of Perjury*, 8 COLUMBIA LAW REVIEW, 399–400 (1827).

49. 6 *Works*, Bowring's ed. 319 (1898), 1 *Rationale of Judicial Evidence*, 399–400 (1827).

50. E.g., *Statute of Frauds and Perjuries*, 29 Car. II, c. 3 (1677); Amos and Walton, *Introduction to French Law*, 200, 347 (1935).

51. 1 Stimson, *American Statute Law*, §§ 1566–1603 (1886); Amos and Walton, *Introduction to French Law*, 103 (1935).

52. *See* Wigmore, *Evidence* (3 ed. 1940) §§ 578, 578a.

53. I have discussed this in *Interests of Personality*, 28 HARVARD LAW REVIEW, 343, 359–64 (1916).

54. *See* Parry, *What the Judge Thought* (1892) chap. 6.

55. Borchard, *Convicting the Innocent* (1932); Watson (editor) *Trial of Adolf Beck* (1924). Andrews, in the first case in Professor Borchard's book, was mistakenly identified in good faith by seventeen witnesses; Beck was so identified by ten.

have spoken already of futile attempts of natural law or of equity at Rome or in England to make moral duties of gratitude or of disinterested benevolence into duties enforceable by courts. In the urban industrial society of today not only duties of care for the health, morals, and education of children, but even truancy, incorrigibility and want of harmony in the family have come under the supervision of Juvenile Courts or Courts of Domestic Relations. But the moment these things are committed to courts, administrative agencies have to be invoked to make the legal treatment effective. Probation officers, boards of children's guardians, detention homes, and the like at once develop.[56] It may be doubted whether such institutions or any that grew out of them will fully take the place of the old-time household discipline by means of which the intangible duties involved in the parental relation were formerly made effective.

A third set of limitations grows out of the subtlety of modes of seriously infringing important interests which the law would be glad to secure effectively if it might. Thus grave infringements of individual interests in the domestic relations by tale-bearing or intrigue are often too intangible to be reached by legal machinery. Anglo-American law has struggled hard with this difficulty. But the result of the action on the case for criminal conversation and alienation of affections, which long ago excited the ridicule of Thackery[57] does not inspire confidence,[58] nor does the American precedent for enjoining a defendant from flirting with the plaintiff's wife[59] assure a better remedy. So also as to the "right of privacy." The difficulties involved in tracing injuries to their source and in fitting cause to effect have compelled some sacrifice of the interests of the retiring and the sensitive.

56. See Young, *Social Treatment in Probation and Delinquency* 2 ed. 52–55, 163, 254–57, 307–35 (1952).

57. *The Newcomes*, vol. 2, chap. 20. See also 3 Campbell, *Lives of the Chief Justices* (1 ed. 1857) 67–68.

58. Many jurisdictions have now done away with the action. Feinsinger, *Legislative Attacks on 'Heart Balm,'* 33 MICHIGAN LAW REVIEW, 1030 (1933).

59. *Ex parte* Warfield, 40 Tex. Cr. 413 (1899). See Pound, *Equitable Relief Against Defamation and Injuries to Personality*, 29 HARVARD LAW REVIEW, 640, 674 (1916).

A fourth set of limitations grows out of the inapplicability of the legal machinery of precept and sanction to many important human relations and to some serious wrongs. One example may be seen in the duty of husband and wife to live together and the claims of each to the society and affection of the other. Today in the western world this interest has no sanction beyond morals and the opinion of the community. That classical Roman law, the modern civil law, and the Anglo-American common law, as a result of experience, each came in the end substantially to this result, speaks for itself.

Finally a fifth set of limitations grows out of the necessity of appealing to individuals to set the law in motion. All legal systems labor under this necessity. But it puts a special burden upon legal administration of justice in an Anglo-American democracy. For our traditional polity depends on individual initiative to secure legal redress and enforce legal precepts. It is true the ultra-individualism of the common law in this connection has broken down. Yet the possibilities of administrative giving effect to legal precepts are limited also and there are grave objections to a general regime of administrative enforcement. On the other hand, legal precepts will not enforce themselves. Human beings must execute them, and there must be some motive setting the individual in motion to do this beyond the abstract content of the precept and its conformity to an ideal justice or an ideal of social advantage. Thus we are brought to consider the social psychological limitations upon enforcement of legal precepts.[60]

What is still the best discussion of the limitations upon law resulting from its dependence upon external agencies to set its machinery in motion — from its dependence upon enforcement by agencies outside of itself — is to be found in Jellinek's Allgemeine Staatslehre.[61] Function-

---

60. 1 Bentham, Works, Bowring ed. 146 (1843); Markby, Elements of Law (6 ed. 1905) §§ 48–59; Salmond, Jurisprudence (9 ed. 1937) § 30; Cohen, Positivism and the Limits of Idealism in the Law, 27 Columbia Law Review, 237 (1927); Chadbourne, Lynching and the Law (1933); Edlin, Rechtsphilosophische Scheinprobleme, II, 2, Das Problem der Sozialen Gesetzmassigkeit (1932).

61. 3 ed. 1914, 332 ff.

ally, he says, what makes a precept law is that it obtains as a rule of conduct and of decision and what makes a legal right is that the precept which stands behind it obtains in action. That means that its psychological efficiency is guaranteed, that is, that the authority which has prescribed it is so backed by social-psychological power as to be in a position to give effect to the precept as a motive for action in spite of counteracting individual motives.

Both judge-made and statutory precepts have failed because they lacked social-psychological guarantee. The difficulty may be: (1) that a precept runs counter to the individual expectations of the greater number or of the more aggressive of a dominant class; or (2) that it runs counter to settled moral ideas of individuals or of an obstinate minority (*e.g.*, the Fugitive Slave Law in the United States before the American Civil War[62] or the National Prohibition Act[63]), or (3) that no immediate interests of individuals are involved and they are indifferent as to the precept.

An example may be found in jurisdictions where some part of the common-law doctrines as to employer's liability still obtains and in those corners of employer's liability in other jurisdictions where recent legislation has left the common law in force. It is notorious that fifty years ago a feeling that employers and great industrial enterprises should bear the cost of the human wear and tear incident to their operations dictated more verdicts in cases of employer's liability than the rules of law laid down in the charge of the court. Most of the new trials directed by American highest courts of review on the ground that the verdicts returned were not sustained by the evidence, were in cases of this sort. Here the body of legal precepts applicable to the facts was settled and defined. But juries so found the facts upon which the court was to proceed that those precepts were not applied and a different result

---

62. See *Ableman v. Booth*, 20 How. 506 (1858); *In re Booth*, 3 Wis. 1 (1854); *Ex parte Booth*, *ibid.*, 145 (1854); *In re Booth and Ryecraft*, *ibid.*, 157 (1854); Boston Slave Riot and Trial of Burns (1854); *The Removal of Judge Loring*, 18 MONTHLY REPORTER, 1 (1855).

63. *National Commission on Law Observance and Enforcement, Report on the Enforcement of the Prohibition Laws of the United States* (1931).

was required. Only the charge of the trial judge, correctly stating the applicable precepts served to preserve an appearance of life in the law in the books. That law ran counter to or, better, ignored the individual expectations of the majority of the community and ran counter to the moral ideas of an increasing number.

More striking still is the divergence between legal theory and current American practice in the handling of persons suspected of crime. It is idle to deny that the so-called third degree has long been all but an everyday feature of investigation by police and prosecuting authorities. According to the books an accused is absolutely protected against official questioning before or at the trial.[64] But prosecuting attorneys and police officers and police detectives manage to conduct the most searching, exhausting and even at times brutal examinations of accused or suspected persons with all the appearance of legality and of having the power of the state behind them.[65] This is done arbitrarily and there is little effective check on it, although the Supreme Court of the United States and the highest courts of a number of the states have been able to do something to discourage it.[66] It is grossly unequal. No business man or manufacturer or railroad superintendent has been subjected to this process to obtain proof of violation of antitrust or rebate legislation nor any powerful politician thus dealt with to obtain proof of bribery or corruption. The malefactor of means, the rogue who has an organization of rogues behind him to provide a lawyer and a writ of *habeas corpus* has

64. 1 Stephen, *History of the Criminal Law of England*, 441 (1863); Train, *Courts, Criminals and the Camorra*, chap. 1 (1912).

65. Although this had been considered an exclusively American practice, the English were astonished not many years ago to find it existing with them also. Rawlinson, *Arrest of Major R. O. Sheppard* (1928); Report of the Tribunal Appointed Under the Tribunals of Enquiry Act, 1921; Parliamentary Paper, CMD. 2497, Inquiry in Regard to the Interrogation by the Police of Miss Savidge (1928); Case of Major R. O. Sheppard (1925) 10 Central Criminal Court Sessions; Case of Irene Savidge (1928) 1 Miscellaneous Trials.

66. *McNabb v. United States*, 318 U.S. 322 (1943); *Lisenba v. California*, 314 U.S. 219, 239–40 (1941); *Ward v. Texas*, 316 U.S. 547, 555 (1942) and cases cited in note to that case.

the benefit of the law in the books. But the ordinary malefactor, and what is worse the ordinary innocent victim of suspicion is too often bullied and even sometimes starved and tortured by officers of the law to obtain a confession.[67] It is no doubt a sound instinct that makes us hesitate to give official interrogation of suspected persons the sanction of legality. We may agree with Sir James Stephen's informant that, to use his words, "it is far pleasanter to sit in the shade rubbing red pepper into a poor devil's eyes than to go about in the sun hunting up evidence."[68] But until the lawmakers can work out some device whereby a properly secured official interrogation can be assured and employed in a proper way in all cases, the weak and lowly and friendless will be at a disadvantage in all cases despite the legal theory.[69] Here the interest secured is the social interest in the individual life which calls for security against oppression of individuals by officials. But it has not proved strong enough to sustain the law in the books as against the pressure of the social interest in the general security, which calls for effective investigation and prosecution.[70]

Cases of doctrines or precepts in advance of popular thought show the same phenomena. For example, take the ultra-ethical ideas of the seventeenth- and eighteenth-century chancellors, such as making unconscionable conduct the sole test in equity, or the exaction of disinterested benevolence from trustees, later applied to the fiduciary relations of directors and promoters of companies. The late nineteenth-century

67. *Wan v. United States*, 266 U.S. 1 (1924); *People v. Shaughnessy*, 184 App. Div. 806 (1918); *Matter of Gaffrey v. Kampf*, 182 Misc. 665 (1944); *National Commission on Law Observance and Enforcement*, Report No. 11 (*Report on Lawlessness in Law Enforcement*); Chafee, Pollak, and Stern, *The Third Degree*, 19–192 (1931); Note, 33 HARVARD LAW REVIEW, 956 (1920).

68. 1 Stephen, *History of the Criminal Law of England* (1883) 442 n. 1.

69. *See* Sir James Stephen's statement of his experience, *ibid.* 442–43.

70. *See* Storey, *Some Practical Suggestions as to the Reform of Criminal Procedure*, 4 JOURNAL OF THE AMERICAN INST. OF CRIMINAL LAW AND CRIMINOLOGY, 495, 500–505 (1913). Pound, *Legal Interrogation of Persons Accused or Suspected of Crime*, 24 *id.* 1014 (1934).

attitude toward specific performance in cases of hard bargains and in cases of sharp practice should be compared with the present-day attitude toward these doctrines.[71] Much of what I have called the "decadence of equity" is to be explained in this way.[72] In both situations, whether the law in the books is behind or is ahead of popular thought on the subject dealt with, the social-psychological guarantee is lacking.

Lawyers have often assumed that most of the divergence between law in the books and law in action was attributable to faulty legislation; that statutes impossible of enforcement, enacted offhand without knowledge of the situation to be dealt with, are chiefly to be blamed. No doubt crude legislation has been a factor of no mean importance. Legislation imposing life imprisonment for possessing a bottle of gin,[73] or imposing a heavier punishment upon one who gives an adult a cigarette than upon serious forms of extortion or upon some forms of corruption most detrimental to the proper conduct of public business,[74] does not impress jurors or prosecutors or even judges with a sense of duty of upholding the written law. No doubt, too, we have had laws made merely to please particular constituents and not seriously intended to be enforced. But these are by no means the whole of the matter. Taught or judge-made traditions, settled habits of legal thought, sometimes fare no better in action. The common law of master and servant, and the ultra-individualist doctrine of contributory negligence long fared badly in the hands of juries and have been modified by legislation in the present century.[75]

Again, the settled judicial doctrine against collusive divorce may be instanced, at least as the matter goes in many American state courts and

71. Pound, *Recent Developments in the Law of Equity* (1933) 38–40.

72. Pound, *The Decadence of Equity*, 5 COLUMBIA LAW REVIEW, 20 (1905).

73. Mich. 1922, Suppl. to Comp. L. 1915, § 7079 (5), Act of June 25, 1919, Act no. 3 of Extra Session of 1919, in view of §§ 11785 and 11786, Comp. L. of 1897.

74. Neb. Act of July 1, 1905, Comp. Stat. 1905, §§ 7960a, 7960b, in view of *State* v. *Greene*, 83 Neb. 84 (1908).

75. Gregory, *Legislative Loss Distribution in Negligence Actions*, chap. 7 (1936); Wilson and Mole, *Comparative Negligence*, 17 CORNELL LAW QUARTERLY, 333, 604 (1932).

began to go recently in England. In many of the United States "extreme cruelty" has become a convenient fiction to cover up that incompatibility of temper which may not unreasonably exist between a respected good citizen and his wife. The legal theory, the judicial decisions defining cruelty and the judge-made rule against collusion remain in the books.[76] But husband and wife agree on a settlement out of court, they came to an understanding that she shall aver and prove cruelty unopposed, the newspapers publish that she is to have a divorce, the ritual of a suit is gone through with, and a decree is entered. A like situation seems to have developed in England: "The judges do their best to enforce the law as it stands, but they struggle in vain."[77] Obviously there is an ill adjustment of the social interest in the security of the social institution of marriage and the social interest in the individual life. Hence there is nothing to induce individuals to move to vindicate the social interest in the institution of marriage as against the strong individual interests involved.

In order to secure enforcement law must largely rely on some immediate and obvious individual advantage which it may use either to bring about obedience to its precepts or to furnish a motive to others to vindicate or enforce it. The legal science of the past century knew of no such problem. To the analytical jurist the whole matter was one of executive efficiency. To the lawyer it was enough that a precept had obtained the guinea stamp of establishment by the sovereign. The jurist had no concern with questions of enforcement. That was for the executive. If the executive did not make the precept effective in action, then the executive was at fault. To the historical jurist the whole matter was one of whether the precept did or did not correctly express human experience.

76. Bishop, *Marriage, Divorce and Separation* (1891) §§ 249–66.

77. Hume-Williams, *The World, the House, and the Bar* (1930) 265. "With his blunt and logical outlook the judge had recognized that divorce by mutual arrangement exists in fact, though not in theory in England." Fay, *Life of Mr. Justice Smith* (1939) 145. See *Woods* v. *Woods*, 4 All E.R. 9, 11 ff.; *Bevis* v. *Bevis* [1935] P. 23, 26, 86, 94; *Russell* v. *Russell* [1935] 39, 49.

If it was a formulation of what had been discovered by experience, enforcement would take care of itself. It would be rooted in habits and customs of mankind and would be secure on that basis. If not, it was a futile attempt to do what could not be done and all attempt at enforcement would in the end prove vain. To the philosophical jurist the whole matter was one of the intrinsic justice of the precept — of its appeal to the conscience of the individual. If as an abstract proposition it was inherently just, its appeal to the reason and conscience of the individual would assure obedience from all but an almost negligible minority who would persist in going counter to their consciences and might have to be coerced. If not, the attempt to enforce an unjust rule contrary to the conscience of the individual ought to fail and we ought not to feel badly if it did fail. Another theory looked at the question in terms of politics. If laws were imposed on the people they would disobey them. If the people themselves made the laws, they would obey the laws they made or assented to.

Such simple theories of making legal precepts effective fall to the ground under the conditions of the urban industrial society of today. We learn quickly that efficient or inefficient executives alike encounter certain obstacles that seem beyond the reach of efficiency. We soon find that in such matters as traffic regulation in a time of motor vehicles the general security requires us to make habits instead of waiting for them to develop by experience at the cost of life and limb. We come to see that the exigencies of the general security and of the individual life require us to prescribe many things the reasons for which are not upon the surface and the justice of which, clear as it may be to the expert, will not appear to every reasonable and conscientious individual. Also the point is not whether the people at large have assented to or have made the precept in question. It is rather what interest will move the individuals, through whose initiative the precept must be made effective, to bestir themselves to see that it is vindicated.[78] Jhering urged the duty of the good citizen to go to trouble and expense to vindicate his legal rights,

78. See Duff, *Spinoza's Political and Ethical Philosophy* (1903) chap. 22.

even on small occasions, as his contribution to maintaining the legal order.[79] But in the busy world of today men are less and less inclined to pursue their legal rights even in matters of no little moment at the expense of time, money, and energy they can more profitably employ in their everyday work.

Herein is the kernel of truth in Savigny's distrust of conscious law-making and the lawyer's distrust of legislation. Abstract formulation of rules is likely to result in empty formulas because there is only speculative interest in them, as propositions, not the living interest on the part of individuals whose demands and desires are affected directly and immediately by observance or nonobservance of the precept.

Establishing a criterion of valuing interests is not the whole of the science of law nor is valuing of interests whether recognized or pressing to be recognized, the whole task of law. Much of that task can be achieved only through what is called positive law — compromises or fixed rules, dictated by the need of some settled disposition of cases of conflicting or overlapping demands or expectations in order to assure uniformity and certainty rather than by any ideal other than predictability. But even then application is governed by an ideal of civilized society and of what the law of such a society should be. In practice interests are recognized and secured and legal precepts are interpreted and applied with reference to ideals of the end of law and ultimately of the ideal relation among men. While philosophers argue as to an absolute measure of values, received ideals of the purpose of the legal order and of justice as the ideal relation among men, received traditionally in the time and place, have to serve. What these ideals have been must be considered in the lectures that follow.

79. *Der Kampf um's Recht* (1872, 19 ed. 1919), English transl. *The Struggle for Law* by Lalor (1879, 2 ed. by Kocourek, 1915). This little book, of which there have been twenty-three translations into seventeen languages was the pioneer discussion of what we can do in the way of social control through law.

FIVE

The End of Law:
Maintaining the Social Status Quo

We turn now to the end or purpose of law, both as legal order and as a body of authoritative norms, *i.e.*, models or patterns of conduct, of decision of controversies, and of predictions or advice by counsellors; or, in other words, to theories of justice.[1]

It has been seen that a body of philosophical, political, and ethical ideas as to the end of law — as to the purpose of social control and of the legal order as a form thereof — and hence as to what legal precepts ought to be in view of this end, is an element of the first importance in the work of judges, jurists, and lawmakers. The history and development of this body of ideas is no less important for the science of law than the history and development of the precepts and doctrines which used to be thought of as making up the whole of the law. Indeed, the history of ideas as to the end of law is part of the very history of legal precepts and legal doctrines. But there is another reason why we should examine the history of these ideas. It used to be said that law is the body of precepts in accordance with which justice is administered by the authority of the

---

1. Pound, *Justice According to Law* (1951) pt. 2; Del Vecchio, *Justice* (1952) (transl. by Lady Guthrie, ed. by Campbell); Radbruch, *Rechtsphilosophie* (3 ed. 1932) §§ 7–9; Binder, *Philosophie des Rechts* (1 ed. 1925) § 12; Kant, *Philosophy of Law* (1887, transl. by Hastie) 45–46; Spencer, *Justice* (1891) chaps. 5, 6; Dewey and Tufts, *Ethics* (1938) rev. ed. chaps. 20–24.

state.[2] This presupposes that the purpose of law (in the sense of the judicial process) is the administration of justice, and the task of the judicial process is to maintain the legal order as an order of justice by applying to decisions of controversies the authoritative norms of decision established or recognized by the state. Thus at the outset of even a purely analytical investigation we are met by the question, what is justice, in the sense of what we are trying to bring about through law.

This is not a question of what justice is when thought of as an individual virtue, nor what it is when thought of as a regime of adjusting relations and ordering conduct. It is a question of what it is that we seek to attain by means of the legal ordering of society. What is the end which we are trying to reach by means of the legal order and hence through judicial decision, juristic discussion and legislation? As has been said hereinbefore, I prefer Radbruch's definition of justice as the ideal relation among men. Even if we cannot dogmatically lay down an unchallengeable universal formulation of that ideal, we may set forth the received formulation which men accept in the time and place as what they believe to be the ideal formulation and we accept as the nearest approximation we may attain for the time being.

We may take up this question of the end of law, or of what is justice, either historically or philosophically. We may inquire as to ideas of the end of law as they have developed in legal precepts and legal doctrines. Or we may inquire about these ideas as they have developed in juristic thought. In the latter connection we are brought to inquire what ought to be conceived as the end of law, and we must ask what do economics, politics, sociology, and ethics point to as the purpose to which the ordering of society is to be directed. As one pursues this last inquiry he soon perceives that juristic theories of the end of law and those which obtain in the other social sciences are not always the same. Thus there was a significant divergence between the idea as to the end of law which had developed in actual legal precepts and doctrines and obtained in juristic thought at the end of the nineteenth century, on the one hand,

2. E.g., Pollock, *First Book of Jurisprudence* (1 ed. 1896) 17.

and, on the other hand, the idea of justice which had then come to obtain in economics, politics, and ethics. Hence we have not merely to ask, what is the legal or at least the juristic idea of justice. It is of no less moment to know how, and when, and why it has differed or may differ from the economic, or political, or ethical idea. To answer such questions we must consider how and why the legal idea of justice came to be what it is.

In studying ideas as to the end of law we must note that actual legal ideas and juristic ideals have acted each upon the other. If ideals of what law ought to be have done much in all ages to shape legal precepts as they were, it is no less true that the actual legal situation for the time being has had a large influence upon the ideals.[3] We must consider the development of each in order to understand the other. Approaching the subject historically I have found it convenient to think of four stages of legal development in systems which have come to maturity: (1) The stage of primitive law, (2) the stage of the strict law, (3) the stage of equity and natural law, and (4) the stage of maturity of law. To these we must now add a fifth stage upon which the law has definitely entered throughout the world, which may be called the stage of socialization.

Perhaps it need not be said that all such divisions into periods or stages must be somewhat arbitrary. Lines drawn to bring out one point would have to be laid out differently if we had our eye on a different point. Also a certain over-emphasis is involved in any classification. Schematic arrangements involve hard-and-fast lines which do not occur in nature. In fact, all periods or stages overlap and shade into one another. It should be said also that the division into stages which I have suggested is made primarily with reference to Roman law, the modern Roman law, the codified law of Continental Europe and its derivatives. It is not a classification of all social control. It begins as near as may be

---

3. This is especially apparent in theories of natural law, as brought out in the second lecture. *See also* my paper, *Natural Natural Law and Positive Natural Law* (1952) 68 LAW QUARTERLY REVIEW, 330.

at the point where there begins to be law in the analytical sense. Also it is made with reference to the law, its methods, scope, materials, and ideals, and not with reference to politics. For the law is made up chiefly of traditional materials, a traditional art, and traditional ideals, transmitted and developed by teaching, which are continually but gradually reshaping to meet conditions of the time and place. The political conditions of the time by no means give them character, although they do exert a gradual influence in remaking them. But this influence is often manifest in its results after these conditions have ceased and a still newer set of conditions have begun to replace them.

I shall not go back to the origins of social control. Such things belong to sociology or anthropology and have relatively a remote bearing on jurisprudence. But as law, in the analytical sense, arises in the transition from a kin-organized society to a politically organized society, or in the transition from religious social control to political social control, and hence its materials in the formative period are the materials of what Vinogradoff calls tribal law[4] or the materials of a religious ordering of society, ideas and institutions of tribal society and of society organized on a religious basis become legal ideas and legal institutions. A good part of the earlier history of a legal system is the story of how these ideas and institutions were made over to the exigencies of politically organized society or even gradually eliminated.

By primitive law I do not mean social control in primitive societies but a stage in which law in the analytical sense is undifferentiated or little differentiated from social control generally. Such an undifferentiated or little differentiated social control may exist even though there is an advanced moral order and effective social control. The law may be primitive in comparison with what the world has known as law since the Romans although the society was not. What I mean, then, is the stage in which law in the analytical sense is gradually emerging from an undifferentiated social control by religion, ethical custom and kin discipline.

4. 1 Vinogradoff, *Historical Jurisprudence* (1920) 158.

Even after transition from a kin-organized to a politically organized society seems complete from a political standpoint, the differentiation of law may be far from complete.

In the beginnings of a legal order the purpose is simply to keep the peace. Unless internal peace can be attained a society cannot subsist. At first the law attempted nothing more affirmatively than to regulate and provide a substitute for revenge. There were three ways in which injured persons, persons who had been wronged, might obtain redress. One was self-help, that is, by the help of oneself and of his kindred. This is the remedy of kin-organized society. Accordingly reprisals, self-help and the blood feud were the ordinary institutions for the redress of injuries.[5] Another mode of obtaining redress was by the help of the gods or of their ministers. This is the remedy of a religious organization of society.[6] The weapons of a religious organization of society were sacrificial execution, expiation, and what might be called excommunication. There seems to have been sacrificial execution in the beginnings of Roman law.[7] Expiation is taken over by the king or magistrate and becomes legal penal treatment.[8] Largely the help of the gods means procuring exclusion of the wrongdoer from the society of the pious unless he makes peace with the gods by repairing the wrong if it is expiable. The oldest monuments of Roman law are *leges sacratae*, precepts sanctioned by the formula *sacer esto* — be he devoted to the gods.[9] A third mode of obtaining redress is by

5. Dareste, *Le droit des représailles, Nouvelles études d'histoire du droit* (1902) 38; Von Maurer, *Altnordische Rechtsgeschichte* (1907) pt. I; 1 Brunner, *Deutsche Rechtsgeschichte* (2 ed. 1905) § 22; 1 Post, *Grundriss der ethnologischen Jurisprudenz* (1884) §§ 58, 62; Fehr, *Hammurapi und das salisches Recht* (1910) chap. 5.

6. Maine, *Early History of Institutions* (1875) lect. 2. *See also* the penances in Maine, *Early Law and Custom* (new ed. 1891) 36–40; *Manu* (transl. by Müller, 1889) 25 SACRED BOOKS OF THE EAST, 430–83. Compare the penitential system of the canon law — the Canones penitentiales, which customarily stand in editions of the Corpus Iuris Canonici next after the Decretum of Gratian.

7. Strachan-Davidson, *Problems of the Roman Criminal Law* (1912) 1–3.

8. Maine, *Early Law and Custom* (new ed. 1891) 36–40.

9. Laws of Romulus, 13, 1 Bruns, *Fontes Iuris Romani Antiqui* (7 ed. 1909) 7; Laws of Servius Tullius, 6, *id.* 14; Twelve Tables, VIII, 21, 33, 2 Bruns, *Fontes*, 34, 35; Festus s.vv. *sacer homo* and *sacratae leges*.

the help of the state, that is, by the help of the king or of magistrates or officials. This is the remedy of politically organized society. Speaking generally, at first this help is extended to prevent the wrongdoer from interfering with self-redress by the injured party. But with the development of political organization public authorities begin to take a more active part to prevent a general disturbance of the peace of the community and to keep self-redress within bounds.

Thus in its beginnings law (in the lawyer's sense) has for its end, and for its sole end, to keep the peace. Other tasks of social control are left to other agencies — religion and kin discipline or the public opinion of one's kinsmen or of his brethren in some primitive brotherhood. The only social interest secured by law is the social interest in the general security in its lowest terms, namely, the interest in peace and public order. Along with religion and morality it is a regulative agency by which men are restrained from violent disturbance of the general security.[10] It retains this character of a regulative agency and of a means of which the end is peaceable ordering, although other ends become manifest as it develops. This end is sought to be attained in a primitive legal order in three ways: By regulating self-redress and private war, by satisfying or endeavoring to satisfy the desire of the injured party for vengeance, and by affording some purely mechanical mode of trial which will obviate all disputes as to the facts.

Accordingly there are four general characteristics of the beginnings of law: (1) The measure of what an injured person may recover is not the injury done him but the desire for vengeance awakened by the injury — the idea is not reparation but composition;[11] (2) the modes of trial are not rational but mechanical;[12] (3) the scope of the law is very limited —

---

10. "Religion, law, and morality cover the area of human action with rules and sanctions." Stubbs, *Lectures on the Study of Medieval and Modern History* (1906) 336.

11. *Gaius*, iii, §§ 183–92, 220–24, iv, §§ 75–78; *Twelve Tables*, VIII, 6, 1, 1 Bruns, *Fontes Iuris Romani Antiqui* (7 ed. 1909) 30; Salic Laws, xiv, §§ 1–3; Laws of Ethelbert, 59, 60; Wade-Evans, *Welsh Medieval Law* (1909) 190–91.

12. Thayer, *Preliminary Treatise on Evidence* (1898) chap. 1; *Glanvill*, ii, chaps. 1, 3, 5, 12 (between 1185 and 1187).

there are no principles or general ideas but only rules attaching definite defined consequences to definite detailed acts;[13] (4) for many purposes the legal unit is not so much the individual human being as a group of kindred.[14]

Many of these characteristics of the beginnings of law persist into the period in which there is a fully differentiated legal order. For a long time the development of law largely consists in getting away from them.

In the beginning, then, the idea of the end of law, one might say the ideal to which lawmaking and the applying of legal precepts was directed, was that the legal order exists to keep the peace. In the earlier part of this stage, law is the feeblest of the agencies of social control. The stronger agencies are religion, made effective by priests, and ethical custom, given effect by the internal discipline of the kin group or of societies or fraternities, on the model of the kindred.[15] The Romans recognized three bodies of precepts: *Fas*, that which accorded with the will of the gods, ascertained through religion, enforced in theory through supernatural sanctions and in practice through pontifical penalties; *boni mores*, that which accorded with the settled customs of men, resting in tradition and sanctioned by social pressure or the discipline of the kin group; and *ius*, law, ascertained by agencies of the state and sanctioned

13. Hippodamus of Miletus (fifth century B.C.) held that there were but three kinds of laws, "as the possible subjects of judicial procedure were but three, namely, assault, trespass, and homicide." Aristotle, *Politics*, ii, 8.

14. Thus the Athenian law of reprisals allowed not more than three of the nearest kinsmen of a murderer to be seized by the nearest relatives of the murdered person and held till justice was done or the murderer was surrendered. Demosthenes, *Oration Against Aristocrates*, § 96; in the Germanic law the feud was the right of the person injured and the duty of the kinsmen of the wrongdoer, 1 Brunner, *Deutsche Rechtsgeschichte* (2 ed. 1906) § 25; 1 Pollock and Maitland, *History of English Law* (2 ed. 1898) 24; Salic Law, tit. 57. "If breach of the peace is committed in a fortified town, let the inhabitants of the town themselves go and get the murderers, living or dead; or their nearest kinsmen, head for head," *Laws of Ethelred*, ii, 6—*see also* id. ix, 53, Laws of Alfred, § 27, Laws of Edmund, 2, 4; also the older Roman law of inheritance spoke of *familia, sui heredes, adgnati*, and *gentiles*. Twelve Tables, V, 5, 6, 7a, 1 Bruns, *Fontes* (7 ed. 1909) 23.

15. *See* Webster, *Primitive Secret Societies* (2 ed. 1932); Schurtz, *Altersklassen und Männerbünde* (1902).

by the force of the state. Where a wrong was an impiety, an affront to the gods, it endangered the community that harbored the offender.[16] Taken over by the legal order, pontifical dealing with such cases could become outlawry.[17] The legal order, too, could put its sanctions behind *boni mores*.[18] Thus there is a gradual differentiation culminating in societies in which the legal order is paramount and other forms of social control must operate in subordination thereto.[19]

In a second state of development the legal order is definitely differentiated from other modes of social control. When this stage has been reached, the legal order, a regime of social control operating according to law, that is, according to authoritative guides to determination, developed and applied by an authoritative technique, has prevailed or has gone a long way to prevailing over organized religion as the regulative agency of society. The state has prevailed over the organized kindred as the organ of social control. Usually, normally men have come to appeal only or ultimately to the state for redress of wrongs. Hence the body of legal precepts determining the cases in which men may appeal to the state for help comes to define indirectly the interests which the legal order recognizes and secures. In this stage the law is characteristically a mass of procedural rules, a system of remedies and of formal procedure to obtain remedies, just as the prior stage is characteristically a tariff of compositions.

16. See, *e.g.*, the plague sent upon the whole host for the wrong done by Agamemnon to the priest of Apollo, and so an affront to the god, *Iliad*, book II. "A new departure is full of danger, not only to the man who takes it, but to those with whom he lives, for the gods are apt to be indiscriminate in their anger." Jenks, *Law and Politics in the Middle Ages* (1898) 57.

17. Strachan-Davidson, *Problems of the Roman Criminal Law* (1912) chap. 1.

18. I Jhering, *Geist des römischen Rechts* (7 and 8 ed. 1924) §§ 18, 18a; Greenidge, *Infamia: Its Place in Roman Public and Private Law* (1844), chaps. 3, 4.

19. Compare a regime of discipline by household, *gens, collegium*, guild, with one of juvenile courts, domestic relations courts, judicial review of ouster from voluntary associations, laws as to professional discipline, and commissions regulating traders and professions.

Two causes in this stage of legal development operate to produce a system of strict law:[20] (1) Fear of arbitrary exercise of the assistance of the state, the rooted repugnance of men to subjection of their will to the arbitrary will of others, and (2) survival of ideas of form and literal application from the earlier period.

In this period the immediate end which the law seeks is certainty in the application of remedies. The cases in which the state will interfere and the way it will interfere are defined in an utterly hard and fast manner. The law is made up of rules and the rules are inflexible. The characteristics of this stage of legal development seem to be five: (1) Formalism — the law refuses to look beyond or behind the form; (2) rigidity and immutability; (3) extreme insistence that every one looks out for himself; (4) refusal to take account of the moral aspects of situations or transactions — to use Ames's phrase, the strict law is not immoral but unmoral; (5) rights and duties are restricted to a narrow category of legal persons — all human beings or natural persons are not legal persons and legal capacity is restricted arbitrarily.

Comparing the strict law with the prior stage of legal development, the beginnings of law: (1) The end of primitive law is to keep the peace. It considers the situation after injury has been done. The strict law has advanced to the broader idea of security. Hence it considers the situation before injury as well as after injury. (2) The resource employed by primitive law is composition. The strict law has advanced to the more general idea of legal remedies. (3) The contribution of primitive law to the legal order is the idea of a peaceable ordering of the community. The contributions of the strict law are the ideas of certainty and uniformity in this ordering and of rule and form as the means thereto.

A stage of liberalization, which may be called the stage of equity and natural law[21] succeeds the strict law. In Roman law this stage is repre-

---

20. II Jhering, *Geist des römischen Rechts* (6 and 7 ed. 1923) §§ 44–47d. I take the name from the *ius strictum*, the Roman law of this stage of development and the element in the later law representing it.

21. The name is taken from Maine, *Ancient Law* (1861) chap. 3. Some have criticized this name as implying that I suppose equity and natural law are identical. But there is a common spirit, which is significant, although of course otherwise they are distinct.

sented by the period from the development of pretorian law to the
monarchy (Diocletian and Constantine) — especially the classical period from Augustus to the end of the first quarter of the third century. In
English law it is represented by the rise of the Court of Chancery and
development of equity and by the rise and absorption of the law merchant — roughly the seventeenth and eighteenth centuries. In the law of
Continental Europe it is represented by the period of the law-of-nature
school, that is again, the seventeenth and eighteenth centuries. The
watchword of the strict law was certainty. The watchword of this stage is
morals or some phrase of ethical import, such as good conscience,
aequum et bonum, or natural law. The strict law insists on uniformity.
Equity and natural law insist on good morals. The strict law insists on
form, equity and natural law on justice in the ethical sense; the strict law
insists on remedies, equity and natural law on duties; the strict law insists on rule, equity and natural law on reason. The capital ideas of this
stage are: (1) The identification of law with morals, (2) the conception
of duty and attempt to make moral duties into legal duties, and (3) reliance upon reason rather than upon arbitrary rule to keep down caprice
and eliminate or minimize the personal element in the administration
of justice.

Four enduring ideas of the first magnitude come into the law in this
period. The first is that legal personality should extend to all human beings; that the moral unit should be the legal unit, not a kin group, as in
the beginnings of law, and not an arbitrarily defined legal person as in
the strict law. In this period equity and natural law insist not only on the
widest extension of rights but upon a like extension of capacity for legal
transactions. Hence there is insistence on throwing over all incapacities
for which a "natural" reason, as distinguished from a historical explanation, cannot be given, and on making capacity for legal transactions coincident with normal will.[22] A third idea is good faith, the idea that jus-

---

22. *Institutes of Justinian*, I, 3, § 2, 8, §§ 1, 2, ii, 2, § 2; *Gaius*, i, §§ 144–45, 158; *Digest*,
i, 5, 4, § 1, i, 5, 17, xxxviii, 10, 4, § 2, 1, 17, 32; *Grotius*, ii, 5, 1–7. *See* especially the way equity in Roman law treated the perpetual tutelage of women and English equity provided
for the separate estate of married women. The classical account is in Maine, *Early History of Institutions* (1 ed. 1875) 11.

tice demands one should not disappoint well-founded expectations which he has created; the idea that it is not so important that rules should be certain as that men's conduct should be certain.[23] A fourth idea of this stage is that one person should not be enriched unjustly at the expense of another; that it is dishonest to take and hold something for nothing unless by way of intended gift. This has a wide application today in the law of restitution, or quasi contract, as we used to call it, and equitable doctrines as to constructive trusts, preventing merger, subrogation, conditions implied in law, required assurance of counter performance, and equivalent doctrines, derived from Roman law, in the law of Continental Europe.

On the other hand, the attempt to make law coincide with morals leads to two difficulties: (1) It leads to an attempt to enforce over-high ethical standards and to make legal duties out of moral duties which are not sufficiently tangible to be made effective by the machinery of the legal order. (2) A more serious difficulty is that the attempt to identify law and morals gives too wide a scope to judicial discretion since whereas legal rules are of general and absolute application, moral precepts must be applied with reference to circumstances and individuals. Hence at first in this stage the administration of justice is too personal.[24] This overwide magisterial discretion is corrected in two ways. One is by a gradual fixing of rules and consequent stiffening of the legal system. Some moral

---

23. Maitland, *Lectures on Equity* (2 ed. 1936) 80–83; *Grotius*, iii, chap. 11, §§ 3–4; Burlamaqui, *Principes du droit naturel* (1791) pt. 1, chap. 7; Pothier, *Obligations* (1806) pt. 1, chap. 1, § 1; Strykius, *Opera* (1785) xxii, 4, 24. The latter says: "Ideo Deus ligetur pacto et diabolus, et princeps."

24. See, *e.g.*, the well-known saying of Selden in the seventeenth century: "Equity in law is the same that the spirit is in religion, what every one pleases to make it. Sometimes they go according to conscience sometime according to law sometime according to the rule of the court. Equity is a roguish thing; for law we have a measure, know what to trust to. Equity is according to the conscience of him that is chancellor, and as that is larger or narrower so is equity. 'Tis all one as if they should make the standard for the measure we call a foot to be the chancellor's foot; what an uncertain measure this would be; one chancellor has a long foot another a short foot a third an indifferent foot; 'tis the same thing in the chancellor's conscience." *Table Talk*, tit. *Equity* (1689), Selden Society ed. 1927, p. 43.

principles in their acquired character of legal principles, are carried out to logical consequences beyond what is practicable or expedient so that a selecting and restricting process becomes necessary, and at length principles are lost in a mass of rules derived from them. Some examples are the old doctrine of equity as to precatory trusts which gave rise to a set of arbitrary distinctions[25] and finally disappeared,[26] and the doctrine of *laesio enormis*[27] which, as Story says, began by "laying down the broadest rule of equity and morals," then came to be applied as a legal rule, and then was turned by legislators, who were "struck with the un-limited nature of the proposition" into a hard and fast mathematical for-mula.[28] The other correcting agency is development of moral proposi-tions as mere abstractions and thus depriving them of their purely moral character. In Anglo-American law, equity is full of examples of this me-chanical treatment of what were once moral principles. It will be enough to cite the rules as to clogging the equity of redemption, which go back to a moral principle that forbids the taking of "unconscientious advantage of a debtor's necessities."[29]

In other words, there comes in time to be a stiffening of the legal sys-tem and we get a fourth stage, represented both in Anglo-American law and in the law of Continental Europe by the nineteenth century, which I have called the maturity of law.

Comparing the stage of equity and natural law with the preceding stages, the controlling idea is, in the beginnings of law public peace, in the strict law security, in the stage of equity and natural law ethical con-duct and conformity to good morals; the means employed are, in the be-ginnings of law, composition, in the strict law, legal remedy, in the stage

25. 1 Perry, *Trusts* (7 ed. 1929) §§ 112–19.
26. *Lambe* v. *Eames*, 6 Ch. App. 597 (1871).
27. *Code* of Justinian, iv, 44, 2 and 9.
28. 1 W. W. Story, *Equity Jurisprudence* (2 ed. 1839) § 247.
29. "The rules of equity may be evaded but must not be infringed." Lord Bramwell in *Marquess of Northampton* v. *Salt* (1892) A.C. 1. Here the court was conscious of ap-plying what had become a technical rule which it had no intention of carrying a whit beyond its letter. It looked at the form, not the intention of the parties.

of equity and natural law, enforcement of duties; and the permanent contributions are, by the beginnings of law, peaceable ordering of society, by the strict law, certainty and uniformity, reached by rule and form, and by equity and natural law, good faith and moral conduct attained by reason.

For the next stage I take from Austin the name "maturity of law."[30] As a result of the stiffening process by which the undue fluidity of law and over-wide scope for discretion involved in the identification of law and morals are gradually corrected, there comes to be a body of law with the stable and certain qualities of the strict law, yet liberalized by the ideas and conceptions developed by equity and natural law.[31]

In this stage of matured legal systems the watchwords are equality and security. The idea of equality is derived partly from the insistence of equity and natural law upon treating all human beings as legal persons and upon recognizing full legal capacity in all persons possessed of normal will. Partly also it is derived from the insistence of the strict law that the same remedy shall always be applied to the same state of facts. Accordingly as used here equality includes two things: (1) Equality of operation of legal precepts, and (2) equality of opportunity to exercise one's faculties and to employ one's substance.[32] The idea of security is derived from the strict law, but is modified by the ideas of the stage of equity and natural law, especially by the idea of insisting on will rather than on form as the cause of legal results, and by the idea of preventing enrichment of one at the expense of another through forms and without will. In consequence, security, as used in the last century included two things: (1) The idea that every one is to be secured in his interests against aggression on culpable injury by others, and (2) that others are to be permitted

---

30. 2 Austin, *Jurisprudence* (3 ed. 1863) 1107–8.

31. On this stage see *Progress of Continental Law in the Nineteenth Century*, 11 CONTINENTAL LEGAL HISTORY SERIES (1918) chaps. 1, 2; First *Report of the Real Property Commissioners* (1924) 6–7; Hanbury, *The Field of Modern Equity*, 45 LAW QUARTERLY REVIEW, 196, 207–13 (1929).

32. *Digest* of Justinian, i, 1, 4; Bentham, *Theory of Legislation, Principles of the Civil Code* (transl. by Hildreth, 5 ed. 1885) pt. 1, chap. 2.

to acquire from him only through his will that they do so, or through his breach of rules devised to secure others in like interests.[33]

In order to insure equality the maturity of law insists strongly upon certainty and in consequence this stage is comparable in many respects to the stage of the strict law. It is greatly in advance of the stage of the strict law, however, because it insists not merely on equality of application of legal remedies but on equality of legal rights, that is, equality of capacities to influence others through the power of politically organized society, and conceives of equality of application of legal remedies as only a means thereto.

To insure security, the maturity of law insists upon property and contract as fundamental ideas. That is, it thinks of all interests in terms of a social interest in security of acquisitions and security of transactions. This is brought out in American state bills of rights which protect the individual in life, liberty, and property. Liberty was taken in the last century to mean that the individual shall not be held legally except for a fault or except as and to the extent that he has willed a relation to which the law in advance attached a liability, whereby another might exact something from him.

Along with liberty the maturity of law puts property, that is, the security of acquisitions. But one of these acquisitions may be a power to exact from a promisor. Accordingly contract acquires a property aspect. The law is regarded as existing to secure, to the furthest possible extent, the right to contract freely and the right to exact a performance freely promised.[34] Indeed in this stage even personality acquires a property aspect.[35]

Although it may be too soon to speak with assurance, the permanent contribution of the stage of maturity of law appears to be the thorough

33. On the idea of security in the maturity of law *see* Bentham, *Theory of Legislation, Principles of the Civil Code* (Hildreth's transl. 5 ed. 1885) pt. 1, chaps. 2, 7; Lorimer, *Institutes of Law* (2 ed. 1880) 367–74; Demogue, *Les notions fondamentales du droit privé* (1911) 63–110; Schulz, *Principles of Roman Law* (1936) chap. 12.

34. So in *Frorer v. People*, 141 Ill. 171, 181 (1892).

35. "For purposes of the civil law of defamation, reputation is regarded as a species of property." Bower, *Code of Actionable Defamation* (1908) 275.

working out of the idea of individual rights. The important institutions of this stage are property and contract.

Finally, we must look at the stage into which the law has moved in the present century, the socialization of law.[36]

Toward the end of the nineteenth century a tendency became manifest throughout the world to depart radically from fundamental ideas which had governed the maturity of legal systems. In 1891, Jhering[37] formulated it thus: "Formerly high valuing of property, lower valuing of the person. Now lower valuing of property, higher valuing of the person."[38] He went on to say that the line of legal growth was, "weakening of the sense of property, strengthening of the feeling of dignity (*Ehre*)."[39] This states the matter well if by *Ehre* we understand the idea of the moral and so legal worth of the concrete human individual.

In the maturity of law the legal system seeks to secure individuals in the advantages given them by nature or by their station in the world and to enable them to use these advantages as freely as is compatible with the free exercise of their faculties and use of their advantages by others. As has been said, to accomplish those ends it reverts in some measure to ideas of the strict law. In consequence a certain opposition between law and morals develops once more, and just as the neglect of the moral aspects of conduct in the stage of the strict law required the legal revolution through infusion of lay moral ideas into law which we call the stage of equity and natural law, so the neglect of the moral worth of the con-

36. As to the name given it, I got the hint from Stein, *Soziale Frage im Lichte der Philosophie* (2 ed. 1903) 457 (1 ed. 1897). The term was used by Charmont in 1903, *La socialisation du droit*, chap. 2. I used it in the present sense in an address in 1912, *Social Justice and Legal Justice*, 1912 Proc. Mo. Bar Assn. 110, and in an article in 1914, *The End of Law as Developed in Legal Rules and Doctrines*, 27 Harvard Law Review, 195, 225. Vinogradoff adopted it for this stage of legal development in 1920, 1 *Historical Jurisprudence*, 158.

37. In the additions to the fourth edition of his *Scherz und Ernst in der Jurisprudenz*. *See* the preface to the fourth edition in that or any subsequent edition.

38. *Scherz und Ernst in der Jurisprudenz* (4 ed. 1891) 418.

39. *Ibid.*, 424. Compare the steady growth in recent years of equitable protection of personality. Pound, *Equitable Relief Against Defamation and Injuries to Personality* (1916) 29 Harvard Law Review, 640. It had long been said that equitable relief was only granted to protect rights of property.

crete individual and of his claim to a complete moral and social life, involved in the insistence upon property and contract in the abstract, which mark the maturity of law, have been requiring a like revolution through absorption into the law of ideas developed in the social sciences.

Let us leave the theory of this stage of legal development for another place and look instead at what has actually been going on in legal systems. Taking them up in chronological order of their appearance in American law, and a like list could be made for English law and for the law of Continental Europe, twelve points appear especially noteworthy: (1) Limitations on the use of property by the owner and on what is called antisocial exercise of his liberties; (2) limitations on freedom of contract; (3) limitations on the owner's *jus disponendi*; (4) limitations on the power of a creditor or injured party to exact satisfaction; (5) impositions of liability without fault, particularly in the forms of liability for getting out of hand of things maintained on the owner's property or work carried on or persons employed; (6) restrictions on use of *res communes* and appropriation of *res nullius*; (7) insistence upon the interest of society with respect to dependent members of the household; (8) a growing tendency to hold that public funds should respond for injuries to individuals through the operations of public agencies; (9) a tendency to read reasonableness into the obligation of contracts or even to remake contracts in the interest of the frustrated; (10) a tendency to replace the purely contentious theory of litigation by one of adjustment of interests; (11) increasing recognition of groups and associations as having interests to be secured, instead of exclusive recognition of certain historical associations and their analogues; (12) a tendency to relax the rules as to trespassers. More than one lecture could be devoted to more than one of these items. They show a profound change in law beneath the surface. Interpretation of them belongs to a subsequent lecture. Our concern with them here is as to their bearing on the ideal of the end or purpose of law and relation to the ideal element in the law of today.

Having attempted to mark the course which the development of law has actually taken in different periods of legal history with respect to the end for which the legal order and law in the second sense exist, we turn next to the course which juristic thinking has taken during these same periods as to the direction in which law ought to develop and what ought to be regarded as the end of law and furnish an ideal for lawmaking, interpretation and application. In other words, from legal history, the end of law as developed in legal precepts and doctrines we turn to philosophy of law, the end of law as developed in juristic thinking.[40]

Until law had been differentiated as such there could be no strictly juristic thinking. But as the legal order developed as a specialized form of social control, philosophical thinking as to the nature and end of social control could furnish a beginning for juristic thinking about the nature and end of law. The Greeks did not achieve a stage of strict law. But they began to think about social control, and their ideas as to its nature and purpose are the starting point of philosophy of law in the West. So we must begin with the Greeks.[41]

It has been seen that the primitive answer to the question of the end of social control and so of law was simply that law was a device to keep the peace. The force of politically organized society was exerted to keep the peace. Whatever served to avert private vengeance and prevent private war was an instrument of justice. The ideal relation among men was a state of peace. Greek philosophy soon got beyond this conception and put in its place an idea of the ordering of society as a device to preserve the social *status quo*, to keep each man in his appointed groove and thus prevent friction with his fellows. The virtue on which Greek philosophers insist is *sophrosyne*, knowing the limits which nature (*i.e.*,

---

40. Pound, *The End of Law as Developed in Juristic Thought* (1914) 27 HARVARD LAW REVIEW, 605, 30 HARVARD LAW REVIEW, 201; id. *Twentieth-Century Ideas as to the End of Law*, HARVARD LEGAL ESSAYS (1934) 357–75; Yntema, *The Rational Basis of Legal Science* (1931) 31 COLUMBIA LAW REVIEW, 925, 934–55; Cairns, *Legal Philosophy from Plato to Hegel* (1949) 6.

41. 2 Berolzheimer, *System der Rechts- und Wirtschaftsphilosophie* (1905) §§ 13–20; Hildebrand, *Geschichte und System der Rechts- und Staatsphilosophie* (1860) §§ 1–121; Myers, *Political Ideas of the Greeks* (1927) lect. 4; McIlwain, *The Growth of Political Thought in the West* (1932) chaps. 1–3; Sauter, *Die philosophischen Grundlagen des Naturrechts* (1932) chaps. 1–2. Aristotle, *Nicomachean Ethics*, book 5, *Politics*, book 7; Plato, *Gorgias*, 470, 477, 504, *Republic*, books 1, 2, 4, *Laws*, books 3, 4, 6.

the ideal) fixes for human conduct and keeping within them. The vice against which they declaim is *hybris*, willful bound-breaking, willful transgression of the socially appointed bounds. Justice, accordingly, was regarded as maintenance of the social *status quo*, and philosophers were busied in planning an ideal society in which every one was put in the right place, to be kept there thenceforth by the law.[42]

The Pythagoreans spoke of anarchy as the greatest evil since it left the social order without security. They compared justice to medicine, holding that the legislative and judicial functions, whereby the life of the state is kept in a normal course, were the analogues of hygiene and medicine, whereby the normal course of bodily life is secured or restored.[43] We are told that Heraclitus held that self-will was to be suppressed and said that the citizen should fight more strenuously for the law which achieved this than for the walls of the city.[44] Plato, too, considered lawlessness the greatest of evils,[45] and compared the function of justice under the laws as the life of the state to that of hygiene and medicine in the individual bodily life.[46]

Plato brings out the idea fully. Speaking of the ideal state he says: "Shall we not find that in such a city . . . a shoemaker is only a shoemaker and not a pilot along with shoemaking; and that the husbandman is only a husbandman, and not a judge along with husbandry; and that a soldier is a soldier and not a moneymaker besides; and all others in the same way."[47] Again he says: "But when the cobbler, or any other man whom nature designed to be a trader . . . attempts to force his way into the class of warriors, or a warrior into that of legislators or guardians, for which he is unfitted; or when one man is trader, legislator and guardian all in one, then I think you will agree with me that . . . this meddling of

---

42. E.g., the doctrine of the Pythagoreans that every citizen should have his special place assigned to him. Aristoxenus, according to Stobaeus, Florilegium, 43, 49.
43. Iamblichus, *Vit. Pythag.* 101.
44. *Diogenes Laertius*, ix, 2.
45. *Gorgias*, 470, 477, 504.
46. *Ibid.* 477–78.
47. *Republic*, iii, 397–98.

the one with the other is the ruin of the state. . . . As there are three distinct classes, any meddling of them with one another or the change of one into the other, is the greatest harm to the state and may most justly be termed evil doing."[48]

In Plato's ideal state the individual is not to find his own level for himself by free competition with his fellows. Every one is to be assigned to the class for which he is determined to be best fitted. Then there will be a perfect harmony and unity both in the state and in every individual.[49] As Grote puts it, in the Republic and the Laws, "king *nomos*" (a broader word than law, including all social control) is "to fix by unchangeable authority what shall be the orthodox type of character and suppress all the varieties of emotion and intellect except such as will run into a few predetermined molds."[50] Hence a universal genius, who could not be kept to his assigned place was not to be tolerated.[51]

The Stoic doctrine of conformity to nature or conformity to universal reason came to much the same practical result.[52]

Aristotle believed that the individual man, apart from the state, became the "most malignant and dangerous of beasts" so that he could "realize his moral destiny only in the state."[53] Accordingly, interests to be protected could exist only between those who were free and equal before the state.[54] Justice demanded an unanimity in which there would be no violation of mutual claims or spheres of authority, *i.e.*, in which

---

48. *Ibid.* 434.

49. *Ibid.* Elsewhere in the *Republic* we are told that justice consists in every part of the soul fulfilling its own proper function and not taking up the function of another. *Ibid.* 433a, 433c, d, e. Also that "justice is doing one's own business and not being a busybody." *Ibid.* 433.

50. 2 Grote, *Plato*, 138.

51. *Republic*, 398a.

52. Epictetus, *Diss.* ii, 5, § 4; ii, 10, § 1; iv, 7, § 2. The Stoic τὸκαθηκο, which might well be rendered duty, consists in denying the individual natural impulses. In ethical theory this might lead to the view of Epictetus that one should not be a citizen. In political and juristic theory it led to repression of individual self-assertion. *See* 1 Erdmann, *History of Philosophy* (Hough's transl. 1910) 190–91.

53. *Politics*, i, 1, 9.

54. *Ibid.* i, 13; i, 3–7; iii, 1; iii, 4–5; iv, 11.

each would keep within his appointed sphere;[55] and right and law took account primarily of relations of inequality, in which individuals are treated in proportion to their work, and only secondarily of relations of equality.[56] The exhortations of St. Paul in which he calls upon every one to do his duty in the class in which he finds himself placed bring out this same idea.[57]

The Greek way of thinking followed the substitution of the city-state political organization of society for the kin organization. The organized kindred were still powerful. An aristocracy of the kin-organized and kin-conscious, on the one hand, and a *demos* of those who had lost or severed their ties of kinship, or had come from without, on the other hand, were in continual struggle for political mastery. Moreover, the politically ambitious individual and the masterful aristocrat were constantly threatening the none too stable political organization through which the general security got a precarious protection. The chief social want, which no other social institution could satisfy, was the security of social institutions.

Roman lawyers undertook to determine the authorities, liberties, and capacities involved in legal personality and position before the law.[58] In doing this they were guided by the Greek ideal of the legal order as a preserving of the social *status quo*. As Courcelle-Seneuil puts it, the Roman ideal was a stationary society, corrected from time to time by a reversion to the ancient type.[59] Cicero finds the basis of social control not

---

55. *Nicomachean Ethics*, viii, 7, 2–4. *See* especially § 3: "For equality in proportion to merit holds the first place in justice."

56. *Ibid.* viii, 6. Compare Plato, *Laws*, 757.

57. Eph. 5:22 ff. and 6:1–5. *See also* 1 Peter, 3:1–6, and compare St. Paul's Epistle to Philemon, sending back the runaway slave Onesimus, although entreating the master to treat him as a brother.

58. 2 Berolzheimer, *System der Rechts- und Wirtschaftsphilosophie* (1905) §§ 17–20; Hildebrand, *Geschichte und System der Rechts- und Staatsphilosophie* (1860) §§ 131–35.

SOURCES are: Cicero, *De republica, De legibus, De officiis*; Seneca, *De clementia, De otio, De beneficiis*, iii; *Institutes* of Justinian, i, 1; *Digest* of Justinian, i, 1.

59. Courcelle-Seneuil's parallel between the Roman and the nineteenth-century ideal may be found in English in Guyot, *Principles of Social Economy* (Leppington's

in enactment but in the moral spirit which is intrinsic in nature, *i.e.*, in the ideal of things.[60] But we must not confound this *lex naturae* or *lex naturalis* with the natural law of the law-of-nature school in modern times. Its basis is in the conception that everything has a natural (*i.e.*, ideal) principle to be deduced from its characteristics and ends. By this is meant adaptation to human ends. Thus it is not the nature of a horse to run wild but to be owned by a man. From this *naturalis ratio* a natural law could be reached. This natural law involves an appeal to substance from form; an appeal to rational principles against traditional forms and arbitrary rules.[61] The natural law of the seventeenth century, appealing to the reason of the individual against authority, and the natural law of the eighteenth century, appealing to the reason of the individual against society and the state, are very different things. A cardinal principle of Cicero's theory of justice is respect for rights acquired under the social order.[62]

This idea appears also in the formula handed down in the Institutes of Justinian: "Justice is the set and constant purpose which gives to every one his own."[63] In other words, the social system has defined certain things as belonging to each individual. Justice consists in rendering him those things and in not interfering with his having and using them within the defined limits. Another formula in the Institutes of Justinian expresses the same idea. "The precepts of right and law are these: to live honorably, not to injure another, to give to every one his own."[64] This formula would reduce the whole end of law to three functions: (1) Maintenance of decency and decorum in men's outward acts, (2) securing of individual interests of personality, (3) securing of individual interests of

---

transl. 2 ed. 1892) 299. *See also* Courcelle-Seneuil, *Préparation à l'étude du droit* (1887) 99, 396.

60. *De republica*, ii, 1; *De legibus*, ii, 4.

61. *See e.g.*, Gaius, i, § 190, iii, § 98.

62. "All justice (*aequitas*) is destroyed if one is not permitted to hold his own." *De officiis*, ii, 22, 78.

63. *Inst.* i, 1. pr.

64. *Inst.* i, 1, 5.

substance. Savigny's much criticized interpretation of this formula seems quite warranted and brings out its point for our purposes. The first precept, to live honorably, that is, to preserve moral worth in one's own person so far as external acts go, is represented in the legal systems by the doctrines as to good faith in transactions, by the rules as to illegality of corrupt bargains, and by the various doctrines which recognize *boni mores* and attach consequences to violations thereof. The second precept, not to injure another, the respecting of another's personality as such, is represented by those rules and doctrines which give practical effect to the individual interest of personality. The third precept, to render to every one his own, that is, to respect the acquired rights of other men, is represented by the rules and doctrines which secure individual interests of substance.[65]

But the insistence on good faith in the first precept maintains the security of transactions and also secures interests of substance, since in an advanced economic order credit is fundamental and a large part of wealth consists in promised advantages. Taken as a whole, the formula in the Institutes of Justinian is a juristic development of the Greek idea of the end of the legal order, namely, the idea that its end is to maintain harmoniously the social *status quo*. It is a further development of the idea of the beginnings of law, the idea of a device to keep the peace. Peace is so fundamental in civilized society resting on division of labor that we must recognize that this original idea cannot be lost sight of. Nor can we ignore the Greek development of it. Both contain a good part of the truth. But we have not so much added to them as found new and broader ideas which include them and much more besides. It may be significant that with the rise of the welfare or service state in the present century, the multiplication of bureaus, and increasing pressure of administration upon the individual, the idea of the importance of political and social institutions in comparison with the individual life has been

---

65. 1 Savigny, *System des heutigen römischen Rechts*, § 59, pp. 407–10. For other views as to the interpretation of these precepts, *see* Affolter, *Das römische Institutionensystem*, 421–50 (1897); Donati, *Il primo precetto del diritto "vivere con honesta"* (1926).

leading to formulas defining the legal order as a peaceable ordering and so coming back in some measure to the Greek idea.[66]

On the breakdown of the Roman empire in the West, Germanic law brought back for a time the primitive conception of merely keeping the peace, with its concomitant ideas of buying off vengeance, of a tariff of compositions and of regulating private war. There is little of consequence for the present purpose until after the revival of the study of Roman law in Italy in the twelfth century. Moreover, when legal development begins the ruling idea is authority. Not only did the medieval universities, from which the law of Continental Europe has come, take the *Corpus Iuris Civilis*, the body of Roman law as given legislative form by Justinian, to be authoritatively binding, so that it could only be interpreted and not added to, but in philosophy, as was pointed out in the second lecture authority was taken as a ground of reason.[67] Thus reason could be established from church doctrine or from the received authority of Aristotle who to the Middle Ages was the philosopher. Hence the idea of justice developed in Greek philosophy and Roman law was received as a matter of course.[68] In the Middle Ages, as in antiquity, we see the idea of social control as an agency of keeping the peace succeeded by the idea of an agency of maintaining the social *status quo*. To Thomas Aquinas, as to Cicero, to the classical Roman jurists, and to Justinian, the principle of justice is to give every one his own.[69] What is one's own is determined by the social order.[70]

---

66. Kohler, *Philosophy of Law* (transl. by Albrecht 1914) 4, 476; id. *Einführung in die Rechtswissenschaft* (5 ed. 1919) § 1; Levi, *Contributi ad una teoria filosofica dell' ordine giuridico* (1914) 234–35.

67. 2 Erdmann, *History of Philosophy* (Hough's transl. 1910) 299.

68. "No feature of the Greek theory was more elaborately developed by the scholastics than that which set up unity and permanence as the prime criteria of excellence in political organization." Dunning, *Political Theory, Ancient and Medieval* (1913) 292.

69. *Summa Theologica*, i–ii, qu. 58, art. 1. *See* the combination of theology with the authority of Justinian's *Institutes* in Azo, *Summa institutionum*, § 19 on *Inst.* i, 1, *justitia quid*, in 1563 ed. p. 1069.

70. *See also* the doctrines of the glossators with respect to the nature of private property. 2 Carlyle, *History of Medieval Political Theory* (1903) 42–49.

There was good reason, apart from authority, why the Middle Ages received the Roman version of the Greek ideal of maintaining the social *status quo*. The medieval situation was very much like that to which the Greek philosophers addressed their theory. In the Greek city-state there was a perennial conflict between oligarchy and democracy. The state was looked to to save the community from anarchy and permit the effective division of labor upon which a civilized society must rest. Philosophy addressed itself to this problem, and Roman law in the era of the civil wars found a usable theory at hand. In the same way when a new development of law began in the later Middle Ages the law once more came in contact with philosophy when both began to be studied in the universities. Following an era of anarchy and disunion and violence men wished for order and organization and peace. Medieval society often swung back and forth between arbitrary despotism, confusion or anarchy because of the absence or retarded development of effective instruments of government. As it has been put: "The history of medieval society constantly impresses upon us the conviction that the real difference between a barbarous and a civilized political system lies in the fact that the latter has an almost automatically working administrative and judicial system while the former is dependent upon the chance of the presence of some exceptionally competent and clear-sighted individual ruler."[71] There was need of a philosophy which would bolster up authority and rationalize men's desire to impose a legal yoke upon society. Again just as in Greece social control was in transition to a differentiated law, in the Middle Ages the time was one of transition from the primitive law of the Germanic peoples to a strict law through reception of the Roman law from the universities as authoritative legislation of a Christian emperor. A strict law grew up through this receiving of the Roman law as codified by Justinian or through compilation of Germanic customary law more or less after the Roman model, as in the north of France, or through declaration of the customary law through reported decisions of strong central courts, as in England.

71. 3 *id.* (1916) 31.

Scholastic philosophy was exceptionally adapted to the needs of such a time. Its method was one of dialectic development of authoritative, unchallengeable premises. It relied upon formal logic. It sought through logical deduction from premises having the authority of reason to put reason as a foundation under legal and political authority. It met the needs of the time so fully that it enabled teachers in the universities to put the Roman law of Justinian in a form to be received and administered in the Europe of nine centuries after him. They made the gloss (standard teachers' interpretation) into law in place of Justinian's text and made over much of it, as it had to be made over if it was to fit a wholly different social order. But the method of formal logical development of absolute and unquestioned premises made it appear that nothing had been done but work out the logical implications of an authoritative text. It was easy to receive the law expounded by Bartolus when it was believed to be the logical unfolding of the binding legislation of Justinian.

Fortescue (about 1468) applied the scholastic method to the rules of English common law in its stage of strict law. He assumed that these rules were the principles (starting points for reasoning) of which he read in the commentators on Aristotle and that they were comparable to the axioms in geometry. The time had not yet come to call rules or principles or axioms in question. The need was to rationalize and satisfy men's desire to be governed by fixed rules and to reconcile, at least in appearance, the change and growth which are inevitable in all law with the need men felt of having fixed, unchangeable, authoritative rules.

In a time when want of efficient government was felt acutely a conception of law as existing to maintain the social *status quo*, the social order as it was or at least as men were trying to make it, could serve as the ideal.

In another respect also maintaining the social *status quo* was eminently adapted to medieval society. Medieval society was relationally organized, organized about the relation of lord and man with reciprocal duties of protection and service. Establishment of strong central administrative and judicial systems was still in the future. The national idea, establishment of the nation as sovereign state and paramountcy of the law of that state over all other agencies of social control, belongs to the sixteenth century. Security was found in the feudal relation until later it could be found in the political relation of sovereign and subject or citizen and state. The feudal system was formative at the time of the dissolution of the Carolingian empire and the confusion due to invasion of the Northmen and the Magyars. Hence it took its final form in a time without well-organized general governments such as to afford adequate security to the individual. As Carlyle says: "In the absence of strong central or national authorities, men had to turn for protection to the nearest power which seemed to be capable of rendering this."[72] Maintaining the social structure was the guarantee of the general security.

But in politics at the end of the Middle Ages, Europe was in transition to an era of strong centralized national governments. Also scholastic philosophy was giving way and was soon superseded by the rationalism which held the ground till the end of the eighteenth century. Medieval thought had begun with an entire subordination of philosophy to theology. It had moved to a harmony of the two which reaches its full development in Thomas Aquinas. With him the effort of scholasticism to be both philosophy and theology seemed to have been achieved. But as in the earlier period more and more was withdrawn from the domain of reason and assigned to that of faith, after the harmony achieved by Thomas Aquinas, in which reason and faith were made to establish the same results by different methods, negative criticism set in and it seemed that scholasticism had failed to rationalize the doctrines of the church. In truth Aristotle's method did not fit a subject for which it was not devised. Christianity was not to be forced into an alien form. When later jurisprudence was set free from theology and law from Justinian, ideas of the end of law could be adjusted to new social, economic, and political conditions.

Except for the theological-philosophical version of natural law, the Middle Ages added nothing of moment to juristic theory. The view of antiquity as to the end of the legal order was accepted. But the way was

72. *Ibid.* 75.

being prepared through philosophy for a new conception of justice which developed in the sixteenth and seventeenth centuries.

Transition marks the era of the Reformation. The great jurists of the Humanist school, which superseded the Commentators and their scholastic construction of a strict law, were Protestants.[73]

For the jurist the significance of the Reformation is to be found in the change from the Roman idea of a universal empire and hence a universal law to the Germanic idea of a territorial state with a national law. In law the Reformation marks a breaking over of Germanic individualism long kept back by Roman authority.[74] Hence, so far as jurisprudence is concerned, the Reformation is a period of clearing away in which the ground is prepared for the constructive period of the seventeenth century through the separation of philosophy, jurisprudence, and politics from theology and the establishment of a science of politics. The main purpose of the Protestant jurist-theologians[75] was to throw over the authority of the church and set up the authority of the state. Accordingly, the most significant feature of their work for the jurist is their insistence on a national rather than a universal law; their insistence on replacing the universal empire of Roman law and canon law by the civil law of each state. We must bear in mind what Beseler calls Germanic *kleinstaatismus.*[76] This led to an ideal of local law; not even national, much less universal. The legal order was to rest on the authority of the divinely

73. Alciatus (1492–1550), Cujacius (1522–1590), Donellus (1527–1591).

74. "Authority is in itself a Roman concept." Werner Jaeger, *The Problem of Authority and the Crisis of the Greek Spirit,* in *Authority and the Individual,* HARVARD TERCENTENARY PUBLICATION (1937) 241; Heinze, 60 HERMES (1925) 348–66.

75. 2 Berolzheimer, *System der Rechts- und Wirtschaftsphilosophie* (1905) § 24; 1 Hinrichs, *Geschichte der Rechts- und Staatsprincipien seit der Reformation* (1848) 1–6; Bluntschli, *Geschichte der neuren Staatswissenschaft* (1881) chap. 3; Gierke, *Althusius und die Entwicklung der natürrechtlichen Staatstheorien,* 18–49, 143–62, 321; Gumplowicz, *Geschichte der Staatstheorien* (1903) §§ 60–61, 64–65, 68, 75.

SOURCES are: Oldendorp, *Iuris naturalis gentium et ciuilis* Σισαγωγή (1539); Hemmingius, *De lege naturae apodictica methodus* (1562); Winckler, *Principiorum iuris libri V* (1615); Johannes Althusius, *Politica methodice digesta* (1603) translated with introduction by Friedrich (1932).

76. *Volksrecht und Juristenrecht* (1843) chap. 4.

ordained state not on an authoritative universal law. Winckler tells us that *lex* and *ius* are cause and effect, *constituens* and *constitutum*, maker and made.[77] This flowed naturally from the break with authority which substituted private interpretation by the individual, each for himself, for authoritative universal interpretation of the Scriptures by the church. The exigencies of this demand for private interpretation led to a claim of independence for the state, for the family, and for the natural man. The logical result in jurisprudence was the opposition of the abstract man to society which developed in the juristic thinking of the eighteenth century. When the starting point of the science of law shifted from society to the individual man, from the general security to the individual life, jurists began to give up the ideal of the social *status quo*. Political organization of society had become effective and paramount. Both the relational-feudal organization and the religious-political organization of the Middle Ages were passing. A new ideal, an ideal of liberty, was growing up.

But the reformers themselves did not perceive the atomistic implications, with respect to jurisprudence and politics, of a world of self-sufficient individuals. Indeed, the need of opposing the state to the church, because the popes had claimed to absolve Christians from allegiance to rulers who were at difference with the church, led the reformers to a political doctrine of passive obedience. Luther and Melanchthon were very severe in their attitude toward rebellious peasants who sought by force to escape from the serfdom imposed on them by the laws of the time.[78] Moreover, the period was one of transition from the strict law to the stage of equity and natural law, which identified law and morals. The strong ethical element in the jurists of the Reformation, and the emphasis which the reformers put on abstaining from sinful conduct rather than on repentance therefor, cooperated with this identification of law and morals to postpone the conclusion that the in-

77. *Principiorum iuris libri* V, tit. 2, cap. 1 (1615).
78. *See* especially the quotations from Luther in Figgis, *Studies of Political Thought from Gerson to Grotius* (1907) 241.

dividual conscience was the sole measure of obligation to obey the law. Even if the Christian needed only the spirit for a guide, the rest of the world needed the secular sword of justice, and obedience to Caesar was expressly enjoined in Scripture. Such, at any rate, is the argument in Luther's tract on secular authority.[79]

In its implications the doctrine of the reformers led to the juristic theory of the eighteenth century. But there was much that had first to be cleared away. This clearing process begins with Melanchthon, who argues that the whole of natural law may be deduced from the Ten Commandments and right reasoning as to the nature of man.[80] This is the twofold basis of natural law referred to *ante* in the second lecture. It has an interesting subsequent history. Grotius, after adopting the divorce of jurisprudence from theology, reverts to the theological and puts natural law on two bases: (1) eternal reason, (2) the will of God who wills only reason.[81] Blackstone takes from Grotius this twofold basis but joins to it the Aristotelian distinction between things which are right or wrong by nature, where the positive law is only declaratory, and things which are indifferent by nature, where the positive law finds its proper field.[82] Thus a great part of the law has lost its theological prop. With James Wilson, Grotius' doctrine is rested on a proposition that God "is under a glorious necessity of not contradicting himself" and so, in effect, of conforming to the exigencies of human reason.[83] Croce's comment on Vico's critique of Grotius is apt: "Vico did not know what to make of a God set side by side with other sources of morality, or set above them as a superfluous source for the sources."[84]

79. 11 Luther's *Werke, Kritische Gesammtausgabe* (1883) 245, 252. Compare 11 Melanchthon, *Opera*, ed. Bretschneider and Bindseil, 451 (1834–60).

80. 16 *Opera*, 424 ff. *See* 1 Hinrichs, *Geschichte der Rechts- und Staatsprincipien seit der Reformation* (1848) 18–19.

81. Grotius, *De iure belli ac pacis*, Prolegomena (1625) §§ 11, 12.

82. 1 Blackstone, *Commentaries* (1765) 40–43.

83. 1 Wilson's *Works* (1804) 140–41.

84. Croce, *The Philosophy of Giambattista Vico*, transl. by Collingwood (1913) 94.

The process of clearing away goes forward with Oldendorp in whom we find the beginning of the attempts at systematic philosophical statement of the bases of law which came to be called systems of natural law.[85] It makes a significant, perhaps decisive, stride when Hemmingsen attempts complete emancipation of jurisprudence from theology, telling us that divine revelation is not necessary to a knowledge of natural law,[86] and asserting that the firm and necessary ground of a legal system is to be found in nature (*i.e.*, rational ideal) and end of the law,[87] and asserting that the ideas of right and wrong may be worked out by reason from the nature (*i.e.*, ideal) of men "without the prophetic and apostolic writings."[88] It gains ground when Winckler seeks to carry out the juristic program outlined by Hemmingsen.[89] On another side it is definitely achieved when Althusius, taking up the idea of a contract between the ruler and the ruled, which had been a controversial weapon in the controversies of temporal sovereigns with the church during the Middle Ages, uses it as the basis of political theory and founds the ethicalpolitical natural law which is to govern political thought for the next two centuries.[90]

No direct change in the idea of the end of the legal order took place in the time of the Protestant jurist-theologians. Luther thought of external peace and order as the purpose for which law exists.[91] Melanchthon found the basis of securing acquired rights in the commandment "Thou shalt not steal," and defined liberty as the condition "in which each is permitted to keep his own and citizens are not compelled to do anything

85. Oldendorp, *Iuris naturalis gentium et ciuilis* Σι'σαγωγη' (1539).

86. Hemmingius, *De lege naturae apodictica methodus* (1562). The passage referred to is in the preface. Kaltenborn, *Die Vorläufer des Hugo Grotius* (1848) pt. II, 31.

87. *Id.* 1564 ed. C. p. 2; Kaltenborn, pt. II, 32–33.

88. *Ibid.* Q. p. 7; Kaltenborn, pt. II, 43–44.

89. *Principiorum iuris libri* V (1615).

90. *Politica methodice digesta atque exemplis sacris et profanis illustrata* (1603).

91. *Tract von weltlicher Oberkeit,* 11 *Werke* (Weimar ed. 1883) 245, 253. *See also* 11 Melanchthon, *Opera,* 435.

contrary to principles of right and to what is honorable."[92] It will be noted that this is not at all the nineteenth-century idea of liberty. To Melanchthon justice, the end of law, required respect for acquisitions and respect for personality.

92. 16 *Opera*, 424 ff. *See* 1 Hinrichs, *Geschichte der Rechts- und Staatsprincipien seit der Reformation* (1848) 18–19.

SIX

Promotion of Free Self-Assertion

1. The Sixteenth to the Eighteenth Century

In an exposition of the radical change in juristic thought, beginning in the sixteenth-century jurists everywhere, of the ideal of a society promoting and assuring a maximum of free individual self-assertion instead of the idea which had been developed in Greek philosophy and Roman law and had governed in the Middle Ages, three points have to be noted at the outset: (1) One is the setting free of philosophy from theology and from the formal logical method of the scholastic theologian-jurists, and consequent primacy of reason and scientific inquiry. (2) Next there is the paramountcy of the positive law of the state as an agency of social control after the rise of the centralized national state in the sixteenth century. (3) Third, and as men think today, we must see chiefly behind the phenomena of legal and of political thinking another profound change in adaptation to the economic conditions of an era of individual opportunity upon the breakdown of the closed relational society of the Middle Ages. The discovery of the new world created new opportunities everywhere. Men were eager to take advantage of these opportunities and sought to be free to do so rather than to be secure in what they had under the closed relational social organization and restricted system of duties in feudal society. Rights came to be insisted on rather than duties. Freedom of competitive acquisition got the emphasis instead of reciprocal duties of protection and service.

Appeal to reason in support of authority led to appeal to reason against authority, and that helped toward a new conception in philosophy, in theology, in politics and ultimately in juristic theory. As a result the legal order came to be regarded as existing to secure a maximum of free individual self-assertion. This movement went along with the social, political, and economic changes which mark the transition to the modern world. It develops along with the revival of learning and resulting faith in reason to become faith in individual reason. It develops along with the emancipation of philosophy and rise of what became the sciences of today with the consequences of consciousness of the powers of the free inquiring mind. It goes along with the rise of nations, Spain, France, England, Austria, leading to ideas of national or local laws to be developed with reference to local situations instead of universal enactments of a universal authority. In the era of discovery and colonization it is fostered by pioneer adventurous individualism. With the rise of trade and commerce and consequent breakdown of local economic restrictions it develops competition where a relationally organized society had relied on relational division of labor. With the dissolution of the rational system it develops faith in individual free activity. The movement culminates in the nineteenth century. But the beginnings of the change are a long way back in philosophy in Erigena's doctrine that reason enabled the fathers of the church to discover what they laid down with authority[1] and in the attempt of Anselm to prove to the unbeliever by reason, as if there had been no revelation, the truth of the Scriptures and writings of the fathers of the church.[2]

Another factor was introduced by the revival of natural law and the consequent appeal to a divinely ordained fundamental law against the positive law.[3] Parallel with the theological-philosophical version of natural law an idea of a fundamental law developed as a political-legal doc-

---

1. Joannes Scotus Erigena (d. 875) *De divisione naturae*, I, 69.

2. St. Anselm (d. 1109) *Cur Deus homo*, preface.

3. "A law of nature is a rule of reason; wherefore a human law partakes of the reason of law in so far as it is derived from a law of nature. And if they disagree in anything, there is no law, but a corruption of law." R. Suarez, *Repetitiones* (1558) 272–73.

trine. Historically it is an idea of Germanic law.[4] Throughout the Germanic law books in the Middle Ages, says Heusler, there runs the idea that law is "a quest of the creature for the justice and truth of his Creator."[5] It rejected all notion of arbitrary will. The doctrine that the will of the sovereign had the force of a law came from Justinian's law books.[6] It came into Continental public law with the rise of the centralized royal government in France in the sixteenth century[7] and spread to general legal theory along with the reception of Roman law. The Germanic conception was instead the one expressed in the phrase attributed to Bracton — that the King ought not to be under any man, but under God and the law.[8]

The Germanic polity postulated a fundamental law above and beyond mere will. It conceived that those who wielded authority should be held to account for the conformity of their acts to that fundamental law. For example, in the Salic law where a creditor has duly appealed to the count for justice and the count, with no sufficient reason fails to act, he has to answer with his life or redeem himself with his *wergeld*, that is, he is liable to a feud, a feud may lawfully be waged against him, or must buy it off with the legally fixed value of his life. But if he does act pursuant to the appeal and goes beyond enforcement of what is due, again, he must answer with his life or redeem himself with his *wergeld*.[9] It is only in England that this conception developed as the basis of public law; and this development has been pushed to the furthest point in American constitutional law. In England three things led to the

4. Perhaps I ought to explain that by 'Germanic' they refer to non-Roman legal and political ideas and legal precepts in the Middle Ages.

5. Heusler, *Institutionen des deutschen Privatrechts* (1885) § 1.

6. *Quod principi placuit legis habet vigorem*, Inst. i, 2, 6; Dig. i, 4, 1. Note however that the word is *lex*, rule of law, not *ius*, which is right-and-law.

7. *See* Brissaud, *History of French Public Law* (transl. by Garner, 1915) § 346.

8. Bracton, *De legibus et consuetudinibus Angliae*, fol. 74, quoted by Coke in Prohibitions del Roy, 12 Co. 63 (1612). Bracton's treatise was written between 1250 and 1258. As to the authenticity of the passage quoted, *see* Maitland, *Bracton's Notebook* (1887) 29, 33; McIlwain, *The High Court of Parliament* (1910) 101, 103.

9. Salic Law, tit. 50, § 3.

common-law doctrine of the supremacy of law: (1) The establishment in the thirteenth century of strong central courts, purporting to administer the common custom of the whole realm, (2) the strong central administrative power of the king and the central organization and authority of the common-law courts administering justice in his name, and (3) the medieval formulation of the feudal duties of the king toward his tenants-in-chief.[10] These afforded an opportunity for the evolution of a legal doctrine of the legal duties and responsibilities of those who wield governmental powers. Taken up by Coke in the seventeenth-century controversies between the courts and the crown, this doctrine was fused with the conception of natural law in American constitutional law in the eighteenth century. Juristic thought of the seventeenth and eighteenth centuries derives from the medieval theological-philosophical natural law. But both the revived natural law of the later Middle Ages and the Germanic fundamental law served to undermine the received Greek-Roman ideal of maintaining the social *status quo*. Where that had been used to criticize legal institutions and doctrines and precepts, now the ideal itself was subjected to the scrutiny of reason or to critique in terms of the fundamental higher law. Where men had thought in terms of authority and duties they began to think in terms of liberty and rights.

Maintaining the stability of social institutions had for its basic ideas authority and duty — the authority of those who had the function of upholding the social order and the duty of those over whom the authority is imposed by the social order. The downfall of authority begins when reason is employed to prop it up and is assured when reason assumes to take its place entirely under the eighteenth-century law-of-nature school. Superseding of authority by reason began with the Protestant jurist-theologian who, however, still taught maintaining the social *status quo* as the end of law. In the feudal mode of thought there were reciprocal duties of lord and man, of ruler and ruled. When the idea of liberty grew strong with the emancipation of the individual from the restrictions of feudal relation society, the idea of reciprocal duties gave

10. Adams, *The Origin of the English Constitution* (1905) chap. 12; Pound, *The Spirit of the Common Law* (1921) 25–26.

way to one of duties as correlative not to other duties but to rights. The beginnings of this were the work of the Spanish jurist-theologians.[11]

Just as Comte, in a period of conspicuous development of the physical sciences, thought of the universe as governed by the principles of mathematics and of physics, and the nineteenth-century sociologists, in the period of Darwin's influence, thought of it as governed by the principles of biology, the Catholic writers of the counter reformation thought of it as governed by the principles of the then rising science of jurisprudence. A theological-philosophical jurisprudence had been taught in the universities alongside of the teaching of law since the twelfth century. Moreover, a generation before the Spanish jurist-theologians wrote, the Humanists, the French School at Bourges, had applied the spirit of the Renaissance to the study of Roman law.[12] Accordingly, in insisting upon the Roman idea of universality the jurists of the Counter Reformation did so in a new way and upon a new basis. The organization of the church, its system of church law and its penitential system, had tended in the hands of clerical writers to give a legal color to both ethics and politics. The spread of Roman law over Continental Europe had in fact made law all but universal. A Catholic jurist, therefore, was predisposed to a legal view of the world, as Thomas Aquinas had taken a legal view of the universe,[13] and a Romanist could vouch everyday fact for a universal view of law. But neither of these views could be maintained longer upon mere authority. Moreover, the separateness of states was no less a fact than the universality of Roman law. It was necessary, therefore, to reconcile the general authority of Roman and canon law, as the common law of Christendom, with the independence and equality of separate states. To effect this reconciliation, the Spanish writers turned to the idea of natural law and sought to join to a theory of

11. Figgis, *Studies of Political Thought from Gerson to Grotius* (1907) lect. 6; Westlake, *Chapters on the Principles of International Law* (1894) 25–28; Scott, *On the Spanish Origin of International Law* (1928).

Sources: Soto, *De iustitia et iure* (1589); Suarez, *De legibus ac Deo legislatore* (1619).

12. 1 Continental Legal History Series, *General Survey* (1913) 147, 154, 252–59.

13. E.g., the *lex aeterna*, the reason of the divine wisdom governing the whole universe. *Summa Theologica*, i, 2, qq. 92–95.

independent, equal states a theory of natural law from which all rules of justice of every description derive their binding force and of which Roman law and canon law are but expressions within their respective fields.

To the Spanish jurist-theologians the law of each state was not an isolated phenomenon, it was a phase of a universal principle by which all things were governed. This appears particularly in the treatise of Suarez on laws and on God as a legislator. Thus he says: "For it appears that the reason of every one has the force of law at least to the extent of the dictates of natural law. Therefore, at least in natural law it is not a necessary condition that it be enacted by public authority."[14] Again he says: "It is of the reason and essence of law that it prescribes what is just. The assertion is not only certain in religion but clear in natural reason."[15] In his treatise there is at first sight no practical distinction between natural law and positive law. Legalist ethics and ethical law go hand in hand. The actual Spanish law, doctrines of the Roman law which he thinks should be, although they are not, in force in Spain, practical morality and the dictates of reason and conscience combine in a universal system. Yet Suarez saw the insufficiency of reason to demonstrate to each man all the rules required for organized society and hence laid down that society might supply the deficiency by declaratory legislation and by customs not in contravention of nature.[16] The identification of law and morals is obviously an incident of the period of infusion of morals into the strict law which was in full vigor at the moment. But the new version of universality was an original contribution of the first magnitude. For one thing it made international law possible. If international law was the work of the law-of-nature school after Grotius, it had its roots in the latter part of the century before and the Catholic jurists of the Counter Reformation were first among its forerunners. Our chief concern, however, is with their relation to the abstract individualist idea of

14. Suarez, *De legibus ac Deo legislatore*, i, 8, § 1.
15. *Ibid.* i, 9, § 2.
16. *Ibid.* ii, 19, § 9, i, 8, § 2, xii, 13. *See* Westlake, *Chapters on the History of International Law* (1899) 25–28.

legal justice which began to develop in the seventeenth century and culminated in the nineteenth century.

A foundation of a new science of law was laid by reconciling the modern and the medieval, by recognizing the political fact of national law and adjusting it to the medieval ideals of unity and the Germanic conception of law as an eternal verity. The skillful combination of modern ideas with conservatism which characterizes the work of the Jesuit jurists enabled them to effect this reconciliation. Law was eternal. Only it was not eternal because of the authority which imposed it (*i.e.*, the academically postulated empire) or by which it imposed itself, but because it expressed eternal principles of justice.[17] The old and the new were fitted to this conception. Recognizing the facts of the political world of their time, they conceived of individual states, and thence ultimately of individual men, as equal (in this departing from Aristotle), since states and men were able to direct themselves to conscious ends and thus their equality was a principle of justice. To a Spanish writer after the centralized absolutism achieved by Charles V, the analogy of state and individual man was palpable.[18] Holding to the idea of the unity and universality of law as a body of eternal principles, they were led to the conception of restraints by which this equality was maintained and in which it might be expressed. Two types of such restraints suggested themselves, restraints upon states and restraints upon individuals, and in an age of absolute personal sovereigns these types were taken to be generically one. The restraints upon states, limitations upon their activities which they might not overpass, since they were imposed by eternal principles, might fix (1) the limits of the activities of sovereigns in their relations with each other,[19] giving us what we now call international law, or (2) the limits of the activities of sovereigns in their relations with their subjects, giving us political theory.[20] The restraints upon individuals

17. Soto, *De iustitia et iure* (1589) i. q. 5, a. 2.

18. *See* Pound, *Philosophical Theory and International Law* (1923) 1 Bibliotheca Visseriana, 75, 76–80.

19. 1 Franciscus de Victoria, *Relectiones theologicae* (1557) 375 ff. *Cf.* 1 *id.* 359 ff.

20. Soto, *De iustitia et iure*, III, q. 3, a. 2; Suarez, *De legibus*, iii, 35, § 8; iii, 9, § 4; iii, 11. The argument for separation of powers in the passage last cited is noteworthy.

had the same basis in eternal principles of universal law and were of the same nature. They (3) fixed the limits of individual activity in the relations of individuals with each other, giving us juristic theory.[21] Accordingly in the next two centuries these three subjects are always taken up together. The treatises on the law of nature and of nations, characteristic of the seventeenth and eighteenth centuries, are treatises on international law, on politics, and on philosophical jurisprudence. The three were not separated until the nineteenth century.

Comparing the juristic theory so developed with the juristic theory of antiquity, it will be perceived that the conception of the end of law has undergone a fundamental change. The theory of antiquity thought of the legal order as a limiting of the activities of men in order to keep each in his appointed place and preserve the social order as it stands. The theory which begins with the Spanish jurist-theologians thinks, instead of a limiting of men's activities in the interest of other men's activities because all men have freedom of will and ability to direct themselves to conscious ends and so are equal. Thus instead of a regime of maintaining a *status quo*, the legal order begins to be thought of as a regime of maintaining a natural (*i.e.*, *ideal*) equality. But it is an equality of action not of condition.

We pass now to the seventeenth century.[22] It is usual to fix the date of a new era in the science of law by the appearance of the great work of Grotius in 1625. That book marks the beginning of the law-of-nature school of jurists which was dominant until the metaphysical jurispru-

21. Suarez, *De legibus* (1612) ii, 12.

22. 2 Berolzheimer, *System der Rechts- und Wirtschaftsphilosophie* (1905) §§ 25–27; 2 Stintzing, *Geschichte der deutschen Rechtswissenschaft* (1880–83) 1–111; Hinrichs, *Geschichte der Rechts- und Staatsprincipien seit der Reformation* (1848–52) I, 60–274, II, III, 1–318; Duff, *Spinoza's Political and Ethical Philosophy* (1903) chap. 22.

SOURCES: Grotius, *De iure belli ac pacis*, especially i, 1, 3–6, and 8–11 (1625); Pufendorf, *De iure naturae et gentium*, especially i, 7, §§ 6–17 (1672); Hobbes, *Leviathan*, chap. 15 (1651), id. *De cive*, especially tit. libertas (1642); Spinoza, *Tractatus theologico-politicus*, especially chap. 16 (1670); id. *Tractatus politicus*, especially chaps. 2, 4 (1678); id. *Ethica*, especially pt. V (1677); 1 Rutherforth, *Institutes of Natural Law*, 2 § 5 (1754).

dence following Kant. Such certainly has been the prevailing opinion. In almost all accounts of the history of jurisprudence Grotius stands out as marking a turning point.

But in recent years many have discounted that prevailing opinion. It is true that Grotius had notable forerunners in the theory of international law and that as one looks into the matter attentively he seems to have added little. It is true also that the divorce of jurisprudence from theology had been achieved before him. Likewise the theory of natural law which has gone by his name was almost if not quite full fledged before him. It is said that he did little more than state clearly and convincingly what was already at the very least in the air. Likewise in recent times even those who are of a liberal juristic creed and urge a renewed faith in creative legal science question the whole attitude and work of seventeenth- and eighteenth-century natural law and in consequence disparage Grotius. In part this is involved in the reaction against formal logical methods of jurisprudence and conceptions through which the legal science of the nineteenth-century maturity of law gave the law in action so many of the unhappy features of the strict law. In part also it has gone along with the renewed quest of individualization in the administration of justice involved in the bigness of things in an urban industrial society. That quest leads to a search for just results through magisterial feelings of right and justice and the individual conscience of the judge. Also the functional attitude characteristic of modern legal science has produced impatience of abstract formulas of justice, distrust of speculation as to the abstract justice of legal precepts, and suspicion of rationalist methods in every connection. In consequence both the right and the left of modern jurisprudence have little use for Grotius. The orthodox historical analytical jurisprudence regards the law of nature as definitely buried. The newer functional science of law thinks of a psychological natural law or a natural law grounded in the social sciences. But a book which has so long, so widely, and so profoundly affected both juristic thinking and the dogmatic law must have much more intrinsic quality than recent critics of Grotius have been willing to acknowledge. It is rather the alien spirit in the revolt against juristic logic as it was developed in the nineteenth-century maturity of law and the reaction from a rational development of legal dogma which has dictated the attitude of recent critics. Leaving international law wholly out of account Grotius was dominant in the literature of natural law well into the nineteenth century. In English exposition of the subject he is recognized as the chief authority from Blackstone (1765) to Lorimer (1860). He was one of the chief authorities recognized by the founders of our American polity, and his ideas are to be found everywhere in American books on public and constitutional law. Through Kent and Story his book entered into much of our thinking in more than one feature of equity and of commercial law. His theory of rights held the ground in one form or another until the middle of the nineteenth century, and however much seventeenth- and eighteenth-century natural law may have been repudiated by historical jurists of the nineteenth century, the Grotian theory was an ingredient of the first importance of what is still the orthodox theory of legal rights.[23]

As Grotius expounded the new doctrine it had two sides. On the one hand, there was a theory of limitations upon human activities, imposed by reason in view of human nature. On the other hand, there was a theory of moral qualities inherent in human nature, or natural rights, demonstrated by reason as deductions, from human nature, *i.e.*, from the ideal of a man. The first had been propounded already by his forerunners. But whereas in Suarez the divine lawmaker has established the eternal and universal principles, Grotius makes reason a sufficient measure of all obligation and basis of all limitations.[24] In part this follows from the definite breaking with theology in which he carries forward the ideas of the Protestant jurists of the Reformation. In part it is an echo of the Renaissance. As Westlake puts it, "the boundless intellectual confidence of that time" led the men of the Renaissance "to regard the dic-

23. *See* Pound, *Grotius in the Science of Law* (1925) 19 AMERICAN JOURNAL OF INTERNATIONAL LAW, 685.
24. *Prolegomena,* §§ 8–16.

tates of natural law as capable of clear and exhaustive enumeration."[25] In part also it is a phase of the infusion of morals into law in the stage of equity and natural law. The main current of seventeenth-century thought followed Grotius, and in the eighteenth century Blackstone made his ideas familiar in England and America with important consequences for Anglo-American juristic and political thinking. For at the very time that the common law under the leadership of Coke had established its doctrine of the supremacy of law and had turned the feudal duties of the paramount landlord toward his tenants into something very like legal duties of the crown toward the subject, a juristic theory of fundamental limitations upon the activities of states, of rulers, and of individuals, dictated by eternal reason, had grown up to furnish the scientific explanation.

As has been said, Grotius and his followers made reason the sufficient basis of obligation. They held that the object for which the law exists is to produce conformity to the nature of rational creatures. His words are: "That is unjust which is contrary to the nature of rational creatures."[26] Note that "nature" is not used here in a psychological sense, such as it bears today when we speak of "human nature" nor in the biological sense to which the doctrine of evolution has made us accustomed. Here the "nature" of a thing means the rationally conceived ideal of it. The ideally perfect thing is taken to be "natural." But Grotius had not thought this out with much precision. He had broken with authority as authority. Yet in the main he accepted the Roman law as embodied reason, and beyond a few bold assertions, such as his famous one that he could conceive of natural law even if there were no God,[27] he ventured little that did not have authority behind it. Hence he and his followers accepted the Roman maxim, not to injure another and to give to every one his own, that is, respect for personality and respect for acquired

25. Westlake, *Chapters on the Principles of International Law* (1894) 28.
26. i, 1, 3, § 1.
27. *Prolegomena*, § 11.

rights, as a formula of conformity to the nature of rational creatures. This, however, raised obvious problems: What is injury to another? What is it that constitutes anything one's own? Grotius and his successors sought to answer these questions by a theory of what we came to call natural rights, not merely natural law as heretofore; not merely principles of eternal validity, but certain qualities inherent in persons and demonstrated by reason, recognized by natural law, to which, therefore, the national law ought to give effect. Thus again, at the very time that the victory of the common-law courts in their contests with the Stuart Kings had established that there were fundamental common-law rights of Englishmen which Englishmen might maintain in court and in which courts would secure them even against the king or his ministers and agents, a juristic theory of fundamental natural rights, independent of and running back of all states, which states might secure and ought to secure but could not alter or abridge, had sprung up independently and was at hand to furnish a philosophical basis when political conditions at and after the American Revolution made it expedient to claim them as men rather than as Englishmen. By a natural transition, the common-law limitations upon royal authority became natural limitations upon all authority and the common-law rights of Englishmen became the natural rights of men.[28] According to the Grotian definition a right is: "A moral quality of a person whereby it is fit that he have something or do something."[29] His English exposition puts it thus: "That quality in a person which makes it just or right for him either to possess certain things or to do certain actions."[30] The medieval idea was that law exists to maintain those powers of control over things and those powers of action which the social system has awarded or attributed to each man. The Grotian idea was that law exists to maintain and give effect to certain inherent moral qualities in every man, discovered for us by reason,

---

28. I have discussed this at length in *The Spirit of the Common Law* (1921) lect. 4.
29. i, 1, 4.
30. 1 Rutherforth, *Institutes of Natural Law* (1754) 2, § 3.

by virtue of which he ought to have powers of control over things (property) or powers of action — capacity for legal transactions and liberties of action free from aggression. Thus, under the influence of the theory of natural law we get the theory of natural rights. A legal right is an institution of the legal order. But according to the theory of the law-of-nature jurists what ought to be law was regarded as law for that all-sufficient reason. No precept could stand as law except as it ought to be, and conversely to show that it ought to be law was to show that it was law. Hence what ought to be a legal right became decisive of what was a legal right.

There was a good side to all this. The insistence on what ought to be as the measure of what is, liberalized and modernized the actual law of the European states through the juristic testing of every doctrine and every category with reference to its basis in reason. But it had a bad side. It led to a confusion between the interests which it is conceived the law ought to secure and the rights by which the law secures interests when recognized, which has been the bane of jurisprudence ever since. It led to confusion of extra-legal ideals with the ideal element in the positive law and of both with the precept element. It led to absolute notions of an ideal development of received legal ideas as the jural order of nature, which more than once have brought legal thought and popular political thought into an obstinate conflict.

Since Jhering's treatment of the subject we have perceived that "natural rights" mean only interests which we hold ought to be secured. It is true that neither the law nor the state creates these interests. But it is destructive of sound thinking to treat the *de facto* interest, before or apart from recognition and delimitation by the legal order, as a legal conception. Rights in the legal sense are among the devices of the legal order to secure these interests so far as they are recognized and as they are delimited by law. Legal rights are the creatures of law, although the interests secured, or which ought to be secured, by legal rights are independent of law and state. Hence we did not get much further immediately when in the seventeenth century justice (in the sense of the end of law) came to be regarded as a securing of natural rights. What were natural rights was determined chiefly from ideas drawn from the existing social order. Presently the natural rights of men became as tyrannous as had been the divine rights of kings and rulers.

Although the theory of natural rights led ultimately in America to a hard-and-fast scheme of individual interests, beyond the reach of the state, which the state was bound to secure by law, it had important consequences in broadening the conception of justice and inducing more liberal views as to the end of the law. It soon became apparent that the theory of inherent moral qualities, while it would serve for interests of personality — for claims to be secured in one's body and life and the interests immediately related thereto — would not serve for the *suum cuique* element of the Roman formula of justice or, as we put it today, for interests of substance. None of the jurists of that time questioned the existing social order. They assumed a natural right of property, with all the incidents of *dominium* in Roman law, as beyond question.[31] They conceived that security of acquisitions, including what one had acquired through the existing social order, was a chief end.[32] At the same time they could not but see a difference between this natural right and such natural rights as those to the integrity of one's body, to free choice of location, and to freedom from coercion. Accordingly jurists turned for an explanation to the idea of contract, already given currency in political thought during the medieval contests between the church and temporal rulers.[33]

It must be remembered that "contract" in this connection has reference to the civil-law conception of what I have been calling a legal transaction (*negotium, acte juridique, Rechtsgeschäft*), an act intended to have legal consequences to which the law attributes the intended result.[34] In the seventeenth and eighteenth centuries this became the

31. Pufendorf, *De iure naturae et gentium* (1672) iv, 4.

32. Grotius, ii, 1, 1; ii, 1, 11; ii, 10, 1; ii, 17, 2, § 1.

33. See Figgis, *Studies of Political Thought from Gerson to Grotius* (1907) 148–51.

34. See Isaacs, *John Marshall on Contracts, A Study in Early American Juristic Theory*, 7 VIRGINIA LAW REVIEW, 413 (1921); Ferson, *The Rational Basis of Contracts* (1949).

staple legal analogy. The idea of the legal transaction was one of the most important of the civilian contributions to systematizing the body of authoritative legal precepts, and in an age when trade and commerce were expanding the law of such transactions was becoming the living part of the law. The juristic problem of the time was to reconcile the needs of business and the ethical ideas of good faith which accompanied the infusion of morals into the law with the traditional categories of contract in Roman law. Naturally contract loomed large in juristic thought for two centuries. How thoroughly this analogy took possession of juristic thought is well shown by a statement in a well-known text book which was still in use by both practicing lawyers and law students when I was studying law. The author said:

"The law of contracts, in its widest extent, may be regarded as including nearly all the law which regulates the relations of human life. Indeed it may be looked upon as the basis of human society. All social life presumes it and rests upon it, for out of contracts, express or implied, declared or understood, grow all rights, all duties, all obligations, and all law. Almost the whole procedure of modern life implies or rather is the fulfillment of contracts."[35]

Obviously this does not use "contract" as we now use the term in Anglo-American law. It refers to a social interest in the fulfilling of reasonable expectations; to good faith as a jural postulate of our civilization.

Moreover, the central point in the theory of a legal transaction was will — the will to produce a possible and legally permissible result. But the central idea in the theory of the law of nature and natural rights was conformity to the nature of reasoning creatures possessed of wills. So the question, how could such creatures acquire rights against one another, seemed easy to answer. How, indeed, could this be except by contract, through a legal transaction? Thus the foundation of the natural rights of property (interests of substance) which the law, it was held, existed to maintain, was taken to be a legal transaction, a compact of all men with

---

35. 1 Parsons, *Contracts* (1855) 3.

all men, by virtue of which rights and corresponding duties were created. When property was once established, it was held that the *ius disponendi*, postulated as a corollary of property, perpetuated it. Justice, therefore, consisted in respecting and observing the terms of this compact, and the business of jurist and lawmaker was to discover and interpret its terms.

This resting of rights upon contract had strong followers among seventeenth-century writers on jurisprudence, politics, and ethics. Thus, Pufendorf says: "It must be observed that the concession of God by which He gives men the use of terrestrial things is not the immediate cause of ownership . . . but it [ownership] presupposes a human act and an agreement, express or implied."[36] So Hobbes: ". . . Where no covenant hath proceeded, there hath no right been transferred, and every man has right to everything, and consequently no action can be unjust. But when a covenant is made, then to break it is unjust; and the definition of injustice is no other than the non-performance of covenant. . . . So that the nature of justice consists in the keeping of valid covenants but the validity of covenants begins not but with the constitution of a civil power sufficient to compel men to keep them; and then it is also that property begins."[37] Likewise, Spinoza: "Again in the state of nature no one is by common consent master of anything, nor is there anything in nature which can be said to belong to one man rather than another. Hence in the state of nature we can conceive no wish to render to every man his own or to deprive a man of that which belongs to him; in other words, there is nothing in the state of nature answering to justice and injustice. Such ideas are only possible in a social state, when it is decreed by common consent what belongs to one man and what to another."[38]

While at first theories of natural rights and of a social contract were used to justify and to preserve the social *status quo*, they invited inquiry

---

36. Pufendorf, *De iure naturae et gentium* (1672) iv, 4, § 4.
37. Hobbes, *Leviathan* (1651) cap. 15.
38. Spinoza, *Ethica*, iv, pr. 37, n. § 2 (1677).

as to the foundation of that *status quo*. They led men to ask, how far does it express the terms of the social compact? How far does it depart from a true interpretation thereof? It is manifest that such juristic theories might become very important for political thought. But their chief importance for our present purpose is to be found in their relation to the abstract individualism that long characterized Anglo-American legal thought. In themselves the theories are thoroughly abstract individualist. The natural rights which are the measure of all law, are the rights of individuals who have entered into a contract. Apart from this contract, and so apart from the individual consent involved therein, there would and could be no law and nothing for the law to secure. Individualism of this sort, beginning with the Reformation and growing with the emancipation of the middle class,[39] obtained throughout Europe from the seventeenth century. Five circumstances reinforced this tendency: (1) Puritanism, with its doctrine of "consociation but not subordination"[40] and its putting of individual conscience and individual judgment in the first place;[41] (2) the victory of the courts in the contests between courts and crown in seventeenth-century England, which seemed to establish that the law was something which stood between the individual and politically organized society and secured his natural rights; (3) political theory in the eighteenth century culminating in the Virginia Bill of Rights in 1776, the prototype of the Bill of Rights in the American federal Constitution, and of the bills of rights in all American state constitutions; (4) the classical political economy; and (5) the philosophy of law in the nineteenth century with its different modes of demonstrating Kant's formula of justice. All these successively developed and reinforced the tendency to abstract individualism. Thus in England, and

39. The relation of the development of individual rights and the emancipation and hegemony of the middle class is considered elaborately by Berolzheimer in his view of the maturity and downfall of the law-of-nature school; 2 Berolzheimer, *System der Rechts- und Wirtschaftsphilosophie* (1905) chap. 5.

40. Lord Acton, *Lectures on Modern History* (1906) 200. *See* Pound, *The Spirit of the Common Law* (1921) 57–59.

41. Lord Acton, *Lectures on Modern History* (1906) 10.

even more in America, there came to be an ultra-individualism in legal thought which persisted in the United States to and even beyond the end of the nineteenth century.

Putting the matter in modern phrase, according to the seventeenth century, law, in all of its three meanings, exists to maintain and protect individual interests — the reasonable expectations of individual men, elevated to the position of legal rights, because they were natural rights. This goes forward in the eighteenth century.[42]

Seventeenth-century theory had taken two directions. On the one hand, it conceived of rights as the outgrowth of a social contract. It held that there would be none without the social organization and that there would be no justice or law without the political organization. From Hobbes and Spinoza this idea passes to Bentham, and thence in the nineteenth century to the English analytical jurists whose theory is in the right line of descent therefrom. On the other hand, there was the Grotian idea of rights as qualities inhering in persons. This put rights above civil society and justice outside of and above civil society as permanent, absolute realities which civil society was organized to protect. It was not that there were justice and right because there was an organized society. There was organized society because there were justice and rights to protect and secure. Historically the latter theory is connected with the Germanic idea that the state is bound to govern by law; the notion of *Rechtsstaat*, the state as subject to legal limitations and legal rules of general and independent validity. It is curious that in England, where the Germanic idea became thoroughly established, except as to

---

42. 2 Berolzheimer, *System der Rechts- und Wirtschaftsphilosophie* (1905) § 29; Jellinek, *Die Erklärung der Menschen- und Bürgerrechte* (3 ed. 1919), English transl. of 1 ed. by Farrand as *The Declaration of the Rights of Men and of Citizens* (1901); Boutmy, *La déclaration des droits de l'homme et du citoyen de Mr. Jellinek, Etudes politiques* (1907); Ritchie, *Natural Rights* (1895) chap. 3; Sauter, *Die philosophischen Grundlagen des Naturrechts* (1932) 151–96. Pound, *The Formative Era of American Law* (1938) lect. 1.

Sources: Montesquieu, *L'esprit des lois* (1749) liv. I; Rousseau, *Le contrat social* (1762) liv. ii, chaps. 6, 9; Burlamaqui, *Principes du droit de la nature et des gens*, i, 1, chap. 5, § 10 and chap. 10, §§ 1–7; Wolff, *Institutiones iuris naturae et gentium* (1754) §§ 74–102; Vattel, *Le droit des gens* (1758) liv. i, chap. 2, §§ 15–17; Rutherforth, *Institutes of Natural Law* (1754) bk. ii, chap. 5, §§ 1–3.

Parliament after 1688, the idea that all rights and all justice, flowed from organized society prevailed in juristic thought, while on the Continent, where the Roman idea prevailed in public law, the Germanic idea got the upper hand in juristic thought. But the latter had apparent warrant in the Roman *ius naturale*. In the eighteenth century the second of the two ideas definitely prevailed. But a reconciliation was sought. The social contract was not the source of rights. It was made for the better securing of pre-existing natural rights. Thus Burlamaqui says: "But how great soever the change may be which government and sovereignty make in the state of nature, yet we must not imagine that the civil state properly subverts all natural society or that it destroys the essential relations which men have among themselves. . . . Government is so far from subverting this first order that it has been rather established with a view to give it a new degree of force and consistency. It was intended to enable us the better to discharge the duties prescribed by natural laws."[43] Both theories are thoroughly abstract individualist.

Eighteenth-century juristic theory, down to Kant, holds to four propositions: (1) There are natural rights demonstrable by reason. These rights are eternal and absolute. They are valid for all men in all times and in all places.[44] (2) Natural law is a body of precepts, ascertainable by reason, which perfectly secures all of these natural rights.[45] (3) Politically organized society exists only to secure men in these natural rights.[46] (4) Positive law is the means by which politically organized society performs this function, and it is obligatory only so far as it conforms to natural law.[47] The appeal is to individual reason. Hence every indi-

---

43. Burlamaqui, *Principes du droit de la nature et des gens*, i, 2, chap. 6, § 2 (1766). *Cf.* Vattel, liv. i, chap. 13, § 158 (1758). This was repeated by lawyers who were brought up on the books of the law-of-nature jurists down to the present century. "Organized society is created to secure antecedent rights of individuals or groups of individuals." Baldwin in *Two Centuries Growth of American Law* (1901) 45.

44. Burlamaqui, i, 1, chap. 7, § 4; Wolff, *Institutiones iuris naturae et gentium*, §§ 68–69.

45. Burlamaqui, i, 2, chap. 4.

46. *Ibid.* ii, 1, chap. 3; Wolff, § 972.

47. Burlamaqui, ii, 3, chap. 1, § 6; Wolff, § 1069; Vattel, liv. i, chap. 13, § 159; 1 Blackstone, *Commentaries on the Laws of England* (1765) 41.

vidual is a judge of this conformity. Also, on this theory natural rights alone are legal rights, except as to certain matters morally indifferent, for law is only a means of securing them.

Pushed to its logical limits, this leads straight to anarchy, and, indeed, the philosophical anarchist of the nineteenth century argued on this very basis.[48] But the eighteenth-century writers, who taught that every man's conscience was the measure of the obligatory force of legal precepts, assumed a sort of standard conscience, a standard man's or conscientious man's conscience, an abstract conscience of an abstract man, analogous to the prudence of the reasonable man in the Anglo-American law of torts. They assumed that if John Doe or Richard Roe asserted that his conscience did not sustain the precepts which the philosophical jurist deduced from the nature (ideal) of a moral being, either he did not know the dictates of his own conscience or he was misrepresenting them. It was only in this way that the social interest in the general security could be maintained effectively under the reign of the abstract individualist natural law. But this meant in practice that the philosophical jurist made his personal ethical views the test of the validity of rules of the positive law, and that the practicing lawyer took an ideal form of the settled legal principles in which he had been trained to be fundamental and eternal. Thus as late as the last decade of the nineteenth century a teacher of law in a leading American law school could write: "The very first and indispensable requisite in legal education . . . is the acquisition of a clear and accurate perception . . . of those unchangeable principles of the common law which underlie and permeate its whole structure and which control all its details, its consequences, its application to human affairs."[49] What such an attitude may lead to in the courts is brought out in the American cases of the formative era (from the American Revolution to the Civil War) holding that legislation could not add new categories of jurisdiction over crimes but

48. Brown, *The Underlying Principles of Modern Legislation* (1912) 7 ff.; Ritchie, *Natural Rights* (1895) 65 ff.

49. Phelps, *Methods of Legal Education* (1892) 1 YALE LAW JOURNAL, 139, 140.

must be held fast forever to the territorial theory of the common law. Thus in a case in which as a result of a felonious assault and battery in New York the victim of the attack died in New Jersey, the judge delivering the opinion of the court said: "But I cannot make myself believe that the legislature . . . intended to embrace cases where the injury was inflicted in a foreign jurisdiction. . . . Such an enactment upon general principles would necessarily be void. . . . An act to be criminal must be alleged to be against the sovereignty of the government. This is of the very essence of crime punishable by human law."[50]

The eighteenth-century philosophical method was of service in jurisprudence in that it led each jurist to work out ideals which could serve as a critique of the positive law and to formulate the ideal element in the law so as to make it effective in an era of growth. On the other hand, it was a hindrance to jurisprudence in America in that it seemed to afford a scientific basis for the lawyer's faith in the finality of the common law. The common law had grown up about an idea that reason, not arbitrary will, should be the measure of action and decision.[51] The eighteenth century, however, was sure that it had the one key to reason, and was fond of laying out philosophical and political charts by which men were to be guided for all time. The lawyer believed that he had this key in the traditional principles of Anglo-American common law and drew his charts accordingly.

There were two sides to the general juristic doctrine of the law-of-nature school, a side making for change, a creative side, and a side making for stability, a systematizing, organizing side. Throughout the hegemony of that school in the seventeenth and eighteenth centuries, the

50. *State* v. *Carter*, 27 N.J. Law, 499, 501 (1859). To the same effect; *State* v. *Knight*, Taylor (N.C.) 65 (1799) s.c. 2 Hayw. (N.C.) 109 (1799); Campbell, J., in *Tyler* v. *People*, 8 Mich. 320, 341 (1860).

51. *Glanvill*, preface, ix, 8 (1187); *Magna Carta*, cc. 4, 7, 14, 20, 28 (1215); Stonore, C.J., in *Langbridge's* Case, Y.B. 19 Ed. 3, 375 (1345); Littleton, *Tenures*, Epilogue (1481); *Doctor and Student* (1523) chap. 5; Coke, *Commentary on Littleton* (1628) 11a, 11b, 97b, 394a–395a; Coke, C.J., in *Prohibitions del Roy*, 12 Co. 63 (1612); Finch, *Law* (1627) bk. i, chap. 3.

two sides clearly stand out, on the one hand the law of nature as an instrument of change, as a weapon in the attack on the authoritarianism of the Middle Ages and on the restrictions on individual freedom of action involved in the feudal relational organization, and on the other hand, as an insurer of stability, as a protection from the personal justice and arbitrary administration in an era in which the old authoritative restraints were giving way and absolute governments were being established.

In the formative era of American law after independence, when a law had to be found for the new world and bodies of law had to be worked out by legislatures, judges, and jurists, in statutes, reported decisions, and law text books, for the new commonwealths which grow up so fast in the expansion of the United States across the continent, the creative side of the law-of-nature school served well. Lord Eldon's work of systematizing equity was still to be done and the reception of the law merchant was not yet complete. Lord Mansfield's creative work was going on during and after the American Revolution. Much of the seventeenth-century English law which was received in America was in the condition in which it had come down from the Middle Ages. The English criminal law of Blackstone's time, on which we in America had to build was full of archaisms and the penal system had hardly been touched by the humane ideas of the classical penologists. Indeed, the legislative reform movement which we associate with the name of Bentham,[52] begins in actual legislation in America rather than in England.[53] American courts had to complete the development of equity and taking

---

52. "The age of law reform and the age of Bentham are one and the same." 2 Brougham's *Speeches* (1838) 287–88.

53. Compare the legislation in New York on corporations, wills and administration, descent and distribution, marriage and divorce, executions against real property, and criminal law between 1811 and 1832, as shown in *New York Revised Statutes* (2 ed. 1836) — vol. I, 591 (1819), 741 (1827), 713 (1828); vol. II, 2 (1827), 27 (1823), 32 (1828), 74 (1830), 288 (1828), 373 (1832), 545 (1828); III, 220 (1811) — with the dates in Odgers (and others), *A Century of Law Reform* (1901).

over of the law merchant concurrently with the English courts. Legislatures and courts and doctrinal writers had to test the English common law at every point, with respect to its applicability to America. Judges and doctrinal writers had to develop an American common law, a body of judicially declared or doctrinally approved precepts suitable to America, out of the old English cases and the old English statutes. Those who did this work, and did it well in the seventy-five years before the American Civil War, were deeply read in the writings of the law-of-nature school. However much the last generation may have railed at that school, nothing which that generation achieved will compare with it.

There came to be a combination of history and philosophy along with the rise of historical thinking in the nineteenth century. It is observable in Kent and well marked in Story. With Kent natural rights have a historical content and the theoretical basis is in transition from natural law to history.[54] In Story's writings the transition is complete from a contract basis of rights and a contract basis of government to a historical basis, confirmed by a constitution, which declares natural rights with a historical content.[55] The stabilizing work of the eighteenth-century law of nature was taken over by history after history had for a time propped up reason, as reason in the later Middle Ages had bolstered up authority. In the later eighteenth century the creative force of the law of nature was coming to be spent. There was a tendency to stagnation of thought till at the end of the century, as Kent put it, philosophy awoke from a dogmatic slumber. There is nothing of consequence in the English eighteenth-century text, Rutherforth's Institutes of Natural Law, which is not in Grotius. Bentham's utilitarianism has nothing in it that was not in the law-of-nature utilitarianism that went before him except his calculus of pains and pleasures. The proposition that the end sought by man is happiness, as a proposition of natural law demonstrated by rea-

---

54. 2 Kent, *Commentaries on American Law* (1827), 1–11.

55. 1 Story, *Commentaries on the Constitution of the United States* (1833) bk. 2, chap. 3, especially §§ 340, 348, 356.

son, goes back to Pufendorf and may be found in Rutherforth, Burlamaqui, and Vattel.[56]

A political idea, that what every one agrees to is declaratory of natural law, is to be found in the writings of James Wilson, member of the convention which framed the constitution of the United States, one of the justices of the Supreme Court of the United States in the beginning, and one of the first juristic expositors of general legal theory in America.[57] As Kent and Story in the passing of the law-of-nature school turned to history, Wilson turns to a democratic version of the contract idea, a consensual law of nature, demonstrated by the customary course of popular action. But this idea, reminiscent of the Roman juristic identification of the *ius gentium* with *ius naturale*, may be found in Grotius. He says, in effect, that whatever cannot be deduced from certain principles by a sure process of reasoning, and yet is clearly observed everywhere, must have a natural origin in consent,[58] for men were morally, ideally, and so legally bound by their free consent. Here was a restraining law of nature which could be invoked to stay institutional waste in times of revolutionary upheaval.

If we ask what were the results of the dominance of the law-of-nature school in American juristic thought in the three generations after independence in which it held the field almost undisputed in America, we must put on the bad side of the account its effect on American attempts at codification in the nineteenth century. Over-confidence in the power of pure reason to discover the one right rule for every problem of the legal order led to neglect of history, that is, neglect of experience, and to expecting too much of a single codifier.[59] But most of all we must put on

56. Pufendorf, *De iure naturae et gentium* (1672) cap. xiii; Rutherforth, *Institutes of Natural Law* (1754) bk. i, chap. 1, § 7; Burlamaqui, *Principes du droit naturel* (1747) pt. 1, chap. 5, § 4; Vattel, *Les droit des gens, préliminaires*, 5 (1758).

57. 1 Wilson's *Works*, Andrews' ed. 57, 74. Lectures delivered in 1790.

58. *De iure belli ac pacis*, i, 1, 12.

59. The Civil Code of Georgia, provided for by statute in 1858 and put in effect in 1860, the Field draft codes in New York, and to some extent the Negotiable Instruments Law, the first of the Uniform State Laws under the auspices of the National Conference

this side the absolute idea of law which prevailed so largely in America in the nineteenth century and the wide gulf between popular thought and lawyers' thought to which it led. That idea came to America from Grotius in two ways. On the one hand, it came through Blackstone, whose section "on the nature of laws in general" is founded on Grotius and Pufendorf.[60] On the other hand, it comes through American jurists of the eighteenth and fore part of the nineteenth centuries who followed the Dutch and French publicists and civilians. Wilson's Law Lectures (1791) and Story on the Constitution (1833) abound in references to Grotius, Pufendorf, Burlamaqui, Vattel, and Rutherforth.

Indeed these books and those following them were the staple of American legal education from the beginning and throughout the formative era.

After the American Civil War historical and analytical jurisprudence supplanted philosophical jurisprudence in American legal thinking. The last quarter of the nineteenth century in the United States and the last half of the century on the Continent called for organization and system and stability in law much more than for creation and change. In England the influence of Bentham and rise of analytical jurisprudence crowded philosophical jurisprudence out until the present century. Discredit of the law-of-nature philosophy in the present generation in America is due chiefly to its effects in constitutional law. In the last of its phases it led to an idea of the constitution as declaratory of an ideal of the common law; as in its main lines and characteristic doctrines an embodiment of universal precepts of absolute validity. In consequence, as was said in a preceding lecture, certain common-law doctrines and traditionally received ideals of the profession were made into a super-constitution by which the social legislation of the last decade of the

---

on Uniform State Laws bring this out. *See* Carter, *Law: Its Origin, Growth and Function* (1907); Dillon, *Laws and Jurisprudence of England and America* (1894) 177–87; Hoadley, *Annual Address Before the American Bar Association* (1889) 11 REP. AM. BAR ASSN. 219; Ames, *The Negotiable Instruments Law* (1902) 14 HARVARD LAW REVIEW, 442.

60. 1 Blackstone, *Commentaries on the Laws of England* (1765) 38–61.

nineteenth century and of the first decade of the present century was to be judged.[61]

On the other side of the account, the ideas of the eighteenth-century law-of-nature school gave the American lawyers of the formative era a belief in the efficacy of effort which emboldened them to do much of outstanding worth. Application of reason to the received common law made the work of the legislative reform movement of enduring value. As has been said heretofore, some of its best achievements were authoritative formulations of what men had reasoned out in the seventeenth and eighteenth centuries.

But what led to abandonment of the juristic theory of natural rights was its extreme abstract individualism. It was, as I have pointed out in another connection, thoroughly abstract individualist in both of its aspects. As a theory of inherent moral qualities of persons it was based on deduction from an ideal of the abstract isolated individual. As a theory of rights based upon a social compact, it thought of natural rights as the rights of the individuals who had made the compact and had thereby set up the social and political order to secure them. In either view the end of the law is to maintain and protect individual interests. This fitted so perfectly the legal theory of the common-law rights of Englishmen that the founders of American political, legal, and judicial systems, who were studying Coke and Blackstone on the one hand and the French and Dutch publicists on the other hand, had no doubt they were reading about the same things. Hence Americans of the end of the eighteenth century argued for either or for both. The Declaration of Rights of the Continental Congress in 1774 asserted the legal rights of Englishmen. The Declaration of Independence two years later asserted the natural rights of man. Yet each claimed the same things.[62]

From this identifying of common-law rights with natural rights it followed that the common law was taken to be a system of giving effect to

61. *See* Lecture II, note 79.
62. *See* Pound and Plucknett, *Readings on the History and System of the Common Law* (3 ed. 1927) 309.

individual natural rights.[63] It was taken to exist in order to secure individual interests not merely against aggression by other individuals but even more against arbitrary invasion by state or society.[64] The bills of rights were declaratory both of natural rights and of the common law.[65] This idea is prominent in American judicial decisions in the nineteenth century, when the ideas of the eighteenth century had become classical. Thus one court told us that natural persons did not derive their right to contract from the law. Hence whatever the state might do in limiting the power of a corporation to make certain contracts, because a corporation got its power from the state, it might not limit the contractual capacity of natural persons who got their right to contract from nature, so that nature alone could remove it.[66] Another court, in passing adversely upon labor legislation infringing liberty of contract, said that any classification was arbitrary and unconstitutional unless it proceeded on the "natural capacity of persons to contract."[67] Another court in a similar con-

---

63. *Fletcher v. Peck.* 6 Cranch (U.S.) 87, 134 (1810); Story, *Commentaries on the Constitution of the United States* (1833) § 1399; Cooley, *Constitutional Limitations* (1868) 358–83. *Cf.* 1 Wilson, *Works*, Andrews' ed. 566, lectures delivered in 1790.

64. "With those judges who assert the omnipotence of the legislature in all cases where the constitution has not interposed an explicit restraint, I cannot agree. Should there exist . . . a case of direct infringement of vested rights too palpable to be questioned and too unjust to admit of vindication, I could not avoid considering it as a violation of the social compact, and within the control of the judiciary." Hosmer, C.J., in *Goshen v. Stonington*, 4 Conn. 209, 225 (1822).

65. "The usual Anglo-Saxon bill of rights, as contained in our state constitutions, is in fact nothing more or less than the written expression of a previously existing but silent limitation upon the power of legislators which is imposed without the writing." Abbot, *Justice and the Modern Law* (1913) 47. On this theory there might be constitutionally adopted but unconstitutional amendment to the constitution. *See* Miller, J., in *Loan Association v. Topeka*, 20 Wall. 655, 662 (1874). Compensation in eminent domain was said to be "a settled principle of universal law reaching back of all constitutional provisions." Harlan, J., in *Chicago B. & Q.R. Co. v. Chicago*, 166 U.S. 226, 237–38 (1897). Police regulations are valid unless they infringe a constitutional provision 'or a natural right.' Field, J., in *Butcher's Union Co. v. Crescent City Co.*, 111 U.S. 746, 762 (1884).

66. *Leep v. Railway Co.*, 58 Ark. 407 (1893).

67. *State v. Loomis*, 115 Mo. 307 (1893). *See* Pound and Plucknett, *Readings on the History and System of the Common Law* (3 ed. 1927) 309.

nection denied that contractual capacity could be restricted except for physical or mental disabilities.[68] It all came to a proposition that the common-law categories of disability were final and that legislation could not add new ones. The bills of rights and the fourteenth amendment to the federal constitution were treated as only declaring a natural liberty which was also a common-law liberty. Hence an abridgment not known to the common law was thought to go counter to their fair construction, if not to the letter.

In the last quarter of the nineteenth century and first quarter of the present century these ideas led to a bitter controversy between courts and legislatures in America which went on long after the basic idea had given way before the critique of Immanuel Kant. Kant's Critique of Pure Reason struck at the root of the whole doctrine of the law-of-nature school. If natural rights were inherent moral qualities to be ascertained by reason, granted that reason could deduce with assurance from given premises, how could reason give us the premises? If, on the other hand, natural rights rested on a social contract, how could the details or the implied terms of a contract of a generation far in the past bind the men of today? The fiction of representation, the doctrine taught by Blackstone, that we were represented when our remote forefathers made the contract and so are bound, was obviously founded on British political theory in which all consent to acts of Parliament through the representatives sent to Westminster to act for them. It would not bear examination. He saw that the legal order could not carry out a plan of assuring complete exercise of all the claims or securing all the expectations which reason was asserting as natural rights. He saw as the ultimate problem the reconciling of conflicting free wills. The principle by which their reconciliation was to be effected was equality in freedom of will, the application of a universal rule to each act which would enable the free will of the actor to co-exist along with the like free will of every one else. In his own words: "Every action is right which in itself, or in the maxim on which it proceeds, is such that it can co-exist along with

68. State v. Fire Creek Coal & Coke Co., 33 W.Va. 188 (1889).

the freedom of each and all in action according to a universal law."[69] The whole course of juristic theory in the nineteenth century was determined by this theory of justice. Kant marks an epoch in philosophical jurisprudence no less than Grotius.

Summarily stated, to the eighteenth-century justice, the end of law, the ideal by which values were to be measured, the idea by which choice of starting points for legal reasoning was to be governed, by which legal precepts were to be interpreted and applied, and by which legislation was to be directed, was the securing of absolute, eternal, universal rights of individuals, determined with reference to the abstract individual man. Kant, on the other hand, held it to mean the securing of freedom of will to every one so far as consistent with freedom of all other wills. Thus the transition was complete from the idea of justice as a maintaining of the social *status quo* to an idea of justice as the securing of a maximum of free self-assertion.

69. Kant, *Metaphysische Anfangsgründe der Rechtslehre* (2 ed. 1798) xxv.

SEVEN

Promotion of Free Self-Assertion

2. Nineteenth Century to the Present

A characteristic juristic achievement of the nineteenth century[1] was the setting off of jurisprudence as a separate science. This was the culmination of a development which began in the sixteenth century in the emancipation of jurisprudence from theology. Up to the seventeenth century, jurisprudence and politics were treated along with theology as applications of its doctrines.[2] In a second stage, jurisprudence, politics, and international law were treated together. The philosophical foundation as expounded by the law-of-nature school was taken to suffice for all three and the details of each subject were supposed to be reached by deduction therefrom.[3] Separation from politics was gradually achieved in the nineteenth century. It is true the metaphysical jurists of that century did not

---

1. I have considered nineteenth-century ideas of the end of law in *The End of Law as Developed in Juristic Thought*, 30 HARVARD LAW REVIEW, 201 (1917); *The Spirit of the Common Law* (1921) lect. 6; *The Philosophy of Law in America* (1913) 7 ARCHIV FUR RECHTS UND WIRTSCHAFTSPHILOSOPHIE, 213, 385.

2. In Hobbes' *Leviathan* two of the four parts are theological. *Cf.* also Spinoza's *Tractatus theologico-politicus* (1670).

3. *See,* for example, the sequence of Burlamaqui, *Principes du droit naturel* (1747) and *Principes du droit politique* (1757); the order of treatment, that is, general philosophical foundation, philosophical jurisprudence, politics, international law, in Wolff, *Institutiones iuris naturae et gentium* (1740–49) and the like order in Rutherforth, *Institutes of Natural Law* (1754–56).

wholly abandon the old connection of jurisprudence, politics, legislation, and international law.[4] But as the three distinct methods of jurisprudence pursued in that century, philosophical, analytical, and historical, were definitely worked out, the English analytical school believed they had achieved a separation of jurisprudence from philosophy and ethics and hence from the science of legislation. Thus Markby says: "What . . . Austin's predecessors do not appear to me to have fully apprehended, at least not with that sure and firm grasp which proceeds from a full conviction, is the distinction between positive law and morals. We find for example that Bentham, when drawing the line between jurisprudence and ethics, classes legislation under jurisprudence, whereas, as Austin has shown, it clearly belongs to ethics. Austin, by establishing the distinction between positive law and morals, not only laid the foundation for a science of law, but cleared the conception of law and of sovereignty of a number of pernicious consequences to which in the hands of his predecessors it had been supposed to lead."[5] The English historical school, conceiving that the traditional element in legal systems was the real law and that law was to be found in the unfolding of the principle of justice in human experience rather than made by legislators, agreed in this separation of jurisprudence and the science of legislation. Accordingly Maine said: "Investigation of the principle on which direct improvement of substantive legal rules should be conducted belongs . . . not to the theorist on jurisprudence but to the theorist on legislation."[6] Note that he speaks of *direct* improvement. In the Hegelian thinking of the historical jurists in the last century, there could be continuous indirect improvement through unfolding of the idea of justice by its inherent power of realizing itself.

4. Lorimer, *Institutes of Law* (2 ed. 1880) bk. ii, chap. 1 and bk. iv, chap. 3; Stahl, *Die Philosophie des Rechts* (5 ed. 1878) bk. iv — politics and public law. But compare Lasson, *System der Rechtsphilosophie* (1882) where the philosophical foundations of public law are discussed but not politics.

5. Markby, *Elements of Law* (6 ed. 1905) § 12. The same proposition is stated with less assurance in the first edition (1871) 5–6. *Cf.* 2 Austin, *Jurisprudence* (3 ed. 1869) 1107; Gray, *Nature and Sources of the Law* (1909) § 213, (2 ed. 1921) 94.

6. Maine, *Early History of Institutions* (7 ed. 1897) lect. 13, p. 345. *Cf.* 1 Pollock and Maitland, *History of English Law* (1895) xxiii.

It has been suggested that a like narrow tendency in nineteenth-century philosophy is to be attributed to division of labor in the universities and the requirements of academic courtesy. No doubt these had some part in the segregation of jurisprudence, and the nineteenth-century Anglo-American tendency to insist upon analytical jurisprudence, where the lawyer required no aid from without and was continually in an atmosphere of pure positive law, as the whole of the science of law. As Sir Henry Maine put it: "The jurist properly so-called has nothing to do with any ideal standard of law or morals."[7] But the expansion of learning in the last century, which prevented any one from taking more than a corner of knowledge for his province, and the general tendency of the time to lay out everything analytically, confine it to defined limits, and reduce it to rule, a tendency which the idea of evolution has not yet wholly succeeded in driving even from the biological sciences, are also to be reckoned with. This extreme division of labor had its good side. Analysis and philosophical generalization from comparative legal history, pursued exclusively and more or less independently for a time, have taught us the possibilities of these methods and have given results upon which new methods may be devised with assurance. The bad side was the abdication of all juristic function of improving the law, as Saleilles termed it, the abandonment of "juridical idealism,"[8] and the reduction of those who were best qualified to take conscious part in legal development to the position of mere observers. Coinciding with a period of maturity and stability in the law, this juristic pessimism coincided also with the doctrine of *laissez faire* in economics. Thus the conception of the end of law as an unshackling of individual energy, as an insuring of the maximum of abstract individual free self-assertion, gave rise to a conception of the function of law as a purely negative one of removing or preventing obstacles to such indi-

7. *Early History of Institutions* (1874) lect. 12. In the 7th ed. (1897) the passage is on p. 370. To the same effect, Holland *Elements of Jurisprudence* (1 ed. 1880) chap. 1; and so in 13 ed. (1924). Compare the more temperate statement of this view by Gray, *Nature and Sources of the Law* (1909) §§ 1–9, somewhat altered in 2 ed. 1921, 140–44.

8. Saleilles, *L'école historique et droit naturel* (1901) 1 REVUE TRIMESTRIELLE DE DROIT CIVIL, 80.

vidual self-assertion, not a positive one of directly furthering social ends or social progress.

Five types of nineteenth-century thinkers require consideration. They may be called (1) the metaphysical jurists, (2) the English utilitarians, (3) the historical jurists, (4) the positivists, and (5) the social individualists.

In order of time we come first to the metaphysical jurists.[9] Metaphysical jurisprudence begins with Kant, who puts in its final form the conception of the end of law which came in with the Reformation. In principle the Reformation denied the authority of any doctrine the evidence of which the individual could not find in his own reason and of any precept which could not be referred to the will of the individual to be bound. Hence the elaborate arguments by which eighteenth-century jurists seek to make out that each individual has consented to the law through his representative or has willed it through a social compact.[10] In Kant's doctrine this fiction of consent of the individual will is replaced by an imposition upon the individual free will through the reciprocal action of free wills whereby they may be reconciled by a universal law, which therefore is imposed by a necessity inherent in the very idea of freedom.[11] To use Kant's own words: "A constitution allowing the greatest possible human freedom in accordance with laws by which the freedom of each is made to be consistent with that of all others . . . is at

9. Kant, *Metaphysische Anfangsgründe der Rechtslehre* (2 ed. 1798), English transl. by Hastie as Kant's *Philosophy of Law* (1887); Fichte, *Grundlage des Naturrechts* (1798) new ed. by Medicus (2 ed. 1922), English transl. by Kroeger as Fichte's *Science of Rights* (1889); Hegel, *Grundlinien der Philosophie des Rechts* (1821), 2 ed. by Gans, 1840, new ed. by Lasson, 1911, English transl. by Knox (Oxford, 1942); Krause, *Abriss des Systemes der Philosophie des Rechtes* (1825); Ahrens, *Cours de droit naturel* (1837, 8 ed. 1892); Green, *Principles of Political Obligation* (lectures delivered 1879–80, reprinted, 1911); Lorimer, *Institutes of Law* (1872, 2 ed. 1880); Lasson, *System der Rechtsphilosophie* (1882); Miller, *Lectures on the Philosophy of Law* (1884); Boistel, *Cours de philosophie du droit* (1899); Herkless, *Lectures on Jurisprudence* (posthumous, 1901).

10. 1 Blackstone, *Commentaries* (1765) 140, 158–59; Wilson, *Works*, Andrews' ed. 88–89 (written in 1790); Wooddeson, *Elements of Jurisprudence* (1792) xvii.

11. *Metaphysische Anfangsgründe der Rechtslehre* (2 ed. 1798) xxii–xxiii. See a good exposition of this in 2 Caird, *The Critical Philosophy of Kant* (1889) 296–300. Cf. Herkless, *Lectures on Jurisprudence* (1901) 14–15. As to the relation of Kant's doctrine to the classical economics, see Cooke, *Adam Smith and Analytical Jurisprudence* (1935) 51 LAW QUARTERLY REVIEW, 326.

any rate a necessary idea, which must be taken as fundamental not only in first projecting a constitution but in all its laws."[12] Thus we realize individual freedom through rules of law, and the end of law is "to keep self-conscious beings from collision with each other, to secure that each should exercise his freedom in a way that is consistent with the freedom of all others, who are equally to be regarded as ends in themselves."[13] It should be noted that this is a Kantian way of putting what Ehrlich calls the inner order of groups and associations.[14]

Kant's separation of each man from what we used to call the social organism, *i.e.*, setting him over against society, was characteristic of the eighteenth century. What Kant saw and felt was the independence of our mental life. We can live our individual mental lives. But there is no such individual independence in our economic or social life. Nor can our mental life be so isolated as Kant felt it was. A mental and moral giant like Kant could live a free life of the spirit. But the mental life of most of us is likely to be shaped by the thought of the time and the pressure of the thinking of our fellow men much as our economic life is shaped by the pressure of the wants and activities of our fellows. Kant's putting of the individual person at the center of juristic theory and the individual conscience at the center of ethical theory, "separated him also from the past out of which his intellectual life had grown."[15] Hegel saw that it was unhistorical and took the moral organism, as it used to be called, for the central point of his ethical theory.[16] Here we have the beginning of a new point of view, which becomes significant in the social-philosophical jurists at the end of the century.[17] But nineteenth-century metaphysical jurisprudence remained thoroughly abstract individual-

12. Kant, *Kritik der reinen Vernunft* (2 ed. 1787) 373, Smith's transl., Smith, Immanuel Kant's *Critique of Pure Reason* (1932) 312.

13. 2 Caird, *The Critical Philosophy of Kant* (1889) 296.

14. Ehrlich, *Fundamental Principles of the Sociology of Law* (1936) transl. by Moll, chap. 2.

15. 1 Caird, 54.

16. *Grundlinien der philosophie des Rechts* (2 ed. 1840) § 33. See Wallace, *Hegel's Philosophy of Mind* (1894) 21–23.

17. *See* Boyd, *Workmen's Compensation* (1913) § 21, as to the influence of Hegel.

ist. It postulated that the end of man was freedom.[18] Said Hegel: "The history of the world is nothing but the development of the idea of freedom."[19] It developed the idea of free will into the practical consequence of civil liberty, an idea of general freedom of action for individuals — an idea of the maximum of abstract free individual self-assertion. Hence the end of law was to secure each individual the widest possible abstract liberty. The justification of law was that there is no true liberty — *i.e.*, abstract universal liberty — except where there is no law to restrain the strong who interfere with the freedom of action of the weak, and the organized many who interfere with the free individual self-assertion of the few.[20] On this basis, in his lectures on political theory at Oxford, Green argued that the value of political institutions lay in their giving reality to capacities of will and reason, enabling them to be really exercised. They made it possible for an individual to be freely determined by the idea of a possible satisfaction, thus giving reality to the capacity called will, and enabled him to realize his reason, *i.e.*, his idea of self-perfection, by acting as a member of a social organization in which each contributes to the better being of all. This he considered was the moral justification of laws.[21] Two points in this doctrine are noteworthy: (1) Law as a restraint on individual abstract liberty had to be justified; (2) law is used here in the lawyer's sense of adjustment of relations and ordering of conduct by the force of a politically organized society. Except where there is law in this sense it was held there was no liberty. The test of justice was the amount of abstract individual liberty secured.[22] Jurists of the end of the century insisted vigorously on these points. It was said that sound doctrine "reduces the power of coercion to what is absolutely necessary for

18. See 2 Stirling, *The Secret of Hegel* (1865); Croce, *Ce qui est vivant et ce qui est mort de la philosophie de Hegel* (1910) 114.

19. Hegel, *Philosophy of History*, transl. by Sibree, rev. ed. pt. IV, chap. 3 (1899).

20. Courcelle-Seneuil, *Préparation à l'étude du droit* (1887) 114; Pulszky, *Theory of Law and Civil Society* (1888) § 170; Emery, *Concerning Justice* (1914) 108–9.

21. Green, *Principles of Political Obligation* (1911) 32–33 — lectures delivered 1879–80.

22. Ahrens, *Cours de droit naturel* (8 ed. 1892) §§ 17–18; Trendelenburg, *Naturrecht* (2 ed. 1808) § 46; Lorimer, *Institutes of Law* (2 ed. 1880) 363, 523; Miller, *Lectures on the Philosophy of Law* (1884) 70–74.

the harmonious co-existence of the individual with the whole."[23] Beudant argued that every rule of law was an evil since it regulated the exercise of rights; but it was a necessary evil.[24] A leader of the American bar, in a set of lectures written for delivery before a law school in 1905, said that it was "the sole function both of law and legislation . . . to secure to each individual the utmost liberty which he can enjoy consistently with the preservation of the like liberty to all others. Liberty . . . is the supreme object. Every abridgment of it demands an excuse, and the only good excuse is the necessity of preserving it."[25]

Though American jurists paid little or no direct attention to the systems of the metaphysical school, its central idea of abstract individual liberty fitted into our eighteenth-century law-of-nature individualism and the spirit of a pioneer society so well that the school had begun to have much influence in the United States when a new and more attractive mode of getting to the same result was furnished by the positivists.[26]

We turn now to the English utilitarians.[27] While the metaphysical jurists were deducing the whole system of rights and the end of the legal order from a metaphysical conception of free will, another school was seeking a practical principle of lawmaking. The metaphysical school was a school of jurists. They had their eyes upon the legal order and the

23. Lioy, *Philosophy of Right* (1891) transl. by Hastie, 121.

24. Beudant, *Le droit individuel et l'état* (1891) 148.

25. Carter, *Law: Its Origin, Growth, and Function* (1907) 337.

26. On the influence of metaphysical jurisprudence in America and the American grafting of metaphysical jurisprudence on positivism, see Pound, *Interpretations of Legal History* (1923) 22–23, 32–37, 71–72.

27. 2 Berolzheimer, *System der Rechts- und Wirtschaftsphilosophie* (1905) § 28; Mill, *On Liberty* (1859) chap. 4; Bentham, *Theory of Legislation, Principles of the Civil Code* (1864, new ed. 1931) chaps. 1–7; Dicey, *Law and Public Opinion in England* (2 ed. 1914) lect. 6; Solari, *L'idea individuale e l'idea sociale nel diritto privato* (1911) §§ 31–36.

Bentham's utilitarianism: *Principles of Morals and Legislation* (1780, reprinted by the Clarendon Press, 1879); *Traités de législation* (ed. by Dumont, 1802, transl. by Hildreth as Bentham's *Theory of Legislation*, 10 ed. 1904); 1 Works, *Principles of the Civil Code* (1839) 295–364.

law as a whole, upon systems of authoritative grounds of decision and measures of conduct which had come down from the past, and they sought the principles upon which such systems and their doctrines could be based philosophically and by which rules of law might be criticized and their further development might be directed. The English utilitarians, on the other hand, were a school of legislators. The metaphysical jurists employed the philosophical method in jurisprudence and did not separate the science of law and the science of legislation. The English utilitarians developed the analytical method in jurisprudence and employed a philosophical method in the science of legislation. Accordingly while the metaphysical jurists sought principles of criticism of what was, the utilitarians sought principles of constructing new rules of law by conscious lawmaking. Bentham's life work was law reform.[28] The practical principle which he laid down, as that which should govern legislative reform of law, was the principle of utility. Does the rule or measure conduce to human happiness? This principle and this criterion might have been used to break down the abstract individualist idea of justice as Jhering used the idea of purpose later.[29] But at this time abstract individualist ideas were too firmly fixed in men's minds to be questioned. For the individualist tradition of seventeenth- and eighteenth-century thought was reinforced by economic reasons in the age of Adam Smith and the great British economists and by political reasons in the reaction from the age of absolute governments which made the period following the French Revolution fearful of centralized authority and jealous of local and individual independence. The criterion of the greatest good of the greatest number might easily be put in a way that would not be far from some recent ideas of justice. Thus, that which serves for the greatest happiness of the greatest number, used as

28. On Bentham's life and work: Atkinson, *Jeremy Bentham* (1905); Phillipson, *Three Criminal Law Reformers*, pt. 2, Bentham (1923); 1 Stephen, *The English Utilitarians* (1900).

29. I have discussed this in *The Scope and Purpose of Sociological Jurisprudence* (1911) 25 HARVARD LAW REVIEW, 140, 140–43.

a measure of the conduct of each, might serve as the basis of a social util-itarianism.[30] But Bentham did not question abstract individualism. He vacillated between an idea of utility as the greatest happiness of the ab-stract individual and an idea of utility as the greatest happiness of the greatest number of concrete individuals. Indeed, he did not need to choose between them since he assumed that the greatest general hap-piness was to be procured through the greatest abstract individual self-assertion.[31] Hence his fundamental principle was not substantially dif-ferent from that of the metaphysical jurists. Dicey formulated it thus: "Every person is in the main and as a general rule the best judge of his own happiness. Hence legislation should aim at a removal of all those restrictions on the free action of an individual which are not necessary for securing the like freedom on the part of his neighbors."[32] Negatively his program was, unshackle men; allow them to act as freely as possible. And this was the idea of the metaphysical school. Positively his program was, extend the sphere and enforce the obligation of contract. This, we shall see presently, was the idea of the historical school.

Bentham's principle, then, was: Allow the maximum of free individ-ual action consistent with general free individual action. Thus the end of law came to the same thing with him as with the metaphysical jurists, namely, to secure the maximum of individual self-assertion. Bentham's theory of the end of the legal order made a strong appeal to the com-mon-law lawyer. The Anglo-American legal system had kept much of the individualism of the strict law. The stage of equity and natural law had by no means made it over and the development of equity was not complete in England when English law was received in America.[33]

30. Cf. Tanon, L'évolution du droit et la conscience sociale (3 ed. 1911) 185–89.

31. Cf. Kant: ". . . the greatest possible human freedom . . . —I do not speak of the greatest happiness, for this will follow of itself." Kritik der reinen Vernunft (2 ed. 1787) 373.

32. Dicey, Law and Public Opinion in England (2 ed. 1914) 146.

33. I have considered this in, The Place of Judge Story in the Making of American Law (1914) 48 AMERICAN LAW REVIEW, 676.

Moreover, in the classical contests between the English courts and the Crown in the seventeenth century the common law had been made to stand between the individual and oppressive state action. Thus the common-law tradition was thoroughly individualist, and this tradition was especially congenial to the Puritan, who was dominant in America down to the time of the Civil War,[34] and was reinforced by the modes of thought of the pioneer.[35] However much the practicing lawyer might affect to despise philosophical theories of law, he could but be content with a theory that put plausible reasons behind his traditional habits of thought. The one difficulty was the English utilitarian's fondness for legislative lawmaking, which was out of accord with the common-law tradition. But this difficulty presently disappeared.

It is a curious circumstance that while Bentham and Austin believed in legislation and hoped for an ultimate codification,[36] the interpretation of utility as requiring a minimum of interference with the individual led the next generation of English utilitarians to the same position as that of the historical school, namely, that except in a few necessary cases legislation is an evil. The historical jurists held it was an evil because it sought to do what could not be done. The neo-utilitarians held it an evil because that government was best which governed least and left men freest to work out their own destiny. Bentham had already put security (meaning, however, security of the individual free existence) as the main end to which the legal order should be directed.[37] It was to be "security to men in the free enjoyment and development of their capacities for happiness."[38] A utilitarian version of the nineteenth-century juristic pessimism was deduced from this idea. We could not achieve any positive good by law; we could only avert some evils. Thus, Markby wrote: "The value of law is to be measured not by the happiness which

34. *See* Pound, *The Spirit of the Common Law* (1921) lect. 2.
35. *Ibid.* lect. 5. *See also* Pound, *The Administration of Justice in the Modern City* 26 HARVARD LAW REVIEW, 302 (1913).
36. 2 Austin, *Jurisprudence* (5 ed. 1885) lect. 39 and *Notes on Codification*, 1021–32.
37. *Theory of Legislation, Principles of the Civil Code* (1864) pt. 1, chap. 7.
38. Sharswood, *Professional Ethics* (5 ed. 1896) 22.

it procures but by the misery from which it preserves us."³⁹ Also: "We shall, therefore, look for happiness in the wrong direction if we expect it to be conferred upon us by the law. Moreover, not only is it impossible for the law to increase the stock of happiness, it is just as impossible for the law to secure an equal distribution of it. Equality may be hindered by the law, it cannot be prompted by it."⁴⁰ I suppose he would say that "loan shark laws" or small loan acts do not further equality. Certainly such laws or the laws against payment of wages in orders on company stores do not further abstract equality. But law is a practical activity and we may look at concrete situations. What the doctrine came to was well put by Chief Justice Sharswood: "There is not much danger of erring upon the side of too little law."⁴¹

It is noteworthy, however, that this changed attitude toward legislation came after the legislative reform movement was at an end. The type of legislation which unshackled the individual, which did away with restrictions which had come down from a relationally organized society, had exhausted its possibilities in England about 1865. From that time legislation of a new type began to impose the restrictions called for by the relatively newly arisen industrial society.

Thus the English utilitarians did not contribute much of moment to the theory of the end of the legal order. They merely strengthened in the minds of lawyers the extreme individualism which the latter had inherited with the common-law tradition. Perhaps their most significant achievement was in definitely driving the eighteenth-century law of nature out of the English books. For example, in discussing condemnation of private property (taking for public use), Blackstone said that the public was in nothing so essentially interested as in securing to every individual his private rights.⁴² This is the natural-rights idea of the eighteenth century. A little more than a century later Sir George Jessel said: "If there is one thing more than another public policy requires, it is that men of full age and competent understanding shall have the utmost lib-

39. Markby, *Elements of Law* (6 ed. 1905) § 58.
40. *Ibid.* § 59.
41. Sharswood, *Professional Ethics* (5 ed. 1896) 23.
42. 1 *Commentaries*, 139.

erty of contracting and that their contracts . . . shall be enforced by courts of justice."[43] Nearly fifty years later an American judge was echoing this identification of the public good: ". . . surely the good of society as a whole cannot be better served than by the preservation against arbitrary restraint of the liberties of its constituent members."

Here we have Bentham's program of unshackling men and extending the sphere of contract. But we have also the free will idea, the individual liberty idea of the metaphysical jurists. It is worth while to reflect that Sir George Jessel wrote the words just quoted in a case involving a contract as to a patent. Not only do we unhesitatingly limit the freedom of contract of whole classes of men of full age and competent understanding at every turn of modern labor legislation, but we are not so sure today that whatever contract as to his patent a patentee may choose to make or to exact is to be upheld at all events.[44]

Turning to the historical jurists,[45] they were more concerned with the nature of law and the content and development of legal systems than with the end of law. They took their philosophical ideas from the metaphysical school and so agreed in holding abstract individual liberty to be the fundamental idea. This is brought out in a series of unequivocal propositions by Puchta, in a book which long had much vogue as an elementary exposition: "Freedom is the foundation of right, which is the essential principle of all law." Again: "In virtue of freedom man is the subject of right and law. His freedom is the foundation of right and all real relations of right and law flow from it." Again: "Law is consequently the recognition of that jural freedom which is externalized and exhibited in persons and their acts of will and their influence upon objects."[46] Accep-

---

43. *Printing Co. v. Sampson*, 19 Eq. 452, 465 (1875).

44. *Bauer v. O'Donnell*, 229 U.S. 1 (1912); *Motion Picture Patents Co. v. Universal Film Mfg. Co.*, 243 U.S. 502 (1917). *Cf.* recent English decisions as to covenants not to exercise the calling for which one has trained himself. *Hepworth Mfg. Co. v. Ryott* [1920] 1 Ch. 1; *Attwood v. Lamont* [1920] 3 K. B. 571; Younger, L.J., in *Dewes v. Fitch* [1920] 2 Ch. 159, 185.

45. Maine, *Ancient Law* (1860) chap. 5; id. *Early History of Institutions* (1874) lect. 11; Carter, *Law: Its Origin, Growth and Function* (1907) 133–35, 333–38; Puchta, *Cursus der Institutionen* (1841) §§ 1–3; Arndts, *Juristische Encyklopädie und Methodologie* (1860) § 12.

46. Puchta, *Cursus der Institutionen*, Hastie's transl. in *Outlines of Jurisprudence* (1887) §§ 2, 4, 6.

tance of this idea was facilitated by, or perhaps rather it resulted in, their adopting the political interpretation of legal history. They conceived that the history of law was a history of the gradual acquisition or recognition of individual liberty. This is the central philosophical idea in the writings of Sir Henry Maine.[47] As I have pointed out elsewhere, Maine's doctrine of the progress from status to contract is a political type of idealistic interpretation of history.[48] For a purely ethical idea of right it substitutes a political idea of individual freedom. It sees in law and in legal history a manifestation and development of that idea. Hence it finds the end of law in liberty conceived in the sense of the widest possible self-assertion. It teaches that a movement from individual subjection to individual freedom, from status to contract, is the key to social and legal development. The goal toward which the law was moving was the maximum of individual liberty; the measure of values for legislation, for judicial finding of law, and for interpretation and application of legal precepts was promotion and maintenance of the maximum of free individual self-assertion.

This is not the place to discuss Maine's proposition from the standpoint of legal history, although it may not be amiss to point out that his materials are drawn from Roman law, and Germanic law and its derivatives in the world of today do not tell the same story. It is enough to note here that Maine carried on the view of the metaphysical jurists that the philosophical basis of law was to be found in the individual free will. Thus metaphysical jurist, utilitarian, and historical jurist, much as they differed in the route by which they got there, came to the same result; the end of law was to secure the widest possible abstract freedom of individual action. The law would automatically move forward, they said, by the inherent power of the idea of liberty to unfold and realize itself.

In truth, the nineteenth-century historical school of jurists was not historical. It was at most metaphysical historical. The reconciliation of the historical with the metaphysical, which was current at the end of the

47. *Ancient Law* (1861) chap. 5 ad fin.

48. Pound, *Interpretations of Legal History* (1923) 46, 53–65; *The Spirit of the Common Law* (1921) lect. 1; *The End of Law as Developed in Legal Rules and Doctrines* (1914) 27 HARVARD LAW REVIEW 201, 209–21; *The Scope and Purpose of Sociological Jurisprudence* (1911) 25 HARVARD LAW REVIEW 140, 164.

century, may be found in Hegel. In an exposition too long to summarize, much less to quote, he concludes: ". . . in the logical progression of [the idea] taken for itself there is, so far as its principal elements are concerned, the progression of historical manifestations. . . . The succession undoubtedly separate itself, on the one hand, into the sequence of time in history, and on the other hand, into succession in the order of ideas."[49] Both the historical jurist and metaphysical jurist were heirs to the law-of-nature theories of the eighteenth century. Each sought a universal, unchallengeable fundamental principle. One studied the unfolding of the principle in human experience manifested in legal institutions and in legal doctrines. The other verified the same process *a priori* and unfolded the principle logically. Hence the juristic pessimism of the metaphysical school — the feeling that conscious attempt to improve the content as distinguished from the form of the law was futile — was fully shared by the historical school. Compare a philosopher with a legal historian: "[the Hegelian philosophy] only proposed to look on and see how the development followed from the inherent impulse of the idea." So said Lotze.[50] Saleilles, looking back over the work of the school of which he had been an adherent, said: "[the historical school] had clipped its wings and as it were disarmed itself in declaring that scientifically it could exert no effect upon the phenomenal development of law; it had only to await, to register, to verify."[51]

We may pass now to the positivists.[52] Somewhat later the doctrines as to the end of law which had become fixed in Anglo-American juristic thought under the influence of the historical school were reinforced in America by the influence of the positivists. Spencer's writings had much vogue in France, Italy, and Spain as well as in America. In many American cases judicial opinions show the effect of his ideas. Indeed,

49. 1 Hegel, *History of Philosophy* (transl. by Haldane, 1892) 80.
50. *Logic*, 50 (English transl. 1884, p. 196).
51. Saleilles, *L'école historique et droit naturel* (1902) 1 REVUE TRIMESTRIELLE DE DROIT CIVIL, 80, 94.
52. Spencer, *Principles of Sociology*, pt. 2, *Inductions of Sociology* (1876); id. *Justice* (1891) chaps. 4–8. See Ardigo, *La morale dei positivisti* (1879); Gumplowicz, *Grundriss der Soziologie* (1885); id. *Soziologie und Politik* (1892); Vanni, *Lezioni di filosofia del diritto* (3 ed. 1908); Lévy-Bruhl, *La morale et la science des moeurs* (1903).

Mr. Justice Holmes was impelled to protest that the Fourteenth Amendment to the constitution of the United States did not enact Spencer's Social Statics.[53] The earlier positivists thought of the universe as governed by mathematical mechanical laws, and hence of moral and social phenomena as referable to such laws also. The next generation of positivists, influenced by Darwin, thought of evolution as governed by some such mechanical laws. Accordingly the purpose of the positivist jurists was to find laws of morals, laws of social evolution, and laws of legal development analogous to gravitation, conservation of energy, and the like. For example, Brooks Adams says: "I always conceive of sovereignty in the abstract as the resultant of several conflicting forces moving in a curve. If law were the will of the strongest it would be logical and direct. Law is not the will of the strongest, for the will of the strongest is always deflected from its proper path by resistance. Sovereignty, therefore, is a compromise, as the earth's orbit is a compromise."[54]

These laws were to be found by observation and experience, verified by further observation. But observation and verification led them to the same result to which metaphysics had led the nineteenth-century philosophical jurists and history had led the historical jurists. Spencer considered by observation of social, political, and legal phenomena he had proved a "law of equal freedom," which he formulated thus: "Hence that which we have to express in a precise way is the liberty of each limited only by the like liberties of all. This we do by saying: Every man is free to do that which he wills provided he infringes not the equal freedom of any other man."[55] A generation before he had said: "They [the positivists] urge that, as throughout civilization the manifest tendency has been continuously to extend the liberties of the subject and restrict the functions of the state, there is reason to believe that the ultimate political condition must be one in which political freedom is the greatest possible; that, namely, in which the freedom of each has no limit but the

---

53. Holmes, J., dissenting in *Lochner v. New York*, 198 U.S. 45, 75 (1905).
54. Brooks Adams in *Centralization and the Law* (1906) 52.
55. Spencer, *Justice* (1891) § 27.

like freedom of all; while the sole governmental duty is the mainte-nance of this limit."[56] So completely was this accepted by a strong group in politics, ethics, and jurisprudence, that a writer on political ethics in the last decade of the nineteenth century could write: "Governments are being remanded, if not into the rubbish heap of the world's back-yard, yet into a secondary and subordinate place. And where men have relied in the past on the sovereign and the statute book for order, safety, prosperity, happiness, they are now coming to rely for them simply on themselves."[57] Purporting to be based on deduction, this exhibits a cu-rious blindness to the legal and political facts of the time when it was written.

Spencer seems to have thought of the progress from status to contract as the rational outcome of the universe. He took abstract freedom of contract to be, as one might say, the ideal to which evolution continu-ally tended. Moreover, the positivists got their data as to legal institu-tions and doctrines from the historical jurists and so looked at the phe-nomena of legal history not independently but through the spectacles of that school. Maine's Ancient Law is the principal juristic authority used in Spencer's Justice.[58] It is hardly a mere coincidence that the idea of the function of law in maintaining the limits within which the free-dom of each is to find the widest possible development[59] so closely re-sembles Savigny's formula: "If free beings are to coexist . . . invisible boundaries must be recognized within which the existence and activity of each individual gains a secure free opportunity. The rules whereby this opportunity is secured are the law."[60] Spencer's formula of justice is a Kantian formula. He had never read Kant.[61] But Kant had become part of the thought of the time so thoroughly that each of the significant nineteenth-century schools—the metaphysical school, the English

56. Spencer, *First Principles* (1863) § 2.
57. Kimball, *Morals in Politics*, in *Brooklyn Ethical Society, Man and the State* (1892) 521–22.
58. *See* the table of references in the American edition pp. 287 ff.
59. Spencer, *First Principles* (1863) § 2.
60. 1 Savigny, *System des heutigen römischen Rechts* (1840) § 52.
61. Spencer, *Justice*, Appendix A (1891).

utilitarians, the historical school, and the positivists — came to his position as to the end of law, though for different reasons and in different ways.[62] Moreover, the juristic pessimism of the other schools was fully shared by the positivists. Spencer said: "We are to search out with genuine humility the rules ordained for us — are to do unfalteringly without speculation as to consequences, whatever these require."[63] Said Brooks Adams: "If society be, as I assume it to be, an organism operating on mechanical principles, we may perhaps, by pondering upon history, learn enough of those principles to enable us to view, more intelligently than we otherwise should, the social phenomena about us."[64]

Finally, we must consider the economic realists.[65] Juristic radicalism in the nineteenth century took two paths. On the one hand, the idea of justice as the maximum of individual self-assertion and the prevailing juristic pessimism led some (the anarchist individualists or philosophical anarchists) to develop to its extreme logical consequences the doctrine that law is intrinsically evil in that it restrains liberty.[66] Hence they advocated a regime of individual action by voluntary cooperation, free from coercion by state-enforced rules. According to Proudhon: "Politics is the science of liberty; under whatever name it may be disguised, the government of man by man is oppression. The highest form of society is found in the union of order and anarchy."[67] Stirner argues that the "liberty" of the metaphysical jurists is but a negative idea. Put positively the end is: "Be your own; live for yourself, according to your individuality." Accordingly, the only justification for society is to contribute to the

62. See Charmont, *La renaissance du droit naturel* (1910) 122. As to Spencer's relation to Kant, *see* 1 Maitland, *Collected Papers* (1911) 279–80.

63. Spencer, *Social Statics, Conclusion* (1866) § 6.

64. Brooks Adams, *Theory of Social Revolutions* (1913) 203. *See* the comments of Del Vecchio, *Formal Bases of Law* (1914) transl. by Lisle, § 70.

65. 2 Berolzheimer, *System der Rechts- und Wirtschaftsphilosophie* (1905) §§ 37–40; Brown, *The Underlying Principles of Modern Legislation*, Prologue — *The Challenge of Anarchy* (1914).

66. Proudhon, *Qu'est-ce que la propriété?* (1840); id. *Idée génerale de la révolution au dix-neuvième siècle* (1851); id. *De la justice dans la révolution et dans l'église* (1858); Stirner, *Der Einzige und sein Eigenthum* (1845) English transl. as *The Ego and His Own* (1907); Grave, *La société future* (7 ed. 1895) 157.

67. Proudhon, *Qu'est-ce que la propriété*, 1 *Oeuvres Complètes* (1878 ed.) 224.

development of the individual and "permit a larger extension of his powers without demanding restrictions upon his personality beyond what already exist in the environment in which he is found."[68] They urged that government and law were in reality but means of economic oppression. Hence they claimed to look at realities and styled themselves realists. As this group argued for a free consensual rather than a legal ordering of society, naturally enough it gave us nothing which is of importance for jurisprudence. On the other hand, the idea of law and government as means of achieving individual liberty [*i.e.*, rather than of letting it achieve itself] was taken by another group,[69] which, rejecting political and juristic pessimism, but holding to the idea of free individual self-assertion as the end, developed what may fairly be called a social individualism. This "leaves intact the individualistic ends, but resorts to collective action as a new method of attaining them."[70] Where the main current of nineteenth-century juristic thought, following the seventeenth- and eighteenth-century tradition, opposed society and the individual and was troubled to reconcile government and liberty, this group sought individual liberty through collective action as the means to a maximum of liberty. It argued that it was the function of the state "to further the development of the human race to a state of freedom"; it was "the education and evolution of the human race to a state of freedom."[71] On another side, in contributing to theories of the social interest in the individual life and in developing the Hegelian idea of the culture-state (a state performing services) as distinguished from the Kantian law-state (a state which simply enables men to be free) the nineteenth-century socialists mark the beginnings of a transition to a new conception of the end of law.

68. Grave, *La société* (7 ed. 1895) 157.

69. Menger, *Das bürgerliche Recht und die besitzlosen Volksklassen* (1889, 4 ed. 1908); id. *Ueber die sozialen Aufgaben Rechts* (1885, 3 ed. 1910); Picard, *Le droit pur* (1899, reprinted 1920); Barasch, *La socialisme juridique* (1923); Panunzio, *Il socialismo giuridico* (2 ed. 1911).

70. Adler, *The Conception of Social Welfare*, PROCEEDINGS OF THE CONFERENCE ON LEGAL AND SOCIAL PHILOSOPHY (1913) 9. See Radbruch, *Grundzüge der Rechtsphilosophie* (1914) 97–98; id. *Rechtsphilosophie* (3 ed. 1932) § 6.

71. Lassalle, *Arbeiterprogramm* (1863) 1 Werke (ed. Blum) 156, 200.

Summing up the juristic theory of the end of law thus far, in the nineteenth century the idea of justice (the ideal relation among men) as the maximum of free individual self-assertion, which began to appear at the end of the sixteenth century, reached its highest development. But at the same time the actual course the development of legal rules and doctrines began to turn toward new ideas of the end of law and the forerunners of some idea, not yet formulated, which will govern in turn, have been appearing.

Although nineteenth-century jurists were in substantial agreement in conceiving of a maximum of free individual self-assertion as the end of the legal order, in the last quarter of the century courts and lawmakers found themselves pushed continually toward a new approach to legal problems because of the pressure of unrecognized or unsecured interests. For a time this affected courts and lawmakers only. It is not too much to say that, except for the systematic work of analytical jurists, from the standpoint of making legal institutions effective for justice, the courts and the leaders of the practicing profession were ahead of the legal science of the last generation. While legislative lawmaking and judicial finding and shaping of law were reaching out for some new conception, the scientific approach and the orthodox professional approach remained either rationalist or historical. Each of these approaches leads back to the rationalism which replaced authoritarianism at the breakdown of the relationally organized society of the Middle Ages.

No doubt it is too soon to form an assured judgment as to theories of the end of law in the twentieth century.[72] Only a small part of the new paths is apparent. But there seems good ground for asserting that twentieth-century law and twentieth-century juristic thinking are taking two new directions: (1) Concern for the concrete individual life rather than for the abstract individual will. (2) Concern for civilization as distinguished from and contrasted with politically organized society. Indeed, two new jural postulates are suggested by the course of legislation, of ju-

72. Pound, *Twentieth-Century Ideas as to the End of Law* in *Harvard Legal Essays* (1934) 357–75; id. *How Far Are We Attaining a New Measure of Values in Twentieth-Century Juristic Thought* (1936); id. *Fifty Years of Jurisprudence* (1938) 51 HARVARD LAW REVIEW 444, 448–72; id. *Social Control Through Law* (1942) 106–34.

dicial decision, and to some extent, of juristic writing. I should tentatively formulate them thus: (1) Every one is entitled to assume that the burdens incident to life in society will be borne by society. (2) Every one is entitled to assume that at least a standard human life will be assured him; not merely equal opportunities of providing or attaining it, but immediate material satisfactions. Thus far some such postulates have been affecting the law here and there chiefly through legislation. They go along with what is called the socialization of law. I do not propose them as what ought to be or as what will come to be received propositions, but only as what seems to be assumed by not a little legislation and some judicial decision today.

Many causes, social, economic and political, have contributed to require shifting of the emphasis from the abstract will of the abstract individual to the concrete claims of concrete human beings. What compelled jurists to this shift of emphasis was the development of psychology in the latter part of the last century. Under attack from modern psychology, the "individual," in the sense of the nineteenth-century metaphysical jurisprudence and the "individual free will" were as insecure foundations as the "natural man" and "the state of nature" had proved to be under the attacks of the critical philosophy a century before.[73] Indeed, before philosophical jurists had begun to think of such things, legislation was tending to show more and more concern for concrete human beings at the expense of abstract individualism. The last quarter of the nineteenth century was marked by a steady growth of such legislation, and the point of view was typical in legislation and administration in the first two decades, and in judicial decision in the second decade of the present century.

For example, although a majority of the Supreme Court of the United States in 1923, going on abstract considerations, held legislation prescribing minimum wages for women arbitrary and unreasonable, and so unconstitutional,[74] it is significant such statutes had then been

73. "Man *in abstracto,* as assumed by philosophies of law, has never actually existed at any point in time or space." 3 Wundt, *Ethics* (1901) transl. by Tichener and others, 160.
74. *Adkins* v. *Children's Hospital,* 261 U.S. 525 (1923).

enacted throughout the English-speaking world.[75] Also the overwhelming weight of opinion among those who reviewed the decision was adverse thereto.[76] The decision was later expressly overruled.[77]

It will be worth while to look into the change just illustrated in some detail. No doubt pioneer conditions were behind homestead laws, forbidding taking the family home in execution for debts, and exemption laws exempting household furniture, workmen's tools, agricultural machinery and needed animals in case of farmers, and the library of professional men, from seizure on execution against the head of a family. But they survived pioneer life and the principle of such legislation is active in the urban industrial life of today. Legislation against payment of wages in orders on company stores was active after 1881, and legislation as to conditions of labor after 1884. Later there was legislation as to hours of labor for women and children, child labor legislation, and as has been said, minimum wage legislation. There were small loan acts or "loan shark laws," workmen's compensation acts, "blue sky laws" protecting investors of savings, and much more of the sort. It is especially instructive to compare the old regime of employer's liability for negligence only, enforced by actions at law, with the new regime of workmen's compensation, made effective by administrative agencies. The former offered a theoretically complete provision for abstract justice to both abstract worker and abstract employer. Yet it failed notoriously to do justice in concrete cases because of the delay and expense involved in exact judicial determination of the facts and the precise measure of damages, because of the unequal actual position of employer and employed,[78] and because of the prejudice of jurors due to dissatisfaction with a system whereby the risk of accidents, inevitable in the conduct of industrial enterprizes, was so largely thrown upon those least able to bear it. In contrast, the regime of workmen's compensation is theoreti-

75. Andrews, *Minimum Wage Legislation* (1914).

76. *See* the collection of reviews in *The Supreme Court and Minimum Wage Legislation,* compiled by the *National Consumers' League* (1925); Powell, *The Judiciality of Minimum Wage Legislation* (1924) 37 HARVARD LAW REVIEW 545.

77. *West Coast Hotel Co. v. Parrish,* 300 U.S. 379 (1937).

78. *See* Smith, *Justice and the Poor* (3 ed. 1934) 87–90.

cally defective in many ways. It seeks a rough and ready justice rather than an equal and exact justice complete for each case. Experience has shown, however, that the interests of the concrete worker and, on the whole, of the concrete employer, are much better secured by the regime which is abstractly defective than by the regime in which the theoretical provision for full and exact justice to all men in the abstract was quite perfect. Yet abstract individualism had become part of American received ideals, and had so strong a hold upon us that many courts obstinately resisted such legislation, and most courts insisted for a generation on full theoretical securing of the abstract individual at the expense of the full human life of concrete human beings.

Take, for example, the attitude of American courts toward homestead and exemption laws. Chief Justice Taney, trained in the classical law of nature, was willing to allow a state to make retroactive exemptions "according to its own views of policy and humanity." He conceived that a state might "direct that the necessary implements of agriculture, tools of the mechanic, or articles of necessity in household furniture shall, like wearing apparel, not be liable to seizure on judgments;" that the state had power in this way to protect its citizens "in those pursuits which are necessary to the existence and well being of every community."[79] This view of Chief Justice Taney was approved by a great text writer and by more than one state court.[80] But a generation later, when the question came directly before the Supreme Court of the United States, the waning of the old ethical law of nature, the rise of the conception of giving effect to the declared will, and the economic development in the northern states after the Civil War, led to interpretation in the light of different ideals, and the view of Chief Justice Taney was rejected.[81] In the Virginia Homestead Cases,[82] the same year, the argument of counsel

---

79. *Bronson* v. *Kinzie*, 1 How. (U.S.) 311, 315–16 (1843). *See also* Woodbury, J., in *Planter's Bank* v. *Sharp*, 6 How. 301, 330 (1848).

80. Cooley, *Constitutional Limitations* (1 ed. 1869); *Morse* v. *Gould*, 11 N.Y. 281 (1854); *Baldy's Appeal*, 40 Pa. St. 328 (1861); *Gunn* v. *Barry*, 44 Ga. 351, 353 (1871); *Re Kennedy*, 2 S.C. 216 (1870); *Sneider* v. *Heidelberger*, 45 Ala. 126 (1871).

81. *Gunn* v. *Barry*, 15 Wall. (U.S.) 610, 620 (1873).

82. 22 Gratt. (Va.) 266 (1872).

brought out clearly and ably the concrete economic situation in the South to which the statutes involved in the two cases were palpably directed.[83] The complete ignoring of this background of fact as wholly irrelevant,[84] should be compared with the weight given to the *de facto* housing situation during and after the first World War in the District of Columbia Rent Cases,[85] and the New York Housing Case,[86] and the judicial recognition of the *de facto* crisis in the railway wage situation in 1916, which controlled the decision on the Adamson Law.[87] The concrete point of view seemed as much a matter of course in the present century as the abstract point of view in the last century and in the dissenting opinions in the District of Columbia Rent Cases. So strongly did homestead and exemption laws run counter to the juristic ideas of the last century that, although they had clear historical warrant in the common law,[88] they were for a time construed strictly, as in derogation of the common law,[89] and so, as it were, in derogation of "common right."[90]

Another useful comparison may be made if we note the spirit manifest in the course of decision in the courts from 1886 to 1900 and in some states down to 1910 upon liberty of contract as affected by what we have since called social legislation.

Two courts in passing adversely upon labor legislation, because it infringed a theoretical equality of free contract, noted the frequency of such legislation at the time as an interesting phenomenon, but said (one of them as late as 1902) that it was not necessary to consider the reasons therefor in order to determine whether the legislation was reasonable.[91] Reasonableness was an abstract question to be determined from the text

---

83. *Ibid.* 267–68, 274–75.
84. See also *Chambliss v. Jordan*, 50 Ga. 81 (1873).
85. *Block v. Hirsch*, 256 U.S. 135 (1921).
86. *People v. La Fetra*, 230 N.Y. 429 (1921).
87. *Wilson v. New*, 243 U.S. 332 (1917).
88. *See* Dick, J., in *Re Volger*, 28 Fed. Cas. 1248, 1249 (1873).
89. *Ward v. Huhn*, 16 Minn. 159, 161 (1870); *Guillory v. Deville*, 21 La. Ann. 686 (1869).
90. *Robinson v. Wiley*, 15 N.Y. 489 (1857).
91. *Low v. Rees Printing Co.*, 41 Neb. 127, 135 (1894); *State v. Kreutzberg*, 114 Wis. 530, 537 (1902). Each court, in later cases, became willing to consider the concrete situation. *Wenham v. State*, 65 Neb. 394 (1902); *Borgnis v. Falk Co.*, 147 Wis. 327 (1911).

of the statute abstractly regarded. Another court asked what "right" —
not what warrant in fact but what abstract justification — the legislature
had to "assume that one class has need of protection against another."[92]
Another court said gravely that the remedy for the company-store evil
was "in the hands of the employee,"[93] since theoretically he was on an
equal footing with the employer, compulsion in concrete economic fact
being irrelevant where it had no place in abstract legal theory. It is instructive to compare the reliance upon abstract equality in the opinion
of the West Virginia court in 1889 with the concrete view of a similar situation taken by Mr. Justice Holmes in 1907. He said: "Probably the
modification of this general principle [assumption of risk] by some judicial decisions and by statutes like [the Federal Safety Appliance Act]
is due to an opinion that men who work with their hands have not always the freedom and equality of position assumed by the doctrine of
laissez faire to exist."[94]

Still another court said that "theoretically there is among our citizens
no inferior class,"[95] and no facts could avail against that theory. Other
courts at the end of the last century spoke of company-store legislation and
laws to insure fair ascertainment of the laborer's work, where he was paid
on the basis of work done rather than of time, as putting laborers under
guardianship,[96] as creating a class of statutory laborers,[97] as stamping industrial laborers as imbeciles,[98] (*i.e.*, as creating status to replace free contract), as insulting to the manhood of laborers,[99] or as making them wards

92. *State* v. *Haun*, 61 Kan. 146, 162 (1899). As to the factual situation as it was at the
time of this legislation, *see* Smith, *Justice and the Poor* (3 ed. 1824) chap. 2.

93. *State* v. *Fire Creek Coal & Coke Co.*, 33 W.Va. 188, 190 (1889).

94. *Schlemmer* v. *Buffalo, R. & P.R. Co.*, 205 U.S. 1, 12 (1907).

95. *Frorer* v. *People*, 141 Ill. 171, 186 (1892) holding adversely to a statute prohibiting
company stores and requiring miners to be paid weekly.

96. *Braceville Coal Co.* v. *People*, 147 Ill. 66, 74 (1893) — coal to be weighed for fixing
wages; *State* v. *Haun*, 61 Kan. 146, 162 (1899) — wages to be paid in money.

97. *People* v. *Beck*, 10 Misc. (N.Y.) 77 (1894), dissenting opinion of White, J., *The
statute fixed hours of labor on municipal contracts.*

98. *State* v. *Goodwill*, 33 W.Va. 179, 186 (1889) — statute against payment of wages in
store orders.

99. *Godcharles* v. *Wigeman*, 113 Pa. St. 431, 437 (1886) — statute required wages to be
paid in money.

of the state.[100] As late as 1908, even the Supreme Court of the United States dealt with the relation of employer and employee in railway transportation as if it were a matter of two neighbors bargaining in the rural, agricultural neighborhood of a century before.[101] This artificial type of reasoning, on the basis of a theoretical abstract equality and abstract liberty of contract, ignoring the facts of the economic order, began to disappear from American law books a generation ago.[102] It no longer needs to be refuted in spite of a temporary recrudescence after the first World War. More and more the courts have been taking for granted that they may, and indeed must, look at life in the concrete and not at man in the abstract.

If this were all, we might still be able to hold to Kant's formula of justice. We could say that in an industrial society, looking the facts of the economic order in the face, it promoted a maximum of individual liberty to put certain limits upon the freedom of contract of the employer in order to give place for a fair amount of liberty of contract on the part of the employee. But it began to be doubted whether liberty, "the permission or power to do what one pleases to do without any external restraint"[103] was all that men could reasonably expect in civilized society; that, as Kant put it, if liberty was secured to men happiness would take care of itself.[104] There ceased to be general agreement that liberty was the sole nor even the supreme human expectation.

In the first decade of the present century economists, sociologists, and students of politics had become aware of this change of front at a time when jurists were still repeating the nineteenth-century formula. It was easy to assume that the Kantian conception was necessarily identified with law. Hence the first attempts to formulate a new theory of the end of law were put in terms of a contrast between social justice and legal

---

100. Peckham, J., in *Lochner v. New York*, 198 U.S. 45, 57 (1905).

101. Harlan, J., in *Adair v. United States*, 208 U.S. 161, 175 (1908).

102. *McLean v. Arkansas*, 211 U.S. 534 (1909); *Chicago B. & Q.R. Co. v. McGuire*, 219 U.S. 549, 560–75 (1911).

103. Carter, *Law: Its Origin, Growth, and Function* (1907) 133.

104. *See ante* note 31. "Of the conditions necessary to enable the individual to attain [pure happiness] I name, without fear of contradiction, as the first liberty, the choicest of human blessings." Carter, *loc. cit. See also* Carter, *op. cit.* 337.

justice.[105] The divergence between the idea which was growing up beneath the surface in actual rules and doctrines, especially through legislation, and the orthodox juristic conception, the difference between the idea which was coming to obtain in the other social sciences and the one which held in jurisprudence, was most acute in the United States at the time of the agitation for recall of judges and recall of judicial decisions.[106] Today the divergence is less marked or has even disappeared, and other ways of formulating a newer idea of the end of law have replaced formulation in terms of contrast. From the side of ethics the change from the nineteenth-century conception has been put as a shifting from an economic standpoint, which regarded primarily individual claims to property and to promised advantages, to a civilization standpoint, which seeks to make possible for each individual a full moral life. Thus we are told: "The old justice in the economic field consisted chiefly in securing to each individual his rights in property and contracts. The new justice must consider how it can secure for each individual a standard of living, and such a share in the values of civilization as shall make possible a full moral life."[107] Here, I take it, the term "eco-

105. Pound, The End of Law as Developed in Legal Rules and Doctrines: 1. Social Justice and Legal Justice (1914) 27 HARVARD LAW REVIEW 195, 195–98; Willoughby, Social Justice (1900) 20–21; Carver, Social Justice (1915) 3–34; Hobhouse, Elements of Social Justice (1922) chaps. 1–4.

106. This agitation was at its height between 1911 and 1914. See PROCEEDINGS OF THE ACADEMY OF POLITICAL SCIENCE OF THE CITY OF NEW YORK, vol. 3 (1913); ANNALS OF THE AMERICAN ACADEMY OF POLITICAL AND SOCIAL SCIENCE (Philadelphia) The Initiative, Referendum, and Recall (1912); Recall of Judges, Senate Document No. 649 (1911); Brown, Judicial Recall—A Fallacy Repugnant to Constitutional Government, ANNALS OF THE AMERICAN ACADEMY OF POLITICAL AND SOCIAL SCIENCE (Philadelphia) also published as Senate Document No. 892 (1912); Taft, Recall of Decisions, a Modern Phase of Impatience of Constitutional Restraints, 33 REP. N.Y. STATE BAR ASSN. 169 (1913); Dodd, The Recall and the Political Responsibility of Judges, 10 MICHIGAN LAW REVIEW 79 (1911); Theodore Roosevelt, The Right of the People to Rule, Senate Document No. 473, 66th Congress, 2nd Session (1912); Thayer, Recall of Judicial Decisions, 4 LEGAL BIBLIOGRAPHY, New Series, 3 (1913); Hornblower, The Independence of the Judiciary the Safeguard of Free Institutions, Senate Document No. 1052, 62nd Congress, 3rd Session (1913); Addresses on the Recall of Judges and the Recall of Judicial Decisions, 1912 PROC. ILLINOIS STATE BAR ASSOCIATION, 174–258.

107. Dewey and Tufts, Ethics (rev. ed. 1938) 496.

nomics" is used to refer to the point of view of the classical economics, which was identical with that of nineteenth-century jurisprudence. The Kantian justice is given up in economics as well as in jurisprudence. Whitehead makes the same case against the one that has been made against the other. He says: "It is very arguable that the science of political economy, as studied in the first period after the death of Adam Smith [1790] did more harm than good. It destroyed many economic fallacies, and taught how to think about the economic revolution then in progress. But it riveted on men a certain set of abstractions that were disastrous in their influence on modern mentality. It dehumanized industry."[108] From the standpoint of economic realism the change has been put as one of a conception of justice in terms of wants rather than of wills. Thus Ward suggested instead of the liberty of each limited only by the like liberties of all, the satisfaction of every one's wants so far as they are not outweighed by others' wants.[109] But that takes us back to the problem of a measure of values, for the wants of each are to be weighed with reference to the wants of others. It is not to be a count of wants but a weighing. Juristically the change might be put as a shift of emphasis from the social interest in the general security (chiefly in the form of security of acquisitions and security of transactions) to the social interest in the individual life.

Our situation in jurisprudence today, as to theory of justice, is much what it was in the sixteenth century. Then the idea of justice as a maintaining of the social *status quo* which had been received along with Roman law and had proved equal to the problems of the science of law in the Middle Ages was failing to meet the exigencies of a world of discovery, adventure, pioneering and wide opportunities, and jurists were casting about for a substitute.

In the seventeenth century the matter was complicated by the breakdown of the twofold organization of medieval society as religious and political, of the coordinate position of church and state as the chief

108. Whitehead, *Science and the Modern World* (1938) 288.
109. Adapted from Ward, *Applied Sociology* (1906) 22–24.

agencies of social control. It was complicated, too, by the divorce of jurisprudence from theology and of law from the text of Justinian and consequent necessity of building a new foundation for legal theory. It was no offhand matter of replacing authority by reason. As one might put it, reason had to be applied to discovery of the content of reason. There had to be a complete remaking of juristic method.

Today the matter is complicated by the rise of the welfare or, as I prefer to call it, the service state; the state which instead of securing men against molestation while they pursue opportunities and discover happiness for themselves, undertakes to serve up happiness to them ready prepared and to save them harmless not merely from attacks by others or risks unreasonably cast on them by others, but from their own negligence, want of foresight, lack of initiative or energy, and lack of capacity equal to their ambition, as well as from the unforeseen and often unforceable accidents and misfortunes to which humanity is heir in any society and the more in highly mechanized urban existence today. A political organization which sets out to relieve mankind from fear and from want, not to mention other freedoms recently urged, and to provide all men with "just terms of leisure," will call for much protracted hard thinking from those who are to expound its juristic theory.

Along with this controversial change of conception as to the function of the state there goes today a controversy with the believers in collectivism, who see all things in terms of — I was going to say through the spectacles of — politically organized society, who identify society with the state, and to whom the individual is wholly merged in society and so in the state. This stands to the reorganization of juristic thought today where the problem of universal law or a separate local law of each state did to the sixteenth century.

In the second place the matter is complicated today by the unification of the social sciences and recognition of jurisprudence as one of them. But whereas in the sixteenth century jurisprudence had to break loose from what, as we look back, we may call the theological social science of the Middle Ages, it has to work with ethics and politics and economics, and sociology in the quest of a fundamental idea and a formula to replace the Kantian one we are giving up.

Finally the matter is embarrassed today by a feeling of the inadequacy of the legal philosophy of the last century without any general agreement upon a substitute.

What we are looking for is the ideal relation among men which, when we have formulated it as an idea, will give a guide for legislation, a sure ground of choosing from among conflicting or competing starting points for legal reasoning, a touchstone of interpretation and a pathfinder in the application of legal standards. The nineteenth century had such a formula but we are giving it up.

In the past the ideal relation among men has been thought of successively in three ways. First, it was put in terms of peace, and from the standpoint of civilization here is a root idea. Unless there is peace and order in a society effective division of labor is impossible and maintenance of a society of any size or complexity of organization becomes impossible. Second, it was put as stability of the social *status quo*. Here again we have something without which the large populations of most parts of the world could not maintain themselves. The economic organization of society depends upon the social organization, and that rests ultimately in the law. But we say that law must be stable although it cannot stand still. Third, the ideal relation among men has been put as liberty; as a social order in which no one is constrained to do or restrained from doing otherwise than as his free will freely expressed dictates except as he thereby restrains the free will of others. Here, also, is something that must have a place in organized civilized society. All social organization is liable to disruption if the rooted repugnance of mankind to having a man's will forcibly subjected to the arbitrary will of others is not taken into account. The second here includes the first and the third presupposes the second.

After the second was giving way it took two centuries to work out a final formulation of the third. Now that after a century of substantial agreement on the third we are agreeing to give it up we may hardly expect to find a generally acceptable substitute at once.

Some are urging an idea of cooperation, many are urging an idea of civilization. Some are urging an idea of maximum satisfaction of material wants. Some urge an idea of promoting a full economic and social individual life.

As a lawyer, not a philosopher, I do not assume to lay out any formula which is to be a permanent substitute for Kant's. But I purpose to examine the different theories which are proposed and to consider them from a lawyer's standpoint.

EIGHT

Maintaining and Furthering Civilization

We have seen that at the end of the nineteenth century and in the beginning of the present century there was a definite shift in juristic thought away from the idea of promoting and maintaining the fullest free individual self-assertion as the end of law. Throughout the last century that idea was all but universally accepted by jurists substantially as Kant had formulated it at the end of the eighteenth century. No doubt the will jurisprudence of the nineteenth century will hang on here and there for a long time to come just as contract jurisprudence of the eighteenth century has been known to darken counsel in out-of-the-way cases even in the twentieth century.[1] But as a real force either in the law or in the science of law the one is as dead as the other.

Movement away from the accepted idea of the last century is clear enough. But while there is general agreement as to from what juristic thought of the present has moved, there is little or no agreement as to what or toward what is moving. Some have been urging an idea of co-operation as the end of law. But cooperation is a process rather than an end. It must be cooperation toward something, and so we must ask, cooperation to what end? Certainly the emphasis today is on an ideal of cooperation rather than on one of free competitive self-assertion. In the western world it is enough to consider as to any of the significant cities,

---

1. *Sinclair v. Brougham* [1914] A.C. 398, holding that an incorporated society unjustly enriched in an innocent *ultra vires* transaction cannot be held to make restitution because a contract for restitution cannot be implied where no express contract to borrow for the purpose for which money was borrowed could be valid.

and in most western countries the bulk of the population has become definitely urban, how many individuals are freely competing and how many more are doing their part cooperatively, in however modest a way, as employees in great enterprises, finding a reflected glory in the greatness of the enterprise and giving it service in return for protection in a relation suggesting the old one of lord and man.[2] Even if cooperation is not to be the whole idea it may well be a large part of it. Cooperation or participation in maintaining the social and so the political order may be what the eighteenth century meant by the social contract. Moreover if instead of saying cooperation we say, with Duguit, interdependence, we must still ask to what end we seek to promote interdependence. We can hardly think of interdependence as the end. I prefer to think that the recognition of cooperation and the new emphasis upon it in all connections is a step toward some ideal involving organized human effort along with free spontaneous initiative, and one could conceive of such an ideal in the idea of civilization. One might think of cooperation toward bringing about and maintaining a balance between independence and interdependence in order to promote civilization. Some such mode of thought has brought many to look on civilization as the end. There has been not a little argument recently as to whether jurisprudence is a "civilization science."[3]

Thus we find theories of the end of law in terms of cooperation,[4] of promoting and maintaining social interdependence,[5] and of maintaining, furthering, and transmitting civilization.[6]

2. See Pound, *The New Feudalism*, 10 AMERICAN BAR ASSOCIATION JOURNAL, 553 (1930).

3. Radbruch, *Rechtsphilosophie* (3 ed. 1832) 119; Horvath, *Rechtssoziologie* (1934) §§ 27–32; Timasheff, *What Is Sociology of Law*, 43 AMERICAN JOURNAL OF SOCIOLOGY (1937) 225; id. *Introduction to the Sociology of Law* (1939) chap. 14.

4. Picard, *Le droit pur* (1899) § 186. See Pound, *Social Control Through Law* (1942) 126–32.

5. Duguit, *L'état, le droit objectif, et la loi positive* (1901) chaps. 4, 5; id. *Le droit social, le droit individuel, et la transformation de l'état* (2 ed. 1911) lect. 2.

6. Kohler, *Lehrbuch der Rechtsphilosophie* (2 ed. 1917) 11; id. *Einführung in die Rechtswissenschaft* (1901) § 3.

Another end urged has been the satisfaction of human material wants on an assumption that when these are satisfied (as Kant thought would happen if desire for individual self-assertion were satisfied happiness would follow as a matter of course) all causes of conflict among men would be eliminated.[7] This postulates that there are no human claims or expectations which will press upon a legal order except those arising from control over the material goods of existence; that there will always be enough of the material goods of existence to give every one as much as he can wish, so that no contentions can arise as to use and enjoyment. Secondly, it postulates that there will be no conflicts or overlappings of the desires or demands or expectations known as interests of personality, or that they will be so simple as not to require more than an offhand commonsense determination for each individual case. Indeed, those who adhere to the Marxian idea or to variants of it, urge that there are no such things as interests to be secured apart from the law. They argue that rights, so-called, are but results of state interference, so that there would be none if the state kept its hands off. They argue that it is not a matter of interests pre-existing and taken up and secured by threats, but one of threats arising from the self-interests of the dominant class, giving rise to demands which are then secured.[8] There is nothing in human experience to warrant faith in any of these propositions. But a doctrine of administrative absolutism is relied on to take the place of the law for such situations as those involved in interference with personality. It is said that the state as an organization of compulsion may go on long after law has disappeared.[9] There is to be no law and but one rule of law, namely, that there are no laws but only administrative orders for the individual case. Expediency is to be the guide for each item of judicial-

---

7. "Law will wholly disappear with the abolition of classes and their opposing interests." Where there are no conflicting interests to be adjusted there is no need of law. Paschukanis, *Allgemeine Rechtslehre und Marxismus* (1929) Intr. and chap. 4.

8. Lundstedt, *The General Principles of Civil Liability in Different Legal Systems*, 2 ACTA ACADEMIAE UNIVERSALIS JURISPRUDENTIAE COMPARATIVAE, 367, 371, 407.

9. Paschukanis, *Allgemeine Rechtslehre und Marxismus* (1929) chap. 5.

administrative action.[10] Experience, however, led to giving up of the doctrine of disappearance of law. It became the Soviet doctrine that while the dictatorship of the proletariat is a power unrestrained by any laws yet it uses laws as an instrument of government.[11] Unrestrained dictatorship of the proletariat, using laws as an instrument of government, puts as an end simply enforcing the will of the dictator for the time being. Nothing more need be said about this as an ideal.

As for the Marxian idea of disappearance of law as not needed under communism, as argued by Paschukanis, all human experience shows that men will fight for their honor at least as much as for the contents of their pocketbooks. It shows that man will fight for his belief no less than for his life and limb and for his honor. The history of religious wars refutes the idea that property is the sole cause of strife. The pious folk who colonized America, and braved the hardships of the wilderness, starvation, and the hostility of savage tribes in order to be able to worship God according to their consciences, gave us a sufficient answer.

It is worth while to notice how jurisprudence has, as one might say, experimented with successive analogues. (1) First, the Greek philosophers used the analogy of the order of physical nature. (2) The scholastic theological philosophers used the analogy of the legislation of Justinian, and thought of divine legislation for the universe of which human lawmaking and application of law were to be a reflection. (3) The rationalists used the analogy of deducing the properties of a triangle from a limited number of axioms. (4) The metaphysical-historical jurists used the analogy of embryology; of the development of a complex organism from a simple embryo through some energy from within. (5) The positivist sociologists used the analogy of the revolutions of the planets in orbits calculable through mathematics. Instead of these sociological jurisprudence turns to analogies which do not postulate determinism and yet remind us that what we do in law is conditioned by

10. *Ibid.* chap. 2.
11. 1 Gsovsky, *Soviet Civil Law* (1948) 187–92.

many things.[12] Accordingly, I have urged an "engineering interpreta-tion" of legal history, using the term "engineering" in the sense with which industrial engineering has made Americans familiar. I have sug-gested thinking of jurisprudence as a science of social engineering, hav-ing to do with that part of the whole field of social control which may be achieved by adjustment of human relations and ordering of human conduct through the action of politically organized society.[13] It is an organized body of knowledge with respect to the means of satisfying human demands and expectations, securing interests, giving effect to claims or desires, with the least friction and waste, so far as these things can be brought about by the legal order; whereby the means of satisfac-tion may be made to go as far as possible. It is the task of the social sci-ences to make this process of satisfying human demands and expecta-tions, of giving effect to human desires, continually less wasteful. They seek to find out how to make this process go on with less friction and to satisfy more effectively a greater total of human demands. As one of the social sciences jurisprudence has for its field to discover what part of this task may be achieved or furthered by the legal order and how. The philosophical jurists of the nineteenth century were not at all in error in thinking of a task of reconciling or harmonizing. Indeed that concep-tion is not the least of Kant's contributions to the science of law.[14] But they did not think of a process. They sought for a universal abstract rec-onciling or harmonizing, where today we conceive of a process giving no more than compromises or adjustments, valid (because effective) for the time and place.

I shall take up the idea of civilization and the idea of social engineer-ing in this lecture. A recent idea beginning to appear in the development of legal rules and doctrines, which for want of any name generally at-tached to it I call the humanitarian idea, will require a lecture for itself.

12. See e.g., Cardozo, Paradoxes of Legal Science (1928) lects. 2, 3.
13. I have discussed this in Interpretations of Legal History (1923) 150–65.
14. See Immanuel Kant, by George Herbert Palmer and others (1925) 81–82.

Civilization as the idea from which to start in the social sciences is a proposition we owe to Kohler.[15] Josef Kohler, Professor at Berlin, 1888 to 1919, had exceptional qualifications as a philosopher of law because of all round knowledge of law and acquaintance with problems of the legal order. He was for a time *Amtsrichter* a term for which we have no English equivalent, but for which the English county court judge as he was before recent extensions of his jurisdiction is not far from comparable. Next he was a *Kreisrichter* or superior judge of first instance. He became professor at Würzburg in 1878, going after ten years to Berlin. His teaching and writing covered a wide field, Roman law, primitive law, in which he became a recognized authority, specialized branches of modern law such as the history of criminal law, patent law and bankruptcy (on each of the two last he wrote standard texts) and the German Civil Code which took effect in 1900, on which he wrote a commentary. Finally in 1904 he turned his attention to philosophy of law. As I have said of him elsewhere, he came nearer than any one else in modern times to taking all law for his province. Four achievements to his credit and to the school of Neo-Hegelian social philosophical jurists which he founded are significant: (1) The theory of law as the product of the civilization of a people, (2) the theory of the relation of comparative legal history and the philosophy of law, (3) the theory of sociological interpretation and application of legal precepts, and (4) the method of formulating the jural postulates of the civilization of the time and place. The four are closely connected and in a measure the three last turn on the first. But our concern here is with the first and the fourth.

Fifty years ago there was a general tendency to say that law was relative. But relative to what? Kohler answered that it was relative to civi-

15. Josef Kohler, 1849–1919, *Einführung in die Rechtswissenschaft* (1902, 5 ed. 1919); *Rechtsphilosophie und Universalrechtsgeschichte*, in Holtzendorf, ENZYKLOPADIE DER RECHTSWISSENSCHAFT (6 ed. 1904, 7 ed. 1915); *Moderne Rechtsprobleme* (1907, 2 ed. 1913); *Lehrbuch der Rechtsphilosophie* (1908, 3 ed. by Arthur Kohler, 1923) the first ed. transl. by Albrecht as Kohler's *Philosophy of Law* (1914); *Recht und Persönlichkeit* in *Der Kultur der Gegenwart* (1914).

lization and that laws were relative to the civilization of the time and place. While there was no body of universal institutions, doctrines and rules, good for all peoples, times and places, there was a universal idea — civilization. Law had a fundamental quest — "the furthering of civilization through a forcible ordering of things."[16] But it was not only a means of maintaining civilization, it was a product of civilization. Hence law had to be looked at in three ways: (1) As to the past, as a product of civilization; (2) as to the present, as a means of maintaining civilization; (3) as to the future as a means of furthering civilization.[17]

By civilization he meant the most complete possible social development of human powers;[18] the most complete human control over both external or physical nature and over internal or human nature.[19] At first sight this looks like the doctrine of the Krauseans. Lorimer saw as the ultimate object of jurisprudence the attainment of human perfection.[20] Ahrens held that the individual was perfecting himself and the law kept others off so that he might do so.[21] To both the individual was the organ of humanity. Humanity was perfected by the individual perfecting himself. To Kohler there was an idea of civilization at work, not simply an aggregate of individuals each for himself. A whole people was striving to develop its powers to the utmost. A comparison with the nineteenth-century idea will tell the story. If we are only to keep the peace while each individual prosecutes his quest of perfection for himself and in his own way, we come to Spencer's denunciation of sanitary laws and factory acts. Indeed, as Kohler saw it, each and all are developing a whole people, even the whole race, by social control, particularly by political and legal institutions which express and are designed to maintain and further civilization as men understand it in the time and place.

16. *Moderne Rechtsprobleme* (1907) § 1.
17. *Lehrbuch der Rechtsphilosophie* (1908) 1–2.
18. *Moderne Rechtsprobleme* (1907) § 1.
19. See *Berolzheimer* in 3 ARCHIV FUR RECHTS UND WIRTSCHAFTSPHILOSOPHIE, 195–96.
20. *Institutes of Law* (2 ed. 1880) 353.
21. *Cours de droit naturel* (8 ed. 1892) § 19.

In an ideal of raising human powers to the most complete unfolding, of bringing about the maximum of human control over both external nature and internal nature, two factors in achieving that control have to be seen: free individual initiative, what the nineteenth century insisted on, and cooperative, ordered activity. If we are to maintain and go forward with and hand down control over nature neither may be left out of account. We are not bound to believe that only one of the two can be the ideal or part of the ideal. By recognizing individual freedom in our picture of what we seek through law we are not bound to exclude coordinated, cooperative, even in no small measure regimented action, nor on the other hand because we recognize cooperation as a factor in civilization are we bound to give up all that we achieved in the nineteenth century in working out a system of individual rights or what was achieved through and since the Puritan Revolution toward securing individual freedom. Here again we have an antinomy such as Radbruch saw as between the ideal relation among men, the ideal development of individual character, and security, and have the perennial problem of balance. Those who complain of the vagueness of the idea of civilization can make the same complaint wherever balance is called for.

As to the method of formulating jural postulates of the civilization of the time and place, the starting point is that the idea of civilization is not one of something fully developed and admitting of detailed formulation in precepts of universal application. As control over physical nature and over human nature develop differently and in different degrees in times and places, the presuppositions of civilized life will differ also from time to time and from place to place. In the Middle Ages in western Europe life in society presupposed relations of protection and service and the beginnings of English common law were built up on or around the idea of relation. It was presupposed that men were in relations involving reciprocal rights and duties. Laws were shaped by or grew up to the exigencies of a social organization of that sort. In the sixteenth century the opening up of wide opportunities of acquisitive activities shaped the law to ideas of liberty which such a society presupposed. The rise of trade and commerce in the seventeenth century brought about a civilization which presupposed the security of transactions and the law of contracts developed accordingly culminating in the proposition of the French Civil Code in 1904 that the making of contract is a legislative act. The parties make laws for themselves governing their relations which the courts can no more alter than they can alter legislature-made laws.[22] After the industrial revolution an industrial society presupposed expectations on the part of employees in the relation of employer and employee. In America, transition from a rural agricultural to an urban industrial society has led to an expectation of a vested right in their jobs on the part of employees which was quite out of line with the ideas of the eighteenth and nineteenth centuries but is now given effect by legislation and judicial decision throughout the English-speaking world. As a general proposition, a legal right is conferred consciously and intelligently as a recognition of reasonable expectations, or what are believed to be reasonable expectations of civilized life. Finding out what these presuppositions are in the time and place and measuring the law of the time by them, realizing that such presuppositions change with changes in society, is a very different thing from setting up universal abstract propositions of natural law and making the basis of criticism and of lawmaking for all time.

Civilization, whether thought of as fact or as idea, is a good starting point for the social sciences. It is said to be the raising of human powers to their highest possible unfolding, or as I put it above, the achieving the maximum control over external or physical nature and over internal or human nature of which man is capable. Thus there is a process, a condition to which the process has brought us thus far, and an idea of the process and of the condition to which the process leads. But this way of putting it is perhaps too much in the manner of Hegel for the present generation. Let us say then the development of human powers to constantly greater completeness. Even if there are intervals

22. *French Civil Code*, art. 1134.

of retrogression, they have been followed by recovery and further advance, so that the history of mankind, looked at as a whole, shows a constant increase in human control both of external and of internal nature. The enormous increase in control over physical nature attained in the past hundred years, in which so much has been gained that one hesitates to say that anything which mankind strenuously seeks to do is impossible, may justify us in thinking, if indeed we can comprehend it, of complete control. At any rate, it is enough to think of the most complete control over external or physical nature which men are able to attain for the time being. They can still look forward to carrying the process on, even if it is to take as long to realize some detail of control as it took from Daedalus to Orville and Wilbur Wright to make good the dream of conquest of the air. This is as true of one side of civilization as of the other.

These two sides of civilization are interdependent. If it were not for the control over internal nature, which men first achieved, they could have done little toward the conquest of physical nature. If men had to go about armed and in constant fear of attack, if it were not a postulate of life in civilized society that men must be able to assume that others will commit no intentional aggressions upon them, and if it were not a further postulate that those who are engaged in any course of conduct will carry it on with due care not to cast an unreasonable risk of injury upon their fellow men, it would not be possible to carry on the research and experiment and investigation which have made possible the harnessing of so much of physical nature to man's use. But without the control of physical nature which has been achieved it would not be possible for the enormous populations which now occupy the earth to maintain themselves. Thus the control over internal nature has enabled man to inherit the earth and to maintain and increase that inheritance. The social sciences have to do with this achieved mastery over internal or human nature. They organize knowledge of what it is, how it has come about, and above all how it may be maintained, furthered, and transmitted.

It has been usual of late to contrast personalism and transpersonalism,[23] or as it is more commonly put, individualism and socialism, as exclusive alternatives and hence many have conceived of the increasing emphasis upon civilization values as a movement toward collectivism. But it has no absolute relation to the controversies between adherents of an atomistic and advocates of an organic conception of society. It is not necessary to make an out-and-out choice once for all between nineteenth-century abstract individualism and nineteenth-century orthodox socialism as inevitable alternatives. It is not necessary to make a thoroughgoing choice, once for all, between, on the one hand, looking at all things from the standpoint of the values in terms of personality value — and, on the other hand, looking at all things from the standpoint of organized society — reckoning personality values and civilization values in terms of community values or political values. It is quite as possible to reckon both personality values and community values in terms of civilization values. Everything that is not abstract individualism is not therefore socialism in any but a propagandist sense of that term. To lump the reckoning in terms of civilization values with the reckoning in terms of community values under an epithet of socialism is superficial. They are quite as distinct from each other as each is distinct from the abstract individualism of the last century. If nineteenth-century abstract individualism carries on the abstract individualism of the law-of-nature school, yet it does go on an organic basis. And if nineteenth-century socialism has a Hegelian philosophical pedigree and a historical juristic pedigree, yet it conceives of the end of law in terms of abstract individualism. The first and second of the three standpoints might with equal truth be lumped as "individualism." Individualist and collectivist or socialist were at one in the last century as to the highest good. Each strove for political and legal institutions which would promote the greatest and freest self-assertion. The one sought it through a regime of political and

23. Lask, *Rechtsphilosophie* (1905) in 1 *Gesammelte Schriften* (1923) 277, 304 ff.; Radbruch, *Grundzüge der Rechtsphilosophie* (1914) 82–158; Binder, *Philosophie des Rechts* (1925) §§ 8, 9.

legal hands off. The other sought it through a regime of all-embracing legal and political action. For, as has been said, the orthodox socialism of the last century was in effect a social individualism. It sought a maximum of free individual self-assertion through a maximum of collective action as orthodox individualism sought it through a minimum of collective action.[24] When individual self-assertion becomes means rather than end, we have something which is neither "individualism" nor "socialism," as those terms got their settled application in the last century, but a distinct tendency more and more characteristic of the present century.

As said in another connection, the method of formulating the jural postulates of the time and place is a means of making the idea of maintaining and furthering civilization practically applicable to the problems in the legal order in a time and place. The postulates are arrived at by study of the law of the time and place to find what its institutions and precepts and doctrines presuppose as being required by the received picture of the ideal relation among men and study of the formulated postulates as to whether they express that picture. As the received picture changes, more here and less there, or more rapidly here and more slowly there, the postulates have to be raised and added to or amended. The postulates are relative to time and place because they are relative to changing conditions and situations in life for which law is devised and to which it must be continually adapted if it is to achieve its end. Hence they are not universal formulations of what it is considered a legal order must presuppose, nor universal formulations of what a given legal order or all legal orders ought to presuppose. As will be seen presently some jural postulates of Anglo-American law of the nineteenth century have stood fast at least since the classical Roman jurists of the third century. Others which seemed settled in the juristic thought of the nineteenth

---

24. "Socialism in all its forms leaves intact the individualistic ends, but resorts to a new method of attaining them. That socialism is through and through individualistic in tendency, with emotional fraternalism superadded, is the point I would especially emphasize." Adler, *The Conception of Social Welfare*, PROCEEDINGS OF THE CONFERENCE ON LEGAL AND SOCIAL PHILOSOPHY (1913) 9.

century can no longer be demonstrated for the actual legislation and judicial decision of today. It would be a rash undertaking to show that any postulate of those which were presupposed by nineteenth-century law are to be held necessary postulates of law even for the next century. If there is any that has stood fast from Roman law, where, indeed, the whole of the actual law did not conform to it, it is that in civilized society men are entitled to assume that men will make good the expectations created by their promises. Natural law from the Greek philosophers assumed this. Roman jurists came to putting all but the whole law of contracts in accord with it. In the fourth century the church announced it as a proposition of Christian morals. In the seventeenth and eighteenth centuries it was made the basis of generally accepted theories of the binding force of positive law. At the beginning of the nineteenth century it was put in emphatic words in the French Civil Code. Today the law everywhere is moving away from it.

Professor Stone considers that there are four difficulties in the method of formulating jural postulates of the civilization of the time and place in that its "perfect operation" assumes four things: (1) A clearly defined civilization in space — "the civilization area"; (2) a clearly defined civilization in time — "the civilization period"; (3) the possibility of finding one set of postulates which will explain substantially all the *de facto* claims in the particular civilization area at the particular civilization period; (4) the availability of human minds at each time and place adequate for the tasks of framing the postulates.[25]

But is it not a good deal to ask of any juristic method that it be equal to "perfect operation" even if perfect operation of a juristic method could be perfectly defined? The analytical method of the English analytical jurist was capable of perfect operation in the sense that the whole body of the law could be laid on the analytical bed of Procrustes and adjusted thereto by the method of Procrustes. The jurisprudence of conceptions of the Pandectists was capable of perfect operation in what

25. Stone, *The Province and Function of Law* (1946) 365.

Jhering called the heaven of juristic conceptions.[26] How perfectly it could operate was illustrated when an American law teacher taught that if a person stood on the street corner and signaled the operator of a tram-car to stop, it was an offer, which the operator accepted by stopping, thus making a contract, which the offeror broke if he then changed his mind and walked off.[27] In law (in the sense of the legal order) we are dealing with a practical activity.

I agree that we cannot fix the "civilization area" of a type of civilization by sharply defined boundaries on the surface of the earth. There may be for some purposes such uniformity in the expectations of life in civilized society in Great Britain, the United States, Canada, Australia, and New Zealand, while on the other hand there may conceivably be some variations of detail if we take up the United States state by state, north and south, and east and west. When we find fixed precepts or doctrines extending over a whole jurisdictional geographical area it may be practically important to consider the expectations of civilized life in the different local jurisdictions. This is what the Declaration of Rights of the Continental Congress in 1774 meant by limiting their claim to the benefit of English statutes to those found applicable by experience to "local and other circumstances."[28] A federal polity takes care of this by leaving to local self-government a large margin for varying local degrees of development.

As to "civilization period" in a sense there is a continuous growth which cannot be arrested at some one point so that postulates can be formulated exactly for, let us say, even a whole century. In a sense law is always in transition just as is the life it governs. But the thirteenth, the eighteenth, and the nineteenth centuries in England, and the nine-

26. *Scherz und Ernst in der Jurisprudenz*, pt. 3, *Im juristischen Begriffshimmel* (1884, 13 ed. 1924).

27. Beale, *The Creation of the Relation of Carrier and Passenger* (1906) 39 HARVARD LAW REVIEW 250, 256.

28. *See* the Declaration in Pound and Plucknett, *Readings on the History and System of the Common Law* (1927) 309.

teenth century in the lands peopled from England, are reasonably well marked civilization periods. No one has seriously supposed that at midnight on December 31 of the last year of a century a civilization period definitely comes to an end and a new period is full fledged on January 1 following. Maitland warns us that when we tell the story of a bit of history we tear a seamless web. But to tell the whole exactly as it happened would take as long to tell as it took to happen.

As to the difficulty of finding one set of postulates which will explain substantially all the *de facto* claims at a particular civilization period, on any theory claims and expectations have to be classified. On Kohler's theory the task of the jurist is to find and formulate the jural postulate behind each class. His difficulty will be as to claims and expectations being newly urged and so pressing on the legal order for recognition. The current law reports will show those which are brought before the courts. For the rest reports of legislative committees, debates in the legislatures, in America the proceedings of all manner of professional, trade, labor and civic organizations, and abundant surveys and investigations under both public and private auspices, are available to show what the jurist must be thinking about. The task of applying an absolute measure of values, when discovered and demonstrated, to each of a multiplicity of conflicting and overlapping claims and demands will not be more easy.

It is said that an absolute element creeps into the method of jural postulates. But it must be said also that a relative element has in the past stood out as controlling in the absolute measures in the past. No doubt one will think with relation to some end or purpose. But it need not be made inexorably a universal end with fixed definition and details. I can think of civilization as the maximum of humanly attainable control of both physical and human nature without assuming some defined maximum as the most of which humanity may prove capable. I can conceive of maintaining the control now attained and furthering increase of that control without feeling bound to go further and lay down dogmatically how far the increase may or can or ought to go. We are told that there is need of weighing the postulates by an absolute measure. In Kohler's theory they are weighed in terms of the idea of civilization — a growing measure in that respect like Stammler's natural law with a changing or growing content. The absolutes by which jurists have measured in the past have been idealizings of the social or economic or legal order of the time, drawings of pictures to the lines of these orders as they were brought up in them, and so have gone no further than the received picture of the end of law for the time being.

In 1910, after eleven years of teaching jurisprudence from the analytical and metaphysical standpoints of the nineteenth century, and some years of teaching law during which I had tried to use Spencer's scheme of eight natural rights deduced from his Kantian "law of equal freedom," I tried my hand at formulating five jural postulates with a corollary of one as the jural postulates of the nineteenth-century Anglo-American law which I had been taught. These were afterward published with some revision of the wording in 1922,[29] in 1942,[30] and in 1943.[31] As an example of method, let me set them forth with some comments.

First I put this: In civilized society men must be able to assume that others will commit no intentional aggressions upon them. An Irish jury in a prosecution for manslaughter is said to have asked the trial judge whether a man who had a weak spot in his skull did not have a right to get killed if he went to the pig fair. Whatever experience might have taught the Irish jury to expect at the pig fair, experience had taught us in the last century that we might go to the county fair with a reasonable expectation of not being hit on the head with a blackthorn cudgel. Mark Twain said that the Leatherstocking Tales [ought] to be called the "broken twig tales" because at the crisis of a story some one always stepped on a broken twig and then the Iroquois fell upon him. In civilized society of today one does not have to keep below the sky line or avoid stepping on broken twigs. Our everyday life presupposes freedom from intentional attack. Again, it is a presupposition, a jural postulate of civilized society that those who are carrying on some course of conduct

29. *Introduction to the Philosophy of Law* (1922) 169–79, 192–94. They were first published in my *Introduction to the Study of Law* (1919).

30. *Social Control Through Law* (1942) 81–83, 112–17.

31. *Outlines of Lectures on Jurisprudence* (5 ed. 1943) 168, 179, 183–84.

will do so with due care not to cast an unreasonable risk of injury upon others. So we cross the street in reasonable expectation that no one will be driving against the lights and run into us. Third, it is a jural postulate that men must be able to assume that those with whom they deal in the general intercourse of society will act in good faith, and hence will make good reasonable expectations which their promises or other conduct reasonably create, will carry out their undertakings according to the expectations which the moral sentiment of the community attaches to them, and will restore specifically or by equivalent what comes to them by mistake or unanticipated situation whereby they receive at another's expense what they could not reasonably have expected to receive under the actual circumstances. It should be noted that the last clause as to restitution was not regarded as anything for the law to insist upon in the stage of the strict law and represents a development of control over internal nature in the stage of equity and natural law.

A further postulate underlies the law of property. It was not hard to formulate this in the last quarter of the nineteenth century. Spencer defined two natural rights, a right of property and a right of incorporeal property, each involving a legal right of possessing, a legal right of excluding others, a liberty of using, a liberty of enjoying the fruits and avails, and a liberty of abusing or destroying, and a power of disposing. Thus there was general agreement that life in civilized society involved full control over things which the social and economic order recognized as owned by individuals.[32] In 1910 I could formulate a postulate thus: In civilized society men must be able to assume that they may control for beneficial purposes what they have discovered and appropriated to their own use, what they have created by their own labor, and what they have acquired under the existing social and economic order. Of the three categories the two first were thought of by Roman jurists as "natural." But they have very little importance in American law of today. Taking of wild game, appropriation of abandoned or lost chattels, and prospecting

32. Spencer, *Justice* (1891) chaps. 12, 13.

for minerals on the public domain are about all that is left of the one, and game laws have greatly restricted the first item. Revival of the whaling industry may preserve for it some importance. As to creation by labor, the minute division of labor in industry precludes reasonable expectation of ownership, for example, of an automobile where the iron ore was scooped out from privately owned land by excavating machines manned by one set of laborers, shipped in boats manned by another, transported to the steel mills by a third set, made into motor cars by a fourth, and the cars transported to market by rail by a fifth, all of these laborers, however, paid for their labor. Yet there is still one case, growing in importance in recent years, namely, literary property, to which natural title by creation is applicable. What is more significant is the qualification of control to exercise for beneficial purposes.

In the present century great changes have gone on with respect to the incidents of ownership. There have been increasing limitations of the liberties of use, of enjoyment, and of abuse or destruction, and limitations of the power of disposing. In America it was taught until the second decade of the present century that an owner of land could dig a well on his land for the sole purpose of intercepting percolating water and dry up the well of his neighbor without having any use for or making any use of the water himself.[33] Also it was taught that an owner who did not like his next-door neighbor could build a fence eight feet high on his side of the boundary line and paint the side next to the neighbor in a hideous camouflage design with no other purpose of this exercise of his liberty of use than spite.[34] But already in the last quarter of the nineteenth century some American courts had balked at the spite well and spite fence.[35] The older French law had gone on a theory of "free exercise of rights." But French jurists worked out a doctrine of "abusive exercise of rights" and saw that the right (or shall we say liberty) ended

33. *Phelps v. Nowlen*, 72 N.Y. 39 (1878).
34. *Letts v. Kessler*, 54 Ohio State, 73 (1896). This case and the preceding were in the casebooks in general use in law teaching as late as 1910.
35. *Chesley v. King*, 74 Me. 164 (1882); *Burke v. Smith*, 69 Mich. 380 (1888).

where the abuse began.[36] The German Civil Code, adopted in 1896 to take effect in 1900, expressly forbade the use of property for the sole purpose of injuring another.[37] By the present century American judicial decisions had moved slowly in the same direction. But the question was still hotly debated in 1909.[38] Today legislation and judicial decision have done away with the spite well and the spite fence. It took longer to bring about a change of front as to surface water and to restrict taking out of percolating water to reasonable use. As late as 1911 a leading text could tell us: "The spirit of the English law is now to leave the parties alone; of the American law it is, on the one hand, to permit a reasonable use of land by all, and, on the other, to prevent an excessive use by any."[39] Today a principle of reasonable use has superseded the old idea that the owner of the surface may do as he pleases.

Legislation has come to extend the doctrine of reasonable use of land in many directions. One is limitations as to building proceeding not on the social interest in the general security but on a newly recognized social interest in aesthetic surroundings.[40] In the United States courts and legislatures long engaged in a sharp struggle over billboard laws and laws against hideous forms of outdoor advertising.[41] A like controversy went on over town planning.[42] But by 1940 it could be said that a policy favoring the aesthetic was established as reasonable and constitutional as against the owner's liberty of use.[43] Indeed a Canadian writer was will-

36. Charmont, *L'abus du droit*, 1 REVUE TRIMESTRIELLE DE DROIT CIVIL (1901) 113; 1 Ripert et Boulanger, *Traité élémentaire de droit civil* (5 ed. 1950) nos. 365–66.

37. *Bürgerliches Gesetzbuch*, § 226.

38. *See* the opinion and dissent in *Barger v. Barringer*, 151 N.C. 433 (1909).

39. 1 Wiel, *Water Rights* (1911) § 744, n. 12.

40. Hardman, *The Social Interest in the Aesthetic and the Socialization of Law*, 29 W.Va. LAW QUARTERLY, 195.

41. *St. Louis Advertisement Co. v. City*, 235 Mo. 99, 249 U.S. 269, 274; *People v. Oak Park*, 266 Ill. 365; *Bill Posting Co. v. Atlantic City*, 71 N.J. Law, 72; *Bryan v. City*, 212 Pa. St. 259.

42. *Village of Euclid v. Ambler Realty Co.*, 272 U.S. 365; *Windsor v. Whitney*, 95 Conn. 357; *State v. Houghton*, 144 Minn. 1; *Piper v. Ekern*, 180 Wis. 586.

43. *General Outdoor Advertising Co. v. Department of Public Works*, 289 Mass. 149; Gardner, *The Massachusetts Billboard Decision*, 49 HARVARD LAW REVIEW 869 (1936).

ing to have a land owner forbidden to cut down for profit a clump of trees on his land which provided the tourist a beautiful view of the Dominion capital,[44] while an American writer thought it probable that we shall eventually make provision by legislation that the houses along certain residence streets shall conform to the artistic sense of the community as expressed by an administrative agency.[45] Hood could no longer write of Englishmen and Frenchmen that "nature which gave them the grout only gave us the gout." Some of the legislative restrictions are based on a social interest in the conservation of social resources, the expectation involved in life in civilized society that the goods of existence will not be wasted; that the means of satisfying human expectations will be made to go so far as possible. Hence there is a recognized policy that acts and courses of action which tend to diminish those goods be restrained. An example of restricting the owner's liberty of enjoying on this ground may be seen in the case where the Supreme Court of the United States upheld a statute denying the owner of land a liberty of taking out natural gas to make lampblack where the gas could be used for heat and light by municipalities.[46] In the same direction there has been a progressive tendency to restrict the liberty of abusing or destroying which the last century attributed to owners. Whereas in 1910 it was debatable whether limiting the presupposition of control by the owner to purposes beneficial to him was reasonable, it is now taken for granted that we presuppose only a control compatible with social interests such as in aesthetic surroundings and in the conservation of social resources.

A power of disposition was regarded by philosophers of the last two centuries as involved in the very idea of ownership. Ownership could not be conceived of without this incident. But here, too, in the stage of socialization of law in the present century there have come to be many significant restrictions. Some are: A requirement in most states that in order to make a valid conveyance of the family home the wife must join

---

44. Note in 8 CANADIAN BAR REVIEW 384.
45. Jenks, *Governmental Action for Social Welfare*, 81.
46. *Walls v. Midland Carbon Co.*, 254 U.S. 300.

even though it is the separate property of the husband;[47] legislation in some states requiring that the wife join in a mortgage of the household furniture by the husband even though it may be his separate property;[48] legislation in some states requiring that the wife join in an assignment of the husband's wages.[49]

A fifth postulate may be put thus: In civilized society men must be able to assume that others who maintain things or employ agencies, harmless in the sphere of their use, but harmful in their normal action elsewhere, and having a natural tendency to cross the boundaries of their proper use, will restrain them or keep them within their proper bounds. As a corollary of the first postulate I have added: One who intentionally does anything which on its face is injurious to another must repair the resulting damage unless he can (1) justify his act under some social or public interest or (2) assert a privilege because of a countervailing individual interest of his own which there is a social or public interest in securing.

Both the fifth postulate and the corollary were long highly debatable and hotly debated. Sixty years ago the weight of American judicial authority denied that there could be legal liability other than under the first and second postulates. But in the urban industrial society of twentieth-century America our civilization presupposes better guarantee of the general security than liability to repair injuries due to fault. The fifth postulate came to express what is now secured by the law everywhere. The corollary of the first postulate was denied as late as 1914. But it expressed what the law had long been moving toward and is now clearly behind our common-law theory of liability.

Professor Stone had no difficulty in showing that I have modified more than once my formulation of the jural postulates of the civilization in the United States in the last third of the nineteenth century which

47. Thompson, *Homesteads and Exemptions* (1878) 465.
48. Illinois, *Laws of 1889*, p. 208.
49. Massachusetts, *Acts of 1908*, chap. 605.

were reflected in Anglo-American law of that century.[50] But the latter part of that century and beginning of the present century was an era of transition from a predominantly rural agricultural to an increasingly urban industrial society. As to one side of civilization that era has seen the coming of the telephone, of electric light and power, of wireless transmission of messages, of the gas engine and automobile transport, of streamlined cars doubling the speed of all vehicles, of air transportation making not only every part of the country but every land the near neighbor of every other, of radio and television, and now the beginnings of a development of atomic energy the results of which no one can foresee. All this has made enormous demands upon the other side of civilization, control over internal or human nature. Moreover that side of civilization in the United States has been profoundly affected by the development of great metropolitan centers and disappearance of the frontier and the pioneer. There are metropolitan centers, economic and social even if not in form political units which in areas less than that of a state in our formative era, have each a population exceeding and infinitely more varied than that of the original thirteen states. Great cities and the social and legal problems to which they give rise are of the last third of the nineteenth century and, indeed, the pressing problems do not begin to be acute till the last quarter of that century. The balance of population between country and city did not shift till the present century was half over. In the meantime a change in men's attitude toward property and promises and duty to respond for injuries suffered by others went on for some time beneath the surface and began to go on conspicuously from the third decade of the century. Jural postulates of an era of transition are not readily discovered and I have not tried to formulate them. Until the change to a distinct civilization era is complete formulation could hardly be profitable. We can see what was presupposed by the civilization of an era on which we can look back as complete for the time being. We can see how the jural postulates of that civilization are re-

50. Stone, *The Province and Function of Law* (1946) 366–68.

flected in the legal institutions and precepts and doctrines which it has left to us. We can see how those postulates are ceasing to be those of the times and places in which we are living and seek to understand those times as well as we may in an era of transition without expecting to lay down final formulations.

Much of what I have suggested elsewhere as to revised or additional postulates[51] belongs to what I have called the humanitarian doctrine which will be taken up in a later lecture.

Thus far we have canvassed the different theories of the end or purpose of law which have served to provide the ideal element which makes the legal order tolerable. What we are to take as the ideal end or purpose of the legal order is an ultimate question for philosophy of law. But there is nothing in experience or in the history of philosophical jurisprudence to justify expectation of converting all men or even all jurists to some one necessary philosophical version of the highest good or some one absolute and unchallengeable measure of values. Certainly jurists cannot be expected to stand by and await the result of philosophical debate or to choose some one of the theories of the moment at their peril. Men have always differed profoundly and so far as we can see ahead are likely to differ profoundly as to the theory and details of a measure of valuing their claims and desires and expectations. Indeed it is largely because they cannot agree on this measure that we must have positive law. As Llewellyn has shown us, if conflicts of individual expectations are not adjusted unsettled controversies tend to break up the social group and "tensions left alone tend to explosion."[52] In the nineteenth century, jurists came for the most part to agree on a conception of the end of law which was consistent or made to consist with the diverse philosophical starting points of the time. But the conception had not been thoroughly worked out before the law began to grow away from it. Perhaps one can do no more in our task of a working guide for a practical activity than

51. *Social Control Through Law* (1942) 115–18.
52. Llewellyn, *Problems of Juristic Method*, 49 YALE LAW JOURNAL 1355, 1375–76 (1940).

seek a juristic conception of the end of law consistent with the dominant philosophies of today and at the same time consistent with modern psychologies. But here again there are fundamental differences not likely soon to be settled, for the solution of which the law cannot wait. What has to be done, consistently with many philosophical approaches and with current psychologies, so far as may be, is to adjust, harmonize, reconcile conflicting or overlapping human demands, desires, expectations in the crowded world of today. William James has shown us how this task may be put in terms of an ethical theory. He says:

"After all, in seeking for a universal principle we inevitably are carried onward to the most universal principle — that *the essence of good is simply to satisfy demand.* . . . Since everything which is demanded is by that fact good, must not the guiding principle for ethical philosophy (since all demands conjointly cannot be satisfied in this poor world) be simply to satisfy at all times *as many demands as we can?* That act must be the best act, accordingly, which makes for the *best whole,* in the sense of awakening the least sum of dissatisfactions. In the casuistic scale, therefore, those ideals must be written highest which *prevail at the least cost,* or by whose realization the least number of other ideals are destroyed. . . . The course of history is nothing but the story of men's struggle from generation to generation to find the more inclusive order. Invent some manner of realizing your own ideals which will also satisfy the alien demands — that and that only is the path of peace! . . . Though some one's ideals are unquestionably the worse off for each improvement, yet a vastly greater total number of them find shelter in our civilized society than in the older savage ways. . . . As our present laws and customs have fought and conquered other past ones, so will they in their turn be overthrown by any newly discovered order which will hush up the complaints that they still give rise to without producing others louder still."[53]

Juristic thought is evidently in transition to some new idea of the end of law. The immediate direction seems to be toward seeking to satisfy the

53. James, *The Will to Believe* (1897) 195–206.

maximum of the whole scheme of human desires (or wants or demands or expectations) so far as it may be done through the legal order without too much sacrifice.

William James tells us that there is a continual search for the more inclusive order. This is illustrated by the history of ideas as to the end of law. Thinkers have gone behind an idea of the past to a more inclusive one. At first they thought of the end as keeping the peace. But why keep the peace? It seemed to be for the purpose of maintaining the social order. Hence the end was taken to be orderly maintaining of the social *status quo*. But why maintain the social order? Because to do that makes division of labor possible and so sets us free to exert our natural faculties — to do things. Hence the end was held to be promoting the maximum of free individual self-assertion. Yet why leave us free to do things? Because freedom to do things is a strong human desire, or want, or demand. Thus we come to the idea of a maximum of satisfaction of human desires or wants. Men wish to be free, but they want much besides. What we have to do in social control, and so in the legal order, is to reconcile these desires, or wants, so far as we can, so as to secure as much of the totality of them as we can. Down to the present that is the more inclusive order.

We come then, for the time being, to an idea of satisfying the expectations involved in life in civilized society. With that we might compare Stammler's substitute for Kant's theory of justice. Kant sought to give the maximum effect to individual wills. Stammler propounds a doctrine of comprehending all possible ends.[54] These ends seem to be the desires or wants of which William James speaks.

One of the Justices of the Supreme Court of the United States, dissenting from the judgment of that Court in the Arizona Employers' Liability Cases,[55] told us that there was "a menace in the . . . judgment to all rights, subjecting them unreservedly to conceptions of public pol-

54. Stammler, *Lehre von dem richtigen Rechte* (1902, new ed. 1926) 196–200.
55. 250 U.S. 400, 432 (1919).

icy."[56] Undoubtedly if certain legal rights were definitely established by the constitution there would be a menace to the general security if the court which must ultimately interpret and apply the provisions of that instrument were to suffer state legislature to infringe those legal rights on mere considerations of political expediency. But it was the ambiguity of the term "right," a word of many meanings, and want of clear understanding of the significance and meaning of the obscure conception of "public policy"—i.e., what the law seeks to achieve through that conception—that made it possible to think of a decision upholding an Employers' Liability Law in such a way. The "rights" of which Mr. Justice McKenna spoke were not legal rights. They were individual wants or claims or demands, that is individual interests, which he felt ought to be secured through legal rights or through some other legal machinery. In other words, there was, as he felt, a policy of securing these interests. The constitution did not set up these or any other individual interests as absolute legal rights. It imposed a standard upon the legislator. It prescribed that if he trenched upon these individual interests he must not do so arbitrarily. His action must have some basis in reason, and that basis must be the one upon which the Anglo-American common law has always sought to proceed, the one implied in the very term "due process of law," namely, a weighing or balancing of the various interests which overlap or come in conflict and a rational reconciling or adjustment. Thus the public policy of which Mr. Justice McKenna spoke is something at least on no lower plane than the so-called rights. As he used the latter term it referred to individual interests which it was felt ought to be secured by law. As he used the former term he referred to social interests which it is felt the law ought to or which in fact the law does secure in delimiting individual interests and establishing legal rights. There is a policy in the one case as much as in the other. The body of the law (in the second sense of the term law) is made up of adjustments or com-

---

56. McKenna, J., dissenting in Arizona Employers' Liability Cases, 250 U.S. 400, 436–37.

promises of conflicting individual interests in which we turn to social interests; under which each may be subsumed, to determine the limits of a reasonable adjustment. In the end there is an adjustment of the individual interests, the claims or demands or expectations asserted in title of the individual life, on the basis of adjustment of the wider claims or demands or expectations asserted in title of social life in civilized society. The measure of delimitation for purposes of the adjustment is found in an ideal of the society of the time and place or an ideal of civilization as understood in the time and place.

Perhaps an integration of the two ideas I have been considering might be put thus: The end is promoting, maintaining, furthering civilization. The means is social engineering.

NINE

Class Interest and Economic Pressure:
The Marxian Interpretation

One phase of the movement away from the nineteenth-century schools near the end of that century was the economic interpretation of legal history, and so, in the reign of historical jurisprudence, economic theory of law. For a time it did not develop a distinct school of jurists, but later, under the influence of positivist mechanical sociology, Neo-Kantian relativism, and Freudian psychology, it has led to what has called itself juristic realism of a number of forms.

In this connection the terms "realist" and "realism" are used as artists use these words rather than in a philosophical sense.[1] Philosophical realism held that the objects of perception were derived from higher realities or formative causes.[2] The juristic realist of today would call this, as applied to jurisprudence, very unreal. In the sense in which he uses the terms, "realist" and "realism" are a boast rather than a description. Each school of jurists in its time has made a like boast. The analytical jurists

---

1. See Pound, *The Call for a Realist Jurisprudence*, 44 HARVARD LAW REVIEW 697–700 (1931); id. *Fifty Years of Jurisprudence*, 51 HARVARD LAW REVIEW 777, 799–800 (1938). Fuller has made the same observation, *American Legal Realism*, 82 UNIV. OF PA. LAW REVIEW, 429, n. 1 (1934).

2. Neither this nor the later epistemological-metaphysical theory, see 2 Baldwin, *Dictionary of Philosophy and Psychology* (1901–5) 421, is what recent juristic realists have in mind.

spoke of the "pure fact of law." Historical jurists spoke of their theories as founded on the "facts of history" instead of pure speculation. The metaphysical jurists considered that they began from an "unchallengeable metaphysical datum."[3] The mechanical positivists argued that they built on laws of social and legal development derived from observation and verified by further observation after the method of the natural sciences and hence as unchallengeable as the laws of physical nature.[4]

No doubt neo-realism is meant to be faithful adherence to the actualists of the legal order as the basis of a science of law. But a science of law must be something more than a descriptive inventory. After the actualities of the legal order have been observed and recorded it remains to see that we have observed and recorded all of them and to do something with them. For one thing must we not consider what of those actualities may be made use of in the science? We may not ignore any of them. On the contrary, we should investigate the shortcomings in the legal order and particularly in the judicial process in order to find their causes and how to eliminate or mitigate them.

What is there in the program of the extreme neo-realists which makes it one of juristic realism? They reject the ideas of the past as to juristic significance. Reason is an illusion. Experience is not the unfolding of principle. No "pure fact of law" is to be found in rules, since the existence of rules of law, as anything outside of the books, is an illusion. Nor have the phenomena of legal institutions among all peoples been observed with enough accuracy and objectivity to allow of formulations of laws of legal development therefrom. One may concede all this, indeed we must concede much of it, and yet be doubtful as to the faith in their ability to find the one unchallengeable basis free from illusion, which many, at least, of the neo-realists seem to have taken over from the illusion-ridden jurists of the past.

As in the disputes of diverse schools of jurists in the past, the difference today is one of emphasis. Received ideals, received conceptions, the quest of certainty, uniformity, and predictability, an authoritative

3. Amos, *Systematic View of the Science of Jurisprudence* (1872) chap. 4.
4. Spencer, *Justice* (1891) chap. 7.

technique of using authoritative legal materials, settled legal doctrines and modes of thought, and a traditional mode of legal reasoning are actual and everyday phenomena of the legal order. The question at bottom is whether a faithful representation of realities shall paint them in the foreground or instead shall put in the foreground the subjective features in the behavior of particular judges, the elements in judicial action which stand in the way of predictability and uniformity, the deficiencies of the received technique, the undefined edges and overlappings of doctrines, and the defects of legal reasoning. Emphasis on the fallings short of these instruments is useful in that it shows us what we have to do toward making them more effective, or toward making their workings accord better with the ends of law, or toward finding better instruments to take their place. But such critical activity is not the whole of jurisprudence, nor can we build a science of law which shall faithfully describe the actualities of the legal order and organize our knowledge of these actualities merely on the basis of such criticism. There is as much actuality in the old picture as in the new. Each selects a set of aspects for emphasis. Neither portrays the whole as it is. Critical portrayals of the received ideal element in a body of law, valuings of traditional ideals with respect to the actualities of the social and legal order of today, are as much in touch with reality, *i.e.*, have to do with things of at least as much significance for the legal order as economic or psychological theories of the behavior of particular judges in particular cases.

As the analytical jurist insisted on the pure fact of law, the neo-realist seeks a pure fact of fact. But facts exist in a multifarious mass of single instances. To be made intelligible and useful, significant facts must be selected. What is significant will be determined by some picture or ideal of the science and of the subject of which it treats. Thus preconceptions will creep in and will determine the choice of pure fact of fact as they determined the pure fact of law of the analytical jurist. The neo-realists have their own preconceptions of what is significant and of what juristically must be. Most of them substitute an economic or a psychological must for an ethical or political or historical must.

Five types of juristic neo-realism may be distinguished: Economic determinism, psychological determinism, logical positivist realism, and phenomenological realism. There is also sometimes a combination of positivist realism with phenomenology.

These types have certain common characteristics. One is a tendency to regard everything which influences a particular judge in a particular case as a source of law. What this comes to is confusion of the judicial process in any given case with the authoritative guides to decision by which the judges at large, the legal professions, and as a general proposition the public, hold it ought to be decided, and normally in the ordinary course of things cases are decided. When these are so confused, there ceases to be any proper criterion for criticizing judicial action. Moreover, the action of the judge who decides on personal animosity in contravention of established legal precepts is likely to be set aside on appeal. In such a case we surely are not to say that each decision in its turn was law; and the animosity surely was not a source of law as to the ultimate decision. Much realist discussion goes upon the psychology of "the judge," forgetting that ultimate determinations proceed from a bench of judges and that therein is a correction of individual eccentricities and prejudices.

Again, the neo-realists in different ways attack logic as a method of judicial decision or juristic thinking. Some of them assume legal or juristic doctrine that every judicial determination necessarily follows by a process of formal logic from an authoritatively given premise and from that only.[5] They assume, what might have been taught in the reign of the jurisprudence of conceptions, that there was, expressly by legislation or by implication derivable from the traditional law, a rule of law for every case. If not in the form of a statute the rule was to be found by formal logic. But it did not need twentieth-century realists to refute such a doctrine, which, if it was ever held at all by common-law lawyers, was shown not to apply to new cases, not covered by an authoritatively formulated precept, as long ago as Austin.[6] Indeed, half a century before

---

5. Oliphant and Hewitt, Introduction to Rueff, *From the Physical to the Social Sciences* (1929) transl. by Green, x ff.

6. 2 Austin, *Jurisprudence* (5 ed. 1885) 638 ff.

Austin, Paley, whom Austin followed, had shown the nature of the choice between competing analogies by which judicial law finding or law making takes place.[7] Others, approaching the subject from the wish-psychology, consider that logic is in truth employed after, not before, a judicial determination in order to give rational color to something arrived at upon a basis quite outside of the supposedly authoritative guides to decision.[8] This proposition must be considered presently in another connection. But it, too, assumes one-judge determinations and the psychology of the postulated one judge as the controlling element. This assumption is perhaps in part attributable to biographies in which all that appears in the reports in the name of a judge is attributed to him individually. It is an easy but fallacious assumption that each decision of the bench of an appellate court is simply the product of the judge who delivered the opinion of the court.

Many of the neo-realists rely upon behaviorist psychology as the basis of attack upon logic, conceptions, principles, and any authoritative guides to decision, holding that "decision is reached after an emotive experience in which principles and logic play a secondary part."[9] Similarly legal terminology is objected to as no more than a sort of smoke screen for concealing the uncertainty attending the judicial process which is taken to be the basic feature of law.[10]

As a result there is a cult of the single determination, an insistence on what is held to be the unique single case rather than on the approximation to a uniform course of judicial action. No one has denied that single cases have unique features and may be in greater or less degree unique. Long ago, experience made this proposition a presupposition of Anglo-American equity, and it is presupposed wherever in the legal system we employ standards rather than rules. But it is no less true that there are common elements in cases which may or may not be significant for a

7. Paley, *Moral and Political Philosophy* (1782) bk. vi, chap. 6.

8. Yntema, *The Hornbook Method and the Conflict of Laws* (1928) 37 YALE LAW JOURNAL 468, 480.

9. *Ibid.*

10. Green, *Judge and Jury* (1930) 43–49.

particular problem or situation. The unique aspects of cases, the common aspects of them, and generalizations from the common aspects may or may not afford useful instruments to attain the ends of the legal adjustment of relations and ordering of conduct, according to the connection in which we look at them and the tasks to which we apply them. None of the three is an absolute and universal solvent. It seems to be assumed that there is no reality in rules or principles or conceptions or doctrines because all judicial action, or at times much judicial action, cannot be referred to them; because there is no definite precept by which we may be absolutely assured that judicial action will proceed on the basis of one rather than of another of two competing principles; because there is a certain no-man's-land about many conceptions so that concrete cases have been known to fall down between them, because much may take place in the process of adjudication which does not fit precisely into the doctrinal plan. Such a view has its use as a protest against the assumption that law is nothing but an aggregate of rules.[11] But nothing is more unreal, *i.e.*, more at variance with what is significant in a highly specialized form of social control through politically organized society, than to conceive of the administration of justice, or the legal adjustment of relations, or even the legislative or judicial or juristic working out of devices for the more efficient functioning of business in a legally ordered society, as a mere aggregate of single, self-sufficient determinations. Such ideas are related to the Marxian doctrine of disappearance of law. They are part of the phenomena going along with the recrudescence of political absolutism throughout the world in the present century. They are urged particularly in America by the proponents of administrative absolutism.[12]

Economic interpretation began in the fifth decade of the nineteenth century when Marx applied the Hegelian dialectic to English political economy, to the theories of French historians of the French Revolution,

11. 1 Bentham's *Works*, Bowring ed. (1843) 141.

12. Pound, *The Place of the Judiciary in a Democratic Polity* (1941) 27 AMERICAN BAR ASSOCIATION JOURNAL 133; id. For the Minority Report, *ibid.* 664; *Report of Special Committee on Administrative Law* (1938) 63 REPORT AMERICAN BAR ASSOCIATION 331, 342 ff.

and to his own experience of the proletarian movement. On this basis he suggested a new way of understanding history. He formulated it in 1859 in what became a much quoted passage.[13] It attracted little notice for a generation, but began to be urged in 1885, and got general currency about 1890. It had much vogue on the Continent in the last decade of the nineteenth century, when it came to be applied to every form of history. It came to America in the decade from 1900 to 1910 and passed over into American juristic thought.[14]

An analytical form of economic interpretation was urged chiefly by Brooks Adams.[15] According to this interpretation all law is made, and is made consciously, by men who make and shape legal precepts to suit the ends of the dominant social class. But these ends are determined by economics. Thus all law is the product of economic causes. Law is thought of as a conscious product of the human will. The basis of its obligation is authority. Thus far it follows Austin. But it is conceived that the will which makes laws is determined wholly by the operation of economic laws.

Brooks Adams regarded law as a manifestation of the will of the dominant social class, determined by economic motives. He asserts that ideals of justice have had nothing to do with the actual course of evolution of law or development of legal doctrines. He says that "the rules of law are established by the self-interest of the dominant class so far as it can impose its will upon those who are weaker."[16] Elsewhere he says that ideals of justice mean only that the dominant class "will shape the law to favor themselves."[17] Law, he tells us, "is the will of the sovereign precisely in the sense that the earth's orbit, which is the resultant of a conflict between centrifugal and centripetal force, is the will of a sovereign.

---

13. Marx, *Zur Kritik der politischen Oekonomie* (1859) iv, v.

14. Seligman, *The Economic Interpretation of History* (1902, 2 ed. 1907).

15. Bigelow and others, *Centralization and the Law*, lecture 1, *Nature of Law*, by Brooks Adams; lecture 2, *Law Under Inequality, Monopoly*, by Brooks Adams (1906); Adams, *The Modern Conception of Animus* (1906) 19 GREEN BAG, 12.

16. *Centralization and the Law* (1906) 45.

17. *Ibid.* 63–64.

Both the law and the orbit are necessities."[18] He attempts to combine the mechanical sociology and the economic interpretation with analytical jurisprudence.

From the standpoint of the neo-realist economic interpretation,[19] jurisprudence has to do with the ends of groups or persons who are in power for the time being and exercise the force of a politically organized society for their own economic advantage. This is an economic-realist version of social utilitarianism. Right and law are simply power. Those in power generalize their ends and put them in universal terms and thus give us rules and principles of law. This interpretation was urged in various forms by socialist jurists, especially in connection with economic determinism. It was subsequently taken up by different types of realists and by some jurists of the Neo-Kantian left.

None of the types of economic interpretation can be accepted as giving a complete account or all-sufficient explanation of the development or the content of law. None can give us more than a partial explanation of certain particular phenomena. What I have said of the historical school and must be said of the mechanical sociologists, applies also to the adherents of the economic interpretation. Their self-imposed limitations preclude a fruitful science of law. But there are three special objections to an exclusive economic interpretation in any of its forms.

In the first place, it is a theory of legislation rather than of law in the sense of the body of authoritative grounds of or guides to decision. It is an explanation of some features of the judicial and administrative processes in action rather than a theory of the legal order. It is a theory of the will element, the imperative element in the body of authoritative precepts rather than of the traditional element, the element of experience developed by reason, which plays much the larger part in legal his-

18. *Ibid.* 23.
19. *See* 2 Berolzheimer, *System der Rechts- und Wirtschaftsphilosophie* (1905) § 40, transl. by Jastrow as *The World's Legal Philosophies* (1912) 298–307; Bohlen, *Old Phrases and New Facts* (1935) 83 UNIV. OF PA. LAW REVIEW 305, 306–7; Myers, *History of the Supreme Court of the United States* (1912) 8.

tory and is in the long run controlling in a system of law. Moreover, it is not an interpretation of that more enduring part of legislation which puts in authoritative form the legal precepts which have developed from experience and have been formulated in judicial or doctrinal tradition. It is rather an interpretation of that less important part of legislation which deals with particular details or special subjects, and lays down precepts for them arbitrarily without regard to general principles of the legal system. Roman imperial legislation extending special privileges to soldiers, the Statute *De Donis*, and like legislative phenomena, are put as typical of all finding or laying down of law.

Much that is vouched for the economic interpretation is legislation to maintain the social interest in the general security. For example, an oft-quoted statement by Jhering has been cited in support of that interpretation. He said: "Every state punishes those crimes most severely which threaten its own peculiar conditions of existence, while it allows a moderation to prevail in regard to other crimes which, not infrequently presents a very stricking contrast to its severity as against the former. A theocracy brands blasphemy and idolatry as crimes deserving of death, while it looks upon a boundary violation as a simple misdemeanor. (Mosaic Law). The agricultural state, on the other hand, visits the latter with the severest punishment, while it lets the blasphemer go with the lightest punishment. (Old Roman law). The commercial state punishes most severely the uttering of false coin, the military state insubordination and breach of official duty, the absolute state high treason, the republic striving after regal power; and they all manifest a severity in these points which contrasts greatly with the manner in which they punish other crimes. In short, the reaction of the feeling of legal right, both of states and individuals, is most violent when they feel themselves threatened in the conditions of existence peculiar to them."[20] It should be noted that in the Mosaic Law the motive was fear of the wrath of God

---

20. Jhering, *The Struggle for Law*, transl. by Lalor, 2 ed. by Kocourek, 48–49 (1915). As Jhering says, that was pointed out long ago by Montesquieu. *Ibid.* 49 n. 1.

against the people which harbored the blasphemer and idolater. In other words, the pressure of the social interest in the general security is a compelling force in lawmaking.

Undoubtedly there is an element of truth in the economic interpretation of legislation. One cannot look into American nineteenth-century legislation without perceiving that organized pressure from groups having a common economic interest is the sole explanation of many anomalous things in the statute books. For example, legislation allowing a lien to one who furnishes material for a building has sometimes been pushed to strange length through the activities of associations of lumber dealers.[21] Credit men's associations have procured laws against sales of stocks of goods in bulk which have sometimes gone very far,[22] and have sought or procured statutory provisions as to preferred claims in bankruptcy to defeat or infringe upon the doctrines of equity as to trusts and constructive trusts.[23] Organized insurers have procured legislation in more than twenty states enabling a debtor to be generous to those he wishes to favor before he is just to his creditors. The real purpose is "to magnify the more desirable aspects of life insurance."[24] Organized farmers have procured legislation against allowing weeds to go to seed on railroad rights of way wherein the farmer was left free to maintain as many weeds as he chose and let them go to seed as much as he chose.[25] Again when interpleader was first made the subject of legisla-

21. See an interesting discussion of a proposal for such legislation in PROC. NORTH DAKOTA BAR ASSN. (1906–8) 44–53; Robertson Lumber Co. v. Bank of Edinburgh, 14 N.D. 511, 515–16, and cases and text books cited n. p. 516.

22. See note in 33 HARVARD LAW REVIEW 717–18 (1920); Note, 42 HARVARD LAW REVIEW 277–78.

23. See McLaughlin, Amendment of the Bankruptcy Act, 40 HARVARD LAW REVIEW 341 n. 2, 383 ff. (1927); Richardson v. Shaw, 209 U.S. 365, 380 (1908); In re Archer Harvey & Co., 289 Fed. 267 (1923); Robinson v. Roe, 233 Fed. 936 (1916).

24. Hanna and MacLachlan, Cases on Creditors' Rights, consolidated 4th ed. note on 79–80 (1951).

25. Indiana, Laws of 1889, chap. 82, p. 146; Texas, Laws of 1901, chap. 107, pp. 283–84. As to the common law see Giles v. Walker, 24 Q.B.D. 656 (1890); Herndon v. Stultz, 124 Ia. 734 (1904).

tion governing the federal courts, the statute extended the scope of the proceeding and did away with technical limitations in the case of insurance companies, surety companies, and fraternal insurance organizations. For the rest, litigants in the federal courts were left where they were before the statute.[26] Insurance companies and surety companies were organized and could urge a remedial act for their cases but were not interested in the cases of litigants generally. Another example may be seen in the state statutes enacted between 1890 and 1917 as to the defense of contributory negligence. These statutes set up a special rule, making the plaintiff's contributing negligence a ground of reducing recoverable damages instead of a bar, in case of actions against railroads.[27] It is clear enough that the statutes were shaped by pressure from unions of railway employees, pressure from those who made money out of actions against railway companies, and the antipathy of farmers toward railroads, very marked at the time and growing out of economic relations. This legislative treatment of the problem of contributory negligence should be compared with judicial treatment of the same problem. Juristic and judicial solutions had been directed toward setting up some general principle, such as comparative negligence, division of the loss, or last clear chance. The legislature made a special provision for a special type of litigant able to exert political pressure. Lord Darling spoke of such legislation as intended to relieve the members of certain

26. Act of February 22, 1917, 39 U.S. St. L. 929; Act of February 25, 1925, 43 U.S. St. L. 976; Act of May 8, 1926, 44 U.S. St. L. 416.

27. Florida, *Laws of 1891*, c. 4071 (No. 62), § 2, pp. 113–14; Iowa, *Acts of 1909*, c. 124, pp. 117–18; Kansas, *Laws of 1911*, c. 239, § 2; Maine, *Public Laws of 1910*, c. 258; Mississippi, *Laws of 1910*, c. 135; Nebraska, *Laws of 1907*, c. 48, § 2, p. 192; Ohio, *Act of 1908*, *Laws of 1909*, p. 25, § 2; South Dakota, *Laws of 1907*, c. 219, § 2; Texas, *General Laws of 1909*, c. 10, § 2, p. 280; Virginia, *Acts of 1916*, c. 444, § 2; Wisconsin, *Laws of 1915*, c. 437, § 2, pp. 553–54.

Significantly, in what was then a mining state, the statutory rule was extended to "every mine and mill owner and operator actually engaged in mining, or milling or reduction of ores." Nevada, *Laws of 1907*, c. 214, § 2, pp. 437–38. I have discussed these statutes in "The Revival of Personal Government" PROCEEDINGS OF THE NEW HAMPSHIRE BAR ASSOCIATION, 1917, 13.

organizations from "the humiliating position" of being upon an equality with the rest of the king's subjects.[28] But these arbitrary precepts, made under pressure of group self-interest, are short-lived, or else are molded into the general legal system so that they get a new shape and even a new content therefrom.

We must not forget that the administration of justice aims consciously at more than the advocates of an exclusive economic interpretation of all the phenomena of the legal order will hear of. We must take account of the extent to which judicial action is moved by the logical exigencies of a traditional system; of the extent to which it is constrained by a tradition of teaching, a traditional technique and what might be called the art of the lawyer's craft, even against self-interest. This must be borne in mind especially when, as in modern times, the administration of justice is in the hands of profession with a long tradition of principles, a received ideal of justice, and a systematic science, in which logical deduction from received principles has become a habit. Thus the common law has proved to have a vitality demonstrated in a long series of contests with the most powerful political and economic forces of time and place.[29] How completely differences of economic and social status, surroundings and associations will be effaced by training in a taught tradition is well brought out if we compare three great judges of the formative era of American law.

Lemuel Shaw (1781–1861) was a staunch Federalist. He was the son of a Congregational minister in a parish so poor that part of his salary was paid in fire wood and the balance supposed to be paid in cash was always in arrear and the arrears accumulated but remained unpaid. He was brought up in a community of farmers and fishermen on Cape Cod, was a graduate of Harvard, a school teacher and newspaper writer while reading for the bar, and lived in his maturity in the commercial environment of Boston of that day. He was a Congregationalist.[30] John Ban-

---

28. *Bussey v. Amalgamated Society of Railway Servants*, 24 TIMES LAW REPORTS, 437 (1908).

29. I have set forth the details in *The Spirit of the Common Law* (1921) 1–6.

30. Chase, *Lemuel Shaw* (1918).

nister Gibson (1780–1853) was a Democrat of Jackson's type. Indeed Jackson wished to put him on the bench of the Supreme Court of the United States. He was the son of a man of business in a frontier community in western Pennsylvania who lost his property in the depression after the American Revolution. He was brought up after his father's death by his mother who had a hard struggle to maintain the family home and conducted a school in order that her children might be educated. He studied at Dickinson College but did not graduate. He practiced law in a developing community and associated while at the bar with the enterprising builders of a relatively new community. He evaded baptism.[31] Thomas Ruffin (1787–1870) was a conservative Democrat, born on a plantation in Virginia. He graduated at Princeton. He was by descent and bringing up one of the landed aristocracy of the old South and in his maturity lived upon his own plantation among his fellow gentlemen planters. He was a zealous member of the Episcopal Church.[32]

Each of these men long dominated the highest court of an important state, from which many newer states took their legal traditions and upon their decisions those newer states built their course of decision. The marked differences in their parentage, bringing up, social environment, political and religious affiliations, and economic surroundings should, according to the economic and psychological determinists of today, have determined their judicial action decisively and so have led to three different judicial traditions. Yet they cooperated in making a consistent body of law on the basis of the tradition they had been taught in the offices of lawyers whose training (through office apprenticeship) ran back to barristers trained in the Inns of Court in England before American independence.

A second point is that the phenomena of legal history which are vouched for the doctrine of the economic interpretation do not sustain it.

---

31. Roberts, *Memoirs of John Bannister Gibson* (1890).
32. Graham, *Life and Character of Thomas Ruffin* (1871).

A chief reliance of those who urge the economic interpretation as the sufficient explanation of every item of judicial finding of law and judicial determination of causes is "the fellow servant rule," the rule of the common law that an employee could not hold his employer liable for injury through the negligence of a fellow employee in the course of their employment. A typical statement of the economic-interpretation thesis was made by Walter Lippman: "Under the old common law of England a workman who was injured could sue the master for damages. If he had been injured by a fellow workman's negligence he could still sue the master because the law held the master liable for his servant's acts. . . . In 1837 this system of law was changed in a decision rendered by Lord Abinger. After that it became the law that the master was not liable for an injury to a workingman when the injury was due to a fellow workingman."[33] There are here two wholly erroneous statements. It was not the common law of England before 1837 that an employer was liable for injury to an employee through the negligence of another employee in the course of their common employment. That question had not then arisen. If it had, it would probably have been held that an employee assumed the risk of negligence of his co-workers as an incident of what they were all doing. At any rate the law was not changed by the decision of the Court of Exchequer in 1837. But apart from the fundamental error in Mr. Lippman's statement, others argue that the rule laid down in 1837 was an arbitrary exception to a settled principle of the common law. This assumes that *respondeat superior*, that the principal or master, although without fault, must answer for the wrongs done by his agent or servant, is a fundamental principle of justice and that the fellow servant rule was an arbitrary exception to it. It would be more true to say that *respondeat superior* was a judge-made exception to what the nineteenth century regarded as a fundamental principle of justice, namely, that liability was based on fault and that the courts refused to ex-

33. Lippman, *The Good Society*, 188, citing Berman, *Employer's Liability* (1931) 3 ENCYCLOPEDIA OF THE SOCIAL SCIENCES, 515.

tend the exception. Mr. Justice Holmes,[34] Dr. Baty,[35] and many others have pointed out that vicarious liability is the exception to what had been taken to be the general principle, not limitation of vicarious liability the exception to the normal precept. Also those who vouch the fellow servant rule for their doctrine ignore the judicial development of encroachments on the principle of no liability without fault in order to respond to a newer idea that an enterprise should bear the human no less than the material wear and tear incident to its conduct, such as the vice-principal doctrine.[36] Also they ignore the judicial working out of duties incident to the relation of employer and employee, such as the duty to furnish safety appliances, and the duty to furnish a safe place to work,[37] which were responding to conditions of employment very different from those involved in the case in 1837. The courts could not have been expected to make at one stroke the radical change to the theory of workmen's compensation. Moreover, the proponents of the economic interpretation, in arguing from the fellow servant rule, overlook the whole setting of *Priestley* v. *Fowler*,[38] the case which is said to have introduced an arbitrary exception to employer's liability. It was an action by the servant of a butcher who was injured by the overloading of the butcher's van. The case came up on the declaration and was argued as one upon contract whether the contract of employment involved an implied duty to "cause the servant to be safely and securely carried." The court said that the mere contract of employment could not be said to involve an implied obligation of the master to take more care of the servant than he could reasonably be expected to do of himself.[39] In other words, so far from introducing an arbitrary exception that case refused

---

34. Holmes, *Agency* (1891) 4 HARVARD LAW REVIEW 345, 5 id. 1.

35. Baty, *Vicarious Liability* (1916) chaps. 1, 5.

36. 4 Labatt, *Commentaries on the Law of Master and Servant* (2 ed. 1913) chaps. 41–44.

37. 3 id. chaps. 36–39; 4 id. § 1497.

38. 3 M. & W. 1 (1837).

39. *Ibid.* 6.

to depart from established traditional lines. It should be noted also that this was not a case of a workman in a factory. The butcher and his apprentice were of the same class. The apprentice expected to become a master butcher when he had served his apprenticeship.

As to the American case of *Farwell v. Boston & Worcester R. Corp.*[40] the case was not argued for the plaintiff as one of a general rule of liability of the master for injuries due to negligence of his servants. It was admitted by counsel for the plaintiff that *Priestley v. Fowler* was rightly decided on the common law. But it was argued that the engineer, who was injured, and the switchman, who was at fault were "engaged in distinct employments."[41] No suggestion was made of an arbitrary exception to *respondeat superior*. Moreover, the same court, in the same volume, in *Commonwealth v. Hunt*[42] refused to depart from the common-law doctrine and hold a labor union a conspiracy, as, according to the economic interpretation, it was bound to do. In that case, to use the words of a leading exponent of the economic interpretation, the court "overthrew the sub-structure upon which a Tory criminal law against labor organizations could respectably have been established."[43] If the first decision was the formulation of the self-interest of a dominant employer class, what of the second? The same mode of juristic thought which led the court to follow *Priestley v. Fowler* led them also to reject a theory of conspiracy out of line with the common law. The best explanation that the advocate of the economic interpretation can give is that the court feared the people would take away the life tenure of the judges and make the bench elective if some case was not decided in favor of workingmen at an early opportunity."[44] The whole judicial career of Chief Justice Shaw refutes such a charge. But if *Commonwealth v. Hunt* had been decided the other way, it would be argued vigorously that his asso-

40. 4 Met. (Mass.) 49 (1842).
41. *Ibid.* 52.
42. 4 Met. (Mass.) 111 (1842).
43. Nelles, *Commonwealth v. Hunt* (1932) 32 COLUMBIA LAW REVIEW 1128, 1151.
44. *Ibid.* 1158–62.

ciates were two old-line Federalists and the appointees of the "Federalist Whigs."

The argument from the fellow servant rule overlooks also the history of the doctrine of *respondeat superior* and its relation to employer's liability. Liability for legal transactions entered into by an agent within the scope of the agency is correlative to a power conferred by the principal upon the agent. Liability without regard to fault for the employee's torts, committed against the instructions of the employer, despite all precautions on the part of the employer and although the employer chose the employee with due care, is not correlative to a power conferred. It is conferred by law and has a historical origin. The explanation that the servant represents the master, so that what the former does must be treated as done by the latter, is a dogmatic fiction.[45] The historical liability has maintained itself because of pressure of the social interest in the general security. But the difference between representation in legal transactions and representation in torts contrary to the intent of the employment has been obvious in all connections except to the partisans of the economic interpretation in discussing the fellow servant rule. "If the law went no further than to declare a man liable for the consequences of acts specifically commanded by him, with knowledge of the circumstances under which those consequences were the natural result of those acts," says Holmes, "it would need no explanation and would introduce no new principle." The new principle requiring explanation, he goes on to say, was introduced into the law when the master without fault was treated as if he was the wrongdoer. There was an old historical liability for the acts of those who were in the household as dependents. In the frankpledge system there was this sort of liability for the acts of others. The master was made to stand as security for the acts of his servants, to hand them over to justice or to pay the fine himself. So far was this carried that the host was liable for the tort of a guest in his house as well as for wrongs done by his servant. Thus liability of a master for the

45. Holmes, *Agency* (1891) 4 HARVARD LAW REVIEW 345, 345–50.

torts of a servant comes down from a primitive liability of the head of a household to buy off the vengeance of the injured person or surrender the wrongdoing dependent.[46]

Neither analytically nor historically was the fellow servant rule an arbitrary exception to the general common-law theory of liability. It was a refusal to extend an exception to what was accepted as that principle. As late as 1891, Mr. Justice Holmes could say that it represented "the revolt of common sense from the whole doctrine" of identification of the master with the servant "when its application is pushed far enough to become noticeable."[47] The same question came up with respect to liability of the master for punitive damages for a wanton and willful wrong done by his servant. More than one court, said Mr. Justice Holmes "impressed by the monstrosity of the result . . . peremptorily declared that it was absurd to punish a man who had not been to blame."[48] The King's Bench had laid down in the sixteenth century that it was contrary to common right and reason to hold one who was not at fault.[49] In 1804, the French Civil Code had laid down that liability was a consequence of fault and causation.[50] The beginnings of a doctrine of general liability for failure to control things maintained or agencies employed came a generation after *Priestly* v. *Fowler* and two decades after *Farwell* v. *Boston & Worcester R. Corp.*, and that doctrine was not generally accepted in America for at least three-quarters of a century after the latter case. What had happened was that a historical liability for those who were in the household was made into a liability for the acts of nondependent employees in order to maintain the general security. But as to liabilities for employees today the idea has not been one of maintaining the general security. It has been one of insuring, at the expense of the one nearest at hand who could bear it and pass it on to the public, those who were in no economic position to bear loss. This is a very re-

46. *Ibid.* 346 ff.
47. Holmes, *Agency* (1891) 5 HARVARD LAW REVIEW 1, 16.
48. *Ibid.* 22.
49. Lord Cromwell's Case, 4 Co. 12*b*, 13*a* (1578).
50. *French Civil Code*, art. 1382.

cent conception as to the requirements of justice, quite out of line with nineteenth-century ideas, and one which the judges of 1837 could not reasonably have been expected to grasp. At that time the idea of using litigation as a means to bring about what Professor Patten called "distribution of the economic surplus" had not occurred to any one. The fellow servant rule, properly superseded by legislation under the conditions of today, was not an arbitrarily manufactured exception to established principles set up in the interest of an economically dominant class in the fore part of the nineteenth century.[51]

Professor Bohlen has given an ingenious economic interpretation of the doctrine of *Rylands* v. *Fletcher*,[52] namely, that one who maintains things likely to get out of hand or to escape and do damage is liable at his peril if they escape or are not kept within their proper bounds. He compared the English decisions with those in the United States.[53] He says that in England the country gentleman was dominant. Consequently security of the holding of land seemed paramount to enterprise in making use of adjoining land. In the United States, on the contrary, those who were engaged actively in enterprise were the dominant class, and it seemed that the claim to use and improve land, using due care, was paramount.[54] This would be well enough if the decision in the United States had uniformly rejected the rule in *Rylands* v. *Fletcher*, or if distinctions between the jurisdictions which follow and those which reject it could be shown to conform to some such proposition. The facts are that *Rylands* v. *Fletcher* was soon followed in Massachusetts.[55] It was adopted by the Supreme Court of Minnesota in the following year.[56] Massachusetts has generally followed English decisions as a matter of authority and at that time many American state courts were inclined to

51. I have discussed this subject at length in *The Economic Interpretation and the Law of Torts* (1940) 53 HARVARD LAW REVIEW 365.

52. 3 Hurlst. & C. 774 (1865), L.R. 1 Ex. 265 (1866), L.R. 3 H.L. 330 (1868).

53. Bohlen, *The Rule in Rylands* v. *Fletcher* (1911) 59 UNIV. OF PA. LAW REVIEW 292, 313.

54. *Ibid.* 318–20.

55. *Shipley* v. *Associates*, 206 Mass. 194 (1891).

56. *Cahill* v. *Eastman*,18 Minn. 255 (1872).

follow the decisions in Massachusetts in the same way. But the next year the question was raised in New Hampshire before Chief Justice Doe, a vigorous and independent mind, who rejected the rule on the basis of a fundamental principle of no liability without fault.[57] Chief Justice Doe's reasoning was so vigorous that for a time it was generally followed in this country. The proposition that American courts rejected *Rylands* v. *Fletcher* was announced by text writers on torts and thus added currency was given to the rejection.[58] Nevertheless after a time the current set in the other way and American jurisdictions came to be not unevenly divided. The English law had been followed in Massachusetts,[59] Minnesota,[60] Ohio,[61] West Virginia,[62] Missouri[63] and Texas.[64] It has been rejected in New Hampshire,[65] Rhode Island,[66] New York,[67] New Jersey,[68] Pennsylvania,[69] Indiana,[70] Kentucky[71] and California.[72] It will be noticed that industrial states are on both sides of the question. Massachusetts is certainly quite as industrial as New York and Ohio as Pennsylvania. Nor can it be said to depend on whether the judges are elective or appointed. Massachusetts and New Jersey on opposite sides of the question each has an appointed judiciary. Nor can it be said that the courts are divided on sectional lines. In New England, Massachusetts and New

---

57. *Brown v. Collins*, 53 N.H. 442 (1873).

58. *E.g.* Burdick, *Torts* (1905) § 543.

59. *Supra*, n. 55.

60. *Supra*, n. 56.

61. *Defiance Water Co. v. Olinger*, 54 Ohio St. 532 (1896).

62. *Weaver v. Thurmond*, 68 W.Va. 530 (1911).

63. *French v. Manufacturing Co.*, 173 Mo. App. 220, 227 (1913).

64. *Texas R. Co. v. Frazer* (Tex. Civ. App.) 182 S.W. 1161 (1912). *See also* the discussion in *Exner v. Sherman Power Constr. Co.* (C.C.A.) 54 Fed. 2d, 510 (1931).

65. *Supra*, n. 57.

66. *Rose v. Socony-Vacuum Corp.* 54 R.I. 411 (1934).

67. *Losee v. Buchanan*, 51 N.Y. 476 (1873).

68. *Marshall v. Welwood*, 38 N.J. Law, 339 (1876).

69. *Pennsylvania Coal Co. v. Sanderson*, 113 Pa. St. 126 (1886).

70. *Lake Shore R. Co. v. Chicago R. Co.*, 48 Ind. App. 584 (1911).

71. *Owensboro v. Knox*, 116 Ky. 451 (1905).

72. *Judson v. Giant Powder Co.*, 107 Cal. 549 (1903).

Hampshire with Rhode Island are on opposite sides. In the Middle West, Ohio and its next neighbor Indiana are on opposite sides. In the South, West Virginia and Kentucky next adjoining are on opposite sides. The explanation is to be found rather in the weight of doctrinal considerations and the tendency of courts to follow certain others on doctrinal questions.[73]

Looking at the subject in another way, there are many cases in which juristic and judicial idealism has produced and enforced rules of conduct in advance of the ideas and interests of the dominant class or the ideas of any other class of the lay community. There are many examples in equity, such as the doctrine of constructive notice, constructive fraud, duties of fiduciaries, and especially duties of trustees.[74] Our courts of equity, so far from taking their ethical views from a dominant class of business men, have enforced traditional doctrinal ideas on that class. They have preserved and enforced the ethical tradition of the stage of infusion of morals into law even to the extent of an idea of disinterested benevolence on the part of fiduciaries which has come down from the clerical chancellors.[75] No dominant economic class in nineteenth-century America had any such ideas of disinterested benevolence in ordinary affairs. Perhaps it is enough to contrast equity doctrines with the notions of business men as to the duties of directors of corporations and promoters.

There are many questions also in which a juristic tradition, logically developed by lawyers drawn from a dominant economic or social class has withstood the interest of the class. Those who have urged the economic interpretation in America have always assumed that the man of

73. I have gone into this subject further in *Interpretations of Legal History* (1923) 105–9.

74. "To the writer the doctrine of the clog on the equity of redemption seems one of the striking examples of the great truth that the ethical standard of our law is often higher than the average morality of the commercial community." Wyman, *The Clog on the Equity of Redemption* (1908) 21 HARVARD LAW REVIEW 457, 475.

75. "Courts of equity . . . had (so to speak) screwed up the standard of reasonableness to what many men would regard as an unreasonable height." Maitland, *Lectures on Equity* (rev. ed. 1936) 99.

business was representative of the dominant economic class in our industrial communities in the immediate past. No branch of the law has been of such vital importance to the business man as the law of corporations. But his needs and desires have made very little impression upon the tradition of American law as to corporations. We have transferred to the ordinary trading company all the jealousies that might have some reason with respect to public service companies. Indeed a traditional jealousy of corporate action, for the beginnings of which we must go back to the formative stage of the common law when municipalities and ecclesiastical foundations were the only corporations,[76] will explain much more of the American law of trading corporations than can be explained by considering the self-interest of any particular class in the nineteenth century. Legislation has had to provide for the needs of business and through the influence of lawyers has often been along common-law lines.[77] Hence it became necessary for business men to go to Delaware or New Jersey or some other of a few states with liberal legislation in order to incorporate their enterprises. But when the business man takes advantage of the more liberal corporations laws of another state, he finds himself doing business through a "foreign" corporation. Outside of the state where incorporated it is potentially an outlaw, suffered to go on simply by the grace of the local authorities. Although the federal constitution guarantees to him that he may do business over the state line, it is interpreted in a way that prevents or at least hinders and embarrasses him when he seeks to do business in the only way that is practicable for any enterprise of magnitude. The reason is that at a time when "corporation" meant a state granted monopoly it was decided, rightly enough, that one state could not thrust its monopolies upon another.[78] If, instead of incorporating, the business man carries on his trading or manufacturing activities by means of a partnership, an institution

76. Even as late as the end of the eighteenth century these are the types of a corporation to the lawyer. 1 Kyd, *Corporations* (1793) 1–37.

77. *See* a typical discussion of limited liability in Proc. California Bar Assn. 1916, 63–91.

78. *See* Henderson, *The Position of Foreign Corporations in Constitutional Law* (1918).

as old as commerce, he finds that he cannot do what is always done in case of partnership—he cannot be a creditor of or debtor to the partnership—because the law on this subject is not determined by the needs of business, nor does it draw its ideas of partnership from the universal understanding and practice of business men, but from the ideas of Roman jurists.[79] Every grievance of the American laborer against American law in the last century can be matched by quite as real a grievance of the American business man and capitalist.[80] There could be no better example of the tenacity of a taught tradition. If nineteenth-century American courts had been only the mouthpiece through which the business men of America promulgated formulations of their self-interest, these things would have come to an end long ago.

A further argument may be drawn from those legal doctrines which have spread over the modern world. The modern Roman law of legal transactions has not become the law of the modern world, nor is the English law of torts becoming a law of the world because either has a world-dominating social class behind it. In each case experience and reason have worked out certain principles which have proved capable of practical applications in the administration of justice and of an orderly, logical juristic development.

We may say, then, that the phenomena of legal history do not admit of an exclusively economic interpretation.

Third, a theory of mechanical causation by the inevitable operation of class conflict wholly eliminates the efficacy of effort. A no less iron-bound science of law results than follows from the conception of a fi-

---

79. *Institutes of Justinian*, ii, 25, pr. and §§ 1–2; *Digest of Justinian*, xvii, 2, 63, pr.; Story, *Partnership* (1841) § 2. *Compare also* the jealousy of Massachusetts trusts and the whole tone of Warren, *Corporate Advantages Without Incorporation* (1929) and the narrow limitation of the second category of *de facto* corporations. *Ibid.* 688–90.

80. *See* Machen, *Do the Incorporation Laws Allow Sufficient Freedom to Commercial Enterprise* (1909) 14 REP. MD. STATE BAR ASSN. 78; *People* v. *Shedd*, 241 Ill. 155 (1909). "I regret that in many commercial matters the English law and the practice of commercial men are getting wider apart." Scrutton, L.J., in *W. N. Hillas & Co., Ltd.* v. *Arcos, Ltd.*, 36 COMMERCIAL CASES, 353, 368 (1931). *See also* Chorley, *The Conflict of Law and Commerce* (1932) 48 LAW QUARTERLY REVIEW 51; Pound, *Fifty Years of Jurisprudence* (1938) 51 HARVARD LAW REVIEW 777, 778.

nally determined natural law or from the extreme theories of nine-teenth-century historical jurisprudence or from the mechanical sociol-ogy. Theories of law readily become theories of making law and of find-ing law. It cannot be a good theory of making law or of the judicial process that legislator and judge sit to formulate the self-interest of the dominant social class. Undoubtedly the ideal element in law is greatly affected by the economic structure of society and thus legal precepts are gradually affected in their content and application. Yet it is significant that the common-law tradition has proved resistant to economic condi-tions. American land law insists that land is to be treated as a fixed and permanent acquisition, as if we were a community of English country gentlemen; not as an asset which can be passed readily from hand to hand, which is the way in which it is regarded by business men. In American pioneer communities there was a time when town lots were the chief subject of commercial activity and men bought and sold and resold lots and speculated in them after the manner of speculation in shares of stock in commercial centers.[81] But no American court in such an environment ever thought of denying specific performance of a con-tract to sell a town lot, although there were a hundred like it in every par-ticular to be had in the real estate market at a moment's notice and its unique character was a transparent dogmatic fiction.[82] Compare also the traditional arbitrary line between real property and personal prop-erty running through the law, making a sale of land subject to one set of doctrines and a sale of chattels to another, and much more of the sort. The controlling shares of stock in the family business may be sold by an administrator without more. But in general there must be a special pro-ceeding in court and showing of insufficiency of personal property to pay debts before such sale of even the most insignificant parcel of land.[83] The legislature in an agricultural state has sometimes made a farmer's

81. For an account of a real estate exchange, "as stocks are now sold on Wall Street" in a pioneer community, see 1 Grant, *Personal Memoirs* (1885–86) 208.

82. 4 Pomeroy, *Equity Jurisprudence* (4 ed. 1919) § 1402.

83. 2 Woerner, *Treatise on the American Law of Administration* (2 ed. 1899) pp. 1020–24.

note payable in corn or potatoes negotiable.[84] No court, even if the judges were elected for short terms by popular vote, ever thought of establishing such a rule for a community of farmers by judicial decision.

Stammler would say that economic conditions help determine the ideals of the epoch. Kohler would say that we must take account of economic conditions when we formulate the jural postulates of the civilization of the time and place. These ways of putting it are much nearer the truth. The influence of the purely economic situation upon the traditional element of the law is indirect. But the traditional element is the most enduring and significant part. The actual role of economics is quite different from that pictured by the usual economic interpretation. Social and economic changes give rise to new wants. New interests press for recognition and security. As a consequence, traditional principles are put to new uses. The taught tradition is gradually adapted to new wants and expectations and made to secure new interests or to secure in new ways those already recognized.

In economic determinism[85] class self-interest takes the place held by individual self-interest in the classical political economy. The social class is made the unit instead of the individual human being. Nothing but class struggle is involved in the legal order nor in the judicial and administrative processes. This goes back to the single explanation of all the phenomena of the legal order characteristic of nineteenth-century thought. It has two sides, one positive, the other negative.

On the positive side economic determinists have been much concerned with substitutes for law in the sense of a body of established or received precepts applied and developed judicially. One such substitute has been seen in administrative absolutism. According to Marx law will disappear with the abolition of private property. Its function is to keep a

---

84. Illinois, *Rev. Stat.* 1845, chap. 73, §§ 3–10.

85. Pound, *Fifty Years of Jurisprudence* (1938) 51 HARVARD LAW REVIEW 777, 779, 800; Hazard, *Soviet Law—An Introduction* (1936) 36 COLUMBIA LAW REVIEW 1236; Paschukanis, *Allgemeine Rechtslehre und Marxismus* (1929) transl. from 3d. Russian edition; Dobrin, *Soviet Jurisprudence and Socialism* (1936) 52 LAW QUARTERLY REVIEW 402; 1 Gsovski, *Soviet Civil Law* (1948) chap. 5.

class of exploited in subjection to a class of those who exploit them. So when classes disappear law too will come to an end.[86] Such minor conflicts of expectations as arise may be dealt with by administrative agencies. There is to be no law, and but one rule, namely, that there are no laws but only administrative orders for the individual case.[87] But later developments in Russia are a sufficient commentary on the Marxian idea of disappearance of law and of replacing the uniform judicial process by *ad hoc* administrative action. It was found that there must be laws and they must be stable and administered by tribunals.[88]

Another substitute for law, which it was assumed would disappear in the society of the future was expected to be provided in Italy by the corporative state, an idea which had some vogue in political-juristic thinking in some parts of the world until the collapse of Mussolini's dictatorship.[89] In such a state the occupational group was to be the unit instead of the individual man, and we were told that in this organization of society disputes would be adjusted by committees of the occupational group, or if controversies arose between members of different groups, by a general committee in which the different groups were to be repre-

86. Marx, *Critique of the Gotha Program* (English transl. 1933) 31.

87. Paschukanis, *Allgemeine Rechtslehre und Marxismus* (1929) chaps. 2, 5.

88. 1 Gsovski, *Soviet Civil Law* (1948) 187–92.

89. Guarnieri-Ventimiglia, *I principii Giuridici Dello Stato Corporativo* (1928); Navarra, *Introduzione al Diritto Corporativo — Storia e Diritto* (1929); Salemi, *Lezioni di Diritto Corporativo* (1929); Id. *Studi di Diritto Corporativo* (1929); Chiarelli, *Il Diritto Corporativo e le Sue Fonti* (1930); Ferri, *L'Ordinamento Corporativo dal Punto di Vista Economico, Caratteri Generali, I Soggetti, Le Associazioni Sindicali* (1933); Barassi, *Diritto Sindicale E Corporativo* (1934); Coniglio, *Lezioni di Diritto Corporativo* (2d ed. 1934); Mazzoni, *L'Ordinamento Corporativo: Contributo Alla Fondazione D'Una Teoria Generale E Alla Formulazione di Una Domestica Del Diritto Corporativo* (1934); Cioffi, *Istituzioni di Diritto Corporativo* (1935); Cesarini Sforza, *Curso di Diritto Corporativo* (4 ed. 1935); Pergolesi, *Istituzioni di Diritto Corporativo* (2 ed. 1935); Chiarelli, *Lo Stato Corporativo* (1936); Zanelli Quarantini, *Le Fonti del Diritto Corporativo* (1936); Aunós Pérez, *Principios de Derecho Corporativo* (1929); Caballero, *La Legislación Vigente Sobre Organización Corporativo Nacional* (1929); Aunós Pérez, *La Organización Corporativo y Su Posible Desenvolvimiento* (1929); Id. *Estudios de Derecho Corporativo* (1930); Zancada, *Programa de Derecho Corporativo* (1931); Fucile, *Le mouvement corporatif en Italie* (1929); Lescure, *Le nouveau régime corporatif italien* (1934); Pitigliani, *The Italian Corporative State* (1933).

sented. This suggests the regime of kin-group discipline and of the king determining disputes between different kin-groups and between kin-groups and kinless men in the earlier societies of antiquity. Law grew out of that process and if the process were repeated with occupational groups law might grow out of it again. But as development of the corporative state went on in Italy there were nothing more than prophecies and projects. Leaving the whole adjustment of relations to committees of occupational groups presupposes that the only significant relations or groups or associations in society are economic. It is true that men in society are united in all kinds or degrees of relations and groups and associations and that the inner order of these relations and groups and associations is the cement of the social order.[90] But we are not each of us in some one of these relations or groups or associations exclusively and for all purposes. We are in many at the same time and they make varied demands upon our allegiance. History of religion has shown more than once that economic relations and groups and associations are not always those with the strongest hold. Very likely a regime of administration of justice by committees of occupational groups, if it had been put in force for the whole domain of human relations would have had no more enduring existence than the theory of no law and a regime of administrative orders proved to have in Russia.

What may be called the negative type is concerned only to demonstrate the deception and superstition involved in the theory and practice of judicial process guided by a body of authoritative precepts developed and applied by an authoritative technique. Its exponents presuppose that the process is in theory one of mechanical application of precepts with an exactly defined content affixing definite detailed consequences to definite detailed states of fact. Starting with this false presupposition, they have no difficulty in showing that judicial application of standards, such as reasonableness or good faith and fair conduct, and application by court and jury of the standard of due care, do not conform to such a theory. But the presupposition that those who are not prepared to con-

90. Ehrlich, *Grundlegung der Soziologie des Rechts* (1913) chap. 2; English transl. by Moll (1936) 26–39.

cede the sufficiency of the economic interpretation or of Freudian psychology to explain the whole judicial process believe or would like to believe in such a theory is quite gratuitous. Equally gratuitous is the assumption that judges and practitioners of this generation, unless they subscribe to the economic determinist or skeptical realist creed, believe in such a theory.[91] The difference between judicial application of a rule of property and judicial application of a standard had been pointed out long before the extreme realists had begun to write.[92] To those who deny there are such things as authoritative precepts or an authoritative technique one may reply: Can there be any doubt that every judge of every appellate tribunal in the land would come to the same result as to any given case when it was sought to make a written promise to pay money negotiable without using the words prescribed by the Negotiable Instruments Law, or the law merchant in the absence of that statute, or in any given case in a jurisdiction where the constitution prescribes a grand jury in which it was sought to maintain a prosecution for a capital crime without an indictment? Much of what seems plausible in the writings of economic determinists gets its effect by confusing application of a standard with application of a rule and assuming that the phenomena of applying a standard are typical of every feature of the judicial process.

In the hands of some economic realists the Marxian disappearance of law becomes a disappearance of private law or rather a swallowing up of private law by public law.[93] This has an attractive sound, suggesting that the law of the past, which was a private possession of individuals, is being superseded by a public law which is something belonging to all of us. But this is not what is meant. According to the Roman books, public law was that part of the law which had to do with the constitution of the

91. See Lummus, *The Trial Judge* (1937) 3–4.
92. I have discussed this matter repeatedly. *Juristic Science and Law* (1918) 31 HARVARD LAW REVIEW 1047, 1060–63; *Theory of Judicial Decision* (1923) 36 id. 641, 643–53; *The Administrative Application of Legal Standards* (1919) 44 REP. AM. BAR ASSN. 443, 454–58; *The Supreme Court and Minimum Wage Legislation* (1925) compiled by the National Consumers' League.
93. E.g., Jennings, *The Institutional Theory*, in *Modern Theories of Law* (1933) 68, 72.

Roman state; private law was that part which had to do with the interest of individuals.[94] According to the expounders of the modern Roman law, private law has to do with adjusting the relations and securing the interests of individuals and determining controversies between man and man, while public law has to do with the frame of government, the functions of public officials and adjustment of relations between the individual and the state.[95] The term "public law" is not in the literature of the common law. In Blackstone's system public law is a part of the private law of persons, officials are persons and the law applicable to them is the law applicable to every one else.[96] In the domain of English law, the law applied by administrative tribunals and agencies was the law applied by other tribunals, namely, statute and common law, developed and applied by a received technique as in a common-law court. The rise and multiplication of administrative agencies and tribunals in the present century have led to a taking up of the term public law in the Roman sense. But something more is meant by those who expect to see private law disappear because of eating up or penetration by public law. We are told that we must start with a contrast between commutative justice, a correcting justice which gives back to one what has been taken away from him or gives him a substantial substitute, and distributive justice, a distribution of the goods of existence not equally but according to merit or a scheme of values. In the positive law this distinction is said to correspond to a contrast between the co-ordinating law, which secures interests by reparation and the like, and the subordinating law which prefers some or the interests of some to others according to its measure of values.[97] Public law is said to be a "law of subordination," subordinating individual interests to public interests (*i.e.*, interests of politically organized society) and identifying some individual interests but not the interests of other individuals with those public interests.[98] It is said to be

94. *Institutes of Justinian*, i, 1, § 4; *Digest of Justinian*, i, 1, 1 § 2.
95. 1 Dernburg, *Pandekten* (7 ed. 1902) § 21.
96. 1 Blackstone, *Commentaries on the Laws of England* (1765) chaps. 3–9.
97. Radbruch, *Rechtsphilosophie* (3 ed. 1932) 31, 125.
98. *Ibid.* 123, 124. *See* an example in *National Labor Relations Board* v. *Sunshine Mining Co.*, 125 Fed. 2d, 757 (1925).

impossible to satisfy the demands of security except by a subordinating type of law which puts a special value on the position of officials in the legal system.[99] When it comes to be applied in the common-law world, this idea of public law as a subordinating law, putting a higher value on officials and on what they do, and allowing them a wide discretion to put higher value on some persons or groups of persons than on others by identifying the interests of those persons with public interests, is in effect a theory of supplanting law (in the sense of a body of precepts serving as guides to decision and developed and applied by an authoritative technique) by an unchecked magisterial and administrative adjustment of relations and ordering of conduct. If the term "law" is retained, it is given the meaning of what those officials do because they do it.[100]

Economic determinism has had one good result. The exponents of the doctrine have called attention to an influence upon the judicial process which operated unperceived in the last century when judges trained in the tradition and modes of thought of pioneer America were quite unconscious of the beginnings and gradual growth of a class of industrial laborers. The realists challenge the best efforts of the bench and of the profession to maintain the tradition of independence and the zealous and unremitting quest of objectivity and impartiality, which have been the strength of the common-law judiciary.[101] No one doubts that we have here an ideal and, indeed, an ideal hard to attain. Nor would those who are unwilling to look upon the Marxian doctrine of economic interpretation, economic domination, and class struggle as the sole explanation of the legal order and of the judicial process think of believing or pretend to believe that the ideal has ever been, or very likely ever can be, wholly realized. But they have warrant in the history of civilization for believing that a steadfast endeavor to do so has increasingly approximated the process to the ideal; that it as nearly conforms to its postulate as any human activity, and that the development

99. Radbruch, *op. cit.* 123.
100. *See* my discussion of this in *Public Law and Private Law* (1939) 24 CORNELL LAW QUARTERLY 469.
101. Lummus, *The Trial Judge* (1937) 8–20.

of and persistence in this endeavor is not the least important achievement of civilization. To assume that objectivity and impartiality in the judicial process cannot exist in the nature of things, to look on the judicial function as political in the same sense as the legislative and executive processes, and invite a conscious exercise of the judicial process in the interest of a class growing in class-consciousness and political power,[102] is to undo the whole achievement of the legal order in the western world since the later Middle Ages.

102. See Gsovski, *The Soviet Concept of Law* (1938) 7 FORDHAM LAW REVIEW 1, 42–43.

TEN

Later Forms of Juristic Realism

In the United States economic determinism ran into psychological realism and skeptical realism and largely merged in the latter. But economic realism has tended to have more of a positive program than the other two.

I. Psychological Realism

Psychological realism is a development of economic realism in the light of Freudian and behaviorist psychology.[1] Its adherents assume that psychology has completely overthrown the jurisprudence of the past. They hold that it is psychologically impossible to do what men believed they were doing by means of law. They hold that law (in the second sense) is not an agency of promoting control over internal nature holding down the prejudices and individual inclinations of judges and officials which might lead to arbitrary and unequal and unjust exercise of the force of

---

1. Frank, *Law and the Modern Mind* (1933) particularly 1–203, 243–52; Robinson, *Law and the Lawyers* (1935) particularly 1–19, 46–121, 284–323; Arnold, *The Symbols of Government* (1935) particularly 1–104, 199–208; Frank, *If Men Were Angels* (1942).

See also Goodhart, *Some American Interpretations of Law*, in *Modern Theories of Law* (1933) 1, 15 ff.; Pound, *The Call for a Realist Jurisprudence* (1931) 44 HARVARD LAW REVIEW 597, 704–7; Pound, *Fifty Years of Jurisprudence* (1938) 51 HARVARD LAW REVIEW 777, 785–90; Mechem, *The Jurisprudence of Despair* (1936) 21 IOWA LAW REVIEW 669; Arnold, *The Jurisprudence of Edward S. Robinson* (1937) 46 YALE LAW JOURNAL 1128.

politically organized society. It is only what judges and officials do, motivated by their prejudices and individual inclinations.[2] Thus psychological realists have been coming to much the same doctrine as the economic determinists, but on a psychological not an economic basis. They insist on the non-rational element in judicial and administrative action as reality and the rational element as illusion. Where the last century stressed uniformity and predictability and certainty and ignored the fallings short of these ideals in practice, they stress the lack of uniformity and the uncertainties, and the influence of personal and subjective factors in particular cases. They assume that mechanical application of rules attaching a definite detailed legal consequence to a definite detailed state or situation of fact is the juristic ideal and that the quite different processes of choice of starting points for analogical reasoning and of application of standards are processes of applying rules and are governed by the same juristic ideal. They attribute to individual psychology the departures from the ideal of applying rules which are necessarily involved in judicial and juristic reasoning from analogy and application of standards.

Einsteinian relativist physics, with its challenge of what had been supposed to be the fixed order of the universe, and Freudian psychology, with its demonstration of the role of the wish in what had passed for reasoning,[3] came as a powerful reinforcement to economic determinism in the spread of Marxian ideas after the Russian revolution. It would be quite in the spirit of psychological juristic realism to suggest that those

2. "This doing of something about disputes, this doing of it reasonably, is the business of the law. And the people who have the doing of it in charge, whether they are judges or sheriffs or clerks or jailers or lawyers, are officials of the law. *What these officials do about disputes* is to my mind the law itself." Llewellyn, *The Bramble Bush* (1930) 3. Here he puts the task of the legal order and then seems to define law in the second sense as the way law in the first sense is carried on instead of as a body of guides to carrying it on. But it is fair to say that he later repudiated the passage as out of balance in its emphasis. *On Using the Newer Jurisprudence* (1940) 40 COLUMBIA LAW REVIEW 581, 603, n. 17. But what he then said was what many were then saying.

3. There is a good concise statement in Holt, *The Freudian Wish and Its Place in Ethics* (1915).

who sought a new social order after the first World War wished to find in the legal order the camouflaged class tyranny and in the judicial process the hypocritical pretense which would justify their overthrow. It might be suggested that they wished to see a complete class domination for the future and so were able to see one more assuredly in the past. It might be suggested that they wished to see an administrative absolutism wielded by a class with which they considered themselves allied and so were the more readily persuaded that it is impossible to think objectively. One might even suggest that on their own doctrine they labor under a like impossibility.[4]

No small share in bringing about a reaction from nineteenth-century juristic thought must be charged to a type of law teaching which sought to reduce the whole body of legal precepts to rules in the narrower sense and the whole judicial process to mechanical application of rules analogous to rules of property. It is very doubtful whether this was ever carried so far or was so generally prevalent in American law teaching as the realists have been asserting or assuming. It did govern the writing of cyclopaedias of law and a type of text book for practitioners and this to some extent affected the work of courts with overcrowded dockets and no time to listen to competent oral argument. Also it found support in the writing of analytical jurists who assumed a statutory rule of property as the type of a law and that law was an aggregate of such laws.[5] Judges and practicing lawyers, on the other hand, knew better.[6]

In its extreme form, psychological realism conceives of each item of the judicial process as shaped wholly and inexorably by the psychological determinants of the behavior of the individual judge. It thinks of the judicial process in terms of "the judge" and is largely taken up with consideration of the abstract psychology of the abstract judge as this is dogmatically assumed to dictate every item of concrete judicial behavior. In a less extreme form it conceives of determination by factors of individ-

---

4. See an interesting psychological interpretation of psychological realism in Goodhart, *Some American Interpretations of Law*, in *Modern Theories of Law* (1933) 1, 16–17.

5. 1 Bentham's *Works* (Bowring ed. 1843) 141.

6. See e.g., Dillon, *Laws and Jurisprudence of England and America* (1894) 17–18.

ual psychology which are largely undiscoverable, and hence of judicial action as unpredictable "in a case of any novelty whatever."[7]

So long as there have been judges and counselors the counselor at law who advises clients has known that he must bear in mind to some extent the idiosyncrasies of particular judges. But he has known also that in the case of appellate and reviewing tribunals such individual idiosyncrasies will be neutralized in the judicial consultation room. The cases which make him the most trouble are those involving the application of a standard and those where there are no near analogies and many remote analogies with no clear guide leading to one more than another. Looking only at the formulas announced tentatively in the development of a doctrine by judicial inclusion and exclusion, there may seem to be a high degree of unpredictability as to where lines would ultimately be drawn. But looking at the results in each case, not at the successive attempts to generalize from the particular result in the case in hand to a universal precept, as a rule it is by no means difficult to put the actual result in the order of reason and be as sure as one can be in any human practical activity how cases of that sort, even if they involve some degree of novelty, will be decided. If this were not true our complex economic order could not stand.

Even when thought of as merely a theory of the judicial process, psychological realism is too dogmatically narrow, ignoring the effect of a bench of judges upon judicial behavior, the checks upon judicial action and the constraint exercised by professional criticism and opinion, the toughness, as Maitland calls it, of a taught tradition,[8] and the effect of received ideals of the social and legal order, and reaction each upon the other of received traditional ideals and subjective ideals. It is significant to note the relative narrowness and rigid adherence to reduction of reasonableness in the application of standards to fixed rules on the part of elective short-term state judges in their treatment of social legislation

7. Moore and Hope, *An Institutional Approach to the Law of Commercial Banking* (1938) 38 YALE LAW JOURNAL 703–4.

8. Maitland, *English Law and the Renaissance* (1901) 25.

between 1880 and 1910 with the relative breadth of view of appointed judges on the same questions at the same time.[9] Current realist doctrine would require us to expect the reverse.

Investigation of the psychology of courts and study of the psychological bases of the persistence and vitality of a taught tradition systematized in received treatises and studied both in the formative student period and, in the case of judges, continuously during long periods of practice before courts and later of sitting in them, is a more practical and profitable program for psychological realism than the elaborate study of the relation of particular individual judges to particular individual cases which has been suggested as the foundation of a science of law.[10] A less rigorously behaviorist method, tempered by the consideration that we must take account also of the restraints upon non-rational individual behavior and that judges as a rule are not likely to do better than they are expected to do, may well yield useful results. There was a psychological efficacy in the nineteenth-century ideal of the judicial process.[11]

Frank has urged that what he calls the "basic legal myth" of the possibility of certainty, uniformity, and predictability in the legal order and in the judicial process is brought about by a need which the grown man feels for rediscovery of his father "through father substitutes." He says: "The law — a body of rules apparently devised for infallibly determining what is right and what is wrong and for deciding who should be punished for misdeeds — inevitably becomes a partial substitute for the Father-as-Infallible-Judge. That is, the desire persists in grown men to recapture, through a rediscovery of a father, a childish, completely controllable universe, and that desire seeks satisfaction in a partial, unconscious anthropomorphizing of law, in ascribing to law some of the

9. Elliot and others, Preliminary Report on Efficiency in the Administration of Justice, made to the National Economic League (1914) 9; Haynes, *The Selection and Tenure of Judges* (1944) chap. 7.

10. Moore and Hope, *An Institutional Approach to the Law of Commercial Banking* (1938) 38 YALE LAW JOURNAL 703, 704–9 (1938).

11. *See* Schofield, *Swift* v. *Tyson*, Uniformity of Judge-Made State Law in State and Federal Courts (1910) 4 ILLINOIS LAW REVIEW 533, 536–37.

characteristic of the child's Father-Judge."[12] This might be compared with Dr. Ranyard West's proposition that the individual needs the law to keep his tendency to aggressive self-assertion to satisfy his desires in balance with his likewise deep-seated tendency toward adaptation to life in groups and associations and relations.[13] The argument from this starting point may be less iconoclastic.

Social psychology has been refuting Marx's proposition that law is only a means by which a dominant class enforces its self-interest upon a class which it is exploiting. It has made clear that the control of individual aggressiveness exercised by organized society is not merely something set up by a ruling class or group to check the activities of a restless group of have-nots or even of a relatively small criminal class. Although the criminal law commonly stands to the layman for the whole, it is not the most significant part of the law. The civil side which adjusts the everyday relations and orders the everyday conduct of normal men is in a highly developed society the most significant part. Llewellyn has shown convincingly the social need of law in that if conflicts of individual expectations are not adjusted societies are disrupted.[14] But if there are not well conceived adjustments, if determinations of controversies are unequal, arbitrary, or prejudiced the unwillingness of men to be subjected to the arbitrary will of others leads to upheavals which impair the social order. No less, however, law is a recognition by social man of one of his chief needs as an individual, namely, to hold back his aggressive urge and adjust it to the exigencies of his social urge.

There is, we may assume, an urge in man, in all the diverse conditions of life, to gratify so far as may be, the different aspects of his nature. The term "instinct" has been overworked and made to cover so much that one hesitates to use it. But using it to mean certain fundamental ten-

12. *Law and the Modern Mind* (sixth printing 1949) 18–20, 41, 81, 91, 141, 156, 162, 167, 193, 199, 200, 219, 235, 246, 256, 292, 354.

13. West, *The Psychological Status of Present International Law*, in 28 GROTIUS SOCIETY, *Problems of Peace and War* (1943) 135.

14. Llewellyn, *The Normative, the Legal and the Law Jobs: The Problem of Juristic Method* (1940) 49 YALE LAW JOURNAL 1355, 1373–83.

dencies of human behavior, appearing in childhood and manifest throughout life, there are two classes of these tendencies, one of which may be called the aggressive or self-assertive instinct, the other which may be called the social instinct. Man's nature is not a harmonious one except as he learns to bring about a working balance through training and experience of life in society. The aggressive or self-assertive instinct leads him to think of his own desires and demands for himself alone and to seek to satisfy them at the expense of others and to overcome all resistance to them. Bringing up and education seek to teach control of this self-assertive instinct. But it is deep-seated and bringing up and education require a backing of force. The exercise of that force, however, itself requires control, since the aggressive instinct of those who wield it may govern its application. Thus we get a problem of balance of force and of control of force which is at the root of an internal contradiction in criminal law and criminal procedure, from which we have thus far found no escape and is in the background of most of the difficulties of government and the legal order. This is external to the man himself. Aggressive self-assertion even to the point of violence is potential in almost every one. It is exercised in different men in different ways and in different degrees, often spasmodically and contrary to their normal intention and mode of conduct and even in ways for which they find it difficult to account. It runs counter to the social instinct of the individual so that he usually repudiates it. But it exists potentially and is frequently manifested. Hence there must be force somewhere to keep it in control. It is a task of social control, and hence of the highly specialized form of social control which we call law, to control this individual tendency to aggressive individual self-assertion to satisfy individual desires and demands and expectations. This is brought out strikingly whenever the force of politically organized society is for a time suspended. When, for example, in case of revolution or police strike or sudden great catastrophe, conflagration, flood, or earthquake, the coercive agencies of politically organized society are for a time in abeyance, violence seems to break out spontaneously.

In the science of law this task of social control is expressed in one way in the theory of interests. An interest, in this theory, is defined as a desire or demand or expectation which human beings either individually or in groups or associations seek to satisfy, of which, therefore the adjustment of human relations and ordering of human conduct must take account. Such desires or demands or expectations to have or use things or to do things, become significant whenever a number of human beings come in contact. There is a conflict or overlapping of desires or demands or expectations. The aggressive self-assertion of individuals to satisfy them requires restraint, and the law must determine which of them are to be recognized and secured, and within what limits, and must order their satisfaction with a minimum of friction and waste. So much for the task of the law from the standpoint of the social order. But the restraint of aggressive self-assertion by social control with an ultimate recourse to force is not only a need of society, it is need of the individual himself.

On the other hand, all normal men desire and show an aptitude for some sort of life in groups and associations and relations, and the tendency toward this is as fundamental, as deep-seated, as that toward aggressive self-assertion. It might be called an instinct of realizing oneself through others as the aggressive instinct is one of realizing oneself against others. It is manifest in the power of the individual conscience, and it is partly through the social instinct and this manifestation of it and partly by social control external to the individual that society succeeds in harnessing the individual instinct of aggressive self-assertion.

I am not competent to say that either one of these instincts is more original and fundamental than the other nor whether there is any original or fundamental balance of them. But whether there is or is not such an original balance, or whichever of the two is original and fundamental, it seems to be true of human behavior that it goes on normally as if in general the social instinct prevails over the instinct of self-assertion. The universality of groups and associations and relations, existence of society and the history of civilization seem to show it. What McDougall calls the instinct of gregariousness and loyalty and veracity as tendencies connected with it,[15] is one way of putting this. Aristotle saw it long ago when he said that man was a political animal, meaning that men naturally associated themselves in organized societies.[16] Indeed, Aristotle pointed out that otherwise man was the fiercest of beasts.[17] Without social control his aggressive self-assertion would prevail over his cooperative social tendency and civilization would come to an end. Society does in this sense master the individual, and this is what is meant when we say that one side of civilization is conquest of internal nature. It is this normal condition of development of the social instinct or tendency to keep in restraint the aggressive self-assertive instinct or tendency which marks civilization. This, I suppose, is what the Neo-Hegelians have in mind when they say that the task of the legal order is to maintain, further, and transmit civilization. It is what has made possible the conditions under which men have been able to gain continually increasing control over internal nature and harness it to the use of mankind and so to inherit the earth and maintain and increase that inheritance.

Nineteenth-century philosophers of law, seeking to base their whole theory on the idea of liberty, looked on agreement or contract and its analogues as the significant legal institutions. These institutions realized liberty as an idea. It was said that the drawing up of contracts, agreements, family settlements, and conveyances was legislative in character. The parties made law for themselves.[18] In the present century, with the rise of social philosophies of law, instead of this, we hear of law as adjusting relations in order to maintain social interests, that is, the desires and demands and expectations asserted in title of social life in civilized society; of ordering conduct in order to maintain the general security, the security of social institutions, and the conservation of social resources. Instead of individual freedom we hear of the social interest in the individual life. Instead of the individual moral unit we hear of the social interest in the general morals. Instead of individual self-direction

15. McDougall, *Social Psychology* (1936).
16. Aristotle, *Politics*, i, 2, McKeon, *Basic Works of Aristotle*, 1129–30.
17. *Ibid.*
18. Miller, *Lectures on the Philosophy of Law* (1884) 71.

by the individual conscience, we hear more of social control. But I suspect this is as one-sided in one direction as the nineteenth-century mode
of thought was in another. In a sense law maintains one set of moral values against another. It results from workable adjustment of human desires and demands and expectations whereby those proceeding upon
one instinct are harmonized in action with those proceeding upon a
conflicting instinct prevailing in the mind of the individual at another
time. In this way law gives external support to the social instinct against
antisocial aggressions resulting from the self-assertive instinct. In this respect the philosophical jurists of the last century were by no means
wholly wrong when they thought of government and law as extensions
of individual self-control.

Recently Dr. West has written instructively of the "inevitability of
prejudice."[19] By prejudice he means "judgment influenced and dis-
torted by emotion, especially by unconscious emotion," and the question he puts is how far prejudiced emotional judgments of mankind can
be corrected. He comes to the conclusion that when certain facts of human nature are fully recognized we may be able to "organize our fundamental human relations securely enough to withstand the disinte-
grating effect of human passion inadequately controlled."[20] Law brings
the two instincts at the roots of human behavior into harmony. Why can
one not believe that as in the history of civilization we have been able to
achieve a considerable degree of control over non-rational aggressive
self-assertion so we may be able to achieve a continually stronger control over prejudice and arbitrariness in the judicial process? Indeed if we
compare the judicial process in action in sixteenth-century England
with what goes on in English courts today we must admit that great progress has been made. Likewise comparison of the law in action in the era
following independence with the law in action today makes it clear
enough that the working out of a body of American law has enabled
courts with the aid of a received authoritative technique to achieve a

19. Ranyard West, *The Inevitability of Prejudice* (1952) 22 ETHICS, 205.
20. *Ibid.* 209.

high degree of objective determination of controversies. Control of the instinct of aggressive self-assertion has not eliminated wholly occasional outbreaks of it in action. Control of the inevitable element of prejudice in arriving at judgments will not wholly eliminate it in action. But if it can be held, and I think we do succeed well in holding it under reasonable control, we are not bound to give up our belief in a judicial process guided by law in the second sense because in times and places it is not as effective as we could wish and perhaps cannot so far as we can foresee come up in practice to one hundred percent of what we postulate.

Combining psychological realism and the economic interpretation, might it be said that class interests bring about wishes and the wishes operate in the judicial and juristic and administrative and legislative processes? Might it be said that the Freudian wish takes the place of the ideal; that an ideal is a picture of things wished for? If the decisive thing is taken to be the wish, could it be said that a wish on the part of judges, brought up in the common law tradition and thoroughly trained in the principles and technique of that system, to conform the administration of justice to the received ideal may be effective in the judicial process as against unconscious wishes the tradition calls on them to repress? Is that ideal given shape and content by the self-interest of an economically dominant class, or is it something developed in the history of civilization which, as a taught tradition, is able to impose a check upon self-interest of every kind?

It was a distinct advance when Jhering's demand for a jurisprudence of actualities led to looking at legal precepts and institutions and doctrines with reference to how they work or fail to work and why. In keeping to this attitude the realists have been carrying on one of the best achievements of jurisprudence in the present century, namely, looking at the legal order, the body of authoritative grounds of or guides to decision, and particular precepts, institutions and doctrines, functionally. Also there is an advance in their frank recognition of analogical or nonrational element in the judicial process which the legal science of the nineteenth century deliberately ignored. But many of the realists ignore and all minimize the logical and rational element and the traditional technique of application which make for stability and uniformity in spite of disturbing factors. There is not and cannot be the perfect uniformity and mechanical certainty of result which the last century postulated. But it was postulated as an ideal of what we sought to attain. An ideal of a process does not presuppose complete theoretical realization in practice. It guides us in seeking to attain the best that we can. The dogma of a complete body of rules, to be applied mechanically (more held where there were codes and under the Roman-law tradition than where the common law obtained) was quite out of line with reality. It is no less dogmatically unreal to shut one's eyes to the extent to which the administration of justice does succeed in attaining certainty and uniformity and predictability through rule and form and the extent to which the economic order rests thereon. It is no less unreal to refuse to see the extent to which authoritative legal technique, with all its faults and in spite of mishandling in less than ideal hands, applied to authoritative legal materials, with all their defects, keeps down the alogical or unrational or holds it to tolerable limits in practice. In the field of the economic life (in the stricter sense) there is incomparably more significance on the one side than on the other. It is this significance which makes legal and economic development go hand in hand.

II. Skeptical Realism

Skeptical realism[21] carries further the rejection of law in any other sense than the aggregate of the items of judicial and official action. Law is

21. Llewellyn, *The Bramble Bush* (1930) 3, but see *supra*, note 2; id. *A Realistic Jurisprudence — The Next Step* (1930) 30 COLUMBIA LAW REVIEW 431; id. *Some Realism About Realism* (1931) 44 HARVARD LAW REVIEW 1222; Bingham, *What Is Law?* (1912) 11 MICHIGAN LAW REVIEW 1, 109; Llewellyn, *Präjudizienrecht und Rechtsprechung in Amerika* (1933) § § 1–16; id. *Legal Tradition and Social Science Methods* in Swann and others, *Essays in Research in the Social Sciences* (1931); Frank, *What Courts Do in Fact* (1932) 26 ILLINOIS LAW REVIEW 645; id. *Are Judges Human* (1931) 80 UNIV. OF PA. LAW REVIEW 17, 233; id. *Mr. Justice Holmes and Non-Euclidean Legal Thinking* (1932) 17

what judges and administrative officials do and what judges and administrative officials do is law. In this extreme rejection of what jurists had thought of as law from the beginnings of a science of law, Einsteinian relativist physics and Neo-Kantian epistemology with its doctrine of irreducible antinomies and the ultimate role of the force of politically organized society cooperate with economic determinism and psychological determinism. Many things lie behind any particular item of human behavior and so of official behavior. But two things are excluded from the motivation of judicial behavior, namely, the body of authoritative guides to decision and the received authoritative technique of developing and applying them. That these in any way determine the actual course of judicial decision or administration is held to be a mere pious wish of jurist or lawyer or else superstition.

CORNELL LAW QUARTERLY 568; id. *If Men Were Angels* (1942); Hutcheson, *The Judge Intuitive* (1928) 14 CORNELL LAW QUARTERLY 274; Yntema, *Rational Basis of Legal Science* (1931) 31 COLUMBIA LAW REVIEW 925; Radin, *Legal Realism* (1931) 31 COLUMBIA LAW REVIEW 829; Arnold, *The Role of Substantive Law and Procedure in the Legal Process* (1932) 45 HARVARD LAW REVIEW 617; Goble, *Law as a Science* (1934) 9 INDIANA LAW REVIEW 294; Marx, *Juristischer Realismus in den Vereinigten Staaten von Amerika* (1936) 10 REVUE INTERNATIONALE DE LA THEORIE DU DROIT, 28; F. Cohen, *Transcendental Nonsense and the Functional Approach* (1935) 35 COLUMBIA LAW REVIEW 809; Auburtin, *Amerikanische Rechtsauffassung und die neueren amerikanischen Theorien der Rechtssoziologie und des Rechtsrealismus*, 3 ZEITSCHRIFT FUR AUSLANDISCHES OFFENTLICHES RECHT (1933) 529, 547–64.

Pound, *Fifty Years of Jurisprudence* (1938) 51 HARVARD LAW REVIEW 777, 790–97; Morris R. Cohen, *Law and the Social Order* (1933) 219–47; id. *On Absolutism in Legal Thought* (1936) 84 UNIV. OF PA. LAW REVIEW 681; Dickinson, *Legal Rules: Their Function in the Process of Decision, Their Elaboration and Application* (1931) 79 UNIV. OF PA. LAW REVIEW 832, 1052; Fuller, *American Legal Realism* (1934) 82 UNIV. OF PA. LAW REVIEW 425; Kantorowicz, *Some Rationalism About Realism* (1934) 43 YALE LAW JOURNAL 240; Harris, *Idealism Emergent in Jurisprudence* (1936) 10 TULANE LAW REVIEW 169; Cardozo, *Address Before the New York State Bar Association* (1932) 55 REP. N.Y. STATE BAR ASSN., 263; Friedrich, *Remarks on Llewellyn's View of Law, Official Behavior and Political Science* (1933) 50 POLITICAL SCIENCE QUARTERLY 419; Kennedy, *Principles or Facts* (1935) 4 FORDHAM LAW REVIEW 53; id. *Functional Nonsense and the Transcendental Approach* (1936) 5 FORDHAM LAW REVIEW 272. See also Lundstedt, *Superstition or Rationality in Action for Peace* (1925) 96–119; id. *Die Unwissenschaftlichkeit der Rechtswissenschaft* (1932–36).

There is more or less complete skepticism as to the systematic character of official action as a quality of the legal order,[22] as to the role of legal precepts in the judicial process,[23] and as to the actuality or even possibility of any degree of objectivity in the administration of justice.[24] Frank says: "The earlier case means only what the judge in the later case says it means. Any case is an authoritative precedent only for a judge who, as the result of his own reflection, decides that it is authoritative."[25] Again, he says: "The rules a judge announces when publishing his decision are, therefore, intelligible only if one can relive the judge's experience while he was trying the case which, of course, cannot be done."[26] Likewise Yntema says: "Of the many things which have been said of the mystery of the judicial process, the most salient is that decision is reached in an emotive experience in which principles and logic play a secondary part. The function of juristic logic and the principles it employs seems to be like language, to describe the event which has already transpired."[27]

It will have been noted that the foregoing extracts are in terms of decisions of a single judge sitting at first instance. But as the law is today, only the decisions of a bench of judges of ultimate reviewing jurisdiction can make the law. In the case of the average American bench of seven judges sitting on appeals in the highest state court it would be hard indeed to find a common denominator of emotive experience for each case. But if the result reached departs from the norm as shown by

22. Llewellyn, *The Bramble Bush*, 3. But see *supra* note 2.

23. Llewellyn, *Some Realism About Realism* (1931) 44 HARVARD LAW REVIEW 1222, 1227.

24. Frank, *Law and the Modern Mind*, pt. I, chap. 12 (1931); id. *Are Judges Human* (1931) 80 UNIV. OF PA. LAW REVIEW 17, 23–31, 34–37, 233, 240–48; id. *What Courts Do in Fact* (1932) 26 ILLINOIS LAW REVIEW 645; Llewellyn, *A Realistic Jurisprudence—The Next Step* (1930) 30 COLUMBIA LAW REVIEW 431, 447–53.

25. Frank, *Law and the Modern Mind* (1931) 149n. *See* Fuller, *American Legal Realism* (1934) 82 UNIV. OF PA. LAW REVIEW 429, 433.

26. Frank, *Law and the Modern Mind* (1931) 150.

27. Yntema, *The Hornbook Method and the Conflict of Laws* (1928) 37 YALE LAW JOURNAL 468, 480.

the general course of decision in common-law jurisdictions the courts in other states will point this out and refuse to follow it, and if the emotive experience of a judge of first instance leads him to a result departing from the norm either in choice of starting point for reasoning, in developing or interpreting the starting point or in applying the precept found, his judgment or decree will be reviewed by a bench of judges and very likely be upset.

That skeptical realism has had its chief development among American teachers of law is due to a condition peculiar to American law and to American law teaching. In the United States, forty-eight states have each their own legislation and, as to questions of private law, their own ultimate law-finding agency in their highest courts. The federal government has also its own system of courts and had until recently an ultimate law-finding authority for much of private law for those courts.[28] Beneath all this there is a fundamental unity through the received English common law, received common-law technique, the common use of doctrinal treatises, and the persuasive authority of the decisions of other common-law courts. But while there is consistency and uniformity in each state, if we seek to think of American law as a unit there is great diversity in detail because of great diversity of local geographical, economic, and social conditions and of historical background, and even much diversity as to elements of the population coming from different parts of the old world. Thus in any state where a question arises for the first time there may be many competing views of equal authority from which to choose. When law was taught in local schools there was little confusion in the local law to attract attention. But as it has come to be taught more and more in schools with a student body drawn from the country at large, and teachers have sought to teach an American law as a whole, there has sometimes seemed a hopeless confusion in subjects in which the several states have diverged in their working out of details. Thus as a teacher sees it there is a want of certainty and predictability and uniformity which the lawyer does not find in the particular juris-

28. *Erie Co.* v. *Tompkins*, 304 U.S. 64 (1938).

diction in which he practices. He knows which of diverging lines of persuasive authority are likely to be followed in his jurisdiction even if the teacher cannot find one which he can hold likely to prevail universally.

There are three possibilities in the discussions of law in terms of the judicial process which go by the name of realism. Realism might be simply a theory of how the judicial process and the administrative process actually take place. If so, like most juristic theories it contains a partial truth. It is a theory of the whole process in terms of the administrative element in the process, and to some, but less extent, of the more or less legislative element involved in "finding the law" by analogical reasoning. Or, second, it might be a theory of what ought to take place in the operation of the judicial process. It might consider that process from the Marxian standpoint of a class enforcing its self-interest. It might assume that a class rapidly rising into power ought to bring about an administration of justice avowedly in its sole interest, and that such is, on the whole, what we must come to in theory and what we ought to come to in practice. Or, third, it might join psychological determinism in a theory of what must be psychologically and what is psychologically impossible in the judicial process. In that event it needs much correction from a theory which will take account of the role of a taught tradition in legal history and experience of the effect of such a tradition upon the judicial process throughout the common-law world.

As has been suggested above, the situations which give aid and comfort to the skeptical realist are, first, cases of the application of standards, and, second, where choice becomes necessary between starting points for legal reasoning which have equal authority, and the question is from which to begin, there being no precept to determine this. If we start with the nineteenth-century postulate of analytical jurisprudence in the English-speaking world, of the French exposition of the civil code in the last century, and of the Pandectists, the postulate that there is a complete system of legal precepts, either expressly or potentially covering every case, and that finding a rule for a new case is nothing more than a logical drawing out of a precept logically contained in or presupposed by some expressed precept — if we apply this postulate to increasingly common situations where the law must be "found" — it may seem to refute any idea of a uniform, predictable course of judicial action. But even in this type of case judicial action is by no means so completely at large or so completely a matter of individual behavior tendencies of some particular judge as skeptical realism has assumed.[29] The assumption ignores the decisive role of received technique and received ideals.

There is a better basis for the demand of men that there be certainty and predictability in the judicial process than persistence of the child's desire to be led.[30] As Saleilles puts it, "the demand of the social order, represented by the rigidity of legal principles as well as by the requirements of individual justice will ever be recognized."[31] In times of liberalization, following upon changes in the social and economic order, the balance between the general security and the individual life becomes disturbed. It is likely to incline for a time strongly toward the individual life, and so lead to a somewhat blundering or unsystematic individualizing judicial process until new practicable generalizations have been worked out. One who looks at the legal phenomena of a time and place only in terms of the phenomena themselves, may well be deceived into thinking them less possible of being put in the order of reason than they are.

A common assumption of the realists is that those who have been unwilling to go with them to the full length of their doctrine seek to rule out discretion from the legal order and from the judicial process. Frank's argument[32] assumes that one who in speaking of law in the sense of the body of authoritative precepts is speaking also and at the same time of law in the sense of the legal order and of law in the sense of the judicial

29. I have considered this point in *The Ideal Element in American Judicial Decision* (1931) 45 HARVARD LAW REVIEW 1361; *A Comparison of Ideals of Law* (1933) 47 HARVARD LAW REVIEW 1; *Hierarchy of Sources and Forms in Different Systems of Law* (1933) 7 TULANE LAW REVIEW 473.

30. Frank, *Law and the Modern Mind* (1931) pt. I, chap. 2, pt. III, chap. 1.

31. Saleilles, *L'individualisation de la peine* (2 ed. 1904) preface, p. vi, English translation, *The Individualization of Punishment*, p. xxvi.

32. Frank, *Law and the Modern Mind* (1931) 140, 141; id. *Are Judges Human* (1931) 80 UNIV. OF PA. LAW REVIEW 17, 19.

process. A judge may exercise discretion only in case or under circumstance where a legal precept requires or permits it. It may be that the law in the second sense requires that discretion in the particular case be guided by principles as in the discretion of a court in granting or denying equitable remedies. But when such guidance is not prescribed legal precepts still require a judge truly to exercise discretion. If he acts arbitrarily his action may be reviewed for abuse of discretion. Thus when a judge is empowered to and does exercise a personal discretion, while his action is not wholly at large, yet, since there is an administrative element in the judicial process, he goes outside of law in the second sense of the term but not outside of his duty or authority under the legal order. Discretion is contrasted with law in the second of its three senses, as one of the instruments of law in the first sense, that is, the legal order. Because one points out this contrast, using the term "law" in the second sense, it does not follow that he is excluding or seeking to exclude discretion from the legal armory.

Because men have believed they could do great things in the way of social control they have been able to do great things. It is idle to say that law in the second sense is futile deception, is a myth, is a superstition, when we see how the work of the Roman jurisconsults from the first to the third century, codified by Justinian in the sixth century, developed in the universities of Continental Europe from the twelfth to the nineteenth century has served and serves today to adjust relations and order conduct in half of the world and was made almost overnight to serve as the basis of a modern regime of justice in Japan. Equally it is idle to make such assertions when we see how experience of determination of controversies in the King's courts in medieval England developed into a reasoned tradition by teaching in the Inns of Court, and further developed by the courts in nineteenth-century England and America, could go round the world as basis of a system of law for the English-speaking peoples. It is idle to say that these two great bodies of rationally developed experience represent nothing more than human self-deception. It is idle to say that the arbitrary, personal, subjective element in magisterial behavior, which these traditions have for centuries shown us how to subdue, is the reality and this systematized and rationally developed experience only sham used to cover up unrational particular determinations resulting from individual prejudice and class self-interest. Experience of social control by the judicial process guided by law is as objectively valid as engineering experience.

More than once it has happened that judges appointed to turn the course of the law out of its channel have found themselves carried along by the current of the tradition. It has become fashionable to sneer at Story, who was renowned in his day as a great scholar and great lawyer, whose books are still standard not only in America after one hundred years but throughout the English-speaking world and even in Continental Europe. He is now held up as an example of reprehensible legal orthodoxy. No doubt he did cooperate with Kent and Marshall in putting our formative American law in the channel of Anglo-American legal development. But it should be remembered that he was appointed to the bench of the Supreme Court of the United States as a young radical, a follower of Thomas Jefferson,[33] and only proved, what has repeatedly been demonstrated, that a good lawyer will keep law and politics in separate compartments; that he may be a radical politician and yet when he becomes a judge will keep to the received legal tradition.

Morris Cohen[34] asks whether the fellow servant rule and the doctrine of assumption of risk would "have been invented if Lord Abinger and Chief Justice Shaw had been laborers?" Waiving a question as to his assumption that the rule and doctrine were inventions of these judges, for, as Mr. Justice Holmes pointed out and has been set forth in a prior lecture,[35] they failed to invent exceptions to established doctrine instead of inventing new doctrine, one might retort by asking whether he means laborers untrained in law or laborers who had been thoroughly trained in the common law and common-law modes of juristic thought, and had after many years of practice in common-law courts been raised to

33. 1 W. W. Story, *Life and Letters of Joseph Story* (1851) 211, 212.
34. Cohen and Cohen, *Readings in Jurisprudence and Legal Philosophy*, 673 (extract from Morris R. Cohen, *Law and the Social Order*, 1933).
35. Lecture IX, notes 46–49.

the bench and been for years applying the common law to the decision of cases? At any rate class self-interest does not seem to have persisted and affected the judicial process in the case of two great judges in English judicial history — Lord Tenterden[36] and Lord St. Leonards,[37] each the son of a barber.

Theories of judicial decision may be worked out for decision at first instance or for decisions of courts of review (which make precedents) or for both, or may be directed to the law-finding or law-declaring function of appellate courts, or to the judicial process as a whole. Huntington Cairns has given an interesting discussion of four theories.[38] Bacon, who as Chancellor, sat at first instance in the Court of Chancery and as one of the judges of first instance in the Court of Star Chamber at a time when equity had not yet been systematized and the law of misdemeanors administered in the Star Chamber was formative, is giving us an idealized version of the judicial process in those courts.[39] He was concerned with the law-finding function of courts for which a body of authoritative guides to decision had still to be developed. Cairns makes an excellent summary of his theory: "Bacon took the view that in order to achieve justice in the cases not clearly provided for by statute or otherwise the judge has three courses open to him. He may proceed on the analogy of precedents, or by the use of examples, or by his own sound judgment and discretion."[40] Cardozo was writing of the process of finding the law in an ultimate court of review where it was necessary to fill gaps in law in the second sense — as Holmes put it to make law interstitially[41] — and was pointing out the difficulty of determining how far a court can go, when filling a gap in the law, "without going beyond the walls of the interstice."[42] This, Cardozo considered he must learn for

36. 4 Campbell, *Lives of the Chief Justices* (3 ed. 1874) 309–11.
37. 2 Atlay, *Victorian Chancellors* (1908) 1–2.
38. Cairns, *Legal Philosophy from Plato to Hegel* (1949) 236–39.
39. 3 Bacon, *Works* (ed. by Spedding, Ellis, and Heath, 1879) 145.
40. Cairns, *Legal Philosophy from Plato to Hegel* (1949) 237.
41. Holmes, J., in *Southern Pacific Co. v. Jansen*, 244 U.S. 205, 221 (1917).
42. Cardozo, *The Nature of the Judicial Process* (1921) 113–14.

himself. "Logic, and history, and custom, and utility, and the accepted standard of right conduct, are the forces which singly or in combination shape the progress of the law. Which of these forces shall dominate in any case must depend largely upon the comparative importance or value of the social interests that will thereby be promoted or impaired." How to weigh these elements of decision will "come with years of habitude in the practice of an art."[43] It will be a matter of intuition born of experience. With this Cairns contrasts what he terms my "severely analytical"[44] theory of judicial decision. But Cardozo and I are not treating of the same thing. He is thinking of finding the applicable precept where because of a gap in the body of authoritative precepts one has to be made for cases like the one in hand. I was thinking of the steps in the judicial process as a whole, and put it thus: "Supposing the facts to have been ascertained, decision of a controversy according to law involves (1) selection of the legal material on which to ground the decision, or as we commonly say, finding the law; (2) development of the grounds of decision from the material selected, or interpretation in the stricter sense of that term; (3) application of the abstract grounds of decision to the facts of the case. The first may consist merely in laying hold of a prescribed text of code or statute, or of a definite prescribed traditional rule; in which case it remains only to determine the meaning of the legal precept, with reference to the facts in hand, and to apply it to those facts. It is the strength of the administration of justice today that in the general run of causes that have to do with our economic life this is all that is called for, or so nearly all, that the main course of judicial action may be predicted with substantial accuracy. But it happens frequently that the first process involves choice among competing texts or choice from among competing analogies so that the texts or rules must be interpreted — that is, must be developed tentatively with reference to the facts before the court — in order that intelligent selection may be made. Often such interpretation shows that no existing rule is adequate to a

43. *Ibid.*, 114.
44. Cairns, *op. cit.* 238.

just decision and it becomes necessary to formulate the ground of decision for the given facts for the first time."[45] Cardozo was speaking of the
proposition in the last sentence. Cairns thinks that I err at one extreme
and Cardozo at the other. He is too elusive while I am too analytical. He
prefers Dewey's analysis.[46] As Cairns applies Dewey's analysis, "The vital point is that the judge does not first find the facts, then ascertain and
develop the law, and then apply the result to the facts. He does even not
know what the operative facts are until the apparently relevant facts have
been tested in conjunction with the ideas that forecast the solution. He
does not know what the law is until he has settled upon the solution
which he believes he will accept. At that point the judge then 'finds the
law,' and it may well be that the provisional solution will have to be
abandoned if the 'law' as the judge 'finds it' will not permit the proposed
solution. The judge will then seek a different solution and again 'find
the law.' This process will continue until a solution is found which will
withstand the test of the law, the facts, and any other materials the judge
deems relevant."[47]

But is this a statement of the judicial process or is it rather one of
the administrative process? The administrative official has a policy to
enforce. He looks upon his problem in the light of that policy and endeavors to effectuate the policy so far as the law will let him. No doubt
he will form an idea of the appropriate determination, shape the facts to
it, and seek to find how to work his predetermined solution into the legal limits of his authority. But cases do not come to a court in that way.
In an appellate court the case comes before the judges on a record in
which the facts have been found in the verdict of a jury or by the findings of a trial judge in a decree or upon trial without a jury. Where the
case is in a court of first instance, if there is trial to a jury, the issues of
fact are settled in advance by the pleadings and the trial judge must in-
struct the jury as to the legal result of finding each issue one way or the

45. Pound, *The Theory of Judicial Decision* (1923) 36 HARVARD LAW REVIEW 940, 945,
946.
46. Dewey, *Logic* (1938) 101 ff. 120–22.
47. Cairns, *op. cit.* 239.

other. He may put special questions to the jury as to details of fact. If the case is in equity very likely the facts will be found by a master in chancery and his findings confirmed upon exceptions before the judge comes to consider and apply the law. But where the case is tried to the court without a jury in any event the issues of fact will be defined by the pleadings, or in the most recent American practice in pretrial proceedings, and the court will be required to make findings of fact and separate findings of the law applicable thereto. Thus even the judge at first instance either has the facts found for him by jury or master or referee, or finds them specially himself, and then proceeds to apply the law to them as he finds it. There was a time in some American states when inadequately staffed courts of review with crowded dockets badly in arrear left many cases to be decided by single judges in a hurry and the administrative method was too often employed. But it was reprobated and has never been the received method in the common-law world.

We must not ignore the power of ideas. The economic interpretation and psychological realism themselves are ideas. In jurisprudence we are dealing ultimately with what ought to be. We are seeking to attain and maintain the ideal relation among men. Ideas of what is affect ideas of what ought to be and *vice versa*. Ideas of what ought to be are apt to be idealizings of what we take it is. We should be careful not to take the ills we encounter for the significant thing and make our picture of what is from them rather than from what we succeed in doing to overcome them. We should make our picture of what ought to be from our achievements rather than from our failures. It is a strange kind of liberalism that would return to absolute rule because of an assumed futility of attempts at elimination of the features of arbitrary exercise of the powers of politically organized society which it had been the job of liberalism to oppose from the beginning.

Political absolutism assumes that the superman leader will be all-wise and hence will always know what the general good demands and how to use his unlimited powers to that end. It assumes that he will not only know how to use them toward the general good but will habitually and steadfastly so use them. In the same way administrative absolutism assumes that any given administrative agency will be made up of and directed by experts of infallible judgment. They, too, will always know in what the general good consists and may be relied upon to reach the results which it demands by intuitions or hunches, unhampered by precepts or technique discovered by experience and developed by reason in advance of determination. The juristic absolutism, so widespread today as a reinforcement of administrative absolutism assumes that in the nature of things it is psychologically impossible for the judicial process to operate objectively and impartially. Hence the apparatus of rules and principles and conceptions by which men have sought to constrain the process to operate uniformly and predictably and objectively is futile. Its supposed achievement of that purpose is a delusion. Our faith in it is superstition. Behind the supposed principles and rules and conceptions the true moving forces of decision are operating independently. It is not scientific to take account of more than the individual decision itself. What is done in the course of judicial decision is law because it is done not done because it is law. Attempt to hold down the individual judge to legally prescribed paths of action is futile. Legislator, administrative official and judge may as well be left free in theory to pursue their own paths to the general good each in his own way since in practice they will do so in any event. If we think in this fashion one way out does seem to be a postulated all-wise leader with no limit to his power. At any rate he can make some one conception of the general good the common objective of the many agencies of adjudication and administration.

More than one people in the present century came to this conclusion. Others have been drifting to it in the movement away from the nineteenth-century idea without any definitely worked-out idea to take its place. It is felt that the nineteenth-century idea left out something that cannot be dispensed with and that the law rigidly compels excluding it. But there is nothing intrinsic in law in any of its senses to tie it irrevocably to the nineteenth-century ideal. Much of the antagonism to law on the part of a group of political scientists comes from not distinguishing between law and laws and from assuming, as the analytical jurists of the last century gave them good reason to assume, that law is an aggregate of laws and that a law is a rule attaching definite detailed consequences to definite detailed states or situations of fact. Adjustment of relations and regulation of conduct in an orderly systematic fashion, in accordance with principles and authoritative guiding conceptions is rejected because it is not distinguished from a rigidly constrained process of adjustment and regulation governed in every detail by a definite prescribed rule. No difference is perceived between a standard of reasonableness and a rule of property. Hence to one of the leading political thinkers of today, who is also one of the leading analytical jurists of today, there is a self contradiction in the nineteenth-century American theory of a democracy which has voluntarily limited itself by a constitution as self-imposed law; which, to use the language of the seventeenth century, when the idea took form, has covenanted not to do certain things and to do certain other things only in certain ways. As the last century looked on liberty as something contradicted by adjustment and direction and regulation, so he looks on the power of a politically organized society as something contradicted by the common-law conception of the law of the land. To give those who exercise the force of the political organization power and yet limit their exercise of the power is a contradiction in terms. In a democracy a majority must speak for the whole. In a democracy the majority must necessarily be an absolute ruler. The absolute majority takes the place of the absolute personal ruler which political theory in Continental Europe postulated from the sixteenth century at least to the French Revolution.[48]

There is a good side to the work of the American skeptical realists. Although they had been anticipated by Jhering and Kantorowicz,[49] they brought home vigorously to bench and bar in the United States the need of thinking about the judicial process and seeking to improve its exercise. Moreover, when it is recognized that there is an alogical, unrational, subjective element in judicial action, and the function of law

48. As to Kelsen and Laun and the Neo-Kantian left *see* Pound, *Fifty Years of Jurisprudence* (1938) 51 HARVARD LAW REVIEW 444, 452.

49. Jhering, *Scherz und Ernst in der Jurisprudenz* (1884) pt. 3; Gnaeus Flavius (Kantorowicz) *Die Kampf um die Rechtswissenschaft* (1906). *See also* Pound, *Mechanical Jurisprudence* (1908) 8 COLUMBIA LAW REVIEW 605.

in the second sense with respect to that element is recognized attempt by study of concrete instances of its operation to reach valid general conclusions as to the kind of cases in which it operates most frequently and where it operates most effectively or otherwise for the ends of the legal order, becomes indicated as an important item in the juristic program. When this subject is studied adequately and the role of the ideal element in law is well brought out, and that element is better organized and is subjected to an adequate critique, jurisprudence will have done much for law in the sense of the judicial process.

Much needs to be done also upon the program indicated by Llewellyn.[50] The judicial and administrative processes are a legitimate and an important part of the field of jurisprudence if we unify the three meanings of "law" by the idea of social control, of which, taken together, they are today the paramount agency. Out of the work of the skeptical realists there may come a better basis for this side of the task of the science of law, even if we cannot admit that the judicial process is all that we mean by law or that a science of law may be built wholly on theories of that process as purely or even primarily independent of guidance by authoritative legal precepts developed and applied by an authoritative technique.[51]

III. Logical Positive Realism

This is a much more sober type.[52] It investigates, from the standpoint of the logical theory of today, the modes of thought, and particularly the

50. Llewellyn, *Some Realism About Realism* (1931) 44 HARVARD LAW REVIEW 1222, 1247, 1250.

51. In this connection note especially Llewellyn's penetrating discussion of certainty in his book on American case law: *Präjudizienrecht und Rechtsprechung in Amerika* (1933) §§ 55–61.

52. Cook, *Scientific Method and the Law* (1927) 13 AMERICAN BAR ASSN. JOURNAL 303; id. *The Possibilities of Social Studies as a Science*, in Swann and others, *Essays in Research in the Social Sciences* (1931) 27; id. *A Scientific Approach to the Study of Law*, in *Essays in Honor of W. W. Willoughby* (1937) 201; id. *The Logical and Legal Bases of the Conflict of Laws* (1942); Dimock, *Le Professeur W. W. Cook et le relativisme juridique* (1932) ARCHIVES DE PHILOSOPHIE DU DROIT ET DE SOCIOLOGIE JURIDIQUE 575, with bib-

solving words and phrases used by lawyers and judges, and has urged a quest of a method of solving problems through a science of law with the same objectivity as physics or mathematical astronomy. Objective value judgments are to be reached, not by rigorous deduction from arbitrarily chosen postulates, but by scientific research in the sense and in the manner of the physical sciences, disclosing a basis for judgments in the facts of the legal order and of the judicial and administrative processes.

In the social sciences we must consider how men do act in their relations and contacts with others, how they ought to act in those relations and contacts in order to maintain, further, and transmit civilization, and how to insure so far as may be by social, economic, political, and legal institutions, or by ethical precepts, a correspondence of what takes place with what ought to be. Undoubtedly the gathering of statistics can show as much as to how justice is administered and how and how far legal precepts are observed and enforced. But some expect them also to show how justice must (*e.g.*, through a psychological necessity) be administered and so expect to dispense with the question how it ought to be administered. This question of ought, turning ultimately on a theory of values, is the hardest one in jurisprudence. Those who seek an exact science, analogous to mathematics or physics or astronomy, have been inclined to essay exactness by excluding this hard problem from jurisprudence altogether. But such a jurisprudence has only an illusion of reality. The significant question is the one excluded.

Two points may be made as to conceiving of jurisprudence in terms of a physical science. For one thing, judging the conception by its results with respect to the end or purpose of law, it seems to lead back to the juristic pessimism of the historical school and the nineteenth-century positivists. Some at least of its advocates seem to regard the harnessing of internal nature, which along with the harnessing of external nature has been taken to be the basis of civilization, as an illusion so far as it is sought to be brought about or maintained deliberately and of set

liography of Professor Cook's writings. *Cf.* Rueff, *From the Physical to the Social Sciences* (transl. by Green, 1929); Oliphant, *Facts, Opinions, and Value Judgments* (1932) 10 TEXAS LAW REVIEW 697, 701–5.

purpose. They are prone to hold that it must come about through economic or psychological laws, operating behind the scene and beyond the reach of conscious effort.

What is more important, however, there is a significant difference between the formulas of the engineer and the formulas of social control of which legal formulas are a specialized type. Legal formulas, or at least those found in the law reports and the commentaries on legislative texts, are formulations of experience no less than those of the engineer. The materials of legal experience are as objective and as valid for scientific treatment as those of engineering experience. The difference is that legal formulas are put to a test to which the engineer's formulas are not subjected. Legal formulas seem to have hazy and indefinite limits and engineering formulas sharp definite limits because the former operate to restrain behavior while the latter are used to make action possible.[53] It is true a type of new juristic realist would treat legal formulas as devices to permit of action.[54] But this is a way of saying that in the endeavor toward a maximum of free individual self-assertion a competition of legal formulas and choice from among them might enable certain items of behavior to escape application of an inconvenient formula. The net result of legal formulas is restraint of behavior, while that of engineering formulas is to make action possible. Hence men are forever pushing to the extreme limits of legal formulas, while engineers steer a conservative middle course between the limits of their formulas. In each case the formula on its face is definite enough. In the legal formula this definiteness is put to a severe test by a steady current of behavior seeking to stretch the formula to the utmost. But no engineer, architect, or builder would think of building up to the theoretical limits of the strength of materials. If he did he would risk prosecution for manslaughter. As a mat-

---

53. Shewhart, *Statistical Method from the Viewpoint of Quality Control* (1939); id. Contribution of Statistics to the Science of Engineering, University of Pennsylvania Bicentennial Conference: *Fluid Mechanics and Statistical Methods* (1941) 97; Pound, *The Relation of Statistical Quality Standards to Law and Legislation*, ibid. 137.

54. I have considered this in *The Call for a Realist Jurisprudence* (1931) 44 HARVARD LAW REVIEW 667, 708–9. *See* Bohlen, *Old Phrases and New Facts* (1934) 83 UNIV. OF PA. LAW REVIEW 305, 307, 311.

ter of course he builds well within them, and so we are able to contrast the certainty of his results with the relative uncertainty of legal results in action. This is not due to a more exact science or more scientific method in the one case than in the other. In both cases experience has been formulated in rules which are valid enough at the core and indefinite or contingent enough in application at the limits. The difference lies in the nature of the tasks imposed upon the respective formulations of experience, whereby the contingent features in the application of the one are tried continually while those of the other are rarely developed.

One feature of the approach from the standpoint of the physical sciences is insistence on exact terminology. The analytical jurists and the Pandectists laid stress on this also. But the utility of precise terminology and exact meanings is more in connection with differentiating problems from pseudo-problems and with formulation of results than in providing solutions. None of the fundamental problems of jurisprudence is solved by terminology. There have been signs that rigid terminology has been used to create an appearance of solution of problems which have been left untouched at the core. It should be added however that the logical attack on the jurisprudence of conceptions carried on for a generation by Professor W. W. Cook, his relentless exposure of *Scheinbegriffe*, and his critique of specious universals and generalities have done a service to the law (in the sense of the body of authoritative precepts and technique of developing and applying them) and make for a more intelligent juristic thought and effective judicial process. Unhappily his program of investigation of the work of the state courts from a positivist economic standpoint had to be given up while its technique was still developing. But a notable beginning was made from which those who come to the study of research method in the future may learn much.[55]

---

55. Publications of the Institute of Law of Johns Hopkins University: *Monographs in the Study of Judicial Administration in Ohio* (1932); *Bulletins of the Study of Judicial Administration in Ohio* (1932); *Monographs in the Study of the Judicial System in Maryland* (1931–32); *Bulletins of the Study of the Judicial System of Maryland* (1931–32); *Monographs of Survey of Litigation in New York* (1931–32); *Bulletins of Survey of Litigation in New York* (1931–32); Yntema, *Analysis of Ohio Municipal Court Acts* (1933). Marshall, *Unlocking the Treasuries of the Trial Courts* (1933); id. *Comparative Judicial Criminal*

IV. Phenomenology

Phenomenology[56] derives the significance and connection of phenomena from the phenomena themselves. It holds that knowing is not a valuing or a critical act but is a mode of existence of actuality. Hence juristic phenomenology styles itself a theory of actuality as its American analogue calls itself realism. Goodness is held to be an ultimate and objective subsisting entity which is intuitively perceived. A right action is one which has on the whole the best actual consequences, the best consequences being those which contain the greatest quantity of ultimate goods which we intuitively perceive to be valuable. Experience recognizes values embodied in social facts in which the values are realized. Justice is the totality of jural values intuitively recognized through collective experience. But these values are extremely variable. Hence in their mode of thought justice has no meaning apart from the facts in which values are realized.

As Sauer has remarked, German juristic phenomenology has not thus far been able to achieve any notable results.[57] It finds significance in the continually changing single phenomena of the judicial and administrative processes. Ends are reached, values are perceived, and so just results are reached intuitively.[58] Some American realists seem to combine this with economic determinism and psychological realism.[59]

Statistics: Six States (1932); id. Comparative Judicial Criminal Statistics: Ohio and Maryland (1932).

56. Reinach, Die apriorischen Grundlagen des bürgerlichen Rechts (1922); Schapp, Die neue Wissenschaft vom Recht (1931–32); Kaufmann, Logik und Rechtswissenschaft (1922); id. Die Kriterien des Rechts (1924); id. Die philosophischen Grundprobleme der Lehre von der Strafrechtsschuld (1929); Schreier, Grundbegriffe und Grundformen des Rechts (1927); translated as Concepto y formas fundamentales del derecho by Garcia Maynes (1942); G. Husserl, Recht und Welt (1930); Treves, Sociologia y filosofia social (1941) chap. 3; Spiegelberg, Gesetz und Sittengesetz (1934). For applications see G. Husserl, Der Rechtsgegenstand (1933); id. Rechtskraft und Rechtsgeltung (1925); Engisch, Zur phänomenologischen Methode im Strafrecht (1937) 30 ARCHIV FUR RECHTS UND SOZIALPHILOSOPHIE, 130.

57. Sauer, Rechts und Staatsphilosophie (1936) 25.

58. Cf. Hutcheson, The Judgment Intuitive — The Function of the "Hunch" in Judicial Decisions (1929) 14 CORNELL LAW QUARTERLY 274.

59. Yntema, Jurisprudence on Parade (1941) 39 MICHIGAN LAW REVIEW 1134.

V. The Swedish Realists

A notable group headed by Axel Hägerström calls for special notice.[60] He proceeds upon an ultra-realist analysis of the lawmaking, judicial, and administrative processes. From this standpoint, law (in the second sense) is an aggregate of independent imperatives establishing behavior patterns for those whom the lawmaking authority wishes to influence. The rules are imperative in form. But they are not commands. No one commands them. They are explained psychologically. They are taken to be binding and are habitually obeyed. Accordingly certain persons are delegated to wield supreme political power. Thus they are in position to put pressure upon men generally and thereby to direct their actions in certain respects.[61] Legal rights and duties are imaginary. Obedience is assured by the belief of people that they have a duty to obey.[62] There is an imaginary bond originally derived from primitive magic.[63] The reality is force applied by officials and the psychological habit of obedience which makes actual application of force largely unnecessary.[64] This is in line with the recent tendency toward a threat theory of the nature of law.

VI. Constructive Juristic Realism

Thus far the achievement of juristic realism in all its forms has been to rouse American jurists and lawyers from what Kant called dogmatic slumber. In this it has carried on the work begun by Jhering. But it

60. Hägerström, *Inquiries into the Nature of Law and Morals*, transl. by C. D. Broad, ed. by Karl Olivecrona (1953). *See also* Olivecrona, *Law as Fact* (1939). There is an excellent short statement in Yntema, *Jurisprudence on Parade* (1941) 39 MICHIGAN LAW REVIEW 1134, 1171–74.

61. Olivecrona, *Law as Fact* (1939) 53.

62. Hägerström, *Inquiries as to the Nature of Law and Morals*, transl. by Broad (1953) iii, 5, pp. 127 ff.

63. Hägerström, *Der römische Obligationsbegriff im Lichte der allgemeinen römischen Rechtsanschauung* (1927) 35 ff.

64. Olivecrona, *Law as Fact* (1939) 142.

should be possible to formulate a constructive program of relativist realist jurisprudence.[65]

American juristic realists with the Anglo-American professional tradition behind them, think in terms of the judicial process. But in contrast to the analytical jurists who thought of that process in terms of development and application of authoritative precepts by an authoritative technique, they think of the administrative element in the judicial process as the type. Continental realists, with the modern Roman academic tradition behind them, think of a codified law, of the legislative process, of administrative enforcement, and of a judiciary with no or very little power of creative finding of law. What is common to both is insistence on the official, wielding the power of politically organized society, as of primary importance.

If their starting point is accepted it would still be quite possible to set up a constructive program. Five points may be suggested: —

(1) By study of the alogical, unrational, subjective element in the administrative and judicial processes useful general conclusions might be reached as to the kinds of cases in which it operates most frequently and when it operates most effectively or most unhappily for the end of the legal order. Sociological jurists have proposed this but it remains undone.

(2) By study of the administrative process in action in comparison with the judicial process it might be possible to reach useful conclusions as to the effectiveness or ineffectiveness of checks upon each process, as to how far checks upon the administrative process and the administrative element in the judicial process are practicable or advisable, and even to indicate the line of development which should be urged for canons of administrative determination.

(3) There might be recognition of the significance of the individual case, as contrasted with the unqualified universalism of the last century, without losing sight of the significance of generalizations and conceptions as instruments toward the ends of the legal order. At this point the

---

65. *See* Pound, *The Call for a Realist Jurisprudence* (1931) 44 HARVARD LAW REVIEW 697, 710–11.

realists have been anticipated by Stammler. But they will approach the subject in a different way through psychology.

(4) There might be a giving up of the idea of a necessary sequence from a single cause in a straight line to a single effect, and hence of the one sovereign legal remedy for every difficulty and one necessary solution of every problem, without giving up principles, conceptions and technique. There will be recognition of a plurality of elements in all situations and of the possibility of dealing with human relations in more than one way. There will be recognition that the test of a legal precept or doctrine or institution is how and how far it helps achieve the ends of the legal order. Here constructive juristic realism would build on Jhering. Hence in the long run I am confident there will be no abandonment of belief that the administration of justice may be improved by intelligent effort. I suspect also that study of single instances, wisely directed and in sufficient number, will show what study of the legal materials of all systems seems to reveal, namely, that the old straight-line thinking is a useful instrument in parts of the field of administration of justice where the economic order demands the maximum of attainable certainty.

(5) There might be recognition that there are many approaches to juristic truth and that each is significant with respect to particular problems of the legal order. Hence there might be an appraising of these approaches, not absolutely or with reference to some one assumed necessary psychological or philosophical basis of jurisprudence, but with reference to how far they aid lawmaker, or judge, or jurist toward the maintaining, furthering, and transmitting of civilization, and how they may aid the jurist toward organizing the materials and laying out the course of the legal order.

Some recent studies of juristic thinking, directed, one might say, to the juristic rather than to the judicial process, and economic-functional study of law and social change, promise a more real realism and augur well for the progress of the science of law.[66]

___

66. Friedmann, *Legal Theory* (1944); id. *Law and Social Change in Contemporary Britain* (1951); Levi, *An Introduction to Legal Reasoning* (1949).

ELEVEN

The Humanitarian Idea

Legal history shows a continually widening circle of recognized interests and continually more effective means of securing the interests recognized. Two conspicuous examples of recognition and securing of interests theretofore unknown to the law, in the two generations since I was admitted to the bar in 1890, will suffice for illustration. The "right of privacy," the demand made by the individual that his private, personal affairs shall not be laid bare to the world and be discussed by strangers, a modern demand growing out of the conditions of life and extended means of communication and organized news-gathering agencies in the cities of today, was first urged in 1890.[1] It was denied by the highest court of New York in 1902.[2] For a time it was recognized indirectly by a theory of infringement of a property interest of breach of the terms of a contract. Sixty years later it could be said: "Modern decisions allow recovery in situations in which it is not possible rationally to use the older cases of recovery, and the interest is now recognized as having an independent existence."[3] Again the claim of the employee in industry to a vested right in his job, as a right to continue in the relation of employer and employee as a relation protected by law not simply a contractual claim during the term of a contract of employment, was not admitted by a majority of the Supreme Court of the United States as late as the second decade of the

---

1. Warren and Brande, *The Right to Privacy* (1890) 4 HARVARD LAW REVIEW 193.
2. *Roberson v. New York Folding Box Co.*, 171 N.Y. 538 (1902).
3. 4 American Law Institute, *Restatement of the Law of Torts* (1949) § 867.

present century.[4] Twenty years later by the National Labor Relations Act[5] the interest was recognized and effectively secured and the statute was upheld by a majority of that court.[6] The courts now talk about "the fundamental right to work for a living," not a liberty of, if and as one likes, for whom one likes, if the employer agrees, but a right secured against the employer.[7] These examples likewise illustrate how wide extensions in the area of recognized interests may be achieved without impairment of the stability of the legal order and without essential impairment of the system of authoritative body of precepts and technique of applying them (law in the second sense). But new wants and expectations pressing for and getting recognition may affect ideas of the end of the legal order.

As I pointed out in a former lecture, a newer and broader idea of security is indicated for a time when the world has ceased to afford boundless conspicuous opportunities which men only need to be free to seize in order to be assured of satisfaction of their reasonable expectations. Where there are on every side opportunities for freely exerting one's will in pursuit of what he takes to be the goods of existence, security means an ordered competition of free wills in which acquisitive competitive self-assertion is made to operate with a minimum of friction and waste. Where this ordered struggle for existence does not leave opportunities at hand for every one, where the conquest of physical nature has enormously increased the area of human wants and expectations without corresponding increase in the means of satisfying them, equality ceases to mean equality of opportunity. Security ceases to mean security of freely taking advantage of opportunity. Men assert claims to an equality of satisfaction of wants which liberty of itself cannot afford them. They begin to assert claims to living a full life in the society of the time and according to the standards which liberty of itself cannot give them. When a generation which had been brought up in the nineteenth-century idea of complete liberty as the ideal relation among men began

4. *Coppage v. Kansas*, 236 U.S. 1 (1915).
5. Act of July 5, 1935, 49 Stat. L. 449, 29 U.S.C.A. §§ 151 ff.
6. *National Labor Relations Board v. Jones & Laughlin Steel Corp.*, 301 U.S. 1 (1937).
7. *James v. Marinship Corp.*, 25 Cal. 2d, 721, 731 (1944).

to speak of four fundamental freedoms of which the last two were freedom from want and freedom from fear a new idea was coming in, if not to replace, at least to include liberty as only an item in a larger idea. Instead of picturing men as ideally free to achieve justice we have been coming to think of them as ideally in that relation. Security, then, is security from all that keeps them from an ideal relation and keeps many of them far from finding themselves in it. The ideal of a world in which all can find themselves in that relation I have been calling the humanitarian ideal. The emphasis has gradually been shifting from liberty to humanity; from leaving men free to help themselves as they can, to aiding them by the institutions of civilized society to obtain a maximum satisfaction of their claims or desires or reasonable expectations in civilized society compatible with satisfaction of the whole scheme of such expectations with the minimum of friction and waste.

What this means for law in the second sense is brought out by changes in such fundamental subjects as torts, contracts, and liability which have gone on steadily in the present century and are still going on.

Let us turn first to the law of torts. When it was taken that the end of law was promoting and maintaining liberty, it was held that individual liberty ought not to be retained except to allow like activity of others. The line of adjustment of the free activities of each to the like free activities of all others was taken to be prevention of and reparation for culpable interference with person or property. In this way equality and security could be assured. We may call this the fault theory of liability. But the security thought of was security against menace to safety, health, peace and order, to acquisitions under the prevailing social and economic order, and to the stability of the legal transactions on which the economic order depends. With the coming of a new conception of security new theories of liability began to be urged. The two which seem to be devised for law proceeding along a new humanitarian path[8] I am calling the insurance theory and the involuntary Good Samaritan the-

8. I take this term from Mr. Justice Holmes, *The Path of the Law*, 10 HARVARD LAW REVIEW 467 (1897).

ory. In practice, however, the former is used to justify what is in reality the latter.

Development of the law as to liability to answer for losses or injuries suffered by others has followed the lines indicated in the preceding lectures by the development of ideas as to the end or purpose of law.

When justice was thought of simply in terms of keeping the peace one who had caused injury to another was thought of as having threatened the peace in that he had awakened a desire of the injured person for vengeance which would lead him and his kindred to seek redress by force from the one who had caused injury and his kindred. Thus causing injury to another was a potential source of private war. Hence the beginnings of law endeavored to satisfy the desire of an injured person for vengeance. The injured person is required to accept a composition for his vengeance and is restrained from helping himself. The next step is to enable him to compel payment of the composition; to compel the wrongdoer to buy off his vengeance. The measure of what the injured party might recover was not the extent of the injury done him but the extent of the desire for vengeance awakened by the injury. The idea is not to restore to the injured person what he has lost by the injury but to give him enough to satisfy his feelings of indignation and induce him to desist from private war; and the tariff of compositions is graded on that principle.[9] Hence in Anglo-Saxon law the established tariff of compositions provided for fifty percent more recovery where a bruise, even if much less severe, is not covered by the clothes than where one, even if much more severe, is covered by the clothes and so not visible to give rise to embarrassing questions derogatory to the victim's dignity.[10] In the same way the Welsh law distinguished between injuries leaving a conspicuous scar and those where the scar was not conspicuous.[11]

Gradually the idea of composition gave way to one of reparation. The idea of keeping the peace, as we have seen, was replaced by one of main-

9. *See* examples in the oldest Roman law: Gaius, iii, §§ 183–92, iv, §§ 75–78; Twelve Tables, viii, 6, 1, 1 Bruns, *Fontes Iuris Romani Antiqui* (7 ed. 1909) 30, and in the Salic Law, xiv, 1–3.

10. Laws of Ethelbert, 59–60.

11. Wade-Evans, *Welsh Medieval Law* (1909) 190–91.

taining the social *status quo* and that required maintenance of individual expectations of ability to assume that others will commit no intentional aggressions upon them. Intentional aggressions are no longer simply threats to the peace. They are breaches of a social order in which men reasonably expect not to be subjected to them. Accordingly, both in Roman law and in Anglo-American common law the law begins with a series of carefully defined named torts by way of aggression upon the person or corporeal property: In Roman law, *furtum, rapina, damnum iniuria datum, iniuria;*[12] in the common law: Assault and battery, false imprisonment, trespass on land, trespass as to chattels, conversion of chattels, malicious prosecution, slander, libel.[13] A general principle as a starting point for dealing with new types of intentional aggression was not formulated till the last quarter of the nineteenth century. The now generally admitted proposition that one who intentionally does something on its face injurious to another is liable to repair the resulting damage unless he can establish a liberty or privilege under some public or social interest, was unheard-of when I studied torts in 1889 and was still debated as late as 1916.[14]

But in a developed civilized society intentional aggression was not the only threat to the general security. With increasingly minute division of labor those whose tasks were but cogs in the machinery of the economic order could not perform them effectively if continually subjected to unreasonable casting upon them of risk of injury by the want of care on the part of others. Roman law provided for culpably caused injuries to person or property. In the common law we came to provide for it by an action for injuries through negligence.

12. Wrongful appropriations of property: theft (as a tort, conversion); robbery (forcible taking from the person), wrongful injury to corporeal property. Injuries to personality: *iniuria* (injury to the physical person or to honor). Inst. iv, 1, pr. and §§ 1–5; Inst. iv. 2; Inst. iv, 3; Inst. iv, 4.

13. *E.g.*, notice the subjects and order of treatment in Ames, *Cases on Torts* (1 ed. 1874). Blackstone treats named torts under the actions of trespass and trespass on the case. *Commentaries on the Laws of England*, vol. 3, Private Wrongs (1768).

14. "That the intentional infliction of injury without justification invariably constitutes a tort may or may not be settled law." Note, *Equitable Relief Against Injurious Falsehoods*, 30 HARVARD LAW REVIEW 172, 174 (1916).

By this time the law as to liability to repair injuries took on a moral aspect. As set forth in a previous lecture, a theory of a universal law of nature which sought to identify law with morals obtained in the classical era of Roman law and in a like era in the law of Continental Europe and in English law in the seventeenth and eighteenth centuries. As men thought then, the basis of liability to repair an injury must be a moral wrong. Liability must follow from culpability. As Ames put it in 1908, contrasting the nineteenth-century law of torts with the older law which had not looked beyond causation of damage, "the ethical standard of reasonable conduct has replaced the unmoral standard of acting at one's peril."[15] The French Civil Code in 1804 made the idea of fault a general theory of delictal liability, saying: "Every act of man which causes damage to another obliges him through whose fault it happened to make reparation."[16] In other words, liability must be based on an act and it must be a culpable act—culpability, causation and damage were the elements. French law came very near to a logically consistent system of liability for fault and civil liability for fault only throughout the whole of what we should call the law of torts. Except for employer's liability and an all but absolute liability for damage by animals,[17] and in certain cases an imposition of the burden of proof that there had been no fault, there was a thoroughgoing attempt to make delictal liability flow exclusively from culpability. But a generation ago French text writers did not hesitate to say that the attempt had failed and that a new theory must be worked out,[18] and the same movement away from the simple theory of liability only for culpable causation of damage went on elsewhere on the Continent. It came to be rejected generally by German and Swiss jurists.[19]

In Anglo-American law in the last century the doctrine of liability for and only for culpable causation of damage seemed to stand upon the re-

---

15. Ames, *Law and Morals* (1908) 22 HARVARD LAW REVIEW 97, 99.

16. Art. 1382.

17. Arts. 1384–85.

18. 2 Baudry-Lacantinerie, *Précis de droit civil* (1922) §§ 815–47; Demogue, *Fault, Risk and Apportionment of Risk in Responsibility* (1921) 15 ILLINOIS LAW REVIEW 369.

19. 1 Cosack, *Lehrbuch des bürgerlichen Rechts* (8 ed. 1927) §§ 147–48; 5 Egger, *Kommentar zum schweizerischen Zivilgesetzbuch* (1916) 4–5.

ceived theory of justice as a maximum of freedom of action consistent with like freedom of action of all others. Free exertion of the will by every one was to be the rule unless the will was exerted culpably. Such was the orthodox doctrine as it was taught me in 1889. But at that time the teacher of the law of torts had much trouble with a number of rules surviving from the medieval liability for mere causation. For example, there was absolute liability for damage done by trespassing cattle.[20] There was absolute liability where one maintained wild animals which did damage.[21] Also there were old cases where it had been held that one must at his peril restrain things he maintained though there was no nuisance and he was not negligent.[22] In England in 1868 this type of liability was extended to a case where one maintained a reservoir on his land and without negligence the water escaped and did damage to a neighbor.[23] Also there was the established doctrine of *respondeat superior* by virtue of which a master or employer was liable without regard to fault for the acts of servants or employees in the scope of their employment. It is true this last doctrine was reconciled with the doctrine of liability only for fault by the fiction of representation, long ago exposed by Mr. Justice Holmes,[24] and now given up by the teachers of the law of agency.[25] Moreover, teachers of the law of torts and writers on the subject in the later years of the last century regarded the old cases as to animals as historical survivals destined to be given up.[26] Strong American courts refused to follow *Rylands* v. *Fletcher*,[27] text writers agreed in doubting or rejecting its doctrine,[28] and in 1894 Sir Frederick Pollock thought he saw a tendency in the English

20. *Tonawanda R. Co.* v. *Munger*, 5 Denio (N.Y.) 255, 267–68 (1848).

21. *Filburn* v. *Peoples Palace Co.*, 25 Q.B.D. 258 (1890).

22. *See* the older cases discussed by Blackburn, J., in *Fletcher* v. *Rylands*, L.R. 1 Ex. 265, 280–87 (1866).

23. *Rylands* v. *Fletcher*, L.R. 3 H.L. 330 (1868).

24. Holmes, *Agency* (1891) 4 HARVARD LAW REVIEW 345, 353–64.

25. Seavey, *Studies in Agency* (1949) 147 ff.

26. "The doctrine is a stubborn archaism." Pollock, *Torts* (8 ed. 1908) 497 note n.

27. *Brown* v. *Collins*, 53 N.H. 442 (1873); *Losee* v. *Buchanan*, 51 N.Y. 476 (1873); *Marshall* v. *Welwood*, 38 N.J. Law, 339 (1876); *Pennsylvania Coal Co.* v. *Sanderson*, 113 Pa. St. 126 (1886); *Judson* v. *Giant Powder Co.*, 107 Cal. 549 (1895).

28. Salmond, *Torts* (4 ed. 1916) 233, arguing that the doctrine has no application if no one has been negligent; Bigelow, *Torts* (1889) 271–72, asserting a tendency in England

decisions to find subtle distinctions in the facts to take cases out of the rule of that case and prophesied that it would become slowly but surely choked and crippled by exceptions.[29] On the contrary, the historical absolute liability of those who maintain dangerous animals and for trespassing animals, supposed to be a disappearing anomaly, has shown unsuspected vitality. The one has been applied to the very verge in England,[30] while the other has been applied to collateral consequences of the trespass.[31] Moreover, the English courts in the present century have consistently followed *Rylands* v. *Fletcher*, applied it to new situations of fact,[32] and even in one case went so far as to apply it by analogy to what in America we should call an automobile tourists' camp where those who came to the camp habitually committed trespasses in the neighborhood amounting to nuisance.[33] American courts have more and more adopted and applied the doctrine, and liability without fault is well established on both sides of the water.[34]

As was pointed out in a prior lecture, the doctrine that liability must flow from fault was so connected with the will theory and the idea of maintaining individual free self-assertion that it came to be regarded as a proposition of natural law. But if instead of beginning with the individual free will we begin with the wants or expectations involved in life in civilized society we come to a very different result. Just as men cannot effectively go about their several businesses in a society dependent

to modify the doctrine; Cooley, *Torts* (1 ed. 1879) 573, arguing that if construction of a reservoir was done with due care escape of water becomes a question of negligence; Burdick, *Torts* (2 ed. 1908) 447, that the doctrine is emphatically rejected by most American courts; Bishop, *Non-Contract Law* (1889) § 839, note 3, "the reasoning so far as it proceeds on grounds other than negligence is . . . not the reasoning of the law."

29. Pollock, *Law of Fraud in British India* (1894) 53–54.

30. *Baker v. Snell* [1908] 2 K.B. 352, 355.

31. *Thayer v. Purnell* [1918] 2 K.B. 333.

32. *Charing Cross Electricity Supply Co.* v. *Hydraulic Power Co.* [1914] 3 K.B. 772, 779, 795; *Musgrove v. Pandolis* [1919] 2 K.B. 43; 32 Halsbury, *Laws of England*, Hailsham's ed. 199, 200, notes *m* and *n*.

33. *Attorney General v. Corke* [1933] Ch. 89.

34 . Winfield, *Text-Book of the Law of Tort* (5 ed. 1950) chap. 19; Prosser, *Handbook of the Law of Torts* (1941) §§ 59–61.

upon a minute division of labor if they must constantly be on guard against the aggressions or want of foresight of their neighbors, so our complex social order based on division of labor may not function effectively if each of us must stay his activities through fear of the breaking loose or getting out of hand of something which his neighbor harbors or maintains. There is danger to the general security in what men fail to do, in not restraining things they maintain or agencies they employ which may get out of hand and do damage, quite as much as in what they do and the way in which they do it.

Thus far, the social interest in the general security is behind every step in the development of liability to repair injury. But some recent developments must give the systematic jurist pause. One is a movement to do away with the doctrine of non-liability for the torts of an independent contractor and impose a liability on the owner with whom he contracts although the latter has no control over him.[35] Second, there are suggestions of imposing an absolute liability on the maker of a manufactured article put on the market for an injury it causes in the hands of an ultimate purchaser without regard to negligence in producing or marketing it. Third, there are suggestions of extension of the principle and method of the Workmen's Compensation Law to accidents in transportation by public utilities and also to motor vehicle accidents generally. Fourth, there is persistent suggestion of shifting all loss or damage falling on those not in an economic position to bear them well to some one else in a better economic position. Some of the things argued under the first three heads seem at times to come in the end to or very close to the fourth. But that is juristically so revolutionary that we may well take it, as a general proposition, up first since, if it can hold at all, it can serve for an all-embracing theory of liability.

Shifting of loss according to the economic status of the parties, was suggested in the first draft of the German Civil Code (1887) in a proposed section as follows: "§ 752. One who is not liable . . . for the injury caused by him because there was no intention or negligence on his part

35. Steffen, *The Independent Contractor and the Good Life* (1935) 2 UNIVERSITY OF CHICAGO LAW REVIEW 501.

shall nevertheless be liable in damages to the extent equity requires this in view of the facts of the case, in particular in view of the property status of the parties provided the person causing the injury is not deprived thereby of means of subsistence." This part was left out of the final draft (1896, took effect 1900) and the section (§ 829) in the Code finally provided for compensation from the property of a minor tortfeasor, where his parents or guardian were not culpable, determining the equity of the person injured to compensation by his property status. It is noteworthy that under the Nazi regime there was a proposal to enact the rule originally proposed in the draft of 1887.[36] The idea of equitable liability (*Haftung aus Billigkeit*) was argued somewhat in Germany. But it was carried much further in the Soviet Civil Code (1922).

Seeking to lay out a new path for social justice those who drafted the Soviet Civil Code provided for the court a power of "making the wealthy pay where the poor are absolved."[37] The Code reads: "§ 406. In situations where under §§ 403–405,[38] the person causing the injury is not under a legal duty to repair, the court may nevertheless compel him to repair the injury, depending upon his property status and that of the person injured."

"§ 411. In determining the amount of compensation to be awarded for an injury, the court must take into consideration the property status of the party injured and that of the party causing the injury."

Although workmen's compensation could be referred to the general security on the idea that holding the employer absolutely liable will impel him to the utmost vigilance and diligence to prevent injury to those in his employ, nevertheless it is in reality a radical departure from the

36. Nipperdey et al., *Grundfragen der Reform des Schadenersatzrechts* (1940).

37. 1 Gsovski, *Soviet Civil Law* (1948) 525.

38. § 403 lays down the doctrine of the French Civil Code, that one whose culpable act causes injury to another must repair the injury. § 404 provides for liability without regard to fault as to individuals and enterprises whose activities involve increased hazard for persons coming in contact with them unless the defendant can show the injury was due to the act of God or intent or gross contributory negligence of the person injured. § 405 provides that minors under 14 and persons of weak mind under guardianship are not liable for injuries they cause, but the person having the duty of supervision is to be liable. 2 Gsovski, *op. cit.*, 207–9.

law of the past in that it does not proceed upon maintenance of the general security but rather upon an idea that accidents are inevitable in the course of employment in the industrial society of today and that the burden of this risk should not be borne by the employee. It proceeds upon a humanitarian idea that we all of us ought to bear the risk of injuries which will inevitably fall on some of us in the vicissitudes of civilized life and not leave them to the luckless individual who chances to be hit. It goes beyond the principles of liability thus far considered. Extension of its principle and methods to accidents in the operations of railroads, trolley lines and bus lines,[39] and, as others propose, to all motor vehicle accidents, would take a huge domain of litigation out of the law of torts, if not out of the law, by entrusting its administration to administrative agencies rather than to the courts.

How is it with the other recent proposals: That as to the doctrine of the independent contractor and that as to liability of the maker of manufactured articles which, let us say, explode in the hands of a servant of the ultimate purchaser? Do these merely propose extended application of the now recognized principle of liability without fault? May they be referred, as the law of torts as it stands today may be referred to maintenance of the social interest in the general security? It would seem that we must answer these questions in the negative. Can we say that in life in civilized society men must be able to assume that those who employ a contractor over whom they have no control will nonetheless prevent the contractor from independently subjecting others to unreasonable risk of injury? Where there is control over the person or thing causing injury, imposing liability on the one who has control constrains him to vigilance and diligence to exercise that control to prevent injury to others.[40] To impose an absolute liability, where there is no control, is to make the person on whom it is imposed an involuntary Good Samari-

39. Report by the Committee to Study Compensation for Automobile Accidents to the Columbia Council for Research in the Social Sciences (1932). *See* Sherman, *Grounds for Opposing the Automobile Accident Insurance Plan*, 2 LAW AND CONTEMPORARY PROBLEMS (1930) 598.

40. As to the nature and extent of control as affecting liability, *see* Douglas, *Vicarious Liability and Administration of Risk* (1929) 38 YALE LAW JOURNAL 584.

tan. Where one employs an independent contractor to do something which he is himself bound to do, the general security is involved. One cannot be allowed to avoid his duty by employing an independent contractor to do it for him. The social interest in the general security requires, if he does not do it himself, that he do it through some one he can control. If not, he has not done his duty of maintaining the general security and should be held. This exception to the doctrine of the independent contractor is sufficiently within the principle of liability. To extend liability to everything done by an independent contractor will require finding a new principle.

As to the second proposal it will be well to consider the leading case in which it was advanced.[41] A bottle of Coca Cola exploded when taken out of the refrigerator by the servant of the ultimate purchaser. It had been put on the market by the manufacturer after, let us say, it had been manufactured with due care and thoroughly inspected to discover hidden defects. There was no proof of the cause of the explosion and nothing in the fragments of the bottle to show it was defective when put on the market. In the actual case the court properly applied the doctrine of *res ipsa loquitur.* The accident, it appeared, could not have happened if the bottle, charged under high pressure, had been properly made and thoroughly inspected for defects before it was put on the market. The making, filling, and inspecting were under the sole control of the manufacturer. Hence there was a necessary inference of negligence, no other ground of negligence appearing. So far we are proceeding on maintaining the general security.

But one of the state judges of today suggested going further. He said: ". . . I believe that the manufacturer's negligence should no longer be singled out as the basis of a plaintiff's right to recover in cases like the present one. In my opinion it should now be recognized that a manufacturer incurs an absolute liability when an article he has placed on the market, knowing that it is to be used without inspection, proves to have a defect that causes injury to human beings. . . . Even if there is no neg-

41. *Escola v. Coca Cola Bottling Co.,* 24 California 2d, 453 (1944).

ligence, however, public policy demands that responsibility be fixed wherever it will most effectively reduce the hazards to life and health inherent in defective products that reach the market. It is evident that the manufacturer can anticipate some hazards and guard against the recurrence of others, as the public cannot. Those who suffer injury from defective products are unprepared to meet its consequences. The cost of an injury and the loss of time or health may be an overwhelming misfortune to the person injured, and a needless one, for the risk of injury can be insured by the manufacturer and distributed among the public as a cost of doing business. It is to the public interest to discourage the marketing of products having defects that are a menace to the public. If such products nevertheless find their way into the market it is to the public interest to place the responsibility for whatever injury they may cause upon the manufacturer, who, even if he is not negligent in the manufacture of the product, is responsible for its reaching the market. However intermittently such injuries may occur and however haphazardly they may strike, the risk of their occurrence is a constant risk and a general one. Against such a risk there should be general and constant protection and the manufacturer is best situated to afford such protection."[42]

It will have been seen that absolute liability of the manufacturer is rested on three grounds: (1) maintenance of the general security, (2) ability of the manufacturer to pass the loss on to the public in the price of manufactured articles, and (3) that the injured person may not be able to bear the loss and it can best be borne by the manufacturer.

As to the first point, it is a gratuitous assumption that the product which may have gone through many hands from the factory to the ultimate buyer, left the factory in a defective condition which caused the injury. If it did and the product was under the sole control of the manufacturer and the defect could not have existed when the article was put on the market, then the doctrine of *res ipsa loquitur* would govern as the court rightly decided in the case under discussion. Under the assump-

42. *Ibid.* 461–62.

tion that the explosion was due to the condition of the bottle when it left the bottling works there was logical proof of negligence on the part of one in sole charge of the situation where there was nothing to avoid the inevitable inference.[43] The general security is amply provided for in such cases by the law of torts as it stood in the last century.

As to the second point, it raises the question as to the so-called insurance theory of liability, which will be taken up in detail presently.

As to the third ground of proposed imposing of absolute liability upon the manufacturer, it is in effect the proposition behind section 406 of the Soviet Civil Code. It imposes an absolute liability on the basis of the comparative economic status of the parties. As I have been in the habit of putting the matter, it makes the manufacturer an involuntary Good Samaritan. In order to relieve one whose economic status is unequal to bearing the loss it seeks to find some one else who can or who can better sustain it. It should be noted, however, that Soviet administration of justice in effect gave up section 406 of the code as not practicable. The Supreme Court held that in the absence of causation it had no rational sense; that one who did not cause the injury could not be sued.[44]

All this does not mean, however, that we must wholly reject the proposals as to giving up the independent contractor doctrine, as to extending the principle and methods of the Workmen's Compensation Act to accidents in transportation and injuries in the operation of motor vehicles, or as to imposing absolute liability upon manufacturers. We are not bound to fight a hard rear-guard action against such extensions such as jurists long fought in vain against a general principle of liability without fault. It must be asked whether we can find a possible basis for them, either a common basis with workmen's compensation, or one on which some at least may stand independently.

Some argument might be made for resting workmen's compensation on maintaining the general security if it were not for the way in which we are more and more today removing the bar of contributory negli-

43. *Kearney v. London Brighton & South Coast R. Co.*, L.R. 5 Q.B. 411 (1870).
44. 1 Gsovski, *op. cit.* 526–27.

gence over the whole field of liability. One might argue that as a certain
number of accidents are certain to occur in all enterprises in which men
are employed, it is a reasonable mode of minimizing the risk to impose
an absolute liability to repair resulting injury or loss. The conclusive answer to this, however, is that the bar of contributory negligence, by the
same reasoning, should stimulate a high degree of vigilance and diligence on the part of the employees to avoid accidents since if they fail
in due care for their own safety the risk of injury will fall wholly or largely
upon them. Not only in workmen's compensation but on every side
of the law of liability, contributory negligence as a defense has been
steadily giving way. We have moved a long way from the doctrine which
was much discussed when I studied the law of torts sixty-three years ago,
that a plaintiff must, in order to recover, aver and prove that he acted
with due prudence and diligence and did not contribute by his own negligence to the injury of which he complains.[45] In two generations it became generally established that contributory negligence was an affirmative defense to be pleaded and proved as such. In that time we have
seen the scope of that defense greatly narrowed by the doctrine of the
last clear chance. We have seen contributory negligence, after allowing
it as a bar at first and then gradually limiting its application, finally discarded in the domain of workmen's compensation, largely eliminated
in employer's liability legislation, and finally, where it still holds on deprived of much efficacy in practice by statutory adoption of a doctrine
of comparative negligence or statutory provision for mitigation of damages in proportion to the negligence of the parties.[46] As to the practical
operation of this last step toward elimination of the common-law bar, experienced observers tell me that under the statutes the wise jury of today, having determined to give the plaintiff $10,000 find he has suffered

45. *Neal v. Gillett*, 23 Conn. 437 (1855); *Chicago R. Co. v. Levy*, 160 Ill. 385 (1896);
Planz v. Boston R. Co., 157 Mass. 377 (1892) but changed by Act of 1914, chap. 53; *My-
ning v. Detroit R. Co.*, 67 Mich. 677 (1888); *Curran v. Warren Chemical Mfg. Co.*, 36
N.Y. 153 (1867) changed by Laws of 1920, chap. 919.
46. Leflar, *The Declining Defence of Contributory Negligence* (1941) 1 ARKANSAS LAW
REVIEW 1.

injury to the extent of $13,500 and then find further that in view of his contributory negligence the recovery should be mitigated in the amount of $3500. Contributory negligence is a disappearing defense.

While workmen's compensation might have been thought of as standing between the old idea of maintaining the general security and some new idea of liability to repair injury, it has actually broken definitely with that idea. The principle behind it is one growing in the law of torts which may yet come to include the three recently proposed changes considered above and eventually either by legislation or judicial decision much more.

Sooner or later we must consider the effect on law of the rise of the service state, the state which does not limit its activities to maintaining peace and order, upholding the general security, and assuring freedom to take advantage of opportunities for acquisition as they present themselves, but instead seeks to secure to all men directly the fulfillment of their expectations. Its advocates recognize no limits to what the state can do to promote human welfare — to provide for all men fulfillment of their expectations in life in society. Much as we may make fun, as I have been inclined to do, of a broad program of mending all human ills and taking care of all human wants, unless perhaps the welfare hereafter of our immortal souls, it must be admitted that that achievements of science in the past hundred years, and especially in the past fifty years, justify some sanguine faith in the efficacy of effort. A generation which has seen the coming of the motor vehicle, wireless, the radio, television, air transportation to every part of the world at incredible speed, and, above all, has seen physicists divide the indivisible, may well doubt whether the impossible, or what has been held impossible, may not be made possible by planned effort in law.

Today throughout the world the idea of satisfying the wants of men in civilized society is leading to a broad humanitarian conception both of liability in tort and of liability upon contract. Confining ourselves for a moment to the former, there is an idea that the law can be made to secure us all against the losses and injuries incident to life in society in a crowded world so that no one shall find himself deprived by accident or mischance of the expectation of individual conditions of life, political, physical, cultural, social and economic, but shall rather find himself not merely secured in these expectations but restored to the full measure of them when loss or injury or frustration befalls him. I am not arguing for such a political and juristic Utopia. But I submit that it is an ideal, a picture, that men have before them today increasingly, that it is something that is affecting and is bound further to affect the law, and that it calls for serious consideration by jurists.

One way in which this ideal has developed in juristic thought is in what has been called the insurance theory of liability. It is a noble humanitarian conception that the misfortunes of each of us should be borne by all of us. The ills that will inevitably affect some of us in life in civilized society ought to be borne by us all. The common purse should be available to aid the luckless victim of injuries caused culpably by no one, or even caused by no one, or perhaps even caused in whole or in part by the unfortunate victim himself. But in view of the ever multiplying services performed by the service state we shrink from imposing the burden of wholesale reparation of all injuries upon the proceeds of taxation. The insurance theory of liability is an ingenious and plausible evasion of putting the burden upon the public directly, as the humanitarian ideal demands it ought to go. We are told that we are all to insure each, but that this does not mean that all the ills of each are to be repaired directly out of the public purse. By imposing absolute liabilities upon utilities, industries, manufacturers, and then why not upon agricultural producers, who employ workers, we impose it ultimately on the public. The utility in rates for services, the industry by prices for manufactured articles, and the farmer in prices for products, can pass on to all of us the loss we have put upon him temporarily. I have said this is ingenious and plausible. But look into it more deeply in its actual application. As it actually operates in the state of today, is the loss really passed back to us who are in theory ultimately to bear it? In fact in the bureau organization of the service state the proposition as to passing damages for losses incurred by no one's fault on to the public by way of employer or public utility or industrial enterprise is fallacious. One bureau or commission fixes rates for service. Another fixes rates for public utilities. Another fixes or may be fixing prices. Another has control of wages and hours. A jury or some special administrative agency fixes responsibility and assesses the damages or the amount of accident compensation. Each of these agencies operates independently, subject to no co-ordinating power. Those that control rates and prices are zealous to keep the cost to the public as low as may be. Those that control the imposition of liability are apt to be zealous to afford the maximum of relief to the injured or to their dependents. With continual pressure upon industry and enterprise to relieve the tax-paying public of the heavy burden that our recent humanitarian programs involve, the practical result is likely to be that the burden is shifted arbitrarily to the most convenient victim. There is little, if any, validity in the proposition that compensation for loss and injury without fault of the utility or enterprise and without regard to the general security is passed on to the public.

Moreover, in the case of industrial enterprises each enterprise is and is compelled by law to be in competition with others. If the burden of loss without fault and for matters out of its control is cast upon it, competition will prevent it from recouping the loss by what it charges for products, since if it raises prices of its products it will lose its business to its competitors. And if we feel that all losses are to be made good to every one, the entrepreneur, who finds his enterprise burdened with ruinous damages without his fault and for what he has no power to prevent, may claim that he too has suffered a serious loss for which our humanitarian principle should afford him relief.

I fear greatly that we are actually, though not in theory, going on some assumed but covered up jural postulate such as this: "In civilized society men are entitled to assume that they will be secured by the state against all loss or injury, even though the result in part or whole of their own fault or improvidence, and to that end that liability to repair all loss or injury will be cast by law upon some one deemed better able to bear it." This was the idea of section 406 of the Soviet Civil Code. But, as we have seen, that provision proved unworkable on its own ground and there is nothing to lead us to assume that it would work better elsewhere in the world under conditions less favorable to its underlying idea.

It has been suggested that a tendency of juries to render verdicts on the basis of relative economic status and ability to pay is a reason for frank recognition, by expressly imposing absolute liability for all loss or damage, of what has long been the law in action. But apart from the want of sound policy in adding unchecked unrational extensions to unrational action of juries in cases arousing sympathy, unrational jury verdicts whenever carried beyond the bounds of "common right and reason" are subject to correction where an unrational rule of wholesale absolute liability would not be. The deceptive proposition that we are all of us insuring each of us by imposing loss and damage upon some one able to bear it makes for growing acceptance of a general doctrine of absolute liability. It has been proposed to incorporate it in the commercial code under the auspices of the Commissioners on Uniform State Laws and the American Law Institute.[47] Also the ground on which a teacher in one of the great American law schools argues for abolition of the doctrine of the independent contractor in the law of agency is that frequently the independent contractor has no means sufficient to be reached on execution. Hence, we are told, losses and injuries are left unrepaired, which must not be.[48] In the same spirit a judge of one of the most important American courts intimates that the requirement that one who is required to repair a loss must have caused it is artificial and should be abrogated.[49] But note what this may mean. Suppose a man determines to commit suicide but wishes to provide for his dependents. He stands at the street corner waiting for a heavy truck as the chosen agent

47. American Law Institute, *Uniform Commercial Code*, Final Draft, § 2.318 and commentary ¶s 3, 4.

48. *Supra* note 35.

49. Because under the Federal Safety Appliance Acts negligence and causation are not in issue, since there is a statutory absolute liability attached to the relation of employer and employee, does not justify pronouncing all idea of causation generally an outworn artificiality. *O'Donnel v. Elgin J. & E.R. Co.*, 338 U.S. 384 (1949); *Urie v. Thompson*, 337 U.S. 163, 166 (1949); *Carter v. Atlanta & St. A.B.R. Co.*, 338 U.S. 430, 437, 438 (1949); *Affolder v. N.Y.C. & St. L.R. Co.*, 339 U.S. 96, 98 (1950).

The term causation became involved in many complications and artificialities in the course of development of the idea of negligence. What is sound is the idea of creation of an unreasonable risk and of the ambit of the risk.

of self-destruction. When one comes along he throws himself beneath its wheels and is killed. If causation and fault as prerequisites of liability are eliminated must not the transportation company repair the loss to the widow and children? We are not looking squarely at all the facts if we turn to a wholesale establishing of liability without regard to fault or causation or control of the situation in the belief that in so doing we are ourselves taking on the burden of repairing all loss and damage suffered by our fellow men. If leaving the luckless victim of loss or injury not attributable to wrongful causation by any one, or failure of any one to exercise a control which he had over the circumstances of the injury, to bear the risk is not satisfying, yet achieving high humanitarian purposes by the easy method of using the involuntary Good Samaritan as the Greek playwright used the god from the machine is unedifying. There ought to be a better method of making the legal order effective for our humanitarian ideals than that of Robin Hood or that of the pickpocket who went to the charity sermon and was so moved by the preacher's eloquence that he picked the pockets of every one in reach and put the contents in the plate.

But the idea that the state is to secure men against all loss or injury even though the result of their own fault or improvidence and to that end that burdens should be shifted to others better able to bear them is having consequences beyond the law of torts.

From the Greek philosophers who thought on social control and ethics and recognized stability and predictability of conduct as fundamental in civilized society, the morally binding force of a promise has been taken for a starting point. This appears in our everyday language. We say the upright man is trustworthy and reliable. We may rely on his constancy in business, political, and domestic relations. On the other hand, we say that the unrighteous man is untrustworthy, unreliable, unprincipled. We cannot trust or rely on his constancy or conformity to principle in business or political or family relations. Hence in political and legal philosophy a starting point has been to refer institutions to a basis in promises. The political theory of the founders of the American constitutional democratic polity held that the government derived its just powers from the consent of the governed. They found its basis in a social compact or social contract by which each of us was bound to his fellow men to uphold the order of society and adhere to its institutions and laws.

While morals from as far back as when men began to think and write about moral obligations insisted on good faith in the performance of promises the law long left enforcement to social control through morality and religion. Politically organized society long had its hands full in keeping the peace and maintaining the framework of the social order. But the law of Continental Europe took over from the church enforcement of promises made as legal transactions, and in spite of historical procedural difficulties, which took form in the requirement of "consideration," Anglo-American law by 1950 had been coming pretty close to this result. Today, however, at the very time when the law had come substantially to the position of morals, that promises as such were to be kept, there was coming to be an increasing breakdown of the strict moral doctrine as to the obligation of a promise and a corresponding relaxation in the law.

A radically different view as to the obligation of a promise begins with orthodox Marxian socialism in the latter part of the nineteenth century. Since law was held to be a result of the division of society into classes and to be nothing more than a device for keeping an exploited class in subjection, Marx taught that it would disappear with the abolition of private property. Although the idea of disappearance of law has been given up, at least until remaking of society through the dictatorship of the proletariat is complete, the law of obligations, or of contracts in the widest sense of that term, which makes up the bulk of the law in the Continental codes and codes elsewhere on their model as well as in the uncodified law of the English-speaking world, finds no place as such in the Soviet codes.

Continental Europe has had a longer experience of the service state than we have had in English-speaking lands. Hence it is instructive to see how the law of contracts has fared in France. Two phenomena in connection with the law of contracts are discussed by French jurists today. One is what Josserand calls "contractual dirigism,"[50] *i.e.*, making contracts for people instead of leaving contracts to be made by the parties for themselves. The other is a humanitarian idea of rendering a service to debtors or promisors by lifting or shifting burdens or losses so as to put them upon those better able to bear them. The two are closely related. When contracts are made for people by the service state they do not feel any strong moral duty to perform them. If the state makes the contract let the state perform it or compensate the disappointed promisee. Hence we read in the French law books of today about "the principle of favor to the debtor" and Ripert speaks ironically of what he calls "the right not to pay debts."[51]

In 1804 the French Civil Code put emphatically the binding force of a contract: "Agreements legally formed take the place of law for those who have made them."[52] In part this represents the idea of the eighteenth-century law of nature. The legal was declaratory of the moral. The moral duty to keep a promise was therefore legal. But it derives also from the will theory of the nineteenth century. The free wills of the parties had made the law for them. The courts could no more change this than any other part of the law. Even the legislator was bound to respect it as to the contracts of the past. This was put in the Constitution of the United States.[53] But this idea has been disappearing all over the world. In France it is gone entirely. This was covered up for a time by what Austin would have called spurious interpretation.[54] By assuming that the will of the parties had not been fully expressed, courts could discover in contracts terms which were not there and were not in the minds of the parties, and could modify the terms which they found there. French legislation went further and gave the judges power to suspend or rescind

50. 1 Planiol et Ripert, *Traité élémentaire de droit civil français*, rev. by Ripert (4 ed. 1952) no. 293; 2 id. no. 161.

51. 2 *ibid.* (1952) no. 1302.

52. *French Civil Code*, art. 1134.

53. "No state shall . . . pass . . . law impairing the obligation of contracts." Const. U.S. art. I, sec. 10.

54. 2 Austin, *Jurisprudence* (5 ed. 1885) 989–1001.

contracts and change their conditions.[55] The parties no longer make law for themselves by free contract. Partly, the French jurists tell us, a moral idea has been at work here. Contracts might be improvident or changes in the economic situation might affect the value of the promised performance or of the given or promised equivalent. This is akin to an idea we may see at work in the law of legal liability everywhere. It is a humanitarian idea of lifting or shifting burdens and losses so as to put them upon those better able to bear them. It is in line with Article 55a of the Charter of the United Nations, which binds the several members to promote "higher standards of living, full employment and conditions of social progress and development." But it needs to be kept in balance with some other ends. Belief in the obligatory force of and respect for the given word are going, if not actually gone, in the law of today.

What French writers speak of as the moral or humanitarian doctrine of the disappearance of free contract has been manifesting itself gradually in Anglo-American law and has been gaining for a generation. There is a notable tendency in recent writing everywhere to insist, not as did the nineteenth century that the debtor keep faith strictly in all cases, even though it ruin him and his family, but that the creditor must take a risk also either along with or in some cases instead of the debtor. The Roman practice of giving a debtor in certain relations a benefit or privilege of not being held for the entire amount but only for so much as he could pay for the time being, was rejected by French law in the nineteenth century.[56] But recent codes and legislation in Continental Europe have provided a number of restrictions upon the power of a creditor to exact satisfaction,[57] which have been likened to the Roman privilege. Later they were referred to an idea of social justice, but they are now generally referred to a general public service of relieving debtors as a function of the state in order to promote the general welfare by freeing men from the burden of poverty.

55. 6 Planiol et Ripert, *Traité pratique de droit civil français* (1934) nos. 391–98.

56. 1 Baudry-Lacantinerie, *Précis de droit civil* (10 ed.) § 529, toned down somewhat in later editions, *see* 13 ed. § 550; Lavet, *La benéfice de la competence* (1927).

57. *German Civil Code* §§ 528–29, 829; *German Code of Civil Procedure*, § 850.

In the United States homestead and exemption laws began to be enacted more than one hundred years ago[58] and have been greatly extended in the present century, chiefly to protect the family and dependents of the debtor, but partly to secure the social interest in the individual life. There is, however, a changed spirit behind these extensions; a spirit of a claim upon society to relieve a man of the burdens he assumed freely, based upon a proposition that so to relieve him is a service to the whole community which the state has been set up to perform. A debtor is by no means always the underdog which high humanitarian thinking postulates. The creditor may be the guardian of orphans or trustee for a widow and the debtor a wealthy speculator who has taken on too much and seeks to shake off an inconvenient load. "Favor to debtors," as the French put their policy of today, may be a great hardship upon creditors who in particular cases may conceivably make a more meritorious appeal.

How far the humanitarian doctrine is taking us is illustrated by a theory of contract now set forth by some teachers of law. They argue what is called the prediction theory of contract.[59] It has not yet been applied to promissory notes. So far as I know, no one as yet has urged as the real text of a promissory note something like this: "Ninety days after date, for value received, I predict that I shall be able and willing to pay to John Doe on order five hundred dollars." But the bonds and notes of municipalities, public utilities, and industrial corporations under American legislation of today as to reorganization come to something very like this, and there is ample provision for allowing every one to unload his obligations.[60]

58. Thompson, *Homesteads and Exemptions*, §§ 40, 379 (1878).

59. Gardner, *An Inquiry into the Principles of the Law of Contracts* (1946) 46 HARVARD LAW REVIEW 1, 4–8.

60 *See* the chapters added to the Bankruptcy Act within a generation: Chap. 8, Provisions for the Relief of Debtors, § 75 Agricultural Compositions and Extensions, § 77, Reorganization of Railroads; Chap. 9, Readjustment of debts of agencies or instrumentalities, *i.e.*, municipal corporations, great and small; Chap. 10, Corporate Reorganization; Chap. 11, Arrangements (*i.e.*, plans of a debtor "for the settlement, satisfaction, or extension of the time of payment of his unsecured debts"); Chap. 12, Real Property Arrangements; and Chap. 13, Wage Earner's Plans. The Bankruptcy Act, enacted July 2,

Legislation impairing or doing away with the practical legal means of enforcing promises is now upheld on the basis of a doctrine that power of the legislature to relieve promisors of liability is implied in the sovereignty of the state.[61] Such relief is one of the services the state is set up to render. But how does that comport with the limitation on state legislation prescribed in our federal constitution?[62]

After resumption of grants and revocation of franchises at every turn of political fortune in seventeenth-century England and of colonial legislation and state legislation in the economic depression after the American Revolution interfering with the enforcement of contracts and revoking charters, a prohibition of state legislation impairing the obligation of contracts (contract being used in its older, wider sense of legal transaction[63]) was put in the federal constitution. But that provision of the constitution has now for the largest part at least become a mere preachment; and the spirit that has led to substitution of a preachment for an enforceable constitutional provision has been affecting regard for the upholding of promises on every side. There is no longer a strong feeling of moral duty to perform. When to lack of this feeling is added impairment of the legal duty as well, it undermines a main pillar of the economic order.

For a generation legislation has increasingly limited the power of the creditor to collect, has created more and larger exemptions, and has added much to the once narrowly limited number who may escape through bankruptcy. This, too, has been rested avowedly on the powers of the service state. Statutes authorizing municipalities to "reorganize" their debts are upheld, as courts tell us, by "extending the police power into economic welfare."[64]

1898, as Amended through December, 1952, with Annotations by Hanna and MacLachlan (5 ed. 1953).

61. *Home Building & Loan Assn.* v. *Blaisdell*, 290 U.S. 398 (1934).

62. *Supra* note 53.

63. *Fletcher* v. *Peck*, 6 Cranch 87 (1810) — a grant of land; *Trustees of Dartmouth College* v. *Woodward*, 4 Wheaton 518 (1819) — charter of a college.

64. When the idea of liberty was the measure of all things in jurisprudence, "the powers of government inherent in every sovereignty," spoken of as the police power, were taken to be limited to the promotion of the public health, safety, and morals. From

But the movement to relieve promisors is not confined to legislation. The courts have been doing their share in building a body of doctrine as to frustration. A law teacher now tells us that there is "a real need for a field of human intercourse freed from legal restraint, for a field where men may without liability withdraw assurances they have once given."[65] Certainly the one-time general proposition that courts cannot make contracts over for the parties, that freedom of contract implies the possibility of contracting foolishly, is giving way to a power of the service state to relieve by judicial discretion persons of age, sound mind, and discretion from their contracts, or make their contracts over for them, or make their contracts easier for them. We are now told that even where a contract contains provisions as to the consequences of particular possible frustrations the courts may recognize other frustrations and apply other consequences to them.[66] Often the words finally written in a contract after a long negotiation are the result of hard-fought compromises. They are not ideal provisions from either side but are what each is willing to concede in order to reach agreement. After some frustrating event has happened and a party who has suffered damage from nonperformance is suing for it, to say that he consented and would have in-

---

that point of view humanitarian legislation as a service to the public seemed to be an extension of the police power. But it had been seen before that the police power was nothing in reality but the residuum of governmental power after constitutional restrictions. Thayer, *Legal Essays* (1908) 27.

65. "There has been an increasing liberality in determining what constitutes a justifiable impossibility or frustration of purpose." 6 Corbin, *Contracts* (1951). The *Restatement of the Law of Contract* under the auspices of the American Law Institute (1932) says nothing about frustration. It speaks only of impossibility and failure of consideration. Professor Corbin two decades later devoted a whole chapter of nine sections and thirty-nine pages to the subject.

66. The doctrine of frustration of contract was given legislative sanction in England in the Law Reform Frustrated Contract Act, 1943. It had been said that the doctrine was invented by the courts in order to supplement the defects in actual contracts. Lord Wright in *Denny, Mott, and Dickson, Ltd. v. Fraser* [1944] A.C. 265, 274.

The doctrine is "a mode by which upon the facts of the case the court does justice in circumstances for which the parties never provided." Webber, *Effect of War upon Contracts* (2 ed. 1946) 414.

tended to insert a condition which a court conjures up to relieve the promisor is to make a new contract under a fiction of interpretation. This sort of interpretation, which has much vogue in the service state, is said by a judge of our highest American court to be a process of distillation. The meaning is distilled from the words. It might be suggested that distilling is often illicit and the product moonshine.

So much in everyday life depends upon reliance on promises that an everyday dependence will lose its effectiveness if promises are to be performed only when it suits the promisor's convenience. A promise which imposes no risk on the promisor belongs to the prediction theory. It is not a promise. A promisee expects the promise to be performed even if it hurts. Why relieve only a promisor? Forty years ago sociologists were saying that social control through law having put down force in the relations of men with each other, must now put down cunning.[67] But all depends on what is meant by cunning. Are we to say that superior knowledge, diligence, ability to foresee and judgment as to persons and things are to be allowed to have no influence in transactions? Undoubtedly men desire to be equal in all respects. But they also desire to be free. They desire to be allowed to use the qualities with which they were born and those they have developed. Carrying out satisfaction of the desire to be equal to its fullest development would reduce all activity to the lowest level. No one would be allowed to exert himself beyond the capacity of the least efficient. It is not in this way that civilization has been promoted or maintained. Men's desire to be equal and their desire to be free must be kept in balance. Either carried to the extreme negates the other. But this need not lead us to condemn the humanitarian movement.

It took nearly two centuries of juristic thought to formulate in Kant's theory of justice what had been started as a new path by the Spanish jurist-theologians. The prophet tells us that he that believeth shall not make haste. The humanitarian juristic thinking of today may well be the forerunner of an ideal of the end of law which shall make for advance in civilization.

67. This was a favorite saying of Professor Edward A. Ross.

TWELVE

The Authoritarian Idea

When in 1897 Mr. Justice Holmes, having begun when editor of the
American Law Review[1] in the analytical school, by a method of logical
analysis of legal precepts as authoritative imperatives prescribed by
those exercising the powers of a politically organized society, and then
in 1881 (in his Lowell lectures on the common law)[2] moved to the
method of the historical school, tracing the historical development of
legal institutions and doctrines and precepts, finally came to the
method of looking at both the legal order and the body of traditional and
of legislatively prescribed models and patterns of decision with reference to their social ends and function, he gave his epoch-making address under the title of "The Path of the Law."[3] Taking the hint from this
title, when I came to consider what has been going forward in juristic
thought and in law since jurists gave up the Kantian theory of justice as
the maximum of free individual self-assertion, I spoke of "New Paths of
the Law."[4] It seemed to me that after leaving what might be called the
path of liberty, two paths were becoming apparent: One a humanitarian
path on which the law had entered and upon which it had made some
progress, the other what, from its course thus far, might be called an
authoritarian path, a path much more divergent from what Anglo-

1. *Early Writings of Mr. Justice Holmes* (1931) 44 HARVARD LAW REVIEW 725–96.

2. Holmes, *The Common Law* (1881).

3. Holmes, *The Path of the Law* (1897) 10 HARVARD LAW REVIEW 443, *Collected Papers* (1921) 210–43.

4. Pound, *New Paths of the Law* (1950, lectures at the University of Nebraska).

American law had followed in the past. Thus far what I am calling the authoritative path is more suggested as one yet to be laid out than as one actually taken. It may prove to be one going on parallel with the humanitarian path. Or it may prove to be one which the humanitarian path will join to make the path of the future. Or it may be one of which the humanitarian path will prove to be but the beginning. The law seems to be moving toward the securing of a full life for every one. One way of doing this is a regime of shifting losses and imposition of liabilities according to greater ability to bear them. Another is to do or seek to do it through complete control of all individual activities and all productive exertion, through a regime of full service to everybody performed exclusively for us by politically organized society. This may conceivably be the path of the law in the maturity of the service state. Another was projected for a time on Marxian lines as one of gradual disappearance of the regime of a legal order and complete substitution of an administrative order maintained by a hierarchy of bureau officials exercising discretion to achieve policies of service. Theoretically this has been officially abandoned in Russia, but perhaps more by giving up the name and shape than by giving up the direction and *de facto* course of the path. For we are brought back to the social individualism of the orthodox nineteenth-century Marxian socialism.

Promoters of the service state are by no means resolving the paradox of nineteenth-century social-individualism. That doctrine taught that a maximum of individual liberty was to be attained by a maximum of state control. Now we are taught that maximum of concern for the individual life calls for maximum satisfaction of the whole scale of human wants or expectations by a maximum of power of public officials over him. Yet the internal contradiction remains. For example, the service state seeks to relieve against frustration by failure to achieve ambitions, to obviate all feelings of inferiority and assure satisfaction of desires to move in the most esteemed social circles. So men are not to choose freely those who are to be in close social association with them. They are not to be allowed to choose congenial companions for such intimate relations as social clubs, college fraternities or private rooming houses for college students, lest some one's social ambitions be frustrated. It does not seem to be thought proper to weigh or seek to put in balance the frustrated sensibilities of those who are to have unwelcome intimate associates in private social organizations thrust upon them, whose psychological tranquility from agreeable intimate social surroundings are to be sacrificed. When Anglo-American courts of equity were confronted with a problem of the injured feelings of persons expelled from social clubs in contravention of provisions of the club's charter or articles of association, they arrived at a significant distinction. Where no property interests were involved and there was nothing but breach of an agreement as to association for social purposes, courts of equity would not interfere. Sir George Jessel said in a leading case: "A dozen people may agree to meet and play whist at each other's houses for a certain period, and if eleven of them refuse to associate with the twelfth any longer, I am not aware that there is any jurisdiction in any court of justice in this country to interfere."[5] But if a member of an organization was expelled in a manner contrary to ordinary principles of justice and in such manner or under circumstances humiliating and injurious to the reputation and feelings of the person expelled, the courts may redress the wrong.[6] In such a case, however, there was an agreement to associate. Now, in the climate of the service state we are asked to require unwanted associates to be taken into such associations lest otherwise their ambitious social expectations be disappointed. One has to go back to the laws of Manu for precedent for what is being urged upon fraternities in American colleges today. According to Manu, one who gave a banquet and did not invite his two nearest neighbors was subject to a penalty.[7]

Social control as state control, the state as an end in itself, the legal order as a regime of ordering all conduct and dictating all adjustment of relations by official application of the force of a politically organized so-

---

5. *Rigby v. Connol*, 14 Ch. D. 482, 487 (1880).
6. *Berrien v. Pollitzer*, 165 Fed. 2d, 21 (1947).
7. *Manu*, viii, 392, Bühler's transl. 25 SACRED BOOKS OF THE EAST (1886) 322.

ciety to the case in hand, law as what those officials do because they do it, the judicial process as simply effective exertion of the power of the state officials; in other words, an omnicompetent state, in contrast with politically organized society carrying on a regime of social control through orderly application of force according to prescribed models or patterns of decision and determination, a law state, gives a new meaning to the term "law." It indicates a path in the development of society wholly divergent from that which had been followed in the West, which I am calling the authoritarian path. The service state in its development seems to threaten to take this path. It seems to threaten to become an omnicompetent state. But as a lawyer I am not concerned with the service state as such. Its general merits and demerits are for the political scientist and economist. What concerns me is the effect of the rise of the service state upon the law.

One effect upon law is suggested whenever we read in pronouncements of the advocates of the service state about what they call "socialization of law," "socialized courts" and "socialized procedure." I, myself, used the term "socialization of law" as far back as 1914.[8] But what I had in mind then was the conscious recognition of social interests where individual interests had been put as rights and social interests relegated to a subordinate category of policies. What the promoters of the service state have in mind is something quite different. In their use of the three phrases set forth above "socialized" is used to mean an extreme of unchecked power of officials and magistrates to make *ad hoc* determinations such as existed in the late totalitarian states and still obtains in Russia. Whether it is necessary to an adequate recognition and securing of social interests I doubt seriously. But in practice it has been following hard in the wake of the service state. It is characteristic of the authoritarian path.

Coke boasted that there could be no infringement of the life or lib-

8. *The End of Law as Developed in Legal Rules and Doctrines* (1914) 27 HARVARD LAW REVIEW 195, 225.

erty or fortune or inheritance of an individual in England and no species of oppression or misgovernment at his expense but that it should be redressed in one or the other of the common-law courts.[9] Today one of the leading exponents of the service state tells us that private law, the law which adjusts the relations of ordinary men and puts those who wield the authority of the estate on the same plane with — not above — the ordinary man, is being swallowed up by a public law which puts the official on a higher plane.[10]

Economic and psychological realist theories of the impossibility of a judicial process operating according to law, Marxian theories of the disappearance of law in the mature socialist state, and theories of superseding of the judicial process by *ad hoc* determinations by administrative agents — in other words, taking the adjusting of relations and ordering of conduct from the legal order and committing them to an administrative order — have largely gone along with and developed side by side with absolute theories in politics. They are concomitants of a movement toward absolute government which has been going on in every part of the world in the present century and despite a setback as a result of the second World War, is still strong and even growing beneath the surface. Theories of law in terms solely of threat and force are part of a general cult of force. Law is the real foe of absolutism. It presupposes a life measured by reason, a legal order measured by reason, and a judicial process carried on by applying a reasoned technique to experience developed by reason and reason tested by experience.

From their experience of absolute absentee government from Westminster as well as from deep reading in political history, the founders of the American constitutional legal polity knew that law alone could save them from dissolution or rule by mere brute power. As I have said elsewhere, "Civilization involves subjection of force to reason, and the agency of this subjection is law."[11] When John Adams put in the Massa-

9. Fourth Institute (1644) 71.
10. Jennings, *The Institutional Theory*, in *Modern Theories of Law* (1933) 68, 72.
11. *The Future of Law* (1937) 47 YALE LAW JOURNAL 1, 13.

chusetts Bill of Rights the ideal of "a government of laws and not of men,"[12] he pointed to government of men guided by law instead of ruling by fiat of governmental authority. "The conception of a government by laws dominated the thoughts of those who founded this Nation and designed its Constitution, although they knew as well as the belittlers of the conception that laws have to be made, interpreted and enforced by men."[13] Mr. Justice Brandeis said: "Checks and balances were established in order that this should be 'a government of laws and not of men.' . . . The doctrine of the separation of powers was adopted by the Convention of 1787, not to promote efficiency but to preclude the exercise of arbitrary power. The purpose was not to avoid friction, but, by means of the inevitable friction incident to the distribution of governmental powers among three departments, to save the people from autocracy."[14]

It is said frequently that the extent to which the separation of powers has been carried in the Constitution of the United States and the constitutions of the several states is to be attributed to a fashion of eighteenth-century thought. But it was not without good reason, based on experience, that Americans, almost at the moment independence was declared, began to set up written constitutions and to put the separation of powers at the foundation of them.[15] From the beginning down to the American Revolution, the colonies had been subjected to a completely centralized government with no distribution of powers and had learned what this sort of government meant. Ultimately all power over what went on in the colonies was centralized in the King in Council. The Privy Council had ultimate legislative power to the extent that it could disallow all colonial statutes. It could thus veto any statute within five years, and at any later time, even if the statute had not been disallowed, could hold it void as in conflict with the colonial charter.[16] It pre-

12. *Constitution of Massachusetts*, Part I, art. 30 (1780).
13. Frankfurter, J., in *United States v. Mine Workers*, 330 U.S. 258, 308 (1947).
14. Brandeis, J., in *Myers v. United States*, 272 U.S. 52, 292–93 (1926).
15. *E.g.*, Virginia Declaration of Rights (1776) § 5; North Carolina Declaration of Rights (1776) § 4; Massachusetts Declaration of Rights (1780) § 30.
16. *Winthrop v. Lechmere* (1727–28) 1 Thayer, *Cases on Constitutional Law* (1895) 34.

vented a necessary organization of courts in Pennsylvania for twenty-one years.[17] It overturned legislation making a modern provision for treating land as part of the estate of a decedent along with personality.[18] It disallowed statutes limiting appeals to Westminster from colonial courts.[19] It insisted that colonial organization of courts follow the English model and forced a regime of separate probate courts and separate courts of equity where the good sense of more than one colony sought to anticipate the unification of courts to which the English themselves came one hundred years later.[20]

Also the Crown in Council itself or through the Board of Trade and Plantations had ultimate administrative power, controlling administration through instructions to the royal governors, requiring that the governors make reports to them, and addressing inquiries to the governors as to what they and the local magistrates were doing.[21] Likewise the Privy Council had ultimate judicial power. Appeals to it lay from the courts of the colonies and it jealously guarded its appellate jurisdiction against colonial legislation as to jurisdictional amount and time for taking appeals. The expense of such appeals was a heavy burden upon litigants and one colony voted an appropriation to an appellee to enable him to defend his judgment at Westminster.[22] Not the least cause of the Revolution was the effort "to exact a stricter obedience from the colonies and to centralize, as had never been done successfully before, authority in the hands of the Crown."[23]

A like condition of centralized powers of government obtained in

17. Pennsylvania Statutes at Large, 148, 156 (1701) — disallowed, 481–82 (1705); 301–31 (1710) — disallowed 548–49 (1750); 299–308.

18. *Winthrop v. Lechmere, supra* note 16.

19. *E.g.,* 1 Acts and Resolves of the Province of Massachusetts Bay, 72 (1692) — disallowed 1695.

20. *See* Pound, *Organization of Courts* (1940) chap. 3. *See also* Trott, *Laws of the Province of South Carolina,* 472 (1736) — disallowance of the statute of 1726 "for the better settling of the courts of justice."

21. 4 Andrews, *The Colonial Period of American History* (1938) 145–46, 175–76, 303–4, 315.

22. 4 *Connecticut Historical Society Collections* (1892) 96n.

23. 4 Andrews, *The Colonial Period of American History* (1938) 375.

most of the colonies. The governor was appointed by the Crown, and the Crown or the governor appointed the Council. In ten of the thirteen colonies more than ninety-five percent of the local administrative officials were appointed by the Crown.[24] The governor and council, if there was one, were the upper house of the legislature. They were the head of administration. They were often the provincial appellate court,[25] subject to review by the Privy Council. One need not say that this undifferentiated authority was exercised in the administrative manner.[26] Experience of this form of government in the seventeenth and eighteenth centuries led lawyers and statesmen who had read Montesquieu and Blackstone to the express and emphatic pronouncements as to separation of powers in the constitutions which followed on the heels of the Declaration of Independence.

Today the idea of separation of powers is under attack. It is "repudiated" by the Soviet regime. "The program of the Communist Party repudiates the principle of the separation of powers." As Dr. Gsovski says justly, this is a logical conclusion from the dictatorial concept of governmental power.[27] With the passing of the abstract individualism of the last century perhaps ethical justification of coercion of individuals by politically organized society is no longer taken to be a serious question. Sociologists instead of ethical justification think of a science of society having to do with group behavior, the relationships between men, and the phenomena involved in or arising from those relationships. To them the state is but one of the groups or associations they are to study as such. Hence they cannot accept the paramountcy of the state which had been increasingly accepted by jurists since the sixteenth century. Instead of identifying state and society, as some jurists were doing in the latter part of the nineteenth century, they consider a politically organized society as one of a hierarchy of power structures,[28] or as one of a series of groups

---

24. *Ibid.* 420.

25. Pound, *Organization of Courts* (1940) 65–66.

26. See e.g., 1 Colonial Records of Georgia, Candler (1904) 451.

27. 1 Gsovski, *Soviet Civil Law* (1948) 75, and see Vyshinsky and Undrevich, *Soviet Constitutional Law* quoted by Dr. Gsovski. *ibid.* 74–75 and 75n., 78.

28. Timasheff, *Introduction to the Sociology of Law* (1939), chap. 10.

or associations through which men seek to realize their expectations or to secure their interests. This mode of thought comports well with the ideal of the state functioning through law. But it has to compete today with the authoritarian idea, the idea of a power structure based on inherent authority and limited only by efficiency in the performance of its tasks. As such it rests upon its control of the force of a politically organized society. On the other hand, recent sociological philosophical theory looks on the state as an organ of the social community as a whole for promoting certain of its common purposes. Accordingly, the coercion exercised by a sovereign political authority is seen as only one means of social control. It is only one means of enforcing upon the individual the supremacy of common ideals. After all in reality it is a moral authority because of the inherent limitations upon effective legal action.[29] Without the guarantee in a general habit of obedience or the backing of the stronger element of the community, coercion by those who exercise the authority of the state cannot continue to be effective.

In the American constitutional polity we have an ideal of a government proceeding according to law, that is, by a systematic reasoned application of principles, as distinguished from a government applying the force of politically organized society by fiat in each case or by rules resting on its authority for the time or the occasion. The ideal in the authoritarian path seems to be efficiency. But efficiency to what end?

A service state, a state which, instead of preserving peace and order and employing itself with maintaining the general security, takes the whole domain of human welfare for its province and would remedy all economic and social ills through its activities, has made much progress toward establishing itself in America since the first World War. It was known earlier in Continental Europe and came to be well developed there with the rise of great centralized nations. But although some writers in England were urging the possibilities at the end of the last century, it was so at outs with ingrained modes of legal and political thought

29. See Pound, *The Limits of Effective Legal Action* (1916) 27 INTERNATIONAL JOURNAL OF ETHICS, 150.

in the English-speaking world that for a time few sought to fit together the pieces of evidence to see what is indicated as to the direction in which we have been moving. In the meantime it has made exceedingly rapid progress and has covered already a very wide field of individual activity and of official promotion of broad welfare programs on every side.

I say service state rather than the usual term "welfare state." The term welfare state has always seemed to me a boast. Governments have always held that they were set up to promote and conserve public Welfare. This is implicit in the synonym "commonwealth"—the common weal or general welfare personified in the state. So far men have agreed. But when it comes to the question how the common weal or general welfare is to be achieved, they have differed and still differ profoundly. Some think the general welfare is best promoted by a government which maintains order and administers justice by adjusting relations and ordering conduct according to law, for the rest leaving men to do things for themselves in their own way so as they do not commit aggressions upon others or subject others to unreasonable risk of injury, and act in good faith in their relations with others. On the other hand, there have always been those who have believed in a benevolent government which helps men instead of leaving them free to help themselves; who have believed in a paternal order or paternal state (one might even say maternal state) doing things for subjects or citizens to the fullest extent.

Let me make it clear that I am not preaching against a service state in itself. Society of today demands services beyond those the state which only maintained order and repaired injuries could perform. In a complex industrial society it becomes more difficult to do by private initiative many things which the public wishes done and wishes done quickly. Administrative agencies of promoting the general welfare have come to be a necessity and have come to stay. It would be futile to quarrel with the idea of a service state in America kept in balance with the idea of individual spontaneous initiative characteristic of the American in the past. What we must question is not state performance of many services which it can perform without upsetting the American legal-political order. Such things may be done while holding to the idea of rights of individuals as legal rights secured by the law of the land, while holding to a doctrine of law governing public servants, state agents, and private individuals alike, and without substituting administrative discipline for legal liability made effective by legal proceedings in the courts. What must be questioned is the idea that all public services must and can only be performed by the government; that politically organized society and that alone is to be looked to for everything and that there is no limit to the services to humanity which it can perform. What I challenge is carrying to the extreme the idea of regimented co-operation for the general welfare as the task of law, so that there ceases to be law. Exaltation of politically organized society to the position of an absolute ruler means that those who exercise the power and authority of that organization are above the law. What they do is law because they do it, which is the very negation of law.

A politically organized society as an absolute ruler presupposes either a body of supermen administrators and a super-superman over them or an all-wise majority or plurality, served by supermen administrators, omnicompetent and equal to taking over the whole domain of the general welfare and to determining in detail what it calls for in every situation. Such a society cannot tolerate questioning of its commands, methods or acts. They have an all-sufficing basis in its authority. One conspicuous service to mankind may be questioning of institutions and doctrines of the service state, and this service of adequate questioning of itself and of its carrying out of the services it performs, cannot be expected reasonably of absolute rulers or ruling oligarchies under an authoritarian ideal.

In the English-speaking world the service state began by performing a few major additional services beyond maintaining order and administering justice. As it has added more and more it has come to be jealous of public service performed by anyone else.

What is to be the effect of the development of the service state and its authoritarian ideal upon the American constitutional legal polity? The service state as it develops as a superstate must be *par excellence* a bureau state. From the very nature of administration the bureau state calls for a highly organized official hierarchy. A hierarchy calls for a superman (although very likely an *ex officio* superman) at its head. Thus it starts a path which may lead to a totalitarian state. The service state has Marxian socialism and absolute government in its pedigree and has grown up along with the totalitarian state in other parts of the world. Liberty — free individual self-assertion, individual initiative and self-help — is looked on with suspicion if not aversion by the service state, and its advocates seek "a new concept of liberty," a freedom from want and freedom from fear, not freedom of self-assertion or self-determination. Self-help by the individual, competing with the service rendered by the state, seems an interference with the regime maintained by the government. Spontaneous individual initiative is frowned on as infringing on the domain of state action. The service state easily becomes an omnicompetent state with bureaus of *ex officio* experts and self-protecting propaganda activities carried on at public expense. If the step to it is gradual, the step from it to an absolute state is easy and may be made quickly. Regulation of the means of communication becomes control of the means of communication. Thus more and more the service state may block effective criticism and at the same time advertise and extoll its good works. Moreover, the remedy of popular uprising is not available as it was formerly. Effective weapons are not part of the furniture of every home as they were once. "Embattled farmers" and volunteer armies springing up spontaneously cannot compete with the fighting planes and tanks and artillery and motor transport which a strong government of today can bring to bear upon them. In his lectures on law in 1790, James Wilson, then one of the Justices of the Supreme Court of the United States, spoke with enthusiasm of a "right of revolution" which, he said, "should be taught as a principle of the Constitution of the United States and of every state in the Union."[30] The editor of his Works and chief recent exponent of his teaching speaks also of the "inherent natural right of revolution."[31] The Bill of Rights in the Constitution of the United States provides that "the right of the people to

30. 1 Wilson's *Works* (Andrews' ed. 1896) 18.
31. Andrews, *American Law* (1900) §§ 143.

keep and bear arms shall not be infringed"[32] and there are like provisions in the several state constitutions. But the bearing of arms by robbers, gangsters, and bandits has required legislation and one state has forbidden unauthorized bodies of men to drill or parade with arms or associate as a military organization.[33] Our leading nineteenth-century authority on the bills of rights wrote that he would not undertake to say how far it was in the power of the legislature to regulate the right which the constitutions say is not to be infringed.[34] It is perhaps noteworthy that totalitarian governments have fallen in the present century under pressure from without rather than from within.

Bills of rights are a characteristic feature of American constitutions. Beginning with the Virginia Bill of Rights of 1776, enacted immediately after the Declaration of Independence, they have been made a part of all our constitutions, state and federal. Our American bills of rights are prohibitions of government action infringing guaranteed rights, that is, guaranteed reasonable expectations involved in life in civilized society. They are laws, part of the Constitution as the supreme law of the land, enforceable in legal proceeding in the courts at suit of those whose rights are infringed or threatened. They are generically distinct from the declarations of rights on the model of the French Declaration of the Rights of Man which are to be found in constitutions outside the English-speaking world. These are mere preachments, declarations of good intentions or exhortations to governmental authority, legally binding on nobody and unenforceable by any one whose interests are infringed. But the service state is beginning to affect our conception of a bill of rights in America. In a recent proposal for a bill of rights for a world government[35] we get the Continental note in the very title, but

32. U.S. Const. Amendment II, ratified 1791.

33. *Commonwealth v. Murphy,* 166 Mass. 171 (1896).

34. Cooley, *Constitutional Limitations* (1871) chap. 10, last section (7 ed. 1903) 449.

35. American Bar Assn., Documents for Study in the 1949 Series of Regional Group Conferences of the American Bar Association under the Auspices of its Committee for Peace and Law Through United Nations (1949). *See also* Essential Human Rights, ANNALS OF THE AMERICAN ACADEMY OF POLITICAL AND SOCIAL SCIENCE (1946) vol. 243, 18–26.

also the note of the service state which is disinclined toward law. There is a declaration of a right of every one to claim for himself "release from the bondage of poverty." It is not that he is to be free to free himself from this bondage, but that the world political organization is to free him without his active help in the process. Also he is declared to have a right to claim reward and security according to his needs. But his claim to needs is likely to have few limits and is sure to conflict with the claims of others to like needs. Such declarations are not merely preachments, not enforceable and not intended to be enforced as law; they are invitations to plundering by rapacious majorities or pluralities quite as much as to rapacious personal sovereigns.

In a recent book[36] Professor Corwin has discussed the decadence of fear of oppression by government which has become very marked. Experience of absolute government by the Stuarts in seventeenth-century England and of government of the colonies from Westminster in seventeenth- and eighteenth-century America had made this fear a dominant consideration in our polity from the beginning until well into the present century. Growth of a feeling of the divine right of majorities, akin to that of the divine right of kings, has led of late to an assumption that concern about oppression by government is something we have outgrown. Yet distrust of an absolute majority or of an absolute plurality is as justified in reason and in experience as distrust of the absolute personal ruler. Indeed, the latter may be given pause by fear of an uprising which an intrenched majority need not fear.

It is characteristic of the service state to make lavish promises of satisfying desires and expectations by giving them the title of rights. If a bill of rights or a constitution declares a right of every individual to "just terms of leisure," the individual who reads it will think that just terms of leisure have not merely been provided him they have been guaranteed him. But those who draft it very likely do not ask themselves whether such a provision is or can be a law, a precept of the supreme law of the land, or only a preachment of policy which no court can enforce and no legislative body can be made to regard. Such preachments enfeeble a

36. Corwin, A *Constitution of Powers in a Secular State* (1951) 57 ff.

constitutional legal structure. As they are not and cannot be enforced, they lend themselves to a doctrine that constitutional provisions generally are not legally enforceable and may be disregarded at any time in the interest of political policy of the moment. Thus they lend themselves to the encroachments of the proponents of political absolutism. They weaken the constitution polity which we in America built up in our formative era.

Let us ask ourselves whether there is enough wealth in the world reachable by taxation by a world government, or even by confiscation by an absolute ruler of the world, to guarantee "just terms of leisure," supposing they could be fixed as an enforceable legal measure for every land and region, to the whole population of the world during life. A bill of rights is much more than a declaration of ideals. The bill of rights is a body of legal precepts binding on the courts and on the legislative and executive to the extent that enactments and executive action in contravention of them will not be recognized or given efficacy by the courts. A declaration of ideals may point out to legislative or executive what they ought to do. It may afford the courts a means of interpreting what is done by legislature or executive. But it will not enforce itself and there is no body with power to enforce it.

Setting forth such things in a constitutional declaration of guaranteed rights makes a farce of constitutions. How can a universal government release the whole world through a political-legal process "from the bondage of poverty"? What organ of government can be made to bring about that enough is produced and is continuously produced to insure plenty for every one (with guaranteed terms of leisure) everywhere? How can any court compel a legislature, an executive, or any individual or organization of individuals to bring this about? How can an executive or a legislature compel either or any one else to do it? The attempt of the Soviet regime to compel farmers to supply adequately the urban population of industrial laborers[37] shows what the most absolute of autocratic governments must do to realize such an ideal of enforced universal

37. *See* 1 Gsovski, *Soviet Civil Law* (1948) chaps. 20, 21.

plenty even for one land. Such pronouncements proceed upon a theory which used to be preached by social workers that law is a protest against wrong. Protests against wrong may be very effective in spurring law-makers to find remedies and enact laws making the remedies effective. But protests themselves lack the qualities of enforceability and the ma-chinery of enforcement which are demanded for a law in any advanced society.

A power to act toward a general equality of satisfaction of wants and a policy of developing such an equality as an ideal are something very dif-ferent from a provision in a bill of rights that a world government guar-antees to bring such a policy to immediate fruition. No one can seri-ously believe that in such time as we can now foresee even the western world can provide complete social security to its furthest extent to the whole and every part of itself. Is the whole world, much of which has al-ways been close to the brink of starvation, reasonably to be expected to do this?

I have spoken at some length of proposals for declarations of rights for a world organization because the propositions drafted by enthusiastic promoters of a world constitution have been followed in recent propos-als for constitution writing in the development of the service state in America. A state which endeavors through law to relieve its people of want and fear without being able to relieve its individual citizens of the many features of human makeup which lead to poverty and fear is at-tempting more than the miracles of science which has divided the indi-visible have been equal to. How can we expect a state to bring about complete satisfaction of all the wants and expectations of everybody in a world in which we all, potentially at least, want the earth and there is only one earth? I agree that we have a noble ideal. But can it be made an ideal element in a system of law? Guarantees which are no more than promissory declarations of policy can do little more than deceive. The service state is a politically organized society. It cannot, as could Baron Munchausen, pull itself up by its own long whiskers. This does not mean, however, that our American nineteenth-century bills of rights cannot be amended or supplemented to meet conditions of the urban industrial America of today or that they are necessarily a model for bills or declarations of rights elsewhere.

Promissory bills of rights, creating expectations of the legally unachieveable and weakening faith in constitutions as the law of the land are a step toward the totalitarian state. The strong selling point of that state is its argument that a strong man, a superman leader, can do what a government hindered by constitutional checks and balances and operating according to law cannot do. When a constitution declares as rights (presumably legal rights which may be realized by effective procedures) claims to be secured by a government which that government cannot secure, it invites centralization of power in an absolute government which professes ability to secure them. The service state, taking over all functions of public service, operating through bureaus with wide powers, and little effective limitation upon exercise of their powers, through government positions for a large and increasing proportion of the population, and through systematic official propaganda and a system of subsidies to education, science, and research, can easily be taking strides toward an absolute government, although under forms of democracy. Indeed, the extreme advocates of the service state insist that constitutional democracy is a contradiction in terms.[38] To them a democracy must be an unrestricted rule of the majority for the time being. The majority must be as absolute a ruler in all things as was the French king of the old regime or the Czar in the old regime in Russia. As the seventeenth century argued that a monarchy must in the nature of things be an absolute not a constitutional monarchy, on the same logical grounds it is argued that a democracy must be an absolute not a constitutional democracy.

General welfare service by the state, becoming service for strong aggressive groups or for politically powerful localities, has been the ladder by which absolute rulers have climbed to power and the platform on which they have been able to stay in power. Louis XIV held down France by holding down Paris by distribution of bread at the expense of

38. The Neo-Kantian left. *See* Pound, *Fifty Years of Jurisprudence* (1938) 51 HARVARD LAW REVIEW 444, 452, and notes 22–27.

the provinces. The Spanish monarchy long held itself in power by using the wealth of the New World for service to its subjects at home. Napoleon III used state workshops. Totalitarian Italy used the theory of the service rendered by the corporative state. Totalitarian Russia promises proletariat rule at the expense of the rest of the community. Indeed in antiquity the Roman emperor held down Italy by extortion of wheat from Egypt.

Since the first World War there has been a great deal of preaching and much promising as to the rights of minorities and of oppressed racial groups. But the lavish promises and administrative absolutism of the service superstate, with the absolute rule of majorities or even pluralities and of leaders in the name of majorities which they involve, are a menace to the guarantees that a constitution which is a legal document, not merely a frame of government promising welfare service which it cannot be made to perform, is able to give these groups. Experience seems to show that the attempt to make all men equal in all respects, instead of in their political and legal rights and capacities, is likely to make them more unequal than nature has made them already. Unless equality is given the practical meaning of the nineteenth-century American bills of rights, we are likely to be thrown back to a proposition that whether or not all men are born equal they are at any rate born equally.

There has been a tendency of men in all history to worship their rulers. In the society of today that takes the form of faith in absolute rule of the majority or, indeed, of the plurality for the time being. We forget that majority or plurality are only a practical way out when we cannot get entire agreement. The founders of our American polity, with long and bitter experience of absolute rule behind them, sought a government of checks and balances by which absolute rule by any one was precluded. As Mr. Justice Miller put it, in the centennial year of the American Revolution, the theory of American governments, state and national, is opposed to the deposit of unlimited power anywhere.[39] Mr. Justice Frankfurter repeated the proposition only the other day. His words were: "Not so long ago it was fashionable to find our system of

39. *Loan Association v. Topeka*, 20 Wallace (U.S.) 655, 663 (1875).

checks and balances obstructive to effective government. It was easy to ridicule that system as outmoded — too easy. The experience through which the world has passed in our own day has made vivid that the Framers of our Constitution were not inexperienced doctrinaires. These long-headed statesmen had no illusion that our people enjoyed biological or psychological or sociological immunities from the hazards of concentrated power. . . . The accretion of dangerous power does not come in a day. It does come, however slowly, from the generative force of unchecked disregard of the restrictions that fence in even the most disinterested assertion of authority."[40]

It is worth while to recall what brought forth Mr. Justice Miller's pronouncement. State legislation had imposed a tax for a subsidy to a particular private manufacturing enterprise. That was rejected as arbitrary and unreasonable in 1875. But in the service state of today expensive service to some at the expense of others is regarded as a service to the public, as indeed it may be in some cases, and this tempts aggressive groups to obtain legislation providing service to them for which others must pay. A group of this sort easily in its own mind identifies itself with the public. Obviously the conception of public service needs to be carefully defined and limited if we are to avoid being led into absolute rule by majority or plurality.

A government which regards itself, under pretext of extending a general welfare service to the public, entitled to rob Peter to pay Paul, and is free from constitutional restraints upon legislation putting one element or group of the people for the whole, has a bad effect on the general morale. If government is a device for benevolent robbery, a would-be Robin Hood of today is not likely to see why his benevolently conceived activities are reprehensible. Based on colonial experience of legislation imposing burdens on some for the benefit of others rather than of the public, the older American state constitutions and substantially all state constitutions in the nineteenth century, forbade special or class legislation. The omission of this provision from recent state constitutions is significant. No doubt the restriction in the nineteenth-

40. Frankfurter, J., in *Youngstown Co. v. Sawyer,* 343 U.S. 579, 593–94 (1952).

century constitutions was applied too rigidly and was at times made to stand in the way of proper welfare legislation. But entire omission points to a feeling that government is devised and intended to be unfair and even oppressive to minorities and that there should be no limit to the ability of organized groups to make their fellow men pay for special service to them.

A service state must be highly bureaucratic. Bureaus are characteristically zealous to get everything in reach under their control. Would it be a high public service to set up a bureau of psychologists to examine us for our aptitudes and assign us whether we like it or not to the calling for which they find us fitted? Before the advent of psychologists such a state was argued for by Greek philosophers. The later Eastern Roman empire stabilized society by putting and keeping men in callings somewhat in this way. An omnicompetent state postulates omnicompetent bureaus. Why in the perfect all-regulating state allow human energy to be wasted by permitting individuals to engage in futile efforts to employ themselves in callings in which they cannot succeed? Is that the next step after subsidizing them in callings in which they are failing and bound to fail?

Perhaps I have said enough to show that the authoritarian path, indicated by the service state, leads away from law. It is true the Soviet polity gave up the Marxian "withering away of law." But what it kept and developed was not law but laws, rules attaching definite detailed consequences to definite detailed states of fact, applied in the administrative manner. At any rate, the authoritarian path leads away from a legal order maintained by a judicial process adjusting relations and ordering conduct by applying according to a received traditional technique authoritative models or patterns of decision. Social control through politically organized society is made a regime of force, not a regime of reason.

Kelsen has argued the identity of state and law, saying that the State is a normative ordering co-extensive with the normative ordering of the system of law.[41] But if we say that the legal order and the political or-

41. Kelsen, *Reine Rechtslehre* (1934) chap. 8.

ganization of a society are co-extensive does that make them identical? Although the services now performed by the state must have the force exerted through the legal order behind them to make them possible, are those services generically like the adjustment of relations and ordering of conduct through systematic employment of the force of the organization? Most of the states of the United States have established state universities. But they compel no one to go there or to teach there, and do not even prescribe what shall be taught or how it shall be taught. Only by holding that whatever officials do is law and that the state, too, is what officials do can it be maintained that all political action is legal. Certainly it is not all compulsion. The building of the Hoover Dam on the Colorado River or the transfer of voluntary immigrants to Alaska from the wheat-raising states during an agricultural depression were not applying threats of state force to specified acts. Seeking to get rid of the idea of the state, Kelsen thinks of the aggregate of the threats of application of the force of politically organized society to individuals in particular situations and on particular states of fact as a unity not to be distinguished into fact and law. This is one way of meeting the question whether we are to say the state postulates the law or the law postulates the state, which Vinogradoff tells us it is idle to argue.[42] Perhaps in Kelsen's pure science of law, for a purely juristic analytical theory, we can ignore the side of politically organized society which renders services other than maintaining the legal order. In Anglo-American law those through whom the services are performed do so subject to scrutiny of the courts and subject to liability for injuries done in performing them otherwise than within their powers and in the legally appointed way. But if we adopt the threat theory of a law are we bound to say that everything which is brought about directly or indirectly by the threats is to be held law?

In connection with the authoritarian path it remains to say something about the corporative state,[43] of which we heard much in the third and

42. 2 Vinogradoff, *Collected Papers* (1928) 357–60.
43. For the juristic doctrine and bibliography *see* Pound, *Fifty Years of Jurisprudence* (1938) 51 HARVARD LAW REVIEW 777, 782–83.

fourth decades of the present century. For the present purpose its significant feature was that the unit was the occupational group, not the individual human being. The idea of occupations as a political unit was
not new. There was something like it in representation of estates in the
Middle Ages. It had been urged by writers on philosophical politics and
theory of the state in the nineteenth century.[44] In America, Calhoun argued for something very like this. "There are," he wrote, "two different
modes in which the sense of the community may be taken; one simply
by the right of suffrage unaided, the other by the right through a proper
organism. Each collects the sense of the majority. But one regards numbers only and regards the whole community as a unit having but one
common interest throughout and collects the sense of the greater number of the whole as that of the community. The other, on the contrary,
regards interest as well as numbers, considering the community as made
up of different and conflicting interests, so far as the action of the government is concerned, and takes the sense of each through its majority
or appropriate organ, and the united sense of all as the sense of the entire community. The former I shall call the numerical or absolute majority; and the latter the concurrent or constitutional majority."[45] There
is something like this in the sociological view of society as made up of
groups and associations and relations.[46] Thus we have three possible
units for the securing of interests: We may look only at the collectivity
and think of them in terms of a politically organized society, or we may
look only at occupational groups as summing up the interests of its
members, or, as the law has done, we may look at the individual human
being and the claims and demands and expectations he urges. Often to
procure a hearing for them he will identify them with those of the
public. But at bottom they are his and he will not be satisfied unless they

44. Hegel, *Grundlinien der Philosophie des Rechts* (1821) § 308; 2 Stahl, *Die Philosophie des Rechts* (5 ed. 1878) §§ 96–100, especially 320–22; 1 Bluntschli, *Allgemeine
Staatslehre* (6 ed. 1886) 552–54.

45. Calhoun, *Disquisition on Government* (1848–49) in 1 *Works* (New York ed. 1854)
28.

46. Ehrlich, *Fundamental Principles of the Sociology of Law* (transl. by Moll, 1936)
chap. 1.

are weighed as he understands and urges them. The task of the law is to adjust relations and order conduct as claims and expectations are actually urged and press for recognition.

After all the social unit in the modern world is the individual human being. Recognition of his moral worth was the great achievement of eighteenth- and nineteenth-century juristic and political philosophy. Appreciation of the social interest in the individual life is the significant achievement of the social philosophy of the present generation. It is not likely that any economic order which may supervene in such time as we can foresee will bring about a legal order which can succeed in ignoring him.

If what I have called the path of liberty has ended or is to end in a blind alley, and if the humanitarian path is but a detour leading the law into the authoritarian path, the Marxian prophecy of the disappearance of law in the ideal society of the future is likely to be fulfilled. But I am unwilling to subscribe to the give-it-up philosophy that leads to this result. Instead I have faith that what was found for civilization while law was treading the path of liberty will not be lost. We shall not make a wholly new start in the humanitarian path. That path will not be a mere bypass to the authoritarian path. The path of the future will find a broader objective in the direction indicated by the humanitarian path. It will find a sure starting point where the path of liberty has seemed to end and will go forward to a fuller development of human powers in what may prove to be a path of civilization. What has been worked out by experience and reason for the adjustment of relations and ordering of conduct toward the satisfaction of human claims and demands and expectations from the classical Roman jurists to the twentieth-century codes, from the King's Hall of Henry II to the Royal Courts of Justice of Victoria, from the courts of the American colonies to the constitutional system of American courts of today, is not to be wholly lost. Out of it, as the law pursues a broader and straighter path of civilization, should come a law of another great age of the law such as were the Roman classical era from Augustus to Alexander Severus, and the maturity of the civil law in Continental Europe, and of the common law in the English-speaking world in the nineteenth century.

Epilogue

It may well be asked why in lecturing in India upon a general topic of the science of law I have gone so much into American experience, cited American decisions, state and federal, so extensively and devoted so much space to legal problems with which courts and legislators and jurists have dealt in America. This certainly calls for explanation if not, I hope, for apologizing.

You have, I take it, in India a like problem to that which obtained in the formative era of American law. We in America had to work out from our inherited English common law of the seventeenth and eighteenth centuries a general body of American common law for what was to be a politically and economically unified land of continental extent but a federal union of locally self-governing states. In India you have a like task before you of working out a common law for a land of imperial dimensions, of local diversities of race, custom, religion and history, on the basis of the English law of the nineteenth century, both codified and in the form of judicial decision, and of Anglo-Indian declaratory promulgation and judicial and doctrinal exposition of your historical customary law. It will be, I take it, a general common law, with much allowance for local, social, economic, political, and historical conditions, much as an American common law had to be in the United States. But it must be a homemade law of India, even if made, largely at least, from the received English materials, as American common law had to be. As Mr. Justice Holmes said, historical continuity is not a duty, but it is a necessity.

In the nineteenth century the historical jurists held that law was a product of the spirit of a people, not something made for a people from without. As Savigny put it: "Stated summarily . . . [the correct view] is that all law arises in the manner which the prevailing (though not wholly accurate) usage calls 'customary law.' That is, it is produced by custom and popular belief and then through course of judicial decision, hence, above all, through silent inner forces, and not through the arbitrary will of a lawmaker."[1]

That Savigny's proposition is not universally valid is shown by the spread of the French Civil Code to twenty-three countries, one state of the United States, and one Canadian province between 1804 and 1889, and the taking over of the German Code by Japan in 1898 and by China in 1930. But in the Central and South American states which substantially adopted the French Civil Code, it was necessary to take on quickly a body of law where there had been no such political and economic development as to require much law in distinction from particular laws. In truth, the Latin American states started from adaptations of the French Civil Code as we in the United States started from the seventeenth-century English law. Also Japan and China had their real legal development ahead of them and needed an immediate basis on which to proceed. The kernel of the historical doctrine is sound. A body of law to govern a people must be a law adapted to that people, expressing its ideals and rooted in its history.

In India you have had some two centuries of development of a body of Anglo-Indian law by legislation and judicial decision—a much fuller development than we in America had had at our independence. But you have a like task of making a law of your own in your own way on the basis of that development.

No more can be claimed for so full a presentation of American doctrine and American experience than that perchance it may be of some value in India by way of illustration of how a similar task to your own was

1. Savigny, *Vom Beruf unsrer Zeit für Gesetzgebung und Rechtswissenschaft* (3 ed. 1840) 13–14.

achieved. It may at any rate show that a land newly arrived at independence may build a law of its own largely upon English materials adjusted to its economic, social, political and geographical conditions and needs.

You in India will not have the same problems in detail. You will have to meet different conditions. But you will be guided, as we were, by a quest of justice as the ideal relation among men and will have to give content to that ideal with reference to your own conditions and your own experience. How we strove to do that in America and with what results may at least suggest some warnings. At all events, the way in which the task has been achieved through ideals by one free people may justify consideration by another free people confronted with a like task.

Glossary

Adgnati. In general, those who are related by blood to a particular father. Roman law was particularly concerned with the degrees of relationship to the father, a consideration in modern law called consanguinity. More specifically, *adgnati* also means those younger children born after a father has written a will, and Pound is alluding to the problem of the law's recognizing or failing to recognize the injustice of a child's loss of an inheritance as a result only of a father's failure to amend the will before death. (146 n. 14)

Adverse user. Now called "adverse use" or "hostile enjoyment," which under certain circumstances entitles a person using an easement over land without title or permission eventually to hold legal title to the use of the easement through the doctrine of "prescription": the person used the easement until the landholder who might have sued to eject, or to bar the person from using the easement, had allowed the statute of limitations to expire. (73)

Aequum et bonum. That which is right and just; a standard according to which a judge is to determine a dispute according to general principles of equity and fairness. This phrase developed in Roman law and is still used in equity and in international law, particularly for settling boundary disputes. (149)

Agnates. The same as *adgnati.* (72)

Agnation. Kinship through the father's bloodline. See *adgnati.* (44)

Bonae fidei. In general, "in good faith." In the sense of actions, an action brought without collusion or fraud but with an honest belief in the rightful entitlement to legal relief. In the sense of judgments, *ex fide bona* is the term by which a judge may give equitable relief to grant a just remedy that would not otherwise be allowed by the technical limits of a law. (86 n. 59)

Prepared by Steve Sheppard, University of Arkansas School of Law

Boni mores. In general, "good morals." In Roman law, obligations arising from morals or honor that may be enforced by law, either through additions to the civil law or through equitable decrees, called the *ius honorarium.* (71)

Cognation. Kinship through the mother's bloodline. See *adgnati.* (44)

Collegium. A college, particularly a school operating under a charter allowing it the privilege of setting the rules of conduct for its members. (147 n. 19)

Composition. The resolution of a dispute through payment of a settlement, based on the nature of the injury and the status of the person injured. An old Germanic concept that has survived in modern law primarily through the method by which a debtor privately settles all debts with all outstanding creditors by making partial payments. (145)

Corpus juris. Originally the books of law collected under Justinian, between A.D. 529 and 565: the *Codex Constitutionum,* or the code of constitutional law; the *Digest* (also known as the *Pandects*), the collection of precedents from earlier decisions; the *Institutes,* or summary of the whole for students; and the *Novels,* or laws made after the collection. In the sense used by Justice Holmes here, it refers merely to the whole body of law. (120)

Damnum iniuria datum. A *delict,* or a wrong actionable under Roman law, for causing an injury by wrongdoing, whether the wrongdoing was intentional or negligent; usually brought for property damage. (325)

Delictal. Relating to a *delict,* or a wrong actionable under Roman law; particular conduct for which a person harmed thereby may sue to recover for injuries that result from it. In the modern sense here, Pound refers to the relationship between a person who commits a tort, or private wrong, and the person who is wronged. (89 n. 67)

Demos. Although usually translated as "the people," the phrase in ancient Greek more specifically means the lower or most common classes of the citizenry; from it came the mob. (159)

Dicasts. Members of a *dicastery* in ancient Athens, after 508 B.C. Roughly six thousand Athenian male citizens were chosen by lottery as *dicasts,* sitting in panels of five hundred for trials of public law or two hundred for matters of private law. Verdicts were by majority vote. (37)

Dolus. Fraud, or intent to deceive. A concept of Roman law still used in modern civil law. (91)

Dominium. The right of ownership in every aspect over some form of property, particularly in civil law. Pound relates most of the categories of *dominium* from the *Institutes*, so that dominion includes *ius possidendi, ius utendi, ius disponendi, ius abutendi, ius fruendi,* and *ius prohibendi,* which is to say the ability lawfully to possess the property, to make use of it, to dispose of it, to consume it, to reap profits from it, and to bar others from the property. (111)

Familia. Literally, "the family"; under Roman law, the whole community subject to the authority of the *paterfamilias,* who was responsible for the conduct of all of his dependants, including his slaves. (146 n. 14)

Fas. That which is permitted under divine law; right conduct. (71)

Frankpledge. The system instituted in early Norman England to ensure the keeping of the peace, requiring every man over the age of twelve to enroll in a *fiborh,* or group of ten men, each of whom pledged to stand as bail for each of the others to appear when summoned to court. (273)

Furtum. Theft, according to Roman law. (325)

Gens. Although *"gens"* ordinarily refers to all people, or at least all the people who were not Roman, in the sense that Pound is using it here it refers to the clans of Romans including all of the families descended from one *paterfamilias.* (147 n. 19)

Gentiles. Generally, a particular people, sometimes the "other people" as in the case of those who are not Roman, not Jewish, etc. In the sense of Roman law used here, however, it refers to the members of any single *gens.* (72)

Iniuria. Generally, in Roman law, any wrongful conduct. As Pound notes, here he means "injury to the physical person or to honor." In such cases, *iniuria* included a range of acts that under modern law would include slander, libel, defamation, battery, and rape. (325)

Interpleader. A special form of action under the modern common law, allowed by statutes and now codified in Federal Rule of Civil Procedure 22, in which a party that is aware of its liability to either of two or more parties may initiate a lawsuit to determine to whom it is liable and to extinguish its liability to the other possible claimants against it. (266)

Ius. The law. *Ius* is often contrasted with *lex* or *leges,* which are the laws. *Ius* is the law in its broadest sense or ideal state. It is above and largely unaffected by the contingent statutes or other laws that the state happens to enact, which are the *leges.* From this difference arise the English terms "justice" and "legislation." This division remains common in civil law through various terms and is continued in the law of the United States, as in the Fourteenth Amendment of the United States Constitution, which distinguishes "due process of law" as in *ius* from "equal protection of the laws" as in *leges*. (33)

Ius abutendi. One of the attributes of *dominium*, or ownership, usually conceived of as the right or power to consume a thing owned, if it is capable of consumption. Pound uses it to illustrate the sense of *dominium* that corresponds to liberty in the sense of an immunity from interference by others under the law, as opposed to a power or a right. (112)

Ius ciuile (civile). In Roman law, the laws that resulted from statutes and decrees governing the citizenry, particularly as elaborated by the commentators of Roman law. Pound is particularly concerned with the distinction between *ius civile* and *ius gentium* employed by Gaius, according to which the *ius civile* is the law that applied only to Roman citizens and not between foreigners or between Romans and foreigners, who were governed by the *ius gentium*. (33 n. 5)

Ius disponendi. One of the attributes of *dominium*, or ownership, usually conceived of as the right or power to dispose of a thing owned. Pound uses it to illustrate the sense of *dominium* that corresponds to liberty in the sense of an immunity from interference by others under the law, as opposed to a power or a right. (112)

Ius fruendi. Another of the attributes of *dominium*, or ownership, in that one who has *dominium* has the right or power to reap fruits or profits, as by harvesting crops or taking rents from the property. Pound uses it to illustrate the sense of *dominium* that corresponds to liberty in the sense of an immunity from interference by others under the law, as opposed to a power or a right. (112)

Ius gentium. This term had a variety of meanings. In early Roman law, it is the law that is followed by all peoples, and so it is closely akin to the *ius naturale*. From this universal sense, it was also used more specifically to describe the international law that governed Rome's relationship with other states. Following the works of Gaius, the term was employed more narrowly to represent the law that applied between foreigners and between Romans and foreigners. Foreigners, and the legal relations of Romans with them, were governed by the *ius gentium*. (39)

Ius naturae. Literally, "the law of nature." In Roman law, very nearly a synonym for *ius naturale*; it is a law that is supported by natural reason, and so it is a law that is, or ought to be, respected by the laws of all nations. Thus, the *ius natu-*

rae was said to support the *ius gentium* in its universal sense, but even this relationship is not always congruent: famously, in the introduction to Justinian's *Institutes*, slavery is forbidden by nature but allowed by the *ius gentium*. Even so, there was the general sense, seized on increasingly from Roman writings throughout the Renaissance and early modern age, that the object of civil law was to reflect the obligations of natural law, especially when natural law required freedom. (44)

Ius naturale or, as the Roman jurist Ulpian said, "that which nature taught all animals." For most writings of classical Roman law, it is synonymous with *ius naturae*. From the writings of Paul, however, the term *ius naturale* acquired the sense of an ideal of law, *quod semper est bonum et aequum*, or that which is always fair and just. It is this sense that is followed in the Thomist conceptions of natural law, or *lex naturalis*. (39)

Ius possidendi. One of the attributes of *dominium*, or ownership, in that one who has *dominium* has the right or power to possess the property. Pound uses it to illustrate the sense of *dominium* that corresponds to liberty in the sense of a right against all others to act to make the interest effective or to forbear from interfering. (111)

Ius prohibendi. Another of the attributes of *dominium*, or ownership, in that one who has *dominium* has the right or power to prohibit others from using the property, whether by possession alone or by growing or harvesting crops or using or taking rents from the property. Pound uses it to illustrate the sense of *dominium* that corresponds to liberty in the sense of a right against all others to act to make the interest effective or to forbear from interfering. (112)

Ius strictum. A very rare term in the materials of classical Roman law, *ius strictum*, or the strict law, is really a Byzantine term, and it occurs in Justinian's *Institutes* in reference to the strict actions of the law, primarily to describe the rigid limitations of the forms of action available under the law, particularly the older laws. The term is often used by later commentators, as it is here by both Jhering and Pound, to distinguish it from the moderating influence of the praetors, or judges who expanded the law through actions *ex fide bona*, or what we would now call equity. (148 n. 20)

Ius utendi. Another of the attributes of *dominium*, or ownership, in that one who has *dominium* has the right or power to use the property, particularly by residing there. Pound uses it to illustrate the sense of *dominium* that corresponds to liberty in the sense of an immunity from interference by others under the law, as opposed to a power or a right. (112)

Jurisconsult. The jurist; *jurisconsulti* were the great scholars of the law. While they were consulted for opinions on particular matters of law in specific cases, their primary influence was through law books collecting and commenting on earlier laws, which had great significance as sources of law in themselves. Although there were many jurisconsults and many more people wrote laws and books about laws, from the *decimvirs* who wrote the Twelve Tables to the last emperors to issue decrees, the technical training and role of the *jurisconsulti* have limited their ranks to a handful of great names whose books are meant here by Muirhead and Pound: Mucius and Sabinus, *circa* 100 B.C. and 1 A.D. respectively; Julian and Pedius, *circa* A.D. 100; the great Gaius, *circa* 150; the classical-era trio of the 220s, Papinian, Paul, and Ulpian; and lastly Justinian's brilliant minister, Tribonian, who oversaw the creation of the *Corpus Iuris* in the early sixth century. (33)

Laesio enormis. Literally, "great injury." A description of merchandise bought for less than half its real value. Pound is following Justice Story's use of the doctrine to illustrate the gradually more technical and less flexible development of legal doctrines in general. Originally, the praetors would allow an unwitting buyer who had been unjustly dealt with by a merchant to have the option of rescinding the sale or securing a better price; by the time of Justinian, this rule required that the price vary at least fifty percent from market value. (151)

Law merchant. The laws governing the transactions between merchants. It was originally a medieval body of customs that evolved among merchants and guilds, with little regard to the limitations imposed by national borders and laws. Over time, national laws both incorporated and enforced these customs, often by name. (53)

Leges. The laws. *Lex*, the singular, or *leges* in the plural, is often contrasted with *ius*, the law in its broadest sense or most ideal state. *Lex* is the law that the state happens to enact as statutes, decrees, rules, or specific obligations on individuals at any given time. In sum these are the *leges*. From this difference arise the English terms "legislation" and "justice." This division remains common in civil law through various terms and is continued in the law of the United States, as in the Fourteenth Amendment of the United States Constitution, which distinguishes "due process of law" as in *ius* from "equal protection of the laws" as in *leges*. (33)

Leges sacratae. Technically in Roman law, laws for which the penalty was to be outlawed, or exiled. One who was a *sacer homo* was beyond the protection of the law, and so anyone could kill him without violating the law. Thus, whatever protection he had was not civil but was divine. *Sacratio* was among the earliest penalties and was given against those who violated institutions under divine protection, such as moving boundary stones, violating the obligations of a patron to a client, and, most importantly, harming a plebeian tribune. Pound's recitation of the *sacer esto* refers back to his discussion of excommunication. (144)

Lex aeterna. A Thomist division of divine natural law. St. Thomas Aquinas, in the *Summa Theologica*, divided natural law into a hierarchy, at the top of which is the eternal law known only to God and which is designed to govern the affairs of the universe. Thus, *ius naturale* included both the *lex aeterna*, known only to God, and the *lex naturalis*, which was derived from the *lex aeterna* but which was designed to govern the affairs of mankind, and which was knowable through the tools of reason. (45)

Lex Iunia. As used here, Pound appears to refer to the *lex Iunia Norbana*, enacted in A.D. 19, which allowed slaves who had been improperly manumitted to be free, rather than being returned to slavery as a result of error in the process of their manumission. Pound may have confused his title, *Lex Iunia*, as this was the title of a decree a century later expelling foreigners who pretended to be Roman citizens. Pound further seems unaware that, under the law of A.D. 19, the freedman lost an essential privilege that had been granted on a case-by-case basis by praetors acting equitably to cure defective manumissions before the decree. The manumitted did not become citizens, but *Latini Iuniani*, and so they could neither receive nor grant property by will, giving their former owners a continuing power over them. (73)

Lex naturae. As Pound uses it, a general term synonymous with *lex naturalis*. (160)

Lex naturalis. A Thomist division of earthly natural law. St. Thomas Aquinas, in the *Summa Theologica*, divided natural law into a hierarchy, the penultimate level of which is the natural law created by God to govern the affairs of mankind, and to be reflected in the positive laws enacted by human governments. Thus, *ius naturale* included both the *lex aeterna*, known only to God and meant to govern the universe, and the *lex naturalis*, which was derived from the *lex aeterna* but which was designed to govern the affairs of mankind, and which was knowable through the tools of reason. (45)

Mala in se. Wrong in itself; one of the great divisions of criminal wrong. From Aristotle to the modern law, the criminal law has recognized a difference between acts that are criminal because they are inherently wrong, such as murder, and those that are only technically wrong, such as driving on the wrong side of the road. Acts that are *mala in se* are said to be evil in themselves. (39)

Mala prohibita. Wrong as prohibited; the other division from *mala in se.* The wrongdoing of these acts is the result of choices made by lawmakers for the welfare of the populace. The classic example is the wrong of driving on the improper side of the road. It is only the result of a legislative choice that requires drivers in the United States to drive in the right lane of a two-way street. Even so, the public welfare required one or the other to be the choice, and the driver who ignores this choice commits a wrong that endangers the populace. It is this blurring of the nature of the wrong as inherent (is not driving on the wrong side of the road inherently wrong?) from the technical (is not driving on the right side only required by law and not nature?) that Pound finds unsatisfactory. (39)

Naturalis obligatio. The legal enforcement of a debt or other obligation, even if the creditor could not bring a direct action at law against the debtor. A number of mechanisms evolved over time to allow the enforcement of these natural obligations in specific circumstances. (45)

Naturalis ratio. Natural reason, or justification based on the nature of things. Gaius asserted that *ius naturae* and, more importantly, the law of all people, *ius gentium,* could be ascertained through the *naturalis ratio.* (43)

Nuda pacta. Informal, legally unenforceable bargains. *Nudum pactum* is the singular; *nuda pacta* the plural. Usually, only *contractio, stipulatio,* or similarly formal commercial undertakings were enforceable, but, as Pound notes, Redoanus points out that citizens could sometimes bring actions under these agreements against money changers and merchants. (48 n. 58)

Pedis possessio. Literally, possession actually performed on land. An old description of actual possession as a requirement for adverse possession. Sometimes actual possession under this title required enclosure by a fence. A person who actually held land for a sufficient period, under a claim of right or in opposition to all others' rights to the land, in open and notorious use, would be the legal owner even against the person who had earlier held title in the land, once the time had expired under the statute of limitations by which the titleholder could sue the actual possessor for trespass or for ejectment. Pound is using the settled custom for miners who had been in actual possession of their claims to have the strongest claim of ownership as a compelling reason for the government to recognize title in their holdings, rather than trying to impose a later regime upon them. (113)

Precatory trust. A trust created in a last will and testament requesting that a survivor of the testator perform some action, particularly a grant of property to one person, asking that it be used for some person's or entity's benefit or given to someone else. There was a considerable evolution of doctrine in determining whether the legatee under the will was bound to the terms of the will, and many technical rules were created and then abandoned in the effort to determine whether the words of the will were mandatory or not. Pound is using the story to illustrate evolution in a single doctrine in the law. (151)

Pretorian law (praetorian law). Roman equity. This is the sum of changes in law introduced by the praetors, who had the power to create relief through decree, even in the absence of a prior law. Subsequent praetors would re-enact the decrees of their predecessors, and these decrees were usually reflected in legal materials over time, particularly in the *Corpus Iuris*. (149)

Rapina. Robbery. A *delict* within the forms of *furtum*, or theft, committed by the taking of movable goods in acts accompanied by violence. (325)

Regum. Literally, "of the monarch." Pound is quoting Holmes for the idea that the final justification for not only private actions but also acts of states is nothing more or less than force. (120)

Res communes. Property held in common. When two or more people each have an interest in a single property, it is held in common. Pound is emphasizing that each of the property holders has a duty to the others not to waste or destroy the property for that holder's single benefit. (155)

Res nullius. Property held by no one, such as abandoned property, wild animals, and uninhabited, unclaimed land. Any person may acquire ownership in it by being the first to take possession of it, *occupatio*. Pound is emphasizing that there were limits on what may be occupied in this way, as there had been since Roman law, when property that was sacred to the gods was exempt from *occupatio*. (155)

Respondeat superior. The obligation of a superior to answer for the acts of an inferior by making good wrongs done by the inferior and, in certain cases, by being held to have knowledge held by the inferior or held to accept agreements made on the superior's behalf. This relationship is particularly recognized by the common law in a principal for an agent, an employer for an employee, or a parent for a child. (98)

Seisin. The form of possession of land with the intent to hold it as a freehold, which is to say that the land is now held by an owner who is not leasing it from someone else. This medieval idea of seisin as immediate possession originated in the ceremonies, called "livery of seisin," in which a new holder of the land was invested with all of the duties that the feudal system demanded of the land-holder of that particular estate, including duties to perform services for the overlord (such as raising troops, maintaining roads, and providing goods to the overlord); he was also given the right to claim services from the tenants (such as service as a soldier, or giving some number of days to road repair, or some percentage of one's harvest to the landholder). The modern concept of "delivery" is a descendant of this idea. (73)

Senatus consulta. Decrees of the Roman senate issued in answer to questions put to it by the consuls, praetors, tribunes, or other high magistrates. Pound is illustrating the propensity for the typical *consultum* not to be known by its name or for its effects but to be important as a part of a body of law, particularly as integrated into the texts of the jurisconsults. (32)

Subsidium (singular), *subsidia* (plural). Literally, assistance or support or a subsidy; the terms in law refer to the actions that might be created through equitable recognition that a person, who has no other legal remedy, would sustain a loss as a result of another's actions. (8)

Sui heredes. Those who are heirs of a dead person, and who succeed to the powers, assets, and liabilities left by the decedent. (146 n. 14)

Sui juris. A person in his legal capacity. The term has a variety of applications, particularly to mean someone with no legal incapacity, such as a person unburdened by insanity or extreme age or youth. Pound here seems to employ the term in both its Roman sense as someone empowered by law to act for themselves and in its common-law sense of someone who is not insane. (86)

Suum cuique. In full, *suum cuique tribuere*, to give every person what is due. One of the three Roman principles of justice in private conduct. The other two were to live honestly and to harm nobody. (184)

Tortfeasor. Any person who commits a tort, which is a wrong that is subject to a private recovery in law by the person injured. The tortfeasor must make good the injuries of the person injured. (330)

Trespass de bonis. An old common-law action for the recovery of stolen goods, brought by the owner against whoever unlawfully carried them off. (73)

Trover. An old common-law action for payment of damages in compensation for the theft of goods, brought by the owner against whoever converted the property or treated it in a way to interfere with the owner's possession or interest in it. (73)

Ultima ratio. The most fundamental justification, the final reasoning. (120)

Ultra vires. Beyond the powers, particularly of a corporation. A corporation is created under a charter to perform certain acts and to pursue certain goals using certain means. Under modern corporate law in the common-law system, a contract or promise by a person on behalf of a corporation that is beyond the limits of the charter is void and unenforceable. (230 n. 1)

Usufructuary. In civil law, a usufruct is the right of one person to use or enjoy the property owned by another person. The usufructuary is the person with the right to use, and Pound is indicating that there are obligations upon the usufructuary to protect the property for the ultimate benefit of the owner. The modern common-law equivalent is personal servitude. (86)

Vice-principal doctrine. A modern, if now largely altered, rule of agency in the determination of what liability a principal has for an agent. When a person entrusts to another the whole of the duty to supervise, as when a business owner delegates all of the decisions in the business or a department of it to a deputy, the deputy is considered a vice-principal, and not an agent or an employee, and the master is liable for the vice-principal's negligence as if the master had committed it. The doctrine was invented to moderate the nineteenth-century limits on *respondeat superior* and other legal barriers to liability of an owner for harmful acts by an employee. In our age of greater liability of businesses for their employees, the result that Pound is arguing toward in this passage, the vice-principal doctrine has become largely a dead letter. (271)

Wergeld (also wergild, weregild, or weregilt). Blood money. The price paid by someone who committed grave crimes to the victim or, in the event of homicide, to the survivors. The concept seems to have become formalized in early medieval Germany, although most medieval states had standards for the appropriate payment due, which usually turned on the status of the criminal, as the payment was a surrogate for the earlier right of the victim or survivors to have him killed. Pound is using the idea to illustrate one stage in the evolution of the law toward a mature understanding of criminal fines and penalties. (173)

Bibliography of Works Cited

Abbot, Justice and the Modern Law, (1913) / 197

Acton, Lord, Lectures on Modern History, (1906) / 187

Adams, The Origin of the English Constitution, (1905) / 174

Adams, Brooks, Law Under Inequality, Monopoly, (Lecture 2 in *Centralization and the Law*, 1906) / 119, 214, 263, 264

———. The Modern Conception of Animus, (1906) 19 Green Bag, 12 / 263

———. Nature of Law, (Lecture 1 in *Centralization and the Law*, 1906) / 119, 214, 263, 264

———. Theory of Social Revolutions, (1913) / 216

Adler, The Conception of Social Welfare, Proceedings of the Conference on Legal and Social Philosophy, (1913) / 217, 241

Affolter, Das römische Institutionensystem, (1897) / 161

Ahrens, Cours de droit naturel, (1837, 8 ed. 1892) / 56, 76, 109, 203, 205, 236

———. Naturrecht oder Philosophie des Rechts und des Staats, (6 ed. 1870) / 70

Allen, Law in the Making, (5 ed. 1951) / 16, 27

Althusius, Johannes, Politica methodice digesta atque exemplis sacris et profanis illustrata, (1603, translated with introduction by Friedrich, 1932) / 166, 169

Ames, Cases on Torts / 325

———. Law and Morals, (1908) 22 Harvard Law Review, 97 / 93, 116, 326

———. The Negotiable Instruments Law, (1902) 14 Harvard Law Review, 442 / 195

Amos, S., Science of Law, (2 ed. 1874) / 5, 81, 95, 128

———. Systematic View of the Science of Jurisprudence, (1871) / 19, 258

The lists of Acts, Reports, Proceedings, etc., and Publications of Various Organizations begin on p. 412.

Bartolus, The Conflict of Laws, (transl. by Beale) (1914) / 24

Baty, Vicarious Liability, (1916) / 98, 271

Baudry-Lacantinerie, Précis de droit civil, (12 ed. 1919) / 83, 84, 326, 343

Beale, Conflict of Laws, (1935) / 110

———. The Creation of the Relation of Carrier and Passenger, (1906) 39 HARVARD LAW REVIEW, 250 / 243

Bentham, Jeremy, Introduction to the Principles of Morals and Legislation, (Clarendon Press ed. 1876) / 76, 94, 118, 119

———. Principles of Legislation, (1865) / 128

———. Principles of Morals and Legislation, (1780, 1879 ed.) Works, (Bowring ed. 1843, 1898) / 1, 8, 27, 74, 130, 132, 206, 262, 290

———. Rationale of Judicial Evidence (1827) / 130

———. Theory of Legislation, Principles of the Civil Code, (transl. by Hildreth, 5 ed. 1885, new ed. 1931) / 94, 128, 152, 153, 206, 209

Berman, Employer's Liability, (1931) 3 ENCYCLOPEDIA OF THE SOCIAL SCIENCES, 515 / 270

Berolzheimer, System der Rechts- und Wirtschaftsphilosophie, (1905), (translated by Jastrow as The World's Legal Philosophies, 1912) / 2, 156, 159, 166, 178, 187, 188, 206, 216, 264

See 3 ARCHIV FUR RECHTS UND WIRTSCHAFTSPHILOSOPHIE, 195 / 236

Beseler, Volksrecht und Juristenrecht, (1843) / 166

Betteridge, 28 CRIMINAL APPEAL REPORT, 171 (1942) / 95

Beudant, Le droit individuel et l'état, (1 ed. 1898, 3 ed. 1926) / 78, 206

Bible, The, Eph. / 159

Peter / 159

St. Paul's Epistle to Philemon / 159

Bierling, Juristische Prinzipienlehre, (1884) / 109

Bigelow, Torts, (1889) / 327

Bigelow and others — Centralization and the Law

Lecture 1 — Nature of Law by Brooks Adams / 263, 264

Lecture 2 — Law Under Inequality, Monopoly / 263, 264

Billington, 28 CRIMINAL APPEAL REPORT, 180 (1942) / 95

Binder, Philosophie des Rechts, (1 ed. 1925) / 140, 240

Bingham, What Is Law? (1912) 11 MICHIGAN LAW REVIEW, 1 / 299

Birkenhead, Fourteen English Judges / 53

Bishop, Criminal Law, (9 ed. 1923) / 91

———. Marriage, Divorce and Separation, (1891) / 137

Blackstone, Commentaries on the Laws of England, (1765) / 5, 11, 12, 40, 50, 51, 91, 100, 168, 189, 195, 203, 210, 285, 325

Bluntschli, Allgemeine Staatslehre, (6 ed. 1886) / 369

———. Geschichte der neuren Staatswissenschaft, (1881) / 166

Bohlen, The Moral Duty to Aid Others as a Basis of Tort Liability, (1908) 56 UNIV. OF PA. LAW REVIEW, 217 / 93
———. Old Phrases and New Facts, (1935) 83 UNIV. OF PA. LAW REVIEW, 305 / / 264, 315
———. The Rule in *Rylands* v. *Fletcher*, (1911) 59 UNIV. OF PA. LAW REVIEW, 292 / 275
Boistel, Cours de philosophie du droit, (1870, new ed. 1899) / 56, 203
Bonnard, L'Origine de l'ordonnancement juridique, in (1929) MELANGES MAURICE HAURIOU, 31 / 61
Bonnecase, La notion de droit en France au dix-neuvième siècle / 56
Borchard, Convicting the Innocent, (1932) / 130
Boutmy, La déclaration des droits de l'homme et du citoyen de Mr. Jellinek, Etudes politiques, (1907) / 188
Bower, Code of Actionable Defamation, (1908) / 153
Boyd, Workmen's Compensation, (1913) / 204
Bracton, De legibus et consuetudinibus Angliae / 121, 173
Brannan, Negotiable Instruments Law, (ed. by Beutel, 1948) / 28
Brissaud, History of French Public Law, (transl. by Garner, 1915) / 173
Brougham, Speeches, (1838) / 192
Brown, Judicial Recall — A Fallacy Repugnant to Constitutional Government, ANNALS OF THE AMERICAN ACADEMY OF POLITICAL AND SOCIAL SCIENCE (Philadelphia) also published as Senate Document No. 892, (1912) / 225
———. The Underlying Principles of Modern Legislation, (1912) (Prologue — The Challenge of Anarchy) / 190, 216
Bruce, Humanity and the Law, 73 CENTRAL LAW JOURNAL, 335 / 93
Brunner, Deutsche Rechtsgeschichte, (2 ed. 1906) / 144, 146
Bruns, Fontes Iuris Romani Antiqui, (7 ed. 1909) / 83, 144, 145, 146, 324
Bryce, Studies in History and Jurisprudence, (American ed.) / 56
Buckland, More Wardour Street Roman Law, (1915) 31 LAW QUARTERLY REVIEW, 193 / 27
———. Text-Book of Roman Law, (2 ed. 1932) / 45, 129
———. Wardour Street Roman Law, (1901) 17 LAW QUARTERLY REVIEW, 179 / 27
Burdick, Torts, (1905, 2 ed. 1908) / 276, 328
Burlamaqui, Principes du droit naturel, (1747) (de la nature et des gens, 1791) / 28, 50, 150, 188, 189, 194, 200
———. Principes du droit politique, (1757) / 200
Burle, Essai historique sur le développement de la notion de droit naturel dans l'antiquité grecque, (1908) / 38
Burton, 28 CRIMINAL APPEAL REPORT, 89 (1941) / 95

Caballero, La Legislación Vigente Sobre Organización Corporativo Nacional, (1929) / 282

Caccialupi, De pactis, xi, 7, 6, (6 TRACTATUS UNIVERSI IURIS, pt. 1, fol. 13) / 48

Caird, The Critical Philosophy of Kant, (1889) / 203, 204

Cairns, Legal Philosophy from Plato to Hegel, (1949) / 156, 307, 308, 309

Calhoun, Disquisition on Government, (1848–49) (in 1 Works, New York ed. 1854) / 369

Campbell, Lord, Lives of the Chief Justices, (1 ed. 1857, 3 ed. 1874) / 53, 131, 307

Cardozo, Address Before the New York State Bar Association, (1932) 55 REP. N.Y. STATE BAR ASSOCIATION, 263 / 300

——. The Growth of the Law, (1924) / 6

——. The Nature of the Judicial Process, (1921) / 3, 104, 307–8

——. Paradoxes of Legal Science, (1928) / 234

Carlo, Il diritto naturale nell' attuale fase del pensiero Italiano, (1932) / 63

Carlyle, History of Medieval Political Theory, (1903) / 162, 163, 165

Carter, Law: Its Origin, Growth and Function, (1907) / 195, 206, 211, 224

Carver, Social Justice, (1915) / 225

Cesarini Sforza, Curso di Diritto Corporativo, (4 ed. 1935) / 282

Chadbourne, Lynching and the Law, (1933) / 132

Chafee and Simpson, Cases on Equity, (3 ed.) / 90

——. Note, (1920) 33 HARVARD LAW REVIEW, 956 / 135

Chafee, Pollak, and Stern, The Third Degree, (1931) / 135

Charmont, L'abus du droit, (1901) 1 REVUE TRIMESTRIELLE DE DROIT CIVIL / 248

——. La renaissance du droit naturel, (1910) / 216

——. La socialisation du droit, (1903) / 154

Chase, Lemuel Shaw, (1918) / 268

Chiarelli, Il Diritto Corporativo e le Sue Fonti, (1930) / 282

——. Lo Stato Corporativo, (1936) / 282

Chorley, The Conflict of Law and Commerce, (1932) 48 LAW QUARTERLY REVIEW, 51 / 279

Cicero, De haruspicum responsis / 42

——. De inuentione / 44

——. De legibus / 5, 42, 44, 159, 160

——. De officiis / 42, 64, 72, 86, 87, 159, 160

——. De republica / 42, 159, 160

——. Partitiones oratoriae / 42

——. Tusculan disputations / 42

Cioffi, Istituzioni di Diritto Corporativo, (1935) / 282

Clark, Australian Constitutional Law, (1901) / 83

——. Constitution of Brazil / 83

——. Practical Jurisprudence, (1883) / 9, 35, 84

Cohen and Cohen, Readings in Jurisprudence and Legal Philosophy

tista Vico (transl. by Collingwood, 1913) / *168*

Dareste, Le droit des représailles, Nouvelles études d'histoire du droit, (1902) / *144*

Delos, La théorie de l'institution, (1931) in ARCHIVES DE PHILOSO-PHIE DU DROIT ET DE SOCIOLOGIE JURIDIQUE, 96 / *61*

Del Vecchio, Formal Bases of Law, (1914) (transl. by Lisle) / *216*

———. Justice, (1952) (transl. by Lady Guthrie, ed. by Campbell) / *140*

Demogue, Fault, Risk and Appor-tionment of Risk in Responsibility, (1921) 15 ILLINOIS LAW REVIEW, 369 / *326*

———. Les notions fondamentales du droit privé, (1911) / *78, 153*

Demosthenes, Oration Against Aris-togeiton, / *37, 146*

Dernburg, Das bürgerliche Recht der deutschen Reichs und Preussens, (1903) / *2*

———. Pandekten, (7 ed. 1902) / *285*

Dewey, Logic, (1938) / *309*

Dewey and Tufts, Ethics, (1908, rev. ed. 1938) / *80, 140, 225*

Dicey, Law and Public Opinion in England in the Nineteenth Cen-tury, (1905, 2 ed. 1914) / *119, 123, 206, 208*

Dickinson, Legal Rules: Their Func-tion in the Process of Decision, Their Elaboration and Applica-tion, (1931) 79 UNIV. OF PA. LAW REVIEW, 832 / *300*

Dillon, Laws and Jurisprudence of England and America, (1894) / *86, 90, 195, 290*

———. Municipal Corporations, (1872) / *30*

Dimock, Le Professeur W. W. Cook et le relativisme juridique, (1932) ARCHIVES DE PHILOSOPHIE DU DROIT ET DE SOCIOLOGIE JU-RIDIQUE, 575 / *313*

Diogenes Laertius / *37, 39, 157*

Dobrin, Soviet Jurisprudence and Socialism, (1936) 52 LAW QUAR-TERLY REVIEW, 402 / *281*

Dodd, The Recall and the Political Responsibility of Judges, (1911) 10 MICHIGAN LAW REVIEW, 79 / *225*

Donati, Il primo precetto del diritto "vivere con honesta," (1926) / *161*

Douglas, Vicarious Liability and Ad-ministration of Risk, (1929) 38 YALE LAW JOURNAL, 584 / *331*

Duarenus, (François Duaren, French jurist, 1509–1559), De pactis, vi, 1, (6 TRACTATUS UNI-VERSI IURIS, pt. 1, fol. 15) / *48*

Duerden, 28 CRIMINAL APPEAL RE-PORT, 125 (1942) / *95*

Duff, Spinoza's Political and Ethical Philosophy, (1903) / *138, 178*

Duguit, Léon, Le droit social, le droit individuel, et la transforma-tion de l'état, (2 ed. 1911) / *60, 231*

———. L'état, le droit objectif, et la loi positive, (1901) / *60, 62, 231*

———. Les transformations du droit privé depuis le Code Napoléon / *60, 62*

Dunning, Political Theory, Ancient and Medieval, (1913) / *162*

Dwarris, General Treatise on Statutes, (Potter's ed. 1875) / 16

Ebersole, The Iowa People's Law Book, (1900) / 28
Edlin, Rechtsphilosophische Scheinprobleme, (1932) II, 2, DAS PROBLEM DER SOZIALEN GESETZMASSIGKEIT / 132
Egger, Kommentar zum schweizerischen Zivilgesetzbuch, (1916) / 326
Ehrenberg, Die Rechtsidee im früheren Griechentum, (1921) / 38
Ehrlich, Grundlegung der Soziologie des Rechts, (1913), English transl. by Moll as *Fundamental Principles of the Sociology of Law*, (1936) / 30, 104, 105, 106, 107, 204, 283, 369
Elliot and others, Preliminary Report on Efficiency in the Administration of Justice, (1914) / 292
Emery, Concerning Justice, (1914) / 205
Engisch, Zur phänomenologischen Methode im Strafrecht, (1937) 30 ARCHIV FUR RECHTS UND SOZIALPHILOSOPHIE, 130 / 317
Epictetus, Diss. / 158
Erdmann, History of Philosophy, (Hough's transl. 1910) / 158, 162
Erigena, Johannes Scotus, (d. 875), De divisione naturae / 45, 172
Everett, Moral Values / 79

Fay, Life of Mr. Justice Smith, (1939) / 137

Fearne, Contingent Remainders, (10 ed. 1844) / 87
Fehr, Hammurapi und das salisches Recht, (1910) / 144
Feinsinger, Legislative Attacks on "Heart Balm," (1933) 33 MICHIGAN LAW REVIEW, 1030 / 131
Ferri, L'Ordinamento Corporativo dal Punto di Vista Economico, Caratteri Generali, I Soggetti, Le Associazioni Sindicali, (1933) / 282
Ferson, The Rational Basis of Contracts, (1949) / 184
Fichte, Grundlage des Naturrechts, (1798), new ed. by Medicus, (2 ed. 1922), English transl. by Kroeger as *Science of Rights*, (1889) / 203
Figgis, Studies of Political Thought from Gerson to Grotius, (1907) / 167, 175, 184
Finch, Law, (1627) / 191
Fineux, in Anonymous, Y.B. Hil. 4 Hen. 7 (1490) / 91
Fitzherbert, Abridgement, / 47
Fortescue, De laudibus legum Angliae / 5
Franciscus de Victoria, Relectiones theologicae, (1557) / 177
Frank, Are Judges Human, (1931) 80 UNIV. OF PA. LAW REVIEW 17 / 299, 301, 304
———. If Men Were Angels, (1942) / 288, 300
———. Law and the Modern Mind, (1930, Sixth printing, 1949) / 120, 288, 293, 301, 304
———. Mr. Justice Holmes and Non-Euclidean Legal Thinking, (1932)

17 Cornell Law Quarterly, 568 / 299–300

———. What Courts Do in Fact, (1932) 26 Illinois Law Rev., 645 / 299, 301

Friedmann, Law and Social Change in Contemporary Britain, (1951) / 65, 320

———. Legal Theory, (1944) / 320

Friedrich, Remarks on Llewellyn's View of Law, Official Behavior and Political Science, (1933) 50 Political Science Quarterly, 419 / 300

Fry, Memoir of Sir Edward Fry, (1921) / 86

Fucile, Le mouvement corporatif en Italie, (1929) / 282

Fuller, American Legal Realism, (1934) 82 Univ. of Pa. Law Review, 429 / 257, 300, 301

Gaius, Institute / 42, 43, 44, 45, 73, 86, 87, 145, 149, 160, 324

Galoanus Bononiensis, De differentiis legum et canonum, (No. 67 in 1 Tractatus Universi Iuris, 1584) / 47

Gardner, An Inquiry into the Principles of the Law of Contracts, (1946) 46 Harvard Law Review, 1 / 344

———. The Massachusetts Billboard Decision, (1936) 49 Harvard Law Review, 869 / 248

Gareis, Enzyklopädie der Rechtswissenschaft, (1887) / 2

Gény, François, Science et technique en droit privé positif, (Vol. I, 1914; Vol. II, 1915; Vol. III, 1921; Vol. IV, 1924) / 60, 61, 62, 110

Gierke, Althusius und die Entwicklung der natürrechtlichen Staatstheorien / 166

Glanvill, (1187) / 145, 191

Goble, Law as a Science, (1934) 9 Indiana Law Review, 294 / 300

Goodhart, Some American Interpretations of Law, in Modern Theories of Law, (1933) / 288, 290

Goodrich, Emotional Disturbance as Legal Damage, (1922), 20 Michigan Law Review, 497 / 97

Graham, Life and Character of Thomas Ruffin, (1871) / 269

Grant, Personal Memoirs, (1885–86) / 280

Grave, La société future, (7 ed. 1895) / 216, 217

Gray, Nature and Sources of the Law, (1909, 2 ed. 1921) / 19, 26, 56, 201, 202

———. Restraints Upon Alienation of Property, (2 ed. 1895) / 20

———. Some Definitions and Questions in Jurisprudence, (1892) 6 Harvard Law Review, 21 / 6

Green, Judge and Jury (1930) / 261

———. Principles of Political Obligation, (Lectures delivered 1879–80, reprinted, 1911) / 75, 128, 203, 205

Greenidge, Infamia: Its Place in Roman Public and Private Law, (1844) / 147

Gregorius de Megalottis, Tractatus securitatis ac salviconductis, (11

——. History of Philosophy, (transl. by Haldane, 1892) / 213

——. Philosophy of History, transl. by Sibree, rev. ed. (1899) / 205

Heinze, 60 HERMES (1925) 348–66 / 166

Hemmingsen (Hemmingius), De lege naturae apodictica methodus, (1562) / 50, 166, 169

Henderson, The Position of Foreign Corporations in Constitutional Law, (1918) / 278

Heraclitus, Diogenes Laertius / 157

Herkless, Lectures on Jurisprudence (posthumous, 1901) / 203

Heusler, Institutionen des deutschen Privatrechts, (1885) / 22, 173

Hieronymus de Zannettinis, De differentiis inter ius canonicum et ciuile / 47

Hildebrand, Geschichte und System der Rechts- und Staatsphiloso-phie, (I, DAS KLASSISCHE ALTER-TUM, 1860) / 38, 156, 159

Hinrichs, Geschichte der Rechts- und Staatsprincipien seit der Re-formation, (1848) / 166, 168, 170, 178

Hoadley, Annual Address Before the American Bar Association, (1889) 11 REP. AM. BAR ASSN., 219 / 195

Hobbes, De cive, (1642) / 178

——. Leviathan, (1651) / 4, 27, 64, 178, 186, 200

Hobhouse, Elements of Social Jus-tice, (1922) / 225

Hohfeld, Fundamental Legal Con-ceptions as Applied in Judicial Reasoning, (1923) / 109–10

Holdsworth, History of English Law, (3 ed. 1922) / 49, 55, 129

——. Sources and Literature of En-glish Law, (1925) / 51

Holland, Elements of Jurisprudence, (1 ed. 1880, 13 ed. 1924) / 57, 202

Holmes, Agency, (1891) 4 HARVARD LAW REVIEW, 345 / 271, 273, 274, 327

——. Agency, (1891) 5 HARVARD LAW REVIEW, 1 / 274

——. Codes, and the Arrange-ment of the Law, See Early Writ-ings of Mr. Justice Holmes, in 44 HARVARD LAW REVIEW, 725 / 348

——. Collected Papers, (1921) / 120, 348

——. The Common Law, (1881) / 56, 87, 348

——. Law in Science and Science in Law, (1899) 12 HARVARD LAW REVIEW, 443 / 25

——. The Path of the Law, (1897) 10 HARVARD LAW REVIEW, 443, 457, 467 / 5, 120, 323, 348

Holt, The Freudian Wish and Its Place in Ethics, (1915) / 289

Hornblower, The Independence of the Judiciary the Safeguard of Free Institutions, Senate Document No. 1052, 62nd Congress, 3rd Ses-sion, (1913) / 225

Horvath, Rechtssoziologie, (1934) / 104, 231

——. Social Value and Reality in Current French Legal Thought, (1952) 1 AM. JOURNAL COMP. LAW, 243 / 61

Hotman, Anti-Tribonianus, (1567)
/ 50

Hume-Williams, The World, the
House, and the Bar, (1930) / 137

Husserl, G., Der Rechtsgegenstand,
(1933) / 317

——. Rechtskraft und Rechtsgeltung, (1925) / 317

——. Recht und Welt, (1930)
/ 317

Hutcheson, The Judgment Intuitive — The Function of the
"Hunch" in Judicial Decisions,
(1928) 14 CORNELL LAW QUAR-
TERLY, 274 / 300, 317

Iamblichus, Vit. Pythag. / 157

Isaacs, John Marshall on Contracts,
A Study in Early American Juristic
Theory, (1921) 7 VIRGINIA LAW RE-
VIEW, 413 / 184

——. The Limits of Judicial Discretion, (1923) 32 YALE LAW JOURNAL,
339 / 87

Jaeger, Werner, The Problem of
Authority and the Crisis of the
Greek Spirit, in Authority and the
Individual, (1937) HARVARD
TERCENTENARY PUBLICATION, 241
/ 166

James, The Will to Believe, (1897)
/ 123, 253

Jellinek, Allgemeine Staatslehre, (3
ed. 1914) / 132

——. Die Erklärung der Men-
schen- und Bürgerrechte, (3 ed.

1919, English transl. of 1 ed. by Farrand as The Declaration of the
Rights of Men and of Citizens,
1901) / 188

——. Die sozialethische Bedeutung von Recht, Unrecht, und
Strafe, (1878, 2 ed. 1908) / 78

Jenks, Governmental Action for Social Welfare / 249

——. Law and Politics in the
Middle Ages, (1898) / 147

Jennings, The Institutional Theory,
(1933, in Modern Theories of Law)
/ 284, 352

Jhering, Geist des römischen Rechts,
(1854, 5 ed. 1891, 7 and 8 ed. 1924)
/ 70, 109, 147, 148

——. Im juristischen Begriffshimmel, (1884, 13 ed. 1924) / 243

——. Der Kampf um's Recht,
(1872, 19 ed. 1919), English transl.
by Lalor as The Struggle for Law,
(1879, 2 ed. by Kocourek, 1915)
/ 139, 265

——. Scherz und Ernst in der Jurisprudenz, (4 ed. 1891) / 154, 243,
312

——. Der Zweck im Recht, (1883)
/ 71, 79

——. Zweck im Recht (3 ed.
1893–98) / 106

Johnsen, Selected Articles on Law —
Enforcement, (1930) / 128

Joseph, Introduction to Logic / 41

Josserand, Cours de droit civil positif
français, (3 ed. 1939) / 64, 101

Justinian, Code / 151

——. Digest / 149, 152, 159, 173, 279,
285

———. Institutes / 149, 159, 160, 162, 173, 279, 285

Kaltenborn, Die Vorläufer des Hugo Grotius, (1848) / 50, 169
Kant, Kritik der reinen Vernunft, (2 ed. 1787) (Smith's transl. Immanuel Kant's Critique of Pure Reason, 1932) / 204, 208
———. Metaphysische Anfangsgründe der Rechtslehre, (2 ed. 1798) / 2, 55, 77, 199, 203
———. Philosophy of Law, (1887, English transl. by Hastie) / 140, 203
Kantorowicz, Gnaeus Flavius, Die Kampf um die Rechtswissenschaft, (1906) / 312
———. Some Rationalism About Realism, (1934) 43 YALE LAW JOURNAL, 240 / 300
Kaufmann, Die Kriterien des Rechts, (1924) / 317
———. Logik und Rechtswissenschaft, (1922) / 317
———. Die philosophischen Grundprobleme der Lehre von der Strafrechtsschuld, (1929) / 317
Kelsen, Reine Rechtslehre, (1934) / 74, 80, 88, 104, 367
Kennedy, Functional Nonsense and the Transcendental Approach, (1936) 5 FORDHAM LAW REVIEW, 272 / 300
———. Principles or Facts, (1935) 4 FORDHAM LAW REVIEW, 53 / 300
Kent, Commentaries on American Law, (1826) / 30, 51, 193
Kimball, Morals in Politics, (in Brooklyn Ethical Society, Man and the State, 1892) / 215
Knight, Life and Works of Hugo Grotius, (1925) / 52
Kocourek, Jural Relations, (1927) / 109
Kohler, Einführung in die Rechtswissenschaft, (1902, 5 ed. 1919) / 2, 59, 162, 231, 235
———. Lehrbuch der Rechtsphilosophie, (1908, 2 ed. 1917, 3 ed. by Arthur Kohler, 1923, 1 ed. transl. by Albrecht as Kohler's Philosophy of Law, 1914) / 59, 80, 124, 162, 231, 235, 236
———. Moderne Rechtsprobleme, (1907, 2 ed. 1913) / 59, 80, 235, 236
———. Rechtsphilosophie und Universalrechtsgeschichte, (in Holtzendorff, Enzyklopädie der Rechtswissenschaft, 6 ed. 1904, 7 ed. 1913) / 59, 80, 235
———. Recht und Persönlichkeit, (in Der Kultur der Gegenwart, 1914) / 235
Korkunov, General Theory of Law, (transl. by Hastings, 1909) / 79, 128
Kornfeld, Soziale Machtverhältnisse, (1911) / 104
Krause, Abriss des Systemes der Philosophie des Rechtes, (1825) / 203
Kyd, Corporations, (1793) / 278

Labatt, Commentaries on the Law of Master and Servant, (2 ed. 1913) / 271
Laertius, Diogenes / 37, 39, 157
Langdell, Summary of Equity Pleading, (2 ed. 1883) / 129

Lundstedt, The General Principles of Civil Liability in Different Legal Systems, The False Idea of Right, (1934) 2 ACTA ACADEMIAE UNIVERSALIS JURISPRUDENTIAE COMPARATIVAE, 371 / 113, 232
——. Superstition or Rationality in Action for Peace, (1925) / 300
——. Die Unwissenschaftlichkeit der Rechtswissenschaft, (1932–36) / 300
Luther, Tract von weltlicher Oberkeit, / 169
——. Werke, (Weimar ed. 1883) / 168, 169
——. Werke, Kritische Gesammtausgabe, (1883) / 168
Lysen, Hugo Grotius, (1925) / 52

Macaulay, Notes to Draft of Indian Penal Code, (in Complete Works, ed. 1875) / 94
Machen, Do the Incorporation Laws Allow Sufficient Freedom to Commercial Enterprise, (1909) 14 REP. MD. STATE BAR ASSN., 78 / 279
Maine, Ancient Law, (1861) / 56, 105, 148, 211, 212
——. Early History of Institutions, (1 ed. 1875, 7 ed. 1897) / 144, 149, 201, 202, 211
——. Early Law and Custom, (new ed. 1891) / 144
Maitland, Bracton's Notebook, (1887) / 173
——. Collected Papers, (1911) / 216
——. English Law and the Renaissance, (1901) / 291
——. Lectures on Equity, (2 ed.

1936, revised by Brunyate, 1947) / 107, 150, 277
——. Selected Essays, (1936) / 107
Malinowski, Introduction to Hogbin, Law and Order in Polynesia, (1934) / 72, 78
Manu, (transl. by Müller, 1889) 25 SACRED BOOKS OF THE EAST, 430 / 144
Bühler's transl., 25 SACRED BOOKS OF THE EAST, (1886), 322 / 350
Markby, Elements of Law, (6 ed. 1905) / 81, 132, 201, 210
Marshall, Comparative Judicial Criminal Statistics: Six States, (1932) / 316–17
——. Unlocking the Treasuries of the Trial Courts, (1933) / 316
Martin, Mendizábaly, El indestructibile derecho natural, (in 2 STUDI FILOSOFICI GIURIDICI DEDICATI A GIORGIO DEL VECCHIO, 92) / 63
Marx, Compulsory Compensation Insurance, 25 COLUMBIA LAW REVIEW, 164 / 97
——. Critique of the Gotha Program, (English trans. 1933) / 282
——. Juristischer Realismus in den Vereinigten Staaten von Amerika, (1936) 10 REVUE INTERNATIONALE DE LA THEORIE DU DROIT, 28 / 300
——. Zur Kritik der politischen Oekonomie, (1859) / 263
Maschi, La concezione naturalistica del diritto, (1937) / 44
Mazzoni, L'Ordinamento Corporativo: Contributo Alla Fondazione D'Una Teoria Generale E Alla

Formulazione di Una Domestica Del Diritto Corporativo, (1934) / 282

McDougall, Social Psychology, (1936) / 296

McIlwain, The Growth of Political Thought in the West, (1932) / 156

———. The High Court of Parliament, (1910) / 173

McLaughlin, Amendment of the Bankruptcy Act, (1927) 40 HARVARD LAW REVIEW, 341 / 266

Mechem, The Jurisprudence of Despair, (1936) 21 IOWA LAW REVIEW, 669 / 288

Melanchthon, Opera (ed. Bretschneider and Bindseil), (1834) / 168, 169, 170

Menger, Das bürgerliche Recht und die besitzlosen Volksklassen, (1889, 4 ed. 1908) / 217

———. Ueber die sozialen Aufgaben Rechts, (1885, 3 ed. 1910) / 217

Mill, On Liberty, (1859) / 206

Millar, Historical View of the English Government, (1879) / 73

Miller, Lectures on the Philosophy of Law, (1884) / 5, 75, 203, 205, 296

Montesquieu, L'esprit des lois, (1749) / 188

Moore and Hope, An Institutional Approach to the Law of Commercial Banking, (1938) 38 YALE LAW JOURNAL, 703 / 291, 292

Muirhead, Historical Introduction to the Private Law of Rome, (1 ed. 1886) / 33

Myers, History of Supreme Court of United States, (1912) / 264

———. Political Ideas of the Greeks, (1927) / 156

Navarra, Introduzione al Diritto Corporativo — Storia e Diritto, (1929) / 282

Nelles, Commonwealth v. Hunt, (1932) 32 COLUMBIA LAW REVIEW, 1128 / 272

Nicolaus Moronus, Tractatus de treuga et pace, (11 TRACTATUS UNIVERSI IURIS, pt. 1, fol. 420) / 48

Nipperdey et al. Grundfragen der Reform des Schadenersatzrechts, (1940) / 330

Odgers and others, A Century of Law Reform, (1901) / 192

Oldendorp, Iuris naturalis gentium et ciuilis, (1539) / 166

Oliphant, Facts, Opinions, and Value Judgments, (1932) 10 TEXAS LAW REVIEW, 697 / 314

Oliphant and Hewitt, Introduction to Rueff, From the Physical to the Social Sciences, (1929), translated by Green / 260

Olivecrona, Law as Fact, (1939) / 318

Paley, Moral and Political Philosophy, (1782) / 261

Palmer, George Herbert, and others, Immanuel Kant, (1925) / 234

Panunzio, Il socialismo giuridico, (2 ed. 1911) / 217

Parry, What the Judge Thought, (1892) / 130

Parsons, Contracts, (1855) / 185

Paschukanis, Allgemeine Rechtslehre und Marxismus, (1929) / 232, 233, 281, 282

Paulsen, Ethics, (Thilly's transl. 1899) / 101

Pergolesi, Istituzioni di Diritto Corporativo, (2 ed. 1935) / 282

Perry, Trusts, (7 ed. 1929) / 151

Petrazycki, Methodologie der Theorien des Rechts und der Moral [in OPERA ACADEMIAE UNIVERSALIS JURISPRUDENTIAE COMPARATIVAE, (1933) Ser. 2] / 104

———. Ueber die Motiven des Handelns und über das Wesen der Moral und des Rechts, transl. from the Russian by Balson, (1907) / 104

Phelps, Methods of Legal Education, (1892) 1 YALE LAW JOURNAL, 139 / 190

Phillipson, Three Criminal Law Reformers, (1923) / 207

Picard, Le droit pur, (1899, reprinted 1920) / 217, 231

Pitigliani, The Italian Corporative State, (1933) / 282

Planiol et Ripert, Traité élémentaire de droit civil français, (11 ed. 1932, revision by Ripert and Boulanger, 4 ed. 1952) / 64, 101, 129, 342, 343

Plato, Gorgias / 156, 157

———. Laws / 156, 158, 159

———. Minos / 37, 70

———. Republic / 64, 156, 157, 158

Plucknett, Bonham's Case and Judicial Review, (1926) 40 HARVARD LAW REVIEW, 30 / 27

Pollock, Essays in Jurisprudence and Ethics / 56

———. First Book of Jurisprudence, (1 ed. 1896, 6 ed. 1929) / 92, 128, 141

———. Law of Fraud in British India, (1894) / 328

———. Torts, (8 ed. 1908) / 327

Pollock and Maitland, History of English Law, (1 ed. 1895, 2 ed. 1898) / 6, 129, 146, 201

Pomeroy, Equity Jurisprudence, (first published in 1881–82, 3 ed. 1905, 4 ed. 1919) / 86, 280

Post, Grundriss der ethnologischen Jurisprudenz, (1884) / 144

Pothier, Robert Joseph, (1699–1772), Obligations, (1806) / 150

———. Traité des obligations, (1761) / 48, 52–53

Pound, Roscoe, The Administration of Justice in the Modern City, (1913) 26 HARVARD LAW REVIEW, 302 / 209

———. Administrative Application of Legal Standards, (1919) 44 REP. AM. BAR ASSN. 445 / 87, 284

———. Administrative Law, (1942) / 86

———. The Call for a Realist Jurisprudence, (1931) 44 HARVARD LAW REVIEW, 597 / 257, 288, 315, 319

———. The Causes of Popular Dissatisfaction with the Administration of Justice, (1906) 29 REP. AM. BAR ASSN. 395 / 101

———. Common Law and Legislation, (1908) 21 HARVARD LAW REVIEW, 383 / 16

———. A Comparison of Ideals of Law, (1933) 47 HARVARD LAW REVIEW, 1 / 304

——. The Decadence of Equity, (1905) 5 COLUMBIA LAW REVIEW, 20 / *136*

——. The Economic Interpretation and the Law of Torts, (1940) 53 HARVARD LAW REVIEW, 365 / *275*

——. The End of Law as Developed in Juristic Thought, (1916) 30 HARVARD LAW REVIEW, 201 / *119, 156, 200*

——. The End of Law as Developed in Legal Rules and Doctrines, (1914) 27 HARVARD LAW REVIEW, 195 / *102, 154, 156, 212, 225, 351*

——. Equitable Relief Against Defamation and Injuries to Personality, (1916) 29 HARVARD LAW REVIEW, 640 / *131, 154*

——. Fifty Years of Jurisprudence, (1938) 51 HARVARD LAW REVIEW, 444 / *52, 59, 60, 119, 218, 257, 279, 281, 288, 300, 312, 364, 368*

——. The Formative Era of American Law, (1938) / *54, 188*

——. The Future of Law, (1937) 47 YALE LAW JOURNAL, 1 / *352*

——. Grotius in the Science of Law, (1925) 19 AMERICAN JOURNAL OF INTERNATIONAL LAW, 685 / *52, 180*

——. Hierarchy of Sources and Forms in Different Systems of Law, (1933) 7 TULANE LAW REVIEW, 473 / *304*

——. How Far Are We Attaining a New Measure of Values in Twentieth-Century Juristic Thought, (1936) / *218*

——. A Hundred Years of American Law, (in 1 *Law: A Century of Progress, 1835–1935*, 8) / *85*

——. The Ideal Element in American Judicial Decision, (1931) 45 HARVARD LAW REVIEW, 1361 / *304*

——. Interests of Personality, (1916) 28 HARVARD LAW REVIEW, 343 / *97, 130*

——. (1915) 26 INTERNATIONAL JOURNAL OF ETHICS, 92 / *110*

——. Interpretations of Legal History, (1923) / *2, 19, 21, 40, 56, 70, 104, 112, 118, 123, 206, 212, 234, 277*

——. Introduction to the Philosophy of Law, (1922) / *102, 104, 112, 245*

——. Introduction to the Study of Law, (1919) / *245*

——. Juristic Science and Law, (1918) 31 HARVARD LAW REVIEW, 1047 / *284*

——. Justice According to Law, (1951) / *140*

——. Justice According to Law — Executive Justice, (1913) 14 COLUMBIA LAW REVIEW, 12 / *86*

——. Legal Interrogation of Persons Accused or Suspected of Crime, (1934) 24 JOURNAL OF THE AMERICAN INST. OF CRIMINAL LAW AND CRIMINOLOGY, 1014 / *135*

——. Liberty of Contract, (1909) 18 YALE LAW JOURNAL, 454 / *12, 64, 114*

——. The Limits of Effective Legal Action, (1917) 3 AM. BAR ASSN. JOURNAL, 55; (1917) 27 INT. JOURNAL OF ETHICS, 150 / *90, 108, 128, 356*

———. Mechanical Jurisprudence, (1908) 8 COLUMBIA LAW REVIEW, 605 / 312

———. Natural Natural Law and Positive Natural Law, (1952) 68 LAW QUARTERLY REVIEW, 330 / 44, 63, 142

———. The New Feudalism, (1930) 16 AM. BAR ASSN. JOURNAL, 553 / 30, 231

———. New Paths of the Law, (1950, lectures at the University of Nebraska) / 65, 348

———. Organization of Courts, (1940) / 354, 355

———. Outlines of Lectures on Jurisprudence, (5 ed. 1943) / 102, 245

———. Philosophical Theory and International Law, (1923) 1 BIBLIOTHECA VISSERIANA DISSERTATIONUM IUS INTERNATIONALE ILLUSTRANTIUM, 71 / 54, 126, 177

———. The Philosophy of Law in America, (1913) 7 ARCHIV FUR RECHTS UND WIRTSCHAFTSPHILOSOPHIE, 213 / 200

———. The Place of Judge Story in the Making of American Law, (1914) 48 AMERICAN LAW REVIEW, 676 / 208

———. The Place of the Judiciary in a Democratic Polity, (1941) 27 AM. BAR ASSN. JOURNAL, 133 / 262

———. Public Law and Private Law, (1939) 24 CORNELL LAW QUARTERLY, 469 / 286

———. Recent Developments in the Law of Equity, (1933) / 136

———. The Relation of Statistical Quality Standards to Law and Legislation / 315

———. The Revival of Personal Government, (in PROCEEDINGS OF NEW HAMPSHIRE BAR ASSOCIATION) / 267

———. The Scope and Purpose of Sociological Jurisprudence, (1911) 24 HARVARD LAW REVIEW, 591, (1911) 25 HARVARD LAW REVIEW, 140 / 57, 207, 212

———. Social Control Through Law, (1942) / 70, 104, 112, 218, 231, 245, 252

———. Social Justice and Legal Justice, (1912) PROC. MO. BAR ASSOCIATION / 154

———. The Spirit of the Common Law, (1921) / 24, 30, 104, 112, 174, 182, 187, 200, 209, 212, 268

———. The Supreme Court and Minimum Wage Legislation, (1925) compiled by the National Consumers' League / 220, 284

———. A Survey of Social Interests, (1943) 57 HARVARD LAW REVIEW, 1 / 104

———. The Task of the Law, (1944) / 128

———. The Theory of Judicial Decision, (1923) 36 HARVARD LAW REVIEW, 641, 940 / 90, 284, 309

———. Twentieth-Century Ideas as to the End of Law, (1934) HARVARD LEGAL ESSAYS, 357 / 156, 218

———. What Is Law, (1940) 47 W.VA. LAW QUARTERLY, 1 / 70

Pound and Plucknett, Readings on the History and System of the

Roosevelt, Theodore, The Right of the People to Rule, Senate Document No. 473, 66th Congress, 2nd Session, (1912) / 225

Rousseau, Le contrat social, (The Social Contract) (1762) / 64, 188

Rueff, From the Physical to the Social Sciences, (transl. by Green, 1929) / 314

Rutherforth, Institutes of Natural Law, (1754–56) / 28, 50, 178, 182, 188, 194, 200

Saleilles, L'école historique et droit naturel, (1901) REVUE TRIMESTRIELLE DE DROIT CIVIL, 80 / 202, 213

———. L'individualisation de la peine, (2 ed. 1904, English transl. as: *The Individualization of Punishment*) / 304

Salemi, Lezioni di Diritto Corporativo, (1929) / 282

———. Studi di Diritto Corporativo, (1929) / 282

Salmond, First Principles of Jurisprudence, (1894) 10 LAW QUARTERLY REVIEW, 89 / 106

———. Jurisprudence, (9 ed. 1937) / 132

———. Torts, (4 ed. 1916) / 327

Salvioli, Storia del diritto italiano, (8 ed.) / 25

Sauer, Rechts und Staatsphilosophie, (1936) / 317

Sauter, Die philosophischen Grundlagen des Naturrechts, (1932) / 38, 156, 188

Savigny, Geschichte des römischen Rechts in Mittelalter / 25

———. Jural Relations, (transl. by Rattigan, a transl. of book 2 of Savigny's System, 1884) / 109

———. System des heutigen römischen Rechts, (1849) (English translation by Guthrie, A *Treatise on the Conflict of Laws*, 2 ed. 1880) / 24, 84, 109, 116, 161, 215

———. Vom Beruf unsrer Zeit für Gesetzgebung und Rechtswissenschaft, (3 ed. 1840) / 372

Schapp, Die neue Wissenschaft vom Recht, (1931–32) / 317

Schofield, *Swift v. Tyson*, (1910) 4 ILLINOIS LAW REVIEW, 533 / 292

Schreier, Grundbegriffe und Grundformen des Rechts, (1927) (transl. as: *Concepto y formas fundamentales del derecho*, by Garcia Maynes, 1942) / 317

Schulz, History of Roman Legal Science, (1946) / 43

———. Principles of Roman Law, (1936) / 153

Schurtz, Altersklassen und Männerbünde, (1902) / 146

Scott, Collisions at Sea Where Both Ships Are at Fault, (1897) 13 LAW QUARTERLY REVIEW, 17 / 99

———. On the Spanish Origin of International Law, (1928) / 175

———. Trusts, (1939) / 107

Seavey, Studies in Agency, (1949) / 327

Selden, Table Talk tit. Equity, (1689, Selden Society ed. 1927) / 150

Seligman, The Economic Interpre-

Stirling, The Secret of Hegel, (1865) / 205

Stirner, Der Einzige und sein Eigenthum, (1845) (English transl. as *The Ego and His Own*, (1907) / 216

Stobaeus, Ecologae / 38, 157

Stone, Law and Its Administration, (1915) / 91

———. The Province and Function of Law, (1946) / 242, 251

Storey, Some Practical Suggestions as to the Reform of Criminal Procedure, (1913) 4 JOURNAL OF THE AMERICAN INST. OF CRIMINAL LAW AND CRIMINOLOGY, 495 / 135

Story, Commentaries on the Conflict of Laws, (Foreign and Domestic) (1834) / 24

———. Commentaries on the Constitution of the United States, (1st ed. 1833) / 26, 193, 197

———. Partnership, (1841) / 279

Story, W. W., Contracts, (1831) / 115

———. Equity Jurisprudence, (1835, 2 ed. 1839) / 87, 95, 151

———. Life and Letters of Joseph Story, (1851) / 306

Strachan-Davidson, Problems of the Roman Criminal Law, (1912) / 144, 147

Strykius, Dissertationes Hallenses, (1715) / 64

———. Opera omnia, (Florence ed. 1839) / 64, 150

Stubbs, Lectures on the Study of Medieval and Modern History, (1906) / 145

Suarez, R., De legibus ac Deo legislatore, (1619) / 175, 176, 177, 178

———. Repetitiones, (1558) / 172

Sutherland, Principles of Criminology, (3 ed. 1939) / 95

Taft, Recall of Decisions, a Modern Phase of Impatience of Constitutional Restraints, (1913) 33 REP. N.Y. STATE BAR ASSN., 169 / 225

Tanon, L'évolution du droit et la conscience sociale, (3 ed. 1911) / 208

Thackery, The Newcomes / 131

Thayer, Legal Essays, (1908) / 345–46

———. Preliminary Treatise on Evidence, (1898) / 145

———. Recall of Judicial Decisions, (1913) 4 LEGAL BIBLIOGRAPHY, *New Series*, 3 / 225

Thomas, 28 CRIMINAL APPEAL REPORT, 21 (1941) / 95

Thomasius, Fundamenta iuris naturae et gentium, (1 ed. 1705, 4 ed. 1718) / 77

Thompson, Homesteads and Exemptions, (1878) / 250, 344

Thorpe, Ancient Laws and Institutes of England, (1840) (Laws of Edward; Laws of Aethelstan) / 67

Tiffany, Persons and Domestic Relations, (3 ed. 1921) / 17

Timasheff, Introduction to the Sociology of Law, (1939) / 104, 106, 231, 355

———. What Is Sociology of Law, (1937) 43 AMERICAN JOURNAL OF SOCIOLOGY, 225 / 231

Tönnies, Thomas Hobbes, (3 ed. 1925) / 105

Winckler, Principiorum iuris libri, (1615) / 166, 167, 169

Winfield, The Chief Sources of English Legal History, (1925) / 110

———. Text-Book of the Law of Tort, (5 ed. 1950) / 328

Woerner, Treatise on the American Law of Administration, (2 ed. 1899) / 280

Wolff, Institutiones iuris naturae et gentium, (1749–50) / 28, 50, 188, 189, 200

Wood, Institute of the Laws of England, (1722) or Laws of England in their Natural Order, (1724) / 33–34, 51

Wooddeson, Elements of Jurisprudence, (1792) / 203

———. Systematical View of the Laws of England, (1792–93) / 51

Wundt, Ethics (1901, transl. by Tichener and others) / 219

Wurzel, Das juristische Denken, (1904) (translated in Science of Legal Method, 9 MODERN LEGAL PHILOSOPHY SERIES) / 104

Wyman, The Clog on the Equity of Redemption, (1908) 21 HARVARD LAW REVIEW, 457 / 277

Xenophon, Memorabilia / 4, 5, 37

Yntema, Analysis of Ohio Municipal Court Acts (1933) / 316

———. The Hornbook Method and the Conflict of Laws, (1928) 37 YALE LAW JOURNAL, 468 / 261, 301

———. Jurisprudence on Parade, (1941) 39 MICHIGAN LAW REVIEW, 1134 / 317, 318

———. The Rational Basis of Legal Science, (1931) 31 COLUMBIA LAW REVIEW, 925 / 156, 300

Young, Social Treatment in Probation and Delinquency, (2 ed. 1952) / 131

Zancada, Programa de Derecho Corporativo, (1931) / 282

Zanelli Quarantini, Le Fonti del Diritto Corporativo, (1936) / 282

Acts, Reports, Proceedings, etc.

Laws of Texas, 1901, c. 107 / 266
Laws of Texas, 1909, (General) c. 10 / 267
Laws of Wisconsin, 1915, c. 437 / 267

Proceedings, Academy of Political Science of City of New York, 1913 / 225
Proceedings, California Bar Association, 1916 / 278
Proceedings, Illinois State Bar Association, (1912) 174: Addresses on the Recall of Judges and the Recall of Judicial Decisions / 225
Proceedings, New Hampshire Bar Association, 1917 / 267
Proceedings, North Dakota Bar Association, (1906–8) / 266

Report by the Committee to Study Compensation for Automobile Accidents to the Columbia Council for Research in Social Sciences, (1932) / 331
Report of Special Committee on Administrative Law, (1938) in 63 REP. AM. BAR ASSN., 331 / 262
Report of the Committee to Study Compensation for Automobile Accidents, *Columbia Council for Research in the Social Sciences,*

(1932) review by Thurston, (1933) 43 YALE LAW JOURNAL, 166 / 97–98
Report of the Real Property Commissioners, 1924 / 152
Report of the Tribunal Appointed under the Tribunals of Enquiry Act, 1921; Parliamentary Paper, CMD. 2497: Inquiry in Regard to the Interrogation by the Police of Miss Savidge, (1928); Case of Major R. O. Sheppard, (1925) / 134
Report on Lawlessness in Law Enforcement, Report No. 11: (*National Commission on Law Observance and Enforcement*) / 135
Report on the Enforcement of the Prohibition Laws of the United States, (1931), (*National Commission on Law Observance and Enforcement*) / 128, 133

Senate Document No. 649, (1911) Recall of Judges / 225
Statute, 34 Hen. 8, c. 34 (1540) / 33
Statute of Frauds and Perjuries, 29 Car. II c. 3 (1677) / 130
Statutes, New York's Revised, (2 ed. 1836) / 192

Uniform Laws, Annotated, (Edward Thompson Co., Brooklyn, N.Y.) / 33

Publications of Various Organizations

(Arranged according to the names of organizations)

AMERICAN ACADEMY OF POLITICAL
AND SOCIAL SCIENCE (PHILADEL-
PHIA):
Essential Human Rights, (1946)
Vol. 243 / *360*
The Initiative, Referendum, and
Recall, (1912) / *225*
AMERICAN LAW INSTITUTE:
Restatement of the Law of Con-
tracts, (1932) / *101, 346*
Restatement of the Law of Torts,
(1934) / *94*
Restatement of the Law of Torts,
(1949) / *321*
Uniform Commercial Code,
Final Draft / *339*
CONNECTICUT HISTORICAL SOCIETY:
Collections (1892) / *354*

INSTITUTE OF LAW OF JOHNS HOP-
KINS UNIVERSITY:
Bulletins of Survey of Litigation in
New York, (1931–32) / *316*
Bulletins of the Study of Judicial
Administration in Ohio, (1932)
/ *316*
Monographs in the Study of the
Judicial Administration in Ohio,
(1932) / *316*
Monographs in the Study of
Judicial System in Maryland,
(1931–32) / *316*
Monographs of Survey of Liti-
gation in New York, (1931–32)
/ *316*

Index

This book is set in 11 on 14 Electra.
Designed in 1935 by William Addison Dwiggins,
Electra has been a standard book typeface since its release
because of its evenness of design and high legibility.
Electra not only is a fine text face
but is equally responsive when set at display sizes.

Printed on paper that is acid-free
and meets the requirements of the American National Standard
for Permanence of Paper for Printed Library Materials, z39.48-1992. ∞

Book design by Betty Palmer McDaniel, Athens, Georgia
Typography by Graphic Composition, Inc., Athens, Georgia
Printed and bound by Worzalla Publishing Company, Stevens Point, Wisconsin